APR   98

Media,
Crime, and
Criminal Justice
Images and Realities

Contemporary Issues in Crime and Justice Series
Roy Roberg, San Jose State University: Series Editor

Media,
Crime, and
Criminal Justice
Images and Realities

Ray Surette
Florida International University

 Brooks/Cole Publishing Company
Pacific Grove, California

Consulting Editor: Roy R. Roberg

Brooks/Cole Publishing Company
A Division of Wadsworth, Inc.

Printed in the United States of America

10 9 8 7 6 5 4 3 2 1

Library of Congress Cataloging-in-Publication Data

Surette, Ray.
Media, crime, and criminal justice : images and realities / Ray Surette.
p.   cm.—(Contemporary issues in ciminal justice series)
Includes bibliographical references and index.
ISBN 0-534-16440-4
1. Mass media and criminal justice. 2. Crime in mass media.
I. Title. II. Series.
P96.C74S87 1991
364.2′54—dc20   91-17613
                                                                                                         CIP

Sponsoring Editor: *Cynthia C. Stormer*
Editorial Assistant: *Cathleen S. Collins*
Production Editor: *Majorie Z. Sanders*
Manuscript Editor: *Lynne Yamaguchi Fletcher*
Permissions Editor: *Mary Kay Hancharick*
Interior Design: *Roy Neuhaus*
Cover Design: *Lisa Berman*
Art Coordinator: *Cloyce J. Wall*
Photo Researcher: *Ruth Minerva*
Typesetting: *The Clarinda Company*
Cover Printing: *Phoenix Color Corporation*
Printing and Binding: *R. R. Donnelley & Sons Company, Crawfordsville*

Cover text courtesy of the *Daily News,* December 9, 1990.

To my parents,
my wife, Susan,
and my children, Jennifer and Paul

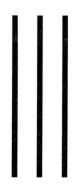

Foreword

Through the Contemporary Issues in Crime and Justice Series, students are introduced to important topics relevant to criminal justice, criminology, law, political science, psychology, and sociology that until now have been neglected or inadequately covered. The authors address philosophical and theoretical issues and analyze the most recent research findings and their implications for practice. Consequently, each volume will stimulate further thinking and debate on the topics it covers, in addition to providing direction for the development and implementation of policy.

The impact of the media on crime and justice has always been of critical importance to a democratic society. The importance of the relationship between the mass media news and entertainment systems and the criminal justice system may be greater today than ever before. This is not only because of the increased interaction between these two powerful institutions in recent years, but also because the mass media have become the most pervasive source of shared knowledge regarding crime and justice in our society. Thus, although these institutions are normally studied separately, it is be-

coming increasingly important that we attempt to understand their influences not only on each another but on society as well. To this end, *Media,
Crime, and Criminal Justice* by Ray Surette is a significant and much needed
contribution to the literature.

The basic premise of the text is that people use knowledge they obtain
from the media to build a picture of the world and then base their actions
on this constructed image. This "social construction of reality" is a particularly important concept, especially regarding how issues are shaped and
policies are determined with respect to crime and criminal justice. The author notes that the primary paradox with respect to the media's relationship
with crime and justice is the "simultaneous perception of the media as both
a major cause of crime and violence and an untapped but powerful potential solution to crime." In an examination of both roles, relevant empirical
and legal data with respect to the media's influence on attitudes and beliefs
about crime and justice, the criminal justice system (i.e., police, courts, and
corrections), the media's impact on crime, and media-designed programs to
reduce crime are reviewed.

Surette's work provides a comprehensive analysis of the relationships
among the media, crime, and the criminal justice system. Contemporary theories and models are explored in interpreting these relationships, and the
liberal use of provocative vignettes of famous (and infamous) media-hyped
personalities and events makes the text a lively and informative reading experience. Through this use of "visual" aids, Surette pragmatically and believ-
ably shows how the media affect crime and criminal justice. The major conclusions drawn are powerful, yet realistic, containing a subtle warning that
improvements with respect to the media, crime, and justice are possible,
but not without a great deal of effort. Early on the author suggests that this
work will be a success if the reader will never again sit through a crime
show or crime news-cast without a thoughtful reaction; in this, he has succeeded admirably.

Roy R. Roberg

Preface

Most people interact with the mass media as passive consumers rather than as thoughtful critical users. We have been conditioned to receive the entertainment and knowledge the media provide without considering where this entertainment and knowledge come from, what effect they have on our attitudes and perceptions, and how they affect society. Still, our attitude toward the media is ambivalent: We frequently point to the mass media as a cause of crime and violence at the same time that we receive most of our facts and impressions of crime and justice through the mass media. In the last few years the relationship between the media and the criminal justice system has devloped rapidly. One can hardly avoid a daily portrayal of crime or justice by the media. In addition, the level of research and interest in crime, criminal justice, and media relations has soared. Despite the widespread, increasing interest in the relationship of the mass media to crime and justice, however, a comprehensive survey has not been available.

One reason is that the relevant reseach is far-flung. Media, crime, and criminal justice relations involve interdisciplinary perspectives. Important research is conducted within the disciplines of criminology, criminal justice, sociology, psychology, psychiatry, political science, law, public administration, communications, and journalism. Research results appear in academic journals as diverse as the *Journal of Sex Research, Criminology,* the *Journal of Communication,* the *American Political Science Review, The Quill,* the *Journal of Broadcasting,* the *New England Journal of Medicine, Judicature,* the *Harvard Civil Rights–Civil Liberties Law Review,* and the *Journal of Personality and Social Psychology,* to name a few. It is not surprising, therefore, that such a multidisciplinary area has no comprehensive general resources. Most research efforts focus on a single aspect of the media, crime, and criminal justice relationship, and the research findings are seldom linked to research outside that area and rarely reach those outside the discipline.

To fill this void and to promote multidisciplinary research, this book explores what is currently known of the total relationship between the mass media, criminal justice, and criminality. It addresses a number of common misconceptions regarding the media's influence on crime and justice and their usefulness in fighting crime.

This book has four goals:

1. To introduce criminal justice students and personnel to the relevant mass media research.
2. To highlight and correct a number of common misconceptions regarding the mass media's effects on crime and justice.
3. To teach readers to be critical media consumers and insightful observers of the relationship between the media and crime and justice.
4. To provide researchers with a broader context for their specific studies and access to a wider range of literature.

Along these lines, the current research is reviewed and examples of ongoing field programs resulting from the research are described. The book is sensitive to the controversies in this area and the fact that various interpretations of the research exist. The words "images and realities" in the title in part reflect competing views of the media's influence on crime and justice and the existence of contradictory research findings.

In addition to the controversies over research, there exist a number of common misconceptions regarding the media, crime, and justice. For example, copycat criminals are normally thought of in connection with violent crime, but property crime appears to be the more influenced. In addition, policies and programs popularized in the mass media are often forwarded as crime cures. The current popularity of shock incarceration programs is a good example.

To create a foundation for readers to become critical media consumers, Chapter 1 introduces basic concepts from the realms of criminal justice and the media, providing a theoretical framework within which to examine the relationship between the media and crime and justice. Many readers will not have had previous exposure to the ideas of criminal justice and the media, and the book assumes no background in criminal justice, communications, or journalism. At the same time, the book is also directed at practicing professionals in both journalism and criminal justice. It provides insights and understanding for each in their dealings with professionals from the other discipline. To accommodate the varied audience, jargon and specialized terminology have been avoided.

This book addresses a major contemporary issue in crime and justice and will be of interest not only within the field of criminal justice but within the mass media and communications fields. It can be used as a primary text in courses that examine crime, justice, and the media, and as a supplemental text in courses in police and community relations, introductory criminal justice courses, and special-topic mass communication, public administration, and journalism courses.

PHILOSOPHY

Guiding this work is the idea that the media constitute a major force for cultural change. The media are also considered to comprise more than television, and print and electronic media are differentiated, with examples drawn from various media. This broad approach is necessary because their multiplicity is one reason the mass media are pervasive. The various media overlap to form a matrix, the many forms and interconections of which must be acknowledged in any discussion of the media's effects.

The mass media are considered to be a part of a process called the "social construction of reality." People use knowledge gained from the media to help construct an image of the world and behave in accordance with the perceived "reality" of that image. The media are felt to be especially important in the social construction of a crime and justice reality.

A book about the media, crime, and justice should encourage further reading and research. At a minimum, this book will induce its readers to ask questions about the media, such as why certain crime images are linked together in newscasts, why one crime story is placed on the front page and another on page 11, and why some explanations of crime and some policies are emphasized over others. This book will be a success if a reader can never again sit through a crime show or crime newscast without reacting thoughtfully.

ORGANIZATION, SCOPE, AND CONTENT

This book is organized into nine chapters. The first introduces and the last reconsiders the entire area. The second through the eighth delve into specific aspects of the media, crime, and justice relationship, beginning with crime and justice in the entertainment media (Chapter 2) and continuing through the news media (Chapter 3), media effects on attitudes about crime and justice (Chapter 4), the media as a cause of crime (Chapter 5), media-based anticrime programs (Chapter 6), the media and the courts (Chapter

7), and finally, the use of media technology in the judicial system (Chapter 8). It is possible to read the chapters independently or in a different order if desired. To obtain a feel for the full range and complexity of the media, crime, and justice relationship, all chapters are recommended.

THE TEXT

Because of the large amounts of research in certain areas, "research summaries" are utilized in places. In contrast, other areas have little research available and must be discussed in hypothetical terms. Hypotheses are distinguished from research conclusions throughout the text; what is proven is separated from what is indicated or only suspected. Examples from the media are included wherever possible, and it is strongly suggested that additional media examples be incorporated into a course plan.

ACKNOWLEDGMENTS

I would first like to thank the individuals at Brooks/Cole who contributed to the development and production of this book. Cindy Stormer was supportive in the early development of the text and Cat Collins was helpful in keeping the developmental process going. Lynne Fletcher did a heroic job as copy editor. Ruth Minerva diligently acquired the photographs. Carline Haga and Mary Kay Hancharick secured the necessary permissions. Roy Neuhaus designed the artwork and graphics. And Marjorie Sanders husbanded the project through to completion. All of them exhibited an attention to detail that I sometimes lack and I thank all of them for their patience and professionalism.

Others deserving thanks include Contemporary Issues in Criminal Justice Series Editor, Roy Roberg, who contributed excellent suggestions during the course of revisions, as did the many reviewers. To William J. Farrell, University of Michigan–Flint; Byron Johnson, Morehead State University; Richard R. E. Kania, Guilford College; Raymond Kessler, Sul Ross State University; Lynette Lee-Sammons, California State University–Sacramento; Lucien X. Lombardo, Old Dominion University; Joan Luxenburg, University of Central Oklahoma; and Joan McCord, Temple University, I extend my sincere appreciation, for the final work is much improved due to their insights and suggestions. I would also want to thank Thomas R. Julin of the law firm of Steel Hector & Davis in Miami, Florida, for his substantive case-law comments on Chapter 7. Lastly, I would be remiss if I did not acknowledge the students in my Crime and the Media classes at Florida International University. Their enthusiasm and interest played a central role in this book coming into existence.

Ray Surette

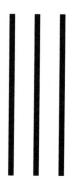

Contents

1 Mass Media, Crime, and Criminal Justice: An Introduction 1

4 The Media's Influence on Attitudes and Beliefs about Crime and Justice 79

5 The Media as a Cause of Crime 107

8 Media Technology and the Judicial System 221

9 Media Justice: From the Past, to the Future 245

1 Mass Media, Crime, and Criminal Justice: An Introduction

OVERVIEW

As indicated in the title, this chapter introduces the topics of the mass media and crime and justice. It opens with a discussion of why it is important to explore and understand the relationships between the mass media, crime, and our criminal justice system. The balance of the chapter examines basic concepts used throughout the book, drawn from the disciplines of criminal justice and mass communications. These concepts will orient the reader to the two disciplines. From the area of criminal justice come the opposing ideas of due process and crime control. From the area of mass communications the distinction between print media and electronic media is explained. These basic ideas are used as a means of bridging the separate realms of the mass media and criminal justice. The concepts of front-stage and backstage behavior are also introduced. These concepts are used in later chapters to explain some of the activities the media have emphasized in portraying crime and justice. Also covered in this chapter is the basic theoretical premise of the book: that people use knowledge they obtain from the media to construct a picture of the world, an image of reality on which they then base their actions. This process, sometimes called "the social construction of reality," is particularly important in the realm of crime, justice, and the media. Closing the chapter is a case study of courtroom television that exemplifies the value of these concepts in the study of the mass media, crime, and justice.

WHY STUDY THE MEDIA, CRIME, AND JUSTICE?

This book concerns a collision between two massive sets of social institutions, both critical to modern society. One set took its present shape only recently but has its roots in the sixteenth century. The other came into its modern elements five centuries ago and can be traced to antiquity. They are, respectively, the mass media's news and entertainment systems and the criminal justice system. Interest in both as independent entities is long-standing, but serious interest in their interaction and mutual effects is relatively recent. Although normally studied as separate and autonomous, the level of interaction between these institutions has soared in recent years, ranging in form from subtle media influences on citizens' attitudes toward crime and justice to the direct use of mass media technology to combat crime. Box 1-1 presents a set of examples showing the range of interaction between the media and the realm of crime and justice. The concerns and issues raised by this increasing and increasingly complex interaction have heightened interest in the relationship between the media and crime and justice.

Despite the heightened interest, however, there are presently no works that discuss the full range of the modern media's effects on the judicial, law enforcement, and correctional systems. This work is offered as a broad introductory survey of the continuing meshing of the mass media and the criminal justice system. It is primarily focused on the media's effects on our system of justice, rather than on a review of the judicial decisions, legislation, and law enforcement efforts that have influenced the mass media (although where relevant the perspectives and concerns of the media are included). The basic question addressed in this book is "How have the mass media changed the reality, and people's perceptions, of crime and criminal justice?"

Beyond academic interest, the study of the media–justice relationship is important for a number of reasons. First, the media are not neutral, unobtrusive social agents providing simple entertainment or news; their pervasiveness alone makes their influence extensive. As of 1987, for example, the television was on more than seven hours a day in the typical American home, and individual Americans watched, on average, more than four hours of television daily (Klain, 1989). Add radio listening and the reading of newspapers and magazines to these figures and it is clear that exposure to the mass media is virtually unavoidable. Indeed, the media's influence is felt to reach even those who do not attend to their messages (DeFleur & Dennis, 1985). Even if one does not watch, listen, or read, one buys products, wears fashions, talks to other persons, and lives under government policies influenced by the media. The media's pervasiveness is commonly acknowledged by a number of commentators on the media, crime, and justice.[1]

It is a basic assumption of this book that the media's changing coverage of and impact on crime and justice can be better understood by recognizing the media's role in the social construction of reality and the inherent nature of media institutions as organizations and businesses (see Box 1-2). An additional premise is that though the media collectively constitute a major force in society, they are more often driven by organizational needs than by political ideologies. In practice, however, in the competition among individuals and groups representing various ideologies to gain media attention, particular perspectives do fare better than others—a fact that is reflected in the way the media cover crime and justice and which has significant impli-

BOX 1-1 How the Media, Crime, and Justice Interact

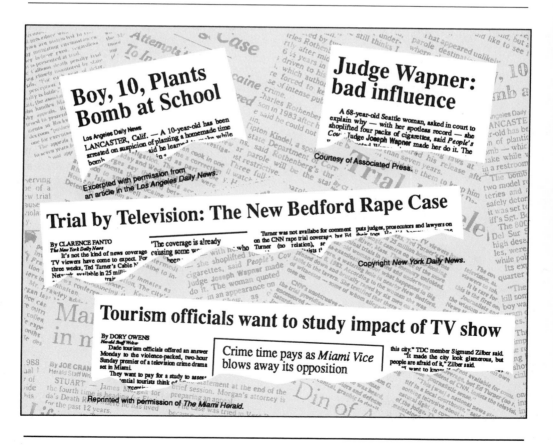

BOX 1-2 The Mass Media and the Social Construction of Reality

The theory known as the "social construction of reality" can help us better understand the socially pervasive and unavoidable mass media.[a] Under this theoretical view of society, people create reality—the world as they believe it exists—based on their individual knowledge and on social interactions with other people. People then act in accordance with their views of reality and society. Individuals gain the knowledge on which they base their social realities from four sources: personal experiences, significant others (peers, family, friends), other social groups and institutions (schools, unions, churches, government agencies), and the mass media (Altheide, 1984; Quinney, 1970; Tuchman, 1978). Through the socialization process, knowledge from all of these sources is mixed together, and from this mix, each individual constructs the "world." This socially constructed world is thus composed of events individuals believe to be happening; facts they believe to be true; causal processes they believe to be operating; relationships they believe to exist; and values, attitudes, and opinions they believe are valid and should be upheld. Not surprisingly, individuals with access to similar knowledge and who interact with one another a lot tend to construct similar social realities.

The sources of knowledge people use to socially construct reality vary in importance, however. The mass media increase in importance as the other sources decline (Cohen & Young, 1981; Lichter, 1988). In addition, the mass media tend to be more important in large industrialized societies like the United States, because other organizations and institutions must depend on the media to disseminate information from and about them (Altheide, 1984). In effect, the media establish powerful frames of reference for perceiving the world and are a strong component in shaping public attitudes and opinions. Their effect has been described as fourfold (Altheide, 1984):

1. History has come to be recorded and analyzed in terms of what media define as significant.

2. People with potential historical importance must rely on media exposure to ensure their place in history.
3. As the influence of media becomes even more widely known and accepted, what [the media report] becomes an essential determination of what is held to be significant.
4. Institutions are forced to present their own message and images within the accepted respectability and familiarity of media-determined formats.

Finally, because the organizations that constitute the media are also businesses, both organizational and economic factors come into play in determining the content of what they broadcast or print and, therefore, the social knowledge that people receive. In practice, the media's organizational nature and "for-profit" business values strongly influence content (Bortner, 1984; Quinney, 1974, p. 161). Thus, in the end, media organizations help construct reality but are bound by organizational constraints in the information that they contribute to the construction.

Associated with this theory is the question of the causal relationship between mass media and culture: Do the media cause cultural change or merely reflect it? As with the question of the chicken or the egg, the media's influence cannot be reduced to a simplistic answer. Rather, the relationship between the mass media and culture is felt to be reciprocal: Changes in one influence changes in the other; thus, the media change the culture, which changes the media, which change the culture, and so on (cf. Altheide & Snow, 1979; Comstock, 1980; Meyrowitz, 1985a). The mass media do not merely reflect behavior; they also establish meaning by presenting topics in formats dictated by the medium being used (Altheide & Snow, 1979, p. 47). They also legitimize people, social issues, and social policies for the general public. The media's depiction of crime-related subjects in particular has been cited as playing a prominent role in this social defining pro-

(continued)

BOX 1-2 (continued)

cess.[b] And though the media do not control the process of cultural change, the fact is that in geographically large, industrialized nations with hundreds of millions of people, cultural change without the media's involvement does not occur. This fact contradicts the popular notion, forwarded by the media industry, that the media simply reflect society. It also contradicts critical and political perspectives on media influence, which state that the media merely uphold, amplify, and extend the cultural status quo.[c] The media in America not only create new social situations but also alter and interact with those already existing (Meyrowitz, 1985a). The media simultaneously change, react to, and reflect culture and society.

---

[a]The ideas included within a social construction of reality fall under the broad umbrella of the sociology of knowledge tradition. See, for example, Karl Mannheim (1952, 1953) and Max Scheler (1926).
[b]See Bortner, 1984; Cohen & Young, 1981; Gerbner et al., 1978, 1979, 1980; Hans, 1990; Quinney, 1970; Surette, 1984a.
[c]See Agree et al., 1982; Curran & Seaton, 1980; DeFleur & Dennis, 1985; Lowery & DeFleur, 1983; Marcuse, 1972; Murdock & Golding, 1977; Quinney, 1970.

---

cations with regard to policies affecting crime and justice (Gorelick, 1989). For example, the Canadian Sentencing Commission concluded in 1988 that "The public . . . is forced to build its view of sentencing on a data-base which does not reflect reality" (1988, pp. 95–96, cited by Roberts & Doob, 1990, p. 452).

The policy implications of the mass media lead to a second reason to study media, crime, and justice. Over the last thirty years, massive amounts of money have been spent in the United States to control crime. Despite these huge sums, however, notable successes against crime have been few. The public's subsequent frustration has paradoxically resulted in the mass media's simultaneously being attacked as contributing to the crime problem while being increasingly utilized as a possible solution to crime. The resultant public policy efforts have worked to both limit and expand the domain of the media with regard to crime and justice in America. The causes of these conflicting and ambiguous perceptions need to be explored and clarified.

Third, amidst all the confusion surrounding the effects of the media, the study of media, crime, and justice also offers a unique potential for increasing our general understanding of society. A society's ideas of criminality and social justice reflect its values concerning humanity, social relationships, free will, and political ideologies. These ideas are put into operation and legitimized within the criminal justice system, and spread and further legitimized through the mass media. And though the mass media are only one source of citizens' knowledge about crime and justice, they have been singled out as the most common and pervasive source of shared information on crime and justice. According to one study, the mass media are credited with providing 95 percent of the information the public receives about crime (Graber, 1979; see also Box 4-1).

From a practical standpoint, a better understanding of the underlying dynamics of society can be gained by examining the points of contact between society's primary information system—the mass media—and its primary system for legitimizing values and enforcing norms—the criminal justice system. The criminal justice system acquires its legitimizing function by serving as a social arena in which the significance and value of social behaviors are designated. It thus serves not only as an institution through which legal disputes may be resolved but also as a mechanism by which a society's laws and system of government are legitimized. Hence anything that influences the public image of the judicial system also influences its legitimizing function and affects the functioning of the total social system (cf. Altheide, 1984). That the advantages of simultaneously studying justice and the media have not been exploited more fully is disheartening. A lack of research in crucial areas has left far more unanswered questions than definitive answers (Newman, 1990).

THE MASS MEDIA AND CRIMINAL JUSTICE: SOME INTRODUCTORY CONCEPTS

Because our focus is the interaction of two sets of institutions normally considered separately, we will use two sets of concepts, drawn respectively from the criminal justice and mass communications disciplines, to bridge the two. An understanding of these concepts will aid in understanding the dynamics and policy ramifications of the ongoing interaction between the mass media and crime and the criminal justice system (see Figures 1-1 and 1-2).

Criminal Justice: Due Process and Crime Control

The concepts of due process and crime control can be used to represent two opposing models of the operation of the criminal justice system. These models serve as conceptual frames for understanding the criminal justice system, its goals, and the mass media's effects on the system (see Packer, 1968). The models are abstract, of course, and do not represent existing criminal justice systems; rather, both models describe organizational case flows. Under the due process model, the criminal justice system is seen as an obstacle course in which the government must prove an accused person's guilt while conforming to strict procedural rules. The system's most important goal under this model is the protection of citizen rights and the prevention of arbitrary and capricious government actions. The key determination in this model is "legal guilt," which is decided at the end of a long and exacting process. In contrast, in the crime control model, the criminal justice system is perceived as an assembly line along which defendants should be processed as quickly and efficiently as possible. The primary goal of the system here is to punish criminals and to deter crime. The key determination in this model is "factual guilt," which is decided early in the pro-

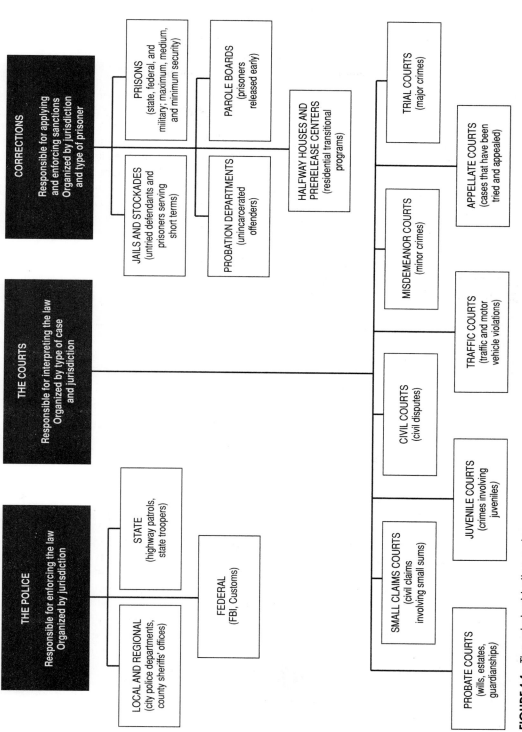

FIGURE 1-1 The criminal justice system

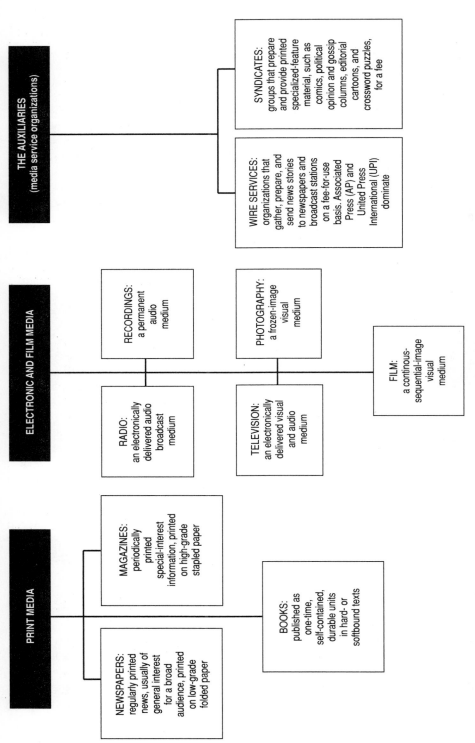

FIGURE 1-2 The mass media. The categories shown are not, of course, mutually exclusive, and there is much overlap among the media. For example, magazines and newspapers often use photographs, films may be shown on television, and recordings are a mainstay of radio.

cess in accordance with the perceived strength of each case and professional discretion.

These models make clear the basic source of conflict between the police and the courts, as police agencies are dominated by crime control advocates and the courts are normally more sensitive to due process considerations. Sometimes, one or the other of these two models dominates social policy; at such times, judicial decisions, too, tend to reflect the dominant model. During the 1960s, for example, the civil rights movement brought due process values to the fore, and the Supreme Court rendered a number of decisions limiting police practices. During the 1980s, when crime control values became dominant, the Court relaxed its position on several earlier strict rulings.

Beyond aiding in understanding the criminal justice system, these models are also useful for understanding the conflicting perceptions that exist within the criminal justice system regarding the mass media and their impact on crime and justice (Tajgman, 1981, p. 509). Conflicts arise because some view the media as mainly promoting due process goals by ensuring that the courts do not exercise power capriciously, while others view them as retarding due process protections by increasing the difficulty of finding impartial juries and conducting fair trials. Paradoxically, some also see the media as promoting the crime control model by educating the public about the functions of the justice system and by enhancing deterrence by publicizing the punishment of criminals, while others see them as hindering crime control efforts by interfering with the efforts of law enforcement to investigate and prosecute crimes, by negatively reporting unethical but effective law enforcement practices, and by withholding information and evidence from the courts.

Given these competing interpretations of mass media's effects, and the lack of empirical data and understanding regarding the media's true effects, the media can be perceived as either enhancing or hindering the criminal justice system depending on whether the effects are thought of as promoting due process or crime control goals. Note that even if people agree on the effects of the mass media on the criminal justice system, they may disagree as to whether these effects are good or bad. The same media effect— for example, making it more difficult for the police to conduct evidence searches—can be seen by some observers as promoting due process and thereby good, while being perceived by other observers as hindering crime control and therefore bad.

The Mass Media

Establishing a conceptual framework for understanding the mass media involves two types of ideas. The first builds on the concept of the social construction of reality and concerns the social behavior that the media report and portray. The second concerns the nature of the mass media themselves.

Front-Stage and Backstage Behavior

Within a socially constructed reality (see Box 1-2), specific types of be-havior are expected of people in specific social roles and places. Front-stage behavior is formal, planned behavior performed in professional and public settings. Such behavior is designed for public observation by a specific au-dience and is usually associated with a formal societal role, such as "stu-dent," "professor," "attorney," or "police officer." Given that a person can have different social roles, his or her front-stage behavior can also differ with the situation and the audience. Thus, a police chief may behave one way in front of patrol officers, another way in front of other lower-ranking officers, another way in front of other police chiefs, and yet another way in front of civilians. In contrast, backstage behavior usually consists of informal, unplanned, private actions that are not normally expected to be observed by anyone but the individual's intimates. Even with backstage behavior, how-ever, individuals may act differently with different audiences. Hence, police chiefs might act differently depending on whether they are with their family members or with personal friends.

As we shall see, these concepts can be used to describe the focus of the media—the type of behavior those who work in the media choose to re-port or portray. When applied to the subjects of media reporting, the con-cepts of front-stage and backstage behavior highlight a seminal difference between the two basic types of mass media: print media and electronic me-dia.[2]

Print and Electronic Media

As used in this work, the term *mass media* refers to media that are eas-ily, inexpensively, and simultaneously accessible to large segments of a pop-ulation. Systems for mass production and mass distribution of information must be in place before a society can have a mass medium. Thus, mass me-dia could not develop until the technology for printing was generally avail-able and a significant proportion of the population was literate—precondi-tions achieved in the United States in the 1800s. Hence, a review of mass media and justice need not begin in antiquity but can appropriately concen-trate on this century.

Note that the first mass medium to develop in the United States was a print medium: newspapers. Today, many people think of the media as a monolithic, singular entity comprising interchangeable parts or, alterna-tively, consisting only of television. But neither view is accurate or adequate. Print media—newspapers, books, and magazines—are still a vital part of the mass media, and print media and electronic media—radio, film, and television—are far from interchangeable.

Until the 1950s, print media dominated the mass media realm (although film and radio were not without influence). With the advent of commercial television in the 1950s, however, came a shift from a print-dominated for-mat to a visual, electronic-dominated one (see McLuhan, 1962, 1964; McLu-han & Fiore, 1967). Although not as dominant as once believed, the electronic visual media have challenged and caused changes in all other media—as well as causing changes in society. Consequently, to be able to follow developments in the relationship between the media and crime and justice, we must understand the basic differences between electronic visual media and print media (see also Real, 1989).

The Shift from Print to Electronic Visual Media

The electronic visual media, exemplified by television, are accessible and easy to comprehend. In contrast, print media, exemplified by newspapers, are difficult to use and distribute and require the learning of a difficult skill—the ability to read. Because print makes controlling the dissemination of information to selective, closed groups easy, it encourages elitism, the division of society into experts and nonexperts, segregated socialization, and social hierarchies. The visual electronic media, however, remove barriers that divide people of different ages and reading abilities. The impact is equivalent to allowing everyone to be present at wars, funerals, courtships, seductions, crimes, and cocktail parties. The electronic media make limiting access to its content to specific groups difficult. Instead, new audience boundaries for events are created, resulting, in essence, in new social events that are no longer shaped by physical location or require physical attendance (Meyrowitz, 1985b, p. 3D).

Another significant change that followed the shift from print to electronic media resulted from the kind of news coverage each medium encourages. The electronic media lend themselves to instantaneous or same-day reporting of events that emphasizes holistic impressions and emotions. In contrast to print media, their holistic nature makes presenting complicated, analytical, fact-heavy reports difficult. Over the long term, this characteristic led to a shift in emphasis, from reporting front-stage behavior to exposing backstage behavior.

When the print media dominated, large aspects of a public person's life were simply not reported. It wasn't that reporters didn't know negative facts

---

Among other effects, the print media's fostering of elitism led to the development of a distinct literature for women, adults, children, academics, practitioners, professionals, and laypersons. The trend toward separate realms of information that was accessible only to a select group was also evident in the proliferation of professional "jargons." Each professional group felt compelled to create special code words and language so that they could communicate in front of clients without revealing "privileged" information. Medicine and law best exemplify this process, and these fields have been the most affected by the electronic media's promotion of common, open communication systems with a minimal use of jargon.

about public personages, but that reporting them would have been seen as in bad taste and beyond the acceptable purview of the media. In addition, though the print media can be more analytical in their reporting and can cover a story in more detail, and thus might seem better able to cover backstage behavior, they are less suited to emotional, visceral reporting than, say, television. As the electronic media became dominant, the scope of acceptable media reporting expanded as a matter of course to include these backstage areas. Under the influence of the electronic media, the social norms regarding what is private and what is fair game for media coverage also changed.

Spurred in the 1960s and 1970s both by competition within the industry to expose new behavior and by the advent of aggressive, investigative, exposé-style reporting, the electronic media, followed by the print media, have pursued and reported more and more backstage, previously private behavior on the part of individuals (Meyrowitz, 1985a, p. 111). This development is most apparent in regard to politicians, who used to be able to control much of what was known about them through selective front-stage events such as speeches and political rallies, and who now try to manage and limit media coverage to these orchestrated events.[3] The pervasiveness and invasiveness of the present-day electronic media, however, coupled with investigative reporting and a journalistic norm under which no behavior is regarded as off limits, has weakened the ability of individuals and institutions to keep backstage events and behavior private. At the same time, this development has paradoxically caused the creation of staged media events (termed "pseudo events" by Daniel Boorstin, 1961) to try to increase the media's coverage of front-stage behavior. But despite the large market for staged media events—events that are visual and appear spontaneous but that are scheduled and planned to meet the electronic media's needs—the long-term trend in both the print and the electronic media has been toward more, and more intensive, coverage of backstage behavior.

The development of the electronic media has also meant the development of sophisticated new communications technology. This work will also discuss media technology and its application in law enforcement and judicial settings. By "media technology" is meant the audio and visual communications equipment that has become available because of the mass media telecommunications advances of the last few decades. In practice, the visual element is emphasized, with videotape, television, and camera technology playing a central role. This technology can be computer enhanced, taped or live, located at a single or several sites, and linked by various methods such as closed circuitry or microwave. In general, the ultimate goal in using the technology in the criminal justice field is to simulate a live person-to-person encounter and conversation.

Compounding the effect of exposing backstage behavior, the electronic media, unlike the print media, are easily available to everyone. The content of modern electronic mass media therefore has the potential to create problems, not because its content is necessarily new but because such information was previously available to fewer people. Even conservative content may be revolutionary when disseminated in new ways to new groups (Meyrowitz, 1985a, pp. 87, 319; see also Foucault, 1977; Goffman, 1961). The social knowledge available to people to construct their realities is simultaneously expanded and homogenized. People now have access to information they previously did not have, and everyone tends to be exposed to the same information. The social effects are multiple.

For one, arcane social realms have been demystified as more information about them has become available. The recent opening of previously closed social institutions (such as prisons, schools, private clubs, courts) reverses a trend several hundred years old, one at least partly supported by the print media's inherent fostering of separate realms of information (Meyrowitz, 1985a, p. 310). Such a trend has also been noted in the judicial system, with some arguing that the use of electronic media has caused legal interactions to become less abstract and more accessible (Katsh, 1989). As the amount of available information has increased, many social roles have become extinct, inappropriate, or severely altered—the "All-American" sports idol, for example. In addition, the idea that a special place is needed for special events is rapidly fading. Like religious services and churches, and teaching and classrooms, the concepts of trials and courtrooms are no longer invariably linked. One need no longer be in the latter place to take part in the former activity. Finally, in a loop effect, information the public receives from the media ultimately affects the information the media distributes. Thus, previously hidden backstage behaviors become acceptable media entertainment content: Bigotry, for example, becomes the central theme of the television show "All in the Family" (Meyrowitz, 1985a, p. 175).

These effects have resulted in a number of paradoxes regarding the media's relationship with crime and justice (see Box 1-3). Chief among them is that the media are simultaneously perceived as both a major cause of crime and violence and an untapped but powerful potential solution to crime. These paradoxes and some common misconceptions about the effects of the media on crime and justice will be explored in later chapters.

The criminal justice system and its institutions have been significantly affected by the pervasiveness and invasiveness of the media. The prognosis is that the legitimacy of the criminal justice system will come to be questioned more and more as more of its daily backstage operations are exposed through the efforts of the media. It is no coincidence that concern over the demystification of the criminal justice system and its attendant loss of legitimacy, and outcries against the prevalence of plea bargains, case delays, and arbitrary discretionary decisions arose as the electronic mass media grew and the social "reality" of crime and justice changed.

BOX 1-3   Paradoxes in the Relationship Between the Media and Crime and Justice

* The media are commonly accused of being a primary cause of crime and violence in society, yet people increasingly turn to them as a possible panacea for crime and the problems of the criminal justice system.

  · In society we look to the media to help reduce violence and drug use, deter crime, and bolster the image of the criminal justice system, especially the courts.
  · In law enforcement we look to the media to aid in criminal investigations, manhunts, and street and vehicle patrols.
  · In the courts we look to the media for assistance in processing criminal cases, reducing case backlogs, conducting trials, and presenting testimony and evidence.
  · In corrections we look to the media to improve security in institutions and help rehabilitate offenders.

* The media more often than not portray the criminal justice system and its people negatively and as ineffective. Yet the cumulative effect of these portraits appears to be increased support for more police, more prisons, and more money for the criminal justice system.
* Although the criminal justice system is not shown positively, crimes are nearly always solved in the media—estimates put the solution rate on television at greater than 90 percent.
* Despite their long history of portraying stories of crime and justice, the media persist in presenting a wholly and often absurdly unrealistic picture of crime and justice.
* The media and the criminal justice system

normally react to criminal events in much the same manner, concentrating their resources on investigating the facts for later presentation to a specific audience. In the end, however, the two systems are often placed in adversarial positions, with, ironically, the judicial system called on to resolve the disputes.

* Trial courts and judges generally use the least effective means available to counteract possible prejudicial effects of media publicity and are encouraged by the Supreme Court to do so.
* The media seek access to government-held information and files while arguing their right to withhold their own information and files from access.
* Although crime news is portrayed as being objective and chosen for its newsworthiness, it is routinely created and prepackaged by and for news agencies, which then present the news within the framework of preestablished stereotypical themes.
* As the technical capability to cover crime news has expanded, media organizations have instead increasingly blurred news and entertainment, and a few have merged their news and entertainment departments. In the process, crime news has become the mainstay of new hybrid news–entertainment, or "infotainment," shows.
* Contrary to their intent, media-based anticrime programs can result in the public's taking fewer crime protection measures.
* The most effective media-based anticrime programs are the most controversial and raise the greatest concerns.

A CASE STUDY: CAMERAS IN THE COURTROOM

The concepts of front-stage and backstage behavior, due process and crime control, and the inherent differences between print and electronic media can be applied to understanding the way the mass media and criminal justice system interact with one another by looking at how attitudes toward televising courtroom proceedings have changed over the last twenty years. Some have argued that the Supreme Court, in its 1965 ruling in *Estes* v. *Texas* (381 U. S. 532), was influenced by its belief that the televising of trials inherently violated the due process rights of defendants—a negative effect that was not, in the Court's view, counterbalanced by any positive crime control effect. In 1981, in *Chandler* v. *Florida* (101 S.Ct. 802), however, the Court appeared to have altered its view of courtroom cameras in accordance with a change in its attitudes regarding the effects of those cameras. Television was now seen as promoting both crime control and due process, and thus was now a positive addition to a proceeding (see Nesson & Koblenz, 1981; Tajgman, 1981). This change in the Supreme Court's attitude can also be understood in terms of front-stage and backstage behavior and the growing influence of the electronically dominated mass media.

First, in the years between *Estes* and *Chandler,* there was growing concern among the judiciary that the public lacked confidence in the courts' ability to control crime and criminals, and that it viewed the courts as partly responsible for the increasing crime rates. In this negative atmosphere,

> televising trials [began to] look to some judges like a possible counter to charges against the judiciary. Trials, after all, show the justice system at its best.

Estes v. *Texas,* 381 U. S. 532 (1965)

Texas financier Billie Sol Estes was accused of a salad-oil swindle. The case was important in Texas due to Estes's political associations, and cameramen crowded into a tiny courtroom with their cameras and seriously disrupted the proceedings. After a trial of great notoriety, which was televised despite his objection, Estes appealed his conviction, arguing that the presence of television cameras denied him a fair trial. The Supreme Court agreed and reversed the decision.

Chandler v. *Florida,* 101 S.Ct. 802 (1981)

Florida policeman Noel Chandler was tried and convicted with another police officer for a series of burglaries. The case received a large amount of regional media attention and was televised over Chandler's objection as part of a Florida pilot program for televising judicial proceedings in the state. The Supreme Court held that if other constitutional due process guarantees are met, a state could provide for television coverage of a criminal trial over the objection of defendants.

The camera's eye will see impartial justice, fair procedure, conviction of the guilty, and the imposition of sentence. Though some may denigrate the trial process, it is impressive. By contrast, the seamy side of the criminal process—plea bargaining, the procedural inefficiency, the arbitrariness inherent in police and prosecutor discretion—will go unseen. Televising trials, in other words, is unlikely to hurt and may help shore up the image of the judiciary. (Nesson & Koblenz, 1981, pp. 408–409)

Thus, the courts saw televised trials as a means of presenting controlled, formal front-stage behavior to the public while protecting their backstage assembly-line processes from further exposure. Furthermore, the basic policy issue underlying the question of whether or not to allow television cameras in the courtroom was not the freedom of the media to report courtroom matters (broadcast journalists can attend and report trials as can other reporters) but the effects of expanding the trial audience to include persons not in the courtroom. At the time of *Estes,* the court feared the effects of this expansion on both the trial participants and the expanded electronic audience.

One reason for this concern is that traditionally in the courtroom information is shared in a form and process different from that preferred by the media. Lawyers extract information point by point in long story lines following strict legal procedures and rules of evidence before a limited audience of a judge or jury (cf. Bennett, Feldman, & Feldman, 1983). In contrast, media stories are outwardly directed and focus on entertainment value rather than on legal relevance. They are brief, time- or space-limited stories that must make their points quickly, and they are selected according to their perceived newsworthiness and built around whatever film or dramatic elements are available (Altheide, 1984).

Thus, the courts have traditionally been an internally controlled front-stage production, but media coverage of the courts focuses on external audiences and dramatic backstage presentations and information. The concern in *Estes* was that the presence of the electronic media would cause courtroom participants to alter the way they present testimony and arguments to suit the media instead of conforming to courtroom format, and that in the process they would delegitimize the whole judicial system by revealing previously shielded information regarding case negotiations and the influence of nonlegal factors (cf. Altheide, 1984; Barber, 1987; Tajgman, 1981). Some also feared that close media coverage would cripple the judicial system by forcing it to rigidly adhere to the formal procedures and by making discretion and plea bargaining impossible. In effect, the social reality of the courts would be changed forever and for the worse.

The basic fear at the time of the *Estes* decision concerned the compatibility of the traditional mission of the judicial system with the addition of television cameras to courtrooms.

The transporting of the sights and sounds of courtroom behavior into a public arena is a qualitative change and not merely journalistic enrichment. The question of whether televising selected trials of great audience appeal improves responsible reporting, enhances public understanding, or hastens needed court reform [is unanswered]. The concern is that an audio-visual element may only enhance dramatic appeal, override other more traditional journalistic considerations, contribute to the pressures for popular rather than fair and dispassionate courtroom behavior, inhibit rather than assist the exposure of less visible justice system needs and problems, and transform television [courtroom] reporting into a dramatic spectacle. (Barber, 1987, pp. xiii, xvi)

However, bolstered by research evidence reported between the *Estes* (1965) and *Chandler* (1981) decisions that indicated that the effects of the presence of television cameras on the traditional trial participants were benign, and acting on its own new attitude that televised trials forwarded both due process and crime control, the Supreme Court decided in *Chandler* that an electronically expanded trial audience was a desirable goal. Whether linking courts to television will enhance or diminish the integrity of the criminal justice system in the eyes of the general public is still to be determined. But whether or not televised trials will remain in judicial favor can

---

BOX 1-4 Arguments for and Against Allowing Television Cameras in the Courtroom

Against (circa 1965 and Estes v. Texas):

1. Trial participants' primary audience would shift from the courtroom to the external public.
2. The judicial system would lose control, mystique, and legitimacy.
3. Courtroom distractions would increase, and witnesses already stressed because of having to appear in court would be further stressed, hampering examination.
4. Jurors, concerned with being on camera, would concentrate less on the proceedings.
5. Lawyers would be tempted to play to the cameras rather than to the jury.
6. A distorted picture of court proceedings would be portrayed, and to a wider audience.
7. Television is inherently biasing: "Television in its present state and by its very nature reaches into a variety of areas in which it may cause prejudice to an accused . . . the televising of criminal trials is inherently a denial of due process" (381 U. S. at 538 and 544).

For (circa 1981 and Chandler v. Florida):

1. There is no research evidence that cameras in the courtroom negatively affect courtroom personnel or trial participants.
2. Modern technology has made equipment less obtrusive and smaller and eliminated the need for cables and special lighting or power.
3. The public has become so used to television as a fact of everyday life that judges no longer consider the fact that jurors are aware of the cameras or that the presence of television cameras indicates to jurors that the trial is significant sufficient to demonstrate prejudice.
4. The televising of trials could bolster the courts' image, as the impressive front-stage ceremony of the courtroom can be seen as the judicial system at its best.
5. Television promotes both crime control and due process.
6. By educating the public about the judicial process, expanding the trial audience would help promote deterrence and increase the legitimacy of the law. In the end, public confidence in the courts would increase.

be predicted by examining whether or not their effects continue to be seen as forwarding due process or crime control goals, which model's values appear to be socially dominant at the time in question, which trial audience (traditional or electronically expanded) is felt to be most affected and in what way, and whether or not trials continue to be the front-stage events that the courts wish to project to the public (see Box 1-4). Should trials come to be seen as expensive, ostentatious, and ineffective events, or as due process mechanisms in a period emphasizing crime control, judicial opposition to their televising will rise. In turn, the mass media will be less attracted to the televising of trials as they become more common and will want instead to reveal newer, backstage behavior within the criminal justice system. Early evidence of this process is shown by the emergence of syndicated television shows such as "Cops," in which real police officers are accompanied on patrols and drug busts by media news crews.

CONCLUSION

The mass media, crime, and criminal justice are seen to be intricately intertwined. An understanding of crime and justice cannot be gained without acknowledging and examining the mass media and their effects. Through the criminal justice models of due process and crime control, and the mass communications concepts of front-stage and backstage behavior and print versus electronic media, many aspects of the contemporary crime and justice scene can be related and better comprehended.

The balance of this book examines the contemporary effects of media on justice. Each chapter deals with a unique facet of the media–justice collision. The concepts of front- and backstage behaviors, due process and crime control models, and the inherent differences between print and electronic media will serve as reference points throughout the chapters.

The next two chapters review the historical development and content of the entertainment and news media. The media have a long history of employing crime themes, and crime's popularity is tied to its being the ultimate backstage behavior, with the associated element of audience voyeurism. Taken together, Chapters 2 (entertainment) and 3 (news) provide the historical foundation and knowledge base necessary to comprehend the contemporary issues and developments in the media justice field.

Notes

1. See, for example, Altheide & Snow, 1979; Comstock, 1980; Gerbner et al., 1980; Gorelick, 1989; Humphries, 1981; Murray, 1980; Newman, 1990.

2. The concepts of backstage and front-stage behavior originate in Erving Goffman's concepts of regions and region behavior (see *The Presentation of Self in Everyday Life,* 1959). Here, however, they are not used precisely as Goffman used them but have been adapted to reflect a change in style and focus in the media over the last thirty years. In their simplest conceptions in this work, backstage behaviors can be thought of as behaviors that a generation ago would have been considered private and in bad taste for the media to portray or report. Front-stage behaviors, on the other hand, are those public behaviors that, if not especially created for the media, are not hidden from the media's attention. Goffman's original concepts described individual face-to-face interactions rather than interpersonal behaviors portrayed and perceived through the media, but by extending and transforming his concepts, we are better able to understand and discuss the development of the relationship between the media and crime and justice (see Goffman, 1959, 1967); for while Goffman's model of back- and front-region behaviors describes a static set of stages and is limited to face-to-face interactions, the principles im-

plicit in it can be adapted to describe the changes in situations and behaviors brought about by new media (Meyrowitz, 1985a, p. 46).

3. Lichter (1988, p. 36) argued that the emergence of the national media is the single most influential factor in transforming the political process and the political culture of late twentieth-century America (see also Dye & Zeigler, 1986).

2 Crime and Justice in the Entertainment Media

OVERVIEW

This chapter covers the historical development and present-day content of the popular entertainment media in regard to crime and justice. First discussed is how crime and justice were portrayed in entertainment prior to the development of the twentieth-century mass media. This review of the "pre–mass media" media shows that the broad stereotypes of criminals and the view of crime as an individual problem found in today's media were established by the late nineteenth century. Also forwarded within this discussion are insights about the long historical popularity of crime and justice themes in entertainment.

Cinema emerged at the turn of the century as the first true mass entertainment medium, and this chapter covers its development and social impact. Major trends in the depiction of crime and justice in film are chronologically traced up to the decline of cinema and its replacement in the 1950s by television as the primary mass entertainment medium. Television's emergence is discussed with a review of its organizational and business roots in commercial radio, its phenomenal growth, and its reliance on crime themes for prime time shows. Crime is seen to be the single most popular story element in the forty-year history of U. S. commercial television, with crime-related shows regularly accounting for one-fourth to one-third of all of the three major networks' prime time shows.

A review and summary of the recent content analysis studies on crime and justice follow. This research has consistently reported a sharp divergence between the crime and justice depicted by the entertainment media and any real-world measures of crime and justice. Detailed in this discussion are the media images of law enforcement, the courts, and corrections—none of which are positive.

The chapter concludes with a discussion of the major implications of the entertainment media's content with regard to the kind of society it describes, the explanation it offers of crime, and the public policies it suggests.

CRIME AND JUSTICE IN THE EARLY POPULAR MEDIA

Crime has been attractive to the entertainment media precisely because it is the preeminent backstage behavior. By nature and necessity, most crime is private, secretive, and hidden, surreptitiously committed and studiously concealed. To the degree that entertainment is escapism and novel, the backstage nature of crime inherently increases its entertainment value and popularity. The more serious the crime, the more backstage it is and the more novel an audience is likely to find its portrayal. Portrayals of crime also allow audiences voyeuristic glimpses of rare and often bizarre acts—often coupled with lofty discussions of justice, morality, and society (Everson, 1964). As a means of showing people new places, new activities, and new perspectives, as escapism and as exposé, the portrayal of crime has been a rich source for the entertainment media.

Crime and justice has been a theme in popular entertainment at least since Apollo successfully defended Orestes on a charge of matricide in Aeschylus's *Oresteia*. English literature continued the trend of the classics, with criminals common figures in ballads, songs, and tales of medieval England, frequently portrayed as romantic and heroic (Stark, 1987, p. 236).[1] Likewise, crime and criminals have been ubiquitous elements in American entertainment since the beginning of the republic (Grenander, 1976, p. 48).

However, with large-scale industrialization, urbanization, and ethnic immigration in the nineteenth century, crime for the first time became one of the nation's principal concerns (Papke, 1987; Stark, 1987). Spurred by growing public worry about crime, by the second half of the nineteenth century the dominant image of the criminal in the popular media had shifted from earlier romantic, heroic portraits to more-conservative, negative images. The media of this "antebellum" period were already presenting the stereotypical portraits and themes of crime and justice that would later dominate movies and television—portraits and themes still to be found in modern entertainment media (Stark, 1987).

Crime and Justice in Nineteenth-Century Print Media

The two most popular genres to emerge in nineteenth-century print media were detective and crime thriller magazine serials and books (dime novels).[2] Both were escapist literature, and by the latter half of the nineteenth century they described crime as originating in individual personality or moral weakness (Papke, 1987, p. 117). By downplaying wider social and structural explanations of crime, these works helped to reinforce the existing social order—the status quo. In addition, the "heroic" detectives in these works closely resembled the criminals they apprehended—calculating, often odd loners, operating in the world of justice but not bound to it (Stark, 1987, p. 237). In contrast to earlier crime fighters, who were harsh social critics and whose concerns about legal fairness were more in line with the due process model, these heroes had become darker agents espousing social order and crime control (Papke, 1987, p. 105). Detective and

The cover from one of the popular nineteenth-century
dime detective novels
Source: Culver Pictures

crime thrillers of the late nineteenth century thus mark the beginning of a trend toward a more violent popular media that is less critical of social conditions and contributes to the construction of a social reality in which crime is predatory and rooted more in individual failure than in social ills (Papke, 1987, p. 108).

It was also in the late 1800s that the popular media industry divided itself into distinct marketing genres (westerns, romantic novels, detective mysteries, crime thrillers, and so forth). It followed up this diversification with extensive advertising and standardization of its products (Papke, 1987, p. 102). By the 1890s, writers for the entertainment mass market were highly specialized professionals working within well-organized branches of an immense "culture industry" in which production, marketing, and consumption were all meshed. The portrayals of crime and justice produced during this time are surprisingly similar to today's, because the crime-and-justice themes established by the late nineteenth century are in many ways the same as those found in today's entertainment media. Both present images that reinforce the status quo, promote the impression that competent, often heroic individuals are pursuing and capturing criminals, and encourage the belief that criminals can be readily recognized and crime ultimately curtailed through direct law enforcement efforts (Papke, 1987, pp. 181–182).

Given this fact, the primary difference between early popular print media and today's electronically based visual entertainment media in terms of the portrayal of crime and justice is the development of new delivery systems. From the nineteenth-century mass media dominated by print (novels and magazine serials) through the media now dominated by electronically delivered visual images (television, cable television, and home video), the broad messages of crime and justice have remained relatively constant, with only a few evolutionary changes. Because of this fact, a review of the development of the contemporary mass entertainment media can safely emphasize movies and television.

Movies and television are commonly acknowledged as the most influential, accessible, and pervasive of the communications media. And because of these characteristics, they have been the subject of the most research, speculation, and public concern. The print media, of course, also present images of crime and justice as entertainment. Novels, magazines, and newspapers have long carried fiction and first-person stories involving criminality, and such stories continually appear on best-seller lists. There exist today a number of specialty magazines (such as *True Detective*) devoted entirely to stories of crime.[3] The history of the novel is intimately bound with depictions of crime, and early in the United States there were even concerns that these portrayals would be imitated by youth (Hartsfield, 1985, pp. 105–106; see also Papke, 1987). In addition, comic books have a long history of crime-and-justice images (see Mooney & Ferell, 1989). Because of space restrictions, however, and because books, comic books, and magazines are inherently different from the modern mass media, which are dominated by newspapers and television, we will not examine these media in depth. With these early media, the consumer made a clear decision to use or not use them, and thus exposure to their content was less "massive" and more selective, unlike with the modern mass media, whose images and messages can hardly be avoided.

CRIME AND JUSTICE IN FILM AND ON TELEVISION

The Development of the Film Industry and Its Social Impact

It was through movies at the beginning of this century that the popular entertainment media were first able to blanket all of society with images of justice and criminality. The movie industry was able to accomplish what the print media, limited to books, newspapers, and magazines, previously could not. It nationalized the content of entertainment by making its portrayals available to every social, economic, and intellectual stratum. Initially silent and inexpensive to go see, the movies did not even require a common audience language. The images were universally available and widely consumed, and the film industry rapidly came to reflect and shape American culture. Within two decades of film's introduction in 1895, the film industry had grown to be the most influential popular entertainment medium in America. By 1923, there were approximately fifteen thousand movie theaters in the United States (Jowett & Linton, 1980, pp. 68–69). By the 1930s, some 80 million people per week in a U. S. population of 122 million attended a movie (Armour, 1980, p. xxi). With their immense popularity, the movies were the first modern mass medium, and their emergence heralded the creation of a twentieth-century mass culture, a culture that is significantly homogeneous across geographic, economic, and ethnic lines (Jowett & Linton, 1980, p. 68; see also Altheide & Snow, 1979).

The social impact of the cinema was pervasive and extensive, affecting the American public's values, political views, social behavior, consumption patterns, and perceptions of the world (see Armour, 1980, pp. xxii–xxiv; Jowett & Linton, 1980, pp. 69, 109; Shadoian, 1977, p. 3). Concerns about the

It was in 1895 in Paris that the first film was shown to a paying audience. By 1905, movies were established, separate, profitable entertainment businesses installed at 5-cent Nickelodeons that showed short features. In 1915, the first major motion picture, *Birth of a Nation*, was released, and the motion picture industry as we conceive it today was established. The studio system, feature films, and stars soon became a staple of the U. S. culture (Armour, 1980, p. xix). By 1917, the motion picture was established as the premier commercial entertainment form in the world. The American film industry began its domination of the worldwide film industry during the 1920s, and movies maintained their dominance of the entertainment media until the advent of commercial television in the 1950s.

movies' widespread influence developed nearly as quickly as the industry (Jowett & Linton, 1980, p. 73). By 1915 the Supreme Court had already considered and ruled that movies were not protected under the First Amendment of the U. S. Constitution as a form of free speech (see *Mutual Film Corporation* v. *Hodges* and *Mutual Film Corporation* v. *Industrial Commission of Ohio*). In a number of localities, people began trying to regulate this new media as soon as it emerged (Jowett & Linton, 1980).

The movies were socially significant for several reasons. By the twentieth century, urbanization, industrialization, and a national communications system made up of the telegraph, postal, and telephone systems had increased our economic and cultural interdependence and social homogeneity, increasing, in combination with the media, the similarity of our socializing experiences and general social knowledge. Movies became a major contributor to this ongoing homogenizing process. As both a social event and a source of social information, movies were the first medium able to bypass the traditional socializing agents of church, school, family, and community and directly reach individuals with information and images (Jowett & Linton, 1980, pp. 69, 71–72).

Film was therefore the first mass medium with the ability to create a mass public—a large homogeneous consumer group comprising individuals from many ethnic, social, and economic strata who, regardless of their differences, now shared much in the way of social information and icons. The movies helped to create a national social perspective and contributed to a collective vision of people and life (Jowett & Linton, 1980, p. 75). Messages about the nature of society and the kinds of individuals it contains were projected again and again to the public. From repeated messages and images related to crime and justice emerged recurring themes (Shadoian, 1977, p. 3).

Historical Trends in the Portrayal of Crime and Justice in Film

Portraits of crime and justice appeared early in film's development, and they have continued to be a popular staple of film. Besides being the central theme of police, detective, robbery, and gangster movies, crime and justice are often secondary plot elements in love stories, westerns, comedies, and dramas. Though, of course, not every movie produced during a particular time frame portrayed the same crime-and-justice theme, dominant themes have been identified with certain periods, and the evolution of the image of crime in film can be conceived of as a dramatized documentary of twentieth-century American history (Rosow, 1978). Thus, the first film criminals were descendants of western outlaws, but unlike the "bandit heroes" of western dime novels, early film criminals were usually portrayed as urban capitalists (Rosow, 1978, p. 37). Most of these early portraits depicted ruthless crooks engaged in corrupt business practices in the pursuit of wealth, a motif that has remained popular to this day (Rosow, 1978, pp. 11–21). Also common in film plots between 1910 and 1920 were nostalgic portrayals of a pure and simple youthful criminality, reflecting street gang experiences among working-class

One of the movies' first criminals in *The Great Train Robbery*
Source: The Bettmann Archive

immigrants.[4] From the 1920s to the 1950s, the film criminal was transformed from an early-twentieth-century immigrant into a returning World War I veteran, into a high-rolling bootlegger and ruthless Depression era gunman, into a modern corporate or syndicate, executive–gangster (Rosow, 1978, p. xiv).

Thus, in the 1920s the media image of criminals was of a socially tolerated "pseudo small businessman."[5] Reflecting the extravagant materialistic lifestyle of the Roaring Twenties, an aura of romantic idolatry surrounded the criminal during this period. This shifted somewhat during the early Depression years, however, when positive portrayals of "Robin Hoods" competed with negative portrayals of "robber barons," and criminals were shown both as heroes and as villains. It is noteworthy that in both the heroic and the villainous portrayals, criminals enjoyed full lives and were often decisive, intelligent, attractive individuals. Whether basically good or bad, criminals were shown as active decision makers who went after what

The theme of the "western," popularized after the West was actually won, reflects a desire for an uncomplicated system of law and order, easily understood and administered, coupled with a distrust of legal nuances of right and wrong that are difficult to decipher and interpret. In westerns, the common man and frontier justice always win (Grenander, 1976, p. 48; Stark, 1987, p. 238). In a way frontier justice reflects a desire for due process "fairness" with crime control "efficiency." Ideally, a man was given a fair opportunity to make things right, but once guilt was established, punishment was quickly and usually violently administered (Newman, 1990, citing Neale, 1980, p. 48). This ideal is best reflected in the popular western books of Louis L'Amour and the classic western films such as *Shane* and *High Noon.*

they wanted, be it money, sex, or power. They controlled their lives, lived well, and decided their own fates, in contrast to the crushing, impoverished helplessness much of the public felt during the Depression. Besides casting criminals in a positive light, this image projected the strong message that worldly success often indicated criminality on the part of the successful individual. To be successful in America, some larceny was acceptable and probably necessary. By extension, this portrait reflected negatively on all real individuals who were successful and powerful, painting them as probable crooks (Rosow, 1978, p. 174).

Concern that such a message could influence people to turn to crime sparked investigations and censorship drives, beginning in the late 1920s. In 1929 the Payne Foundation underwrote the first large-scale study of the impact of mass media—in this case, the consequences of movies.[6] The research was especially aimed at examining the effects of movies on deviant, asocial, and violent behavior on the part of juveniles. These research efforts, combined with the public's concerns about the influence of the cinema, helped prompt the film industry to create its own internal review panel, the Hays Commission, to oversee the content of films and thereby quell increasing calls for government intervention (see Hays, 1932). In response to these developments, in the 1930s the movie industry shifted to "G-man" films in which federal law enforcement agents rather than criminals were made the heroes, a shift mirrored in the radio crime dramas of the time as well (Stark, 1987, p. 240). Stars such as James Cagney who had previously played only criminals now found themselves cast as crime fighters. However, this was a limited change in that local police continued to be portrayed negatively: as incompetents in the "Keystone Cops" and Charlie Chaplin films of the 1940s, as heavies in the film noir of the 1930s and 1940s, and as good guys only on television. Early portrayals of the police so upset the International Association of the Chiefs of Police that its members passed a resolution at their 1913 meeting, pledging to do as much as possible to change those depictions (see Stark, 1987, p. 239, citing R. Fogelson, *Big-City Police,* Harvard University Press, 1977).

James Cagney *(right)* portraying the dynamic, shrewd criminal in *Public Enemy*
Source: Culver Pictures

In the 1940s, depictions of violence, terrorism, and murder became more graphic, as gangsters, policemen, and detectives (many now with weapon fetishes) became more violent (McArthur, 1972, pp. 29–30, 46; Rosow, 1978, pp. 253, 262–268). In response to the introduction of television in the 1950s, Hollywood began marketing crime syndicate films and using a pseudo-documentary style and biographies to enhance movies' realism and suggest that deeper, truer backstage criminality was being revealed. As with the earlier gangster movies of the 1920s, the tendency in these organized-crime films was to romanticize the criminal lifestyle as the way of life within violent criminal brotherhoods (Rosow, 1978, p. 319).

The decline of film as the primary mass medium portraying images of crime and justice began in the late 1940s with the introduction of commercial television, a medium even more pervasive, direct, and influential than

Radio drama, particularly at its height during the 1930s and 1940s, also included a substantial—though never a dominant—proportion of crime-related programming, carrying such programs as "The Shadow," "Sherlock Holmes," and "True Detective." Television programmers also borrowed from this tested set of plots and themes in developing their shows. Radio's portrayals of criminality were not significantly different from film's, the primary difference being, of course, that violence could not be shown.

The "Keystone Cops" portraying the traditional law enforcers of the criminal justice system
Source: Culver Pictures

film. Criminality in the cinema (and in radio), however, had provided a fifty-year pool of plots, themes, and portraits for television to develop. Not surprisingly, television entertainment largely continued the images of crime and justice that had been created in film.

Television's Emergence

Introduced between 1948 and 1951, television soon replaced radio as the primary home entertainment medium, and as already noted, forced the movie industry to restructure (Dominick, 1978). Television's growth and public acceptance was phenomenal and it quickly dominated the media industry. The existence of established business and organizational models in commercial radio facilitated television's rapid emergence. CBS and NBC already existed as radio networks, and "broadcasting" was unquestioningly accepted as a legitimate "for-profit" business venture. Because the nature and needs of the market dominated programming decisions from television's beginnings, television programming has always been aimed at attracting and holding the largest possible audience (Stevens & Garcia, 1980, pp. 97, 141, 143). The medium television quickly came to be criticized for the role that ratings and competition, over advertising dollars, had in determining its programming content. Borrowing its basic themes and programming ideas from film, radio, and stage, and reformatting them in broadly palatable, noncontroversial products, television has been commonly described as a vast wasteland of recycled, mediocre programs.

A key to understanding television and its content is to remember that it is made up of competing business organizations that have to make a profit. The shows (news shows included) that are broadcast must as a first priority attract and hold viewers to retain the show's sponsors. The larger the audience, the more that sponsors are willing to spend for advertising and the greater the profits. Television shows themselves are therefore best thought of as packaging or vehicles for commercials and only secondarily as entertainment. From a business perspective, a mediocre show that has a large audience is a better product than a high-quality show with a small audience. A successful television show is one that is not turned off; it does not need to be well done, accurate, or enlightening. This does not mean that the television industry or its executives are ideologically opposed to high-quality programming. Networks will sometimes carry excellent shows at a loss, but overall they must make money in a highly competitive business. In television, where networks must attract the same viewers week after week, this means not alienating, irritating, or angering viewers. Content must also not be ideologically offensive, and so an ideological bias that supports the status quo emerges. The end result is largely noncontroversial, bland, poor-to-average shows that attract and hold without engaging or stimulating. It is only recently, in response to home video and cable television, that network programming has ventured into controversial areas.

As for packaging, television executives apparently found a gold mine in crime programming. Remember that although television was modeled after radio, crime was never a dominant part of radio programming (ranging from 4 percent in 1932 to a peak of 14 percent in 1948). Television programming, however, developed differently. As noted by Joseph Dominick (1978, p. 113), crime shows became

> a staple of prime time [television] entertainment [in] the late 1950s, when, prompted by the introduction of "adult Westerns" on ABC, and later by the success of a program called "The Untouchables," crime shows began to account for around one-third of all prime time [shows] from 1959–1961. This trend leveled off during the 1960s but began to increase again during the early 1970s until it reached its peak in 1975, when almost 40 percent of the three networks' prime time schedules contained shows dealing with crime and law enforcement.[7]

Table 2-1 details this historical trend, showing that after the decline of westerns in the sixties, crime programming came to average about one-fourth to one-third of all prime time television entertainment through the 1970s (see also Dominick, 1978, p. 113). The proportion of crime shows declined somewhat in the early 1980s. By 1985, however, their level had again surged, with the largest number of crime and justice shows aired in 1987. Crime-related programming has remained at a similarly high level through the 1980s and into the 1990s (Kania & Tanhan, 1987; Stark, 1987, p. 269).

On average, then, about one-fourth of all prime time shows from the 1960s to the 1990s have directly focused on crime or law enforcement. Overall, the proportion of television time devoted to crime and violence makes crime the largest single subject matter on television, with crime themes found across all types of programming (see Gerbner, 1980; Kania & Tanhan, 1987; Lewis, 1984). Special programming, such as television movies and miniseries, shows a similar proportion of crime-related plots (Baily, 1970). There is little question that a significant amount of crime-related programming has been offered on television for a long time. The potential impact of such programming has been heightened by the clear increase over the years in the amount of daily viewing of television, especially by children (Murray, 1984; Peterson & Zill, 1980). The popular mass entertainment media, first in the form of film and today led by television, have thus become a significant social factor, conveying thematic messages and lessons about whom to emulate and fear in society, what the basic causes of crime are,

TABLE 2-1   Prime Time Programming Related to Crime and Law Enforcement on the Three Major Networks, 1953–1990

Year	Number of shows	Number of hours	Percent of prime time programming*
1953	5	2.5	4.0
1954	6	3.0	4.8
1955	3	1.5	2.4
1956	2	1.0	1.6
1957	7	3.5	5.6
1958	8	4.5	7.1
1959	13	8.5	13.5
1960	13	10.0	15.9
1961	13	12.5	19.8
1962	7	6.5	10.3
1963	5	5.0	7.9
1964	3	3.0	4.8
1965	5	4.5	7.1
1966	4	3.0	4.8
1967	7	5.5	8.7
1968	10	8.0	12.7
1969	7	5.5	8.7
1970	12	9.0	14.3

(continued)

Television viewing ranks as the third most time-consuming activity (after sleep and work or school) for Americans (Lewis, 1984; Pearl et al., 1982, vol. 2), and Americans spend nearly half of their free time watching television. More Americans now have televisions than have refrigerators or indoor plumbing (Kubey & Csikszentmihalyi, 1990). As an indication of how much time Americans spend watching television, for every ten years an average American will watch one solid year of television. In 1977, the ratio of television sets to Americans reached 1 to 1 and has never declined (Stevens & Garcia, 1980, p. 143).

TABLE 2-1 (continued)

Year	Number of shows	Number of hours	Percent of prime time programming*
1971	12	10.5	16.7
1972	13	13.5	21.4
1973	18	18.0	28.6
1974	17	17.0	27.0
1975	20	21.0	33.3
1976	16	17.0	27.0
1977	12	12.0	19.0
1978	9	9.0	14.3
1979	12	12.0	19.0
1980	10	10.0	15.9
1981	10	10.0	15.9
1982	12	12.0	19.0
1983	10	10.0	17.5
1984	19	18.5	29.4
1985	22	21.5	34.1
1986	19	17.5	27.8
1987	25	23.5	37.3
1988	15	15.0	23.8
1989	14	14.5	23.0
1990	16	15.5	24.6

Source: Compiled by author from Complete Directory to Prime Time Network TV Shows, 1946–Present *(Eds.) Tim Brooks and Earle Marsh, 1953 through 1984,* TV Guide *fall preview issues for 1985–1990. The hours 8 to 11 were chosen to standardize "Prime Time" to the same 3 hours each evening across all years. If a crime show began at 7:30 and ran to 8:30 it was counted as ½ hour. Classification of a show as crime or criminal justice was taken from the classification scheme and description provided in the* Complete Directory to Prime Time Network TV Shows. *This table does not include westerns, war, horror, adventure, or spy programs such as "Gunsmoke," "Combat," "Alfred Hitchcock," "MacGyver," "A-Team," "Knight Rider," or "Scarecrow & Mrs. King." It also does not include programming on the DuMont network in the early 1950s or the Fox network from the late 1980s. This table therefore under-measures the total amount of crime and criminal justice related programming on television, estimated to be as high as 80 percent in the mid 1980s by one reviewer (Newman, 1990, citing Berman, 1987). By standardizing the prime time hours and the crime and criminal justice classification, the table does show the relative emphasis on crime and criminal justice from one year to the next and over the history of U. S. television.*

*Based on a total of 63 hours of prime time programming per week for the three networks (ABC, CBS, and NBC) combined.

and how crime should be fought. An overview of these lessons from the entertainment world of crime and justice follows.

PORTRAITS OF CRIME AND JUSTICE IN THE MODERN ENTERTAINMENT MEDIA

Of the many themes to be found in the media—love, death, married life, coming of age—that of crime and justice is said to be the most revealing about society, because it encompasses notions of good and evil, morality, social achievement, and social structure (Everson, 1964, p. xi). In addition, criminality is an area about which the viewing public has limited alternative sources of information (everyone knows married people; few personally know convicted criminals), in part because of its backstage nature. As stated earlier, the backstage nature of crime increases its entertainment value and popularity—hence, the enormous number of media portraits of crime and justice. There has been a persistent interest in the content of these portraits since the 1930s, and a number of studies analyzing the content of the entertainment media have been carried out. Most of these studies, and the most recent, thorough, and enlightening, focus on television, since its pervasiveness and ready availability, especially to children, raise the most concern.[8] Accordingly, this discussion will focus on television, cautiously extrapolating the findings to the general popular entertainment media.[9]

What are viewers likely to see in the media? Are they exposed to situations and behaviors they might not experience in reality? In terms of crimes, the offenses that are most likely to be emphasized on television are those that are least likely to occur in real life, with property crime underrepresented and violent crime overrepresented.[10] Media portraits of crime also greatly overemphasize individual acts of violence.[11] If one looks at combined criminal and noncriminal violence on television, the levels are even higher. The 1969 National Commission on the Causes and Prevention of Violence found violent episodes in more than 80 percent of shows (NCCPV, 1969; see also Newman, 1990). Murder and robbery dominate, with murder accounting for nearly one-fourth of all television crimes (see Estep & MacDonald, 1984, p. 115; Lichter & Lichter, 1983, p. 10). In a recent representative content study by Lichter and Lichter (1983), murder, robbery, kidnapping, and aggravated assault made up 87 percent of all television crimes (see Table 2-2). In contrast, murders account for only one-sixth of 1 percent of the FBI Crime Index. At the other extreme, thefts account for nearly two-thirds of the FBI index crimes, but only 6 percent of television crime.

Thus, a large difference exists between what viewers are likely to experience in reality and what they are likely to be exposed to in the media (Lewis, 1984). This perhaps would not be a concern if the portrayals of crime and justice in the media were balanced in other aspects and presented various competing views of the world. That, however, is not the case.

For example, there is also almost no correspondence between media portraits of criminals and official statistics of persons arrested for crimes

TABLE 2-2 Serious Crimes on 1981 TV Entertainment Programs Compared to 1980 Reports (Percent)

	TV	FBI
Murder	36	*
Rape	3	*
Kidnapping	13	*
Aggravated assault	13	5
Robbery	23	4
Burglary	6	28
Larceny-theft	6	62
Total	100	100
Violent crime	88	10
Property crime	12	90
Total	100	100

Source: From Prime Time Crime, by L. S. Lichter and S. R. Lichter, p. 16. Copyright © 1983 by The Media Institute. Reprinted by permission.

*Less than 1 percent
Note: Figures are percentages of all FBI Crime Index listings; larceny category includes motor vehicle theft.

(Garofalo, 1981). The typical criminal as portrayed in the media is demographically older, white, and male, and has a high social status, whereas statistically the typical arrestee is young, poor, black, and male.[12] The single most common television portrait of a criminal has been described as an upper-middle-class person gone berserk with greed (Estep & MacDonald, 1984, pp. 122–123; Pandiani, 1978). Indeed, greed is the basic motivation for criminality in three-quarters of the crimes on television (Lichter & Lichter, 1983, p. 30). The repeated message in the visual entertainment media (film and television) is that crime is largely perpetrated by individuals who are basically different from the majority, that criminality stems from individual problems, and that criminal conduct is freely chosen behavior (see Box 2-1). In effect, the media limit viewers to two types of criminals: the professional deviant who lives a life of crime and the apparent community pillar who uses crime to maintain or better his standard of living (Lichter & Lichter, 1983, p. 57). Both of these types are social predators not bound or restrained in any way by normal social rules and values. In contrast, the media portray victims of crime as passive and helpless. Television crime victims are also predominantly white, and mostly young women, far in excess of the real victimization rates for both groups (see Carlson, 1985, p. 50; Estep & MacDonald, 1984, pp. 122–123; Gerbner & Gross, 1976).

Equally distorted are media portraits of the criminal justice system and its procedures. The early steps of the justice process—law enforcement, investigation, and arrests—are emphasized in entertainment programming to the near exclusion of subsequent steps (Carlson, 1985, p. 117; Garofalo, 1981). And when the rest of the criminal justice system is referred to, the depiction is rarely positive. Law enforcement not only dominates, but dom-

BOX 2-1   Portraits of Criminals in Film

In the cinema, as in television, most criminals are portrayed as predatory, greed-driven individuals. However, other images of criminals appear in film as well, portrayed within themes ranging from that of hero, supermale (most criminals are still portrayed as male), victim, businessman, or working professional to psychopath. Cinematic criminals, who frequently dominate their films, and their antagonists— crime fighters—often share many characteristics (see Parish & Pitts, 1976; Pate, 1978, p. 5).

Psychopaths and Supermales

The psychopathic criminal has been a theme in many films and television programs. In addition, filmmakers sometimes combine a psychopathic antagonist with a supermale theme to create seemingly indestructible murderous supercriminals such as have become popular in recent slasher films. Psychotic supermales generally possess an evil, cunning intelligence, and superior strength, endurance, and stealth. Crime in these films is generally an act of twisted, lustful revenge or a random act of meaningless violence. A historical trend in such films has been to present psychotic criminals as more and more violent and bloodthirsty and to show their crimes more and more graphically. Hence, murderous violence that once took place completely off screen (for example, in *M* in 1931) came first to be represented in scenes that were violent but not graphic (the shower murder in *Psycho* in 1960) and then to be shown in graphic close-up (*The Texas Chainsaw Massacre* in 1978).*

Victims and Heroes

Although the themes of the criminal as hero and the criminal as victim appeared early on in the cinema and have been presented regularly, they have always been less frequent in number than portrayals of the criminal as a psychopath or supermale. These themes usually have the common element of portraying the criminal in either a sympathetic or an envious light. Films that portray criminals in such light often also portray crime in a similar light. Thus, films in which the criminal is a "hero" (*Robin Hood,* 1922, 1938; *The Mark of Zorro,* 1922) usually present crime as either a moral crusade or a thrilling adventure. Films such as *High Sierra* (1941), *I Am a Fugitive from a Chain Gang* (1932), *Billy Budd* (1962), and *A Bullet for Pretty Boy* (1970), which portray the criminal as a helpless "good" victim of external factors, present criminality as an unavoidable, unchosen career.

Businessmen and Professionals

The theme of the criminals as professional is also sometimes combined with that of the supermale, with the criminal businessman characterized as a shrewd, ruthless, violent ladies' man. The professional-criminal theme extends from portrayals of the corporate syndicate executive (*The Godfather,* 1978) through those of the skilled technician (*The Mechanic,* 1972) to those of the working-class day laborer (*Thief,* 1978). The central message of such films is that crime is simply work, similar to other common careers but often more exciting and more rewarding.

---

*Full descriptions of the movies cited can be obtained from the following anthologies: R. Armour, *Film* (Westport, CT: Greenwood Press, 1980); W. Everson, *The Bad Guys* (New York: Citadel Press, 1964); W. Everson, *The Detective in Film* (New York: Citadel Press, 1972); C. McArthur, *Underworld U. S. A.* (New York: Viking Press, 1972); J. Parrish & M. Pitts, *The Great Gangster Pictures* (Metuchen, NJ: Scarecrow Press, 1976); E. Rosow, *Born to Lose* (Oxford, England: Oxford University Press, 1978); J. Shadoian, *Dreams and Dead Ends* (Cambridge, MA: MIT Press, 1977); and J. Tuska, *The Detective in Hollywood* (Garden City, NY: Doubleday, 1987).

inates as a glamorous action-filled process of detection, one that often legitimizes the use of violence (Culver & Knight, 1979). The media's portrayal of the criminal justice system usually ends with the arrest or killing of the offender (Dominick, 1978, p. 116). This emphasis on law enforcement allows the entertainment media to forward the illusion that they are revealing backstage crime-fighting techniques and criminal behavior and simultaneously implies that the criminal justice process after arrest is relatively unimportant. A consideration of the content of the media's direct and indirect depictions of the individual components of the criminal justice system—law enforcement, the courts, and corrections—is revealing.

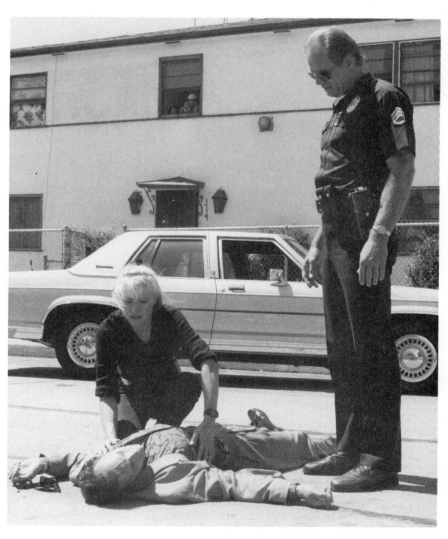

A present-day media crime fighter deals with crime
Source: Photo courtesy of The National Broadcasting Company, Inc.

Law Enforcement: The Police and Crime Fighters

Regarding those who fight crime in the entertainment media, the basic distinction is whether the crime fighter is a member of the established criminal justice system or an outsider. Outsiders are far more common than criminal justice system personnel, but whether an outsider or not, the successful crime fighter is most frequently a heroic white man of action. Media crime fighters are the dramatic embodiment of American individualism and romanticism (Bortner, 1984, p. 19, citing Parenti, 1978, and Sennet & Cobb, 1973). Indeed, crime fighters are usually portrayed as antisocial, unattached loners even when they are members of an established law enforcement agency—*Dirty Harry* being a prime example from film. The media supercop is accordingly usually not a regular cop at all but someone from outside the system or a maverick officer within it (Culver & Knight, 1979; Lichter & Lichter, 1983).

The main message these crime fighters convey about crime is that the traditional criminal justice system is unable to cope with it. The system needs the assistance of either a rebellious law enforcement insider who is willing to bend the law or, more often, a civilian outsider—private eyes being the most popular and successful. Justice, which in the entertainment media means law enforcement, is achieved by individual stars, not by the justice system as a whole (Bortner, 1984, p. 19). Effective conformist law enforcement officers are rare, and when they are portrayed, they often have to resort to innovative special tactics, weapons, technology, and enforcement units to successfully fight crime. Furthermore, in the investigation and apprehension stages of fighting crime, civil liberties are often violated and due process procedures ignored (Culver & Knight, 1979, p. 209; Dominick, 1978, p. 117). The message is that standard police practices are not effective and that extraordinary and extralegal means are necessary to successfully fight crime (Arons & Katsh, 1977). These "extraordinary means" often include such absurd practices as when detectives stick a finger in a substance, taste it, and pronounce it "pure heroin" or the like. Not only is this impossible to do, but real law enforcement officers simply do not taste unknown substances, not wanting to sample powdered LSD, PCP, cyanide, arsenic, or other drugs.

Though the entertainment media continue to portray the police as largely ineffective—a tradition that can be traced to Poe's seminal detective stories, in which the French police fumble and fail while hero–detective Dupin, outsider to the system, solves crimes—Lichter and Lichter (1983) found that on television the police are portrayed more positively—and more often—than other criminal justice personnel such as attorneys, judges, and correctional officers. Even so, the Lichters (1983, p. 45) found that for every heroic police officer, two others performed incompetently and another two actually broke the law. And nearly half the time, the police shown on television are not engaged in solving crimes but just perform other minor tasks.

Who does solve crimes in the media? The Lichters found that private investigators did well, surpassed only by interested private citizens. Every other type of crime fighter failed to capture the criminal more often than they succeeded. By contrast, private eyes proved almost incapable of failure, and involved private citizens were 100 percent successful in the Lichters' study. The high failure rate of most law enforcement officers, combined with the fantastic success of private eyes and private citizens, is striking. In the media, clearly, it is the outsider who saves the day when ordinary law enforcers prove unequal to the task (Lichter & Lichter, 1983, pp. 51–52).

Significant in media portrayals of law enforcement is the use of violence. Violence has been an element in the depiction of crime and justice throughout media history, but in the twentieth century the entertainment media have come to portray both crime fighters and criminals as more violent and aggressive and to show this violence more graphically. Indeed, so brutal have media crime fighters become over the course of this century that they are now more gangsterlike and violence-prone than law abiding (Rosow, 1978, pp. 326–327; Shadoian, 1977, p. 212). In film portraits such as *Dirty Harry* and *Death Wish* and television shows such as "Hunter" and "Kojak," the distinction between the crime fighter and criminal disappears in regard to who initiates violence and how much force is used. The increasing emphasis on graphic violence has also resulted in a kind of weapons cult within the entertainment media, with weapons made increasingly more technical and sophisticated but less realistic over the years. Furthermore, weapons, especially handguns, tend to be portrayed as either ridiculously benign, so that misses are common and wounds minor and painless (usually when the hero is shot at), or ridiculously deadly (usually when the hero is shooting), so that shots from handguns accurately hit moving, distant people, killing them quickly and without extensive suffering (cf. Bortner, 1984; Stark, 1987).

The Courts: Lawyers and Judges

According to the most prominent media image of lawyers and judges, all law school graduates secretly want to be police officers. Although shown less frequently than police officers in the entertainment media, attorneys and judges, when they star, often spend as much effort solving crimes and pursuing criminals as they do interpreting and practicing law.[13] And although criminal law is only one aspect of the field of law and most attorneys practice other specialties, most media lawyers are criminal lawyers. Thus, in the media, officers of the court usually specialize in criminal law and are often crime fighters and crime solvers. And solving crimes is clearly more demanding and significant than their legal work. When the primary advocates of due process in real life are thus portrayed, it is small wonder that the entertainment media's overall portrait of crime and justice is pro–crime control. Overall, Lichter and Lichter (1983, pp. 42, 44) found that lawyers are shown negatively nearly as often as positively (31 percent versus 44 percent of the time). Compared with police officers, they are more likely to be shown as greedy but slightly less likely to be directly involved in crimes.

In accordance with the media's myopic concentration on criminal law, court procedures, when shown at all, emphasize the rare-in-reality adversarial criminal trial (Stark, 1987; Surette, 1989). In contrast to real court systems, in media courts one can expect to go to trial. Seldom are preliminary procedures or informal plea bargaining shown, and posttrial steps are even rarer. The media image of the courts and the law as directly portrayed is thus that of a high-stakes, complicated, arcane contest practiced by expert professionals and beyond the understanding of everyday citizens. The confrontations, the oratory, and the deliberations in the media courtroom are in stark opposition to the criminal justice system's daily reality of plea bargains, compromises, and assembly-line justice (Snow, 1984). Furthermore, in that people are often wrongly accused in the entertainment media's judicial system, the fairness of the real-world judicial system is brought into question. As one researcher noted in referring to the 271 cases tried by Perry Mason in his ten-year law practice on television, "What would you think of a police force that always accuses the wrong subjects, or a district attorney who unquestioningly prosecutes them?" (Stark, 1987, p. 229).

Directly and indirectly, the media paint distorted images of the courts. In shows focused on law enforcement, the courts are often alluded to as soft-on-crime, easy-on-criminals, due process–laden institutions that release the obviously guilty and dangerous (cf. Lichter & Lichter, 1983; Stark, 1987). The fact that most media criminals are recidivists implies that they have been through the court system at least once and have been returned to the streets undeterred. When shown directly, court officers are often engaged in fighting crime or in highly dramatic criminal trials. None of these images comes close to representing the reality of the courts (Brenner, 1989; Rosen,

Though trials still dominate media portrayals of the courts, recent courtroom portraits (exemplified by the television show "L. A. Law") have evolved from focusing on the highly unrealistic courtroom of "Perry Mason" to showing more nontrial backstage aspects of practicing law in the increasingly popular "soap opera" format (Stark, 1987). The soap opera format became popular in police shows as well, exemplified by "Hill Street Blues." This general trend can be traced to the television industry's need to revitalize the crime show genre following a decline in the early 1980s. To appeal to an audience that had been raised on television, program developers looked to add more realism to their shows by revealing more of the backstage behavior and private lives of their crime fighters and criminal lawyers (Stark, 1987, p. 275). The next step has been to develop courtroom docudramas in which real cases are reenacted, tried, and "entertainmentized" in seemingly realistic courtroom scenes in such daytime television shows as "The People's Court" and "Trial by Jury" (see Brenner, 1989; Rosen, 1989).

1989). Indeed, Harvard Law School professor Alan Dershowitz once quipped, "Perhaps the most realistic TV show on 'justice' is a situation comedy—'Night Court'(*TV Guide,* May 25, 1985).

Corrections: Prisons, Guards, and Prisoners

In entertainment programming, corrections is the least shown component of the criminal justice system—and therefore presumably the least important. The few television programs that have featured jails or prisons have either been slapstick comedy or featured the inmates rather than staff (Schwartz, 1989, p. 38). The last serious attempt to focus on corrections on television was a recent show, "Miriah" (1987), which lasted less than a season. More often, corrections is portrayed through indirect negative allusions to its alumni of ex-con offenders in law enforcement shows. With habitual criminals outnumbering first offenders by more than 4 to 1, the entertainment media show the corrections system as at best only marginally equipped to rehabilitate offenders (Lichter & Lichter, 1983, p. 29). Instead, the media imply that the corrections system simply provides way stations for criminals, from which they frequently return at the end of their sentences worse criminals than when they were sentenced.

The film industry, in contrast to television, has not ignored corrections. Unfortunately, the image portrayed there is as negative as that indirectly conveyed on television. The most common corrections films show either harsh, brutal places of legalized torture or uncontrolled human zoos that barely contain their animalistic criminals (Zaner, 1989). Films of women's prisons focus chiefly on lesbianism and sexual relations. And unlike crime films, which at least focus as often on crime fighters as on criminals, correctional movies usually focus on the inmates, ignoring the staff and administration or showing them negatively. Reflecting on these media images, Zaner (1989, pp. 64–66) commented:

> The bad rap corrections takes in the movies may translate into a lack of public support for real-life correctional institutions. . . . The perpetuation of the stereotype that correctional officers and administrators are "disgruntled, alienated hacks prone to violence under pressure" misleads the public, giving it an unrealistic view of the corrections professions. . . . Many of the films made about prisons in the early '30s and '40s highlighted the harshness of inmates' lives. Yet, movies made in the [1970s and 1980s] show little progress. What's really bad, is that the inmates often end up as more sympathetic characters than the [correctional] officers. The pervasive attitude is that the crowd should be rooting for the kept, not the keepers.

In sum, the criminal justice system is not well presented in the entertainment media, and the further one moves into the system, the worse the image becomes. If not shown as corrupt and brutal, the system is shown as bureaucratic, cumbersome, and ineffective, so burdening its few good employees that only those who are willing to bend the rules and the law can be effective. More effective are people completely outside the system, who do not have to consider department rules or government policies and are unconstrained by due process considerations. Now, to enhance the system's "reality" to viewers, the entertainment media present more backstage behavior within the criminal justice system, and this paradoxically shows a media world of crime and justice that has little basis in reality. From these images of crime and justice emerges a recurrent picture of social reality.

THE BIG PICTURE: CONCERNS REGARDING THE ENTERTAINMENT MEDIA'S PORTRAIT OF SOCIETY

The Law of Opposites

The entertainment media's pattern with regard to portraying crime and justice can be summarized as follows: Whatever the media show is the opposite of what is true. In every subject category—crimes, criminals, crime fighters, the investigation of crimes, arrests, the processing and disposition of cases—the media presents a world of crime and justice that is not found in reality. Whatever the truth about crime and violence and the criminal justice system in America, the entertainment media seem determined to project the opposite (Carlson, 1985; Dominick, 1973, pp. 244–245). Their images are wildly inaccurate and inevitably fragmentary, providing a distorted reflection of crime within society and an equally distorted reflection of the criminal justice system's response to crime (Bortner, 1984; Pandiani, 1978). The lack of realistic information further mystifies the criminal justice system, exacerbating the public's lack of understanding of it (Dominick, 1978; Estep & MacDonald, 1984).

Underlying these portraits is a persistent, if often unstated, explanation of crime that has ideological and policy implications. The media consistently point to individual personality traits as the cause of crime, and to violent interdiction as its solution. If one accepts the media's explanation of crime as being caused by predatory personality traits, then the only valid approach to stopping crime is to hold individual offenders responsible for their past crimes and forcibly deter them from committing future ones. In the entertainment media's simplistic notion of crime, the most effective solution is dramatic, individual action (Bortner, 1984, p. 19). Media solutions emphasize individual violence and aggression, with a preference shown for weapons and sophisticated technology (Culver & Knight, 1979, pp. 207–209; Garofalo, 1981). In so depicting crime and its solution, the entertainment media also depict a particular social structure.

The Social Ecology of Crime in the Media

Media analysts' concern is that repeated viewing of these portrayals imposes on the audience a "media reality" view of the world (Altheide & Snow, 1979). Such a portrait of the world has been associated with the development of a "mean worldview"—the feeling that the world is a violent, dangerous place—and attitudes of fear, isolation, and suspicion (Gerbner et al., 1978, 1979, 1980; see also Chapter 4). The social dynamic underlying the image of crime forwarded by the media—an image that has not changed much over the eighty-year history of the mass entertainment media—is one of a trisected society composed of "sheep," "wolves," and "sheepdogs." As Figure 2-1 shows, in the mass entertainment media's vision of society, evil, cunning predator "wolves" create general mayhem and prey on weak, defenseless, often stupid "sheep" (women, the elderly, the general public), while good, middle-class, white, male hero "sheepdogs" intervene and protect the sheep in the name of retributive justice (cf. Carlson, 1985, p. 50). Over the course of this century the character of these portraits has changed. Media criminals have become more animalistic, irrational, and predatory—a change paralleled in media crime fighters—and their crimes more violent, random, senseless, and sensational; conversely, victims have become more innocent. Thus, the differences portrayed between the general public and criminals have swollen. In a subtle shift, the earlier predatory but rational criminal wolves have become unpredictable, irrational mad dogs, while over the years the noble sheepdogs have become wolflike vigilantes for whom the law has become an impediment to stopping crime.

By depicting the social dynamic shown in Figure 2-1, the entertainment media project messages to the audience, both criminal and law abiding, concerning whom to trust, whom to victimize, and how victims and criminals should act. The consistent message is that crime is caused by predatory individuals who are basically different from the rest of us—more ruthless, greedy, violent, or psychotic. Combating these predators requires a special person, an equally tough, predatory, and, most important, unfettered crime fighter. Criminality is an individual choice and other social, economic, or structural explanations are irrelevant and ignored. Tracing this portrait of

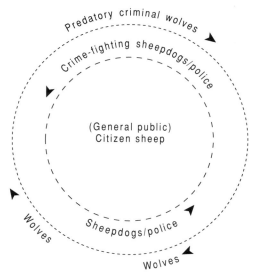

FIGURE 2-1 The social ecology of crime in the entertainment media

criminality back through our literary heritage, reviewers have found few writers or works that have presented criminals as not personally responsible for their own fates (Grenander, 1976, p. 55). Furthermore, by focusing attention on contests between individual criminals and crime fighters, the media's crime ecology ignores the broader social connections underlying crime—for example, the origins and destinations of illegal monies. The flow of money through the underworld has continued to be obscured (Rosow, 1978, p. 319). Though films are generally more explicit than other entertainment media, even filmmakers have consistently remained vague as to the uses of illegal income and the business tactics and organizational activities of criminals. The media may allude to illegal sources of money (bootlegging, drugs, extortion, prostitution, and so forth), but few media portraits spell out details about how the money is made or depict the connection between such sources and businesses and government. Instead, a highly individualistic picture of the genesis and conduct of crime continues to be projected. The result is backstage glimpses of criminal behavior without true backstage knowledge of crime.

Limited to this simplistic, incomplete picture of crime as mostly individual, socially isolated acts, members of each group involved (criminals, crime fighters, and the public) have for generations been receiving misleading lessons in how to engage in and respond to crime. For all three groups, role models are provided (Greene and Bynum, 1982; Stark, 1987, p. 276). Criminals can learn how to actually commit crimes, whom to victimize, and when to use violence and weapons and disdain sympathy. Crime fighters and the public are shown that counterviolence is the most effective means of combating crime, that due process considerations hamper the police, and that in most cases the law works in the criminal's favor. The public is further instructed to fear others, for criminals are not always easily recognizable and often are rich, powerful, and in positions of trust.

These images of society and criminality, combined with the emphasis on the front end of the justice system, investigations and arrests, ultimately promote pro–law enforcement and crime control policies (Carlson, 1985, pp. 52, 117; see also Bortner, 1984). Crime shows may be about law and order, but they are light on law and heavy on order (Stark, 1987, p. 282).

Letkemann (1973; cited by Sherizen, 1978, p. 221) reported that experienced bank robbers feel their work is made more difficult, and the victim's situation more dangerous, by the tendency of the mass media to depict bank robberies as phony, "toy-gun stuff." Robbers feel that they must now first convince their victims the event is "not a joke." This may require more brutal action on their part than they would otherwise need to use. They must secondly convince any potential "heroes" among their victims that they cannot be subdued—TV dramas to the contrary.

Paradoxically, although the media portray the criminal justice system unfavorably, the solutions they depict as being the most effective—harsher punishments and more law enforcement—both entail expansion of the existing criminal justice system. The entertainment media's representation of reality further teaches that the best defense is an aggressive offense, the best protection is a gun, and the safest course is to trust no one (Bortner, 1984; Lichter & Lichter, 1983). The development of these attitudes is fully discussed in Chapter 4.

CONCLUSION

The entertainment media are seen to be distorted, erroneous sources of crime and justice information and images, historically and consistently reversing the real world of crime and justice in their media world. In this entertainment reality, traditional criminal justice systems and practices suffer. The images are not a monopoly and some images conflict, but the prevalent ones show persons outside of the criminal justice system to be the most effective in fighting crime and support crime control-based approaches. In the end, a stark society composed of predator criminals, violent crime fighters, and helpless victims is painted.

Of course, the media do not claim that entertainment programming is accurate or realistic in the first place, and although this does not absolve the entertainment media from responsibility for their effects on society—finding significant disparities between media portrayals and actual crime and justice is not surprising. On the other hand, the news media do claim to depict the world objectively and realistically. It is therefore more disconcerting to find considerable correspondence between the images of crime and justice put forth by the entertainment media and those put forth by the news media. The most stunning portrait of crime in the news media is found in the "media trial," a news media event that utilizes elements of entertainment and drama within a purportedly objective report of crime and justice. It is this concept and the history of news coverage of crime and justice that Chapter 3 discusses.

Notes

1. A listing of the world's great literature would include many works in which the commission of a crime and its aftermath are central themes. Examples include Dostoyevski's *Crime and Punishment;* many of Shakespeare's plays, notably *Macbeth;* and Hawthorne's *The Scarlet Letter.*

2. The detective genre in the United States has been traced to Edgar Allen Poe's stories, beginning in 1841 with "The Murders in the Rue Morgue" (Stark, 1987, p. 231; Tuska, 1987, p. 1; see also Papke, 1987, Chapter 6).

3. Magazines were first published in 1741 but until the late 1800s were targeted chiefly at an elite, affluent social group.

4. Such films reflected the social impact of large immigrations (McArthur, 1972, p. 4; Rosow, 1978, pp. 36–52, 72–86). Their sentimentality mirrored an earlier pattern in the presentation of criminals in crime novels, which began with sentimental portraits of criminals and later moved toward more negative depictions (Hartsfield, 1985, p. 129).

5. Also popular in the early 1920s was a secondary crime theme in which criminality was portrayed in the form of evil, twisted, satanic beings—perhaps reflecting the popularization of Freud's theories. This portrayal soon waned in popularity, however.

6. See Blumer, 1933; Blumer & Hauser, 1933; Charter, 1933; Dale, 1935a; Holaday & Stod-

dard, 1933; Peterson & Thurstone, 1933; and Shuttleworth & May, 1933; see also Chapter 3. For a summary discussion of the Payne Fund studies from a communications perspective, see Lowery & DeFleur, 1983, Chapter 2.

7. Dominick's data reflect the programming on NBC, CBS, and ABC and varying definitions of "prime time." If the DuMont Network, which broadcast from 1948 to 1954, is included and varying definitions of crime and justice shows are taken into account, a peak in crime-related shows appears in the early 1950s (see Kania & Tankan, 1987).

8. The more ambitious have tried to find a link between viewing content and subsequent viewer behavior, particularly aggression. See Chapter 5.

9. Though the other media do not precisely mirror television's content with regard to crime and justice, the content of television programming does seem to reflect the emphasis of the broader spectrum of entertainment media. There is certainly no evidence that the dominant crime-and-justice portraits in other media differ significantly from television's, and there are theoretical and historical reasons why they would not (see Altheide & Snow, 1979; Jowett & Linton, 1980; Meyrowitz, 1985a; Papke, 1987; Stark, 1987; Stevens & Garcia, 1980).

10. See Carlson, 1985; Dominick, 1978; Estep & MacDonald, 1984; Gerbner, 1976.

11. See Antunes and Hurley, 1977; Bortner, 1984; Graber, 1980; Jones, 1976; Pandiani, 1978; Sherizen, 1978.

12. See Dominick, 1973; Estep and MacDonald, 1983; Graber, 1980; Hauge, 1965; Roshier, 1981.

13. See Brenner, 1989; Chase, 1986; Lichter & Lichter, 1983; Rosen, 1989; Stark, 1987. Media lawyers who concentrated on practicing law enjoyed their highest popularity during the 1960s, a period when police shows were at their lowest level. By the late 1960s, police shows had regained their popularity and lawyer shows had declined (Stark, 1987, p. 229).

3 Crime and Justice in the News Media

OVERVIEW

Similar in approach to Chapter 2, Chapter 3 covers the historical development and present-day content of the news media in regard to crime and justice. The first section discusses news coverage of crime and justice prior to the creation of the modern mass media, noting the historical interest in crime and that one can find items about crimes and trials in some of the earliest Western news media. The chapter then traces the development of crime news through the first mass distribution newspapers in the United States, the "penny press," to the standardization of news reporting styles and the creation of modern, corporate newspapers at the end of the nineteenth century.

The unique task that news organizations face in producing daily news is discussed first relative to news in general and then relative to crime news in particular. Concerning news in general, three competing models of the news creation process are compared—the manipulative model, the market model, and the organizational model, of which the organizational model arguably best describes how news is actually created. Within this discussion, the concepts of newsworthiness, routinization, and gatekeeping are developed and related to the selection of crime news. Lastly, two case studies of crime news are summarized to illustrate how the general process of news creation applies to crime.

Having examined how the news comes to exist, the chapter presents a review of the content of present-day news. First considered is the amount of total news that is devoted to crime; then how criminals are portrayed in the news. And third, the chapter looks more closely at how the criminal justice system and its component parts—law enforcement, the courts, and corrections—are portrayed. Crime is seen to constitute a significant portion of the total news, and that the news media normally portray criminals as either predatory street criminals or dishonest businessmen and professionals, and the criminal justice system as an ineffective, often counterproductive means of dealing with crime. Of particular note is the merging of the news and entertainment perspectives as exemplified by two recent phenomena: "infotainment"—tabloid-style television programs that mix news and entertainment formats in exploitative depictions of crime—and the multimedia co-optation of the justice system in heavily covered, miniseries-like "media trials." With the increased merging of news and entertainment, it is no surprise that the research shows the portraits of crime and justice in the news and entertainment media to be more alike than different.

The final section of this chapter highlights various concerns about news coverage of crime and justice. Noted first is the recognized potential of news media to disrupt trials. The chapter then concludes with a listing of other, lesser known matters of concern, including the potential for media-induced social panics and public crusades about relatively rare forms of crime, and general systemwide "echo" effects from news coverage. Also of concern are the possible miseducation of the public about crime and justice, the increased manipulation of crime as a political issue because of the media's high profile–low analysis style of coverage, and, lastly, the likelihood that the combined news and entertainment, multimedia image of crime and justice has negatively influenced public attitudes and support for public policies.

EARLY CRIME AND JUSTICE NEWS

News, if defined as information about the world, has existed for as long as there has been communication. Formal news, however, originated in governmental and religious decrees announcing laws or special events (cf. Park, 1940). Printed news about crime and justice is nearly as old as printing, and a detailed account of a witchcraft trial can be found in an English newsletter as early as 1587. Indeed, after 1575, "it hardly seems possible that a really first-rate murder, especially if it was complicated by an illicit love affair, or the hanging of any notable criminal, went unreported, while the very best of

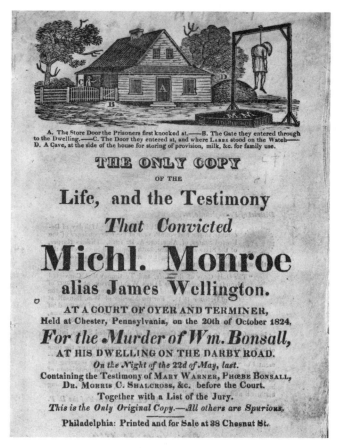

A. The Store Door the Prisoners first knocked at.——B. The Gate they entered through to the Dwelling.——C. The Door they entered at, and where Laaas stood on the Watch—— D. A Cave, at the side of the house for storing of provision, milk, &c. for family use.

THE ONLY COPY
OF THE
Life, and the Testimony
That Convicted
Michl. Monroe
alias James Wellington.
AT A COURT OF OYER AND TERMINER,
Held at Chester, Pennsylvania, on the 20th of October 1824.
For the Murder of Wm. Bonsall,
AT HIS DWELLING ON THE DARBY ROAD.
On the Night of the 22d of May, last.
Containing the Testimony of MARY WARNER, PHŒBE BONSALL, DR. MORRIS C. SHALCROSS, &c. before the Court.
Together with a List of the Jury.
This is the Only Original Copy.—All others are Spurious.

Philadelphia: Printed and for Sale at 38 Chesnut St.

The front page of a nineteenth-century crime news pamphlet, showing the traditional symbolic hanging at upper right and the four stages of a crime at upper left
Source: Harvard Law Library, Special Collections

them inspired numerous effusions of the popular press and many ballads" (Drechsel, 1983, p. 35, citing Shaaber, 1929). By the mid-1600s, some weekly newspapers (termed "broadsheets," or "broadsides") were regularly printing accounts of court activities, generally consisting of terse one-to-two-line announcements, primarily concerning criminal cases (Drechsel, 1983, p. 36).

Through the eighteenth century and into the early nineteenth, crime-related "street" literature (broadsides, pamphlets, sermons, speeches) were the main vehicles for news of crime and justice. Foreshadowing recent television shows, these various print media appeared to often fulfill an entertainment function using an informational format (Papke, 1987, p. 22). However, even though many early examples of detailed coverage of crime and criminal trials exist,[1] until well into the 1800s, crime and justice news was dominated by brief reports about trials involving commercial or political matters and coverage of a few select murders (Drechsel, 1983, p. 41, citing Lee, 1937). No American newspaper published regular police court stories until the 1830s, when they became leading features in the first daily city papers in the eastern United States (Bleyer, 1927). Prior to the emergence of these dailies, early crime and justice news is best characterized as docketlike calendar listings with rare forays into detailed coverage. Long, usually front-page editorials rather than reports of factual events dominated these media. In addition, by modern standards, their distribution and readership were small, so the reach and probable social impact of this early crime and justice news did not approach that of the modern mass media until the penny press emerged in the 1830s (cf. Drechsel, 1983; Papke, 1987).

The Penny Press

Before a modern printed news medium can develop, a society must first have a generally literate population and mass distribution systems in place. In the United States, these conditions were first met in the 1830s. In the eastern cities of New York, Boston, Baltimore, and Philadelphia, the nation's first mass distribution newspapers appeared as municipal penny press newspapers distributed on street corners (Stevens & Garcia, 1980, pp. 121–122). One of the first such papers, the *New York Sun,* began to include a daily police-court news column in 1833 and experienced a notable circulation boost (Gordon & Heath, 1981, p. 227; Sherizen, 1978, p. 208). Other penny dailies followed suit, and human-interest crime stories quickly became a staple of these inexpensive and popular newspapers. The penny press dailies were aimed at the new urban social groups (mechanics, artisans, small merchants) of the emerging literate middle class of the 1800s. Class oriented, these early papers portrayed crime as the result of class inequities and often discussed justice as a process manipulated by the rich and prominent (Papke, 1987, p. 35). They often contained due process arguments and advocated due process reforms, presenting individual crimes as examples of larger social and political failings needing correction.

In response to the newspapers' need for a steady supply of specific types of news, reporters began to specialize. Crime reporters became a prominent, though not highly regarded, specialty.[2] The emergence of specialized reporters marks the beginning of the journalistic construction of news and the marketing of social information to the general public (cf. Altheide & Snow, 1979, p. 63). With the penny press, news became a marketable commodity, and the evolution of newspapers since has been toward perfecting the newspaper as a salable commodity (Hughes, 1940, p. 23). Over time, newspapers changed from being argumentative, politically oriented literature emphasizing editorials and openly advocating political programs to politically neutral, less confrontational sources of general information that tend to perpetuate the status quo (Papke, 1987).

A front page from an 1833 issue of *The Sun,* a New York penny press daily
Source: Museum of the City of New York

The Emergence of a Standard Reporting Style

Despite the early emergence of crime reporters, from the 1830s to the Civil War reporting on crime and justice remained a mixture of stenography and journalism. Often coverage was taken verbatim from court records. However, the restraints of reporting the Civil War from the battlefield and the postwar completion of the cross-continental telegraph system led to the development of the modern journalistic style of brevity and neutrality and the use of the standard lead paragraph. In a standard lead, the main points of the story are quickly summarized in the first paragraph, allowing for rapid news editing. Journalistic reporting was further refined after the Civil War, when news came to be organized and presented according to a preset formula (Altheide & Snow, 1979, p. 67; Desmond, 1978). The news became less analytical and evaluative and more factual and descriptive.

For a brief time during the 1880s, newspaper coverage of crime declined in emphasis. Following this transitional period, newspapers came to be produced in multiple editions within modern corporations with large advertising revenues, staffs, and circulations. Crime coverage rose again in the 1890s with the introduction of a new type of mass entertainment journalism, known as "yellow journalism" (Papke, 1987, p. 35). This new style of journalism, exemplified by the Hearst and Pulitzer newspapers in New York, gave space and importance to disasters, scandals, gossip, and crime, particularly violent personal crime.[3] Large headlines; melodramatic depictions of heroes, villains, and innocent victims; and front-page crime reports became so common that by 1892, crime reporters in New York had their own room in the courthouse (Drechsel, 1983, p. 49). The developing "news industry" emphasized standardized and increasingly generic crime reporting. Newspapers were still marketed as informational, but in reality they had become significantly more entertaining and lively in their content (Papke, 1987, p. 54).

By the end of the 1800s, and persisting to this day, two types of newspapers dominated and competed: "informational" newspapers aimed at upwardly mobile members of the middle class and at the elite (modern examples are the *New York Times* and the *Wall Street Journal*) and "entertainment" newspapers aimed at the lower-middle and working classes (modern examples are the *New York Daily News* and *USA Today*). Unlike the earlier and cheaper penny press newspapers, however, both of these varieties were conservative and supported the status quo. They also depicted crimes as individual acts, in portraits that promoted crime control (Papke, 1987). In con-

---

Despite the relative dryness of its content, police court reporting came under early criticism from people who feared it would cause others to commit copycat crimes. The *New York Evening Post* of June 6, 1828, complained that it was "of little benefit to the cause of morals thus to familiarize the community, and especially the younger parts of it, to the details of misdemeanor and crime. . . . Besides, it suggests to the novice in vice all the means of becoming expert in its devices" (quoted in Bleyer, 1927, p. 157). Bleyer also noted that the penny papers were lamented as promoting licentiousness and the general corruption of young people. In 1859 some of the first published criticism complaining that court reporting interfered with the administration of justice appeared (see Wilmer, 1859). And during the last quarter of the nineteenth century, law journals began to criticize the press for inaccuracies and poor taste and began to address fair-trial issues. By 1892, an attorney was stating flatly in *Criminal Law Magazine* that it had become a question of trial by newspaper or trial by the law (Forrest, 1892, p. 553). By the end of the nineteenth century, criticism of the press by the bar focused more and more on the danger of prejudicial publicity (Drechsel, 1983, p. 68).

trast to earlier crime news, in which the description of individual crimes played a small role and crime was frequently reported as a result of political and social factors, the new journalism emphasized the details of individual crimes and less frequently discussed crime as a social issue. News reports became more important than the editorials that had dominated the earlier press, and police departments and police officers replaced the courts and court personnel as the primary source of information about crime (Drechsel, 1983, p. 68; Papke, 1987, p. 54). Drechsel (1983) has reported that throughout the eighteenth century newspapers gave considerable attention to local court proceedings. In the nineteenth century, however, reporters became far more active, particularly in pursuing official sources outside of court. In Drechsel's view, the increased reliance on official sources to substantiate the news marks the beginning of the skewing of news toward the most accessible, cooperative sources. He offered the following explanation for this shift: Early in this country's history, crime was synonymous with sin and trials were ceremonies of status degradation. And since the goal of justice was to reteach and heal the erring soul, confession, public humiliation, and infamy—all of which publicity could enhance—were valuable social goals. Hence, publicity was seen as part of the sin-cleansing process, and newspapers were willing and encouraged to publicize even such distasteful activities as incest or infanticide. But though sin/crime and its punishment were to be noted, lurid details were not to be sensationalized. The emphasis on editorial moralizing over factual details that was found in these early court stories follows as a logical extension of this view. In sum, in this early period the discovery and punishment of a deviant act might reasonably be regarded as a favorable sign from Providence and its publicity a useful example of the wages of sin to others.

During the nineteenth century, however, crime began to be perceived as a secular problem. Though neither crime nor sin was a laughing matter, as crime came to be perceived as distinct from sin, being entertained by crime came to be seen as less harmful than being entertained by sin. Marked increases in crime and concern over immigration and industrialization during the 1800s, plus a faith in the rehabilitative power of institutions (see Rothman, 1971), also help to explain the increased humor and melodrama to be found in crime coverage and the relative lack of concern expressed over press interference with trial fairness throughout much of the nineteenth century. Americans, fearful of crime in a violent era in which due process rights were not strongly and specifically established, saw little wrong with publicity that, at worst, might help get social undesirables off the streets and into correctional institutions (Papke, 1987; cf. Rothman, 1971). By the late nineteenth century, the shift to reporting crimes as individual, often entertaining acts rather than as manifestations of societal failures was complete. Modern corporate newspapers supplying descriptive, factual crime news were firmly established (Stevens & Garcia, 1980, p. 124). Once set, the format and style of reporting on crime and justice did not change much until the development of investigative journalism in the 1960s.

As with the entertainment media, the primary developments affecting news media in the first half of this century had to do not with content but with the development of new visual and electronic means of delivering the news.

In the 1920s, radio came into dominance as the home entertainment and information medium, with the number of stations growing from 32 to 254 between 1921 and 1922 alone (DeFleur & Ball-Rokeach, 1975, p. 84). Exemplified by coverage of the Hindenburg disaster and the Lindbergh kidnapping and Scopes trials, radio news established itself as the first live, "on-the-scene" reporting medium. The current television news format of short, thirty-to-sixty-second news spots presented within established categories (the world, the nation, sports, weather, economics, crime, and so forth) also originated with radio programming. Within these news categories, temporary themes would periodically prevail: The electronic news would give a topic saturation coverage for a short time, then would slack off and turn to something new (Altheide & Snow, 1979). Together with the producers of the film industry's news reels, which brought weekly visual coverage of news to the public, radio producers created the style that television would embellish: short-term, visceral, emotional news coverage. Ultimately, the presentation styles developed for both print and electronic media and the competitive, profit-driven nature of media organizations set the parameters for how crime and justice news would come to be created and what it would contain.

THE PRESENT-DAY CREATION OF NEWS

On total examination, entertainment and news media are remarkably similar in the distorted image of criminality they project (Bortner, 1984). This is somewhat surprising in that news agencies market their news reports as realistic, objective, and true reports of the world and strive to maintain reputations for accuracy. An examination of the process and criteria by which most news is created, however, reveals the origins of this paradox.

Cohen and Young (1981) have described two models for the process of news creation: the "market" model and the "manipulative" model. The key concept for both models is "newsworthiness"—that is, the criteria by which news producers choose which of all known events are to be presented to the public as news events. In the market model, newsworthiness is determined largely by public interest, and journalists simply and objectively report and reproduce the world in the news. Accordingly, under this model, reporters are regarded as news collection agents who meet the needs of the public interest, and the media, as mechanisms that provide the public with objective and realistic information about the world. In the manipulative model, news is selected not according to general public interest but according to the interests of the news agencies' owners. Under this model, the media are purposefully seen as distorting reality and using the news as a means of shaping public opinion in support of large conservative social institutions (Cohen & Young, 1981, pp. 17–18).

Cohen and Young have argued (and this author agrees) that both news models are simplistic and inadequate, because they presume that an objective reality exists and can be reported and because they ignore the organizational realities of news production. Theorists now consider the assumption that there is an objective world and that the news media can (under the market model) or could (under the manipulative model) report it accurately to be inherently flawed (Terry, 1984). It is flawed because the organizational process of transforming social events into news, by its very nature, makes rendering an objective, unbiased, mirror image of a reality that is at best relative impossible (cf. Cohen & Young, 1981, pp. 18–32). Rather, what the public receives as news is capsulized, stylized information that limits the publisher's liability and is deemed newsworthy by whatever standard the agency uses (Martens & Cunningham-Niederer, 1985, p. 62; see also Pritchard, 1985). These factors have more to do with the organizational needs of news agencies than with the criteria of the manipulative or market model. Hence, because of the organizational nature of its birth, crime news, like other news, is inherently subjective, though not necessarily ideologically biased (cf. Hall et al., 1981). It displays characteristics that can be interpreted as indicative of both the manipulative and market models but that can also be understood within an organizational model of news production—a model that better fits the historical development of news about crime and justice as just outlined.

The bulk of news, then, is less discovered than formed by journalists. But journalists do not make up facts, they select facts "created" for them by individuals or bureaucracies. They offer a reality constructed in part by their selection of some sources and not others. There is nothing necessarily pernicious about this, but the fact is that news sources produce their own idealized versions of reality—versions that when presented as news may be

The adage "there are two sides to every story" reflects the common recognition of the inherent subjectiveness of reality. In that no one can directly observe or experience all of the events that occur in the world, our individual "objective" reality is limited to the small part of the world we personally interact with. In order to "know" about the rest of the world and to tell others about our experiences, we depend on communication. The process of communication involves the selection, assessment, evaluation, summarizing, and translation of events into "accounts" of events. These "accounts" are shared and provide the bulk of our knowledge of the world. The construction of these accounts reflects cultural, personal, and social influences. Our reality is thus composed of personal experiences of some events and the acquired accounts of a larger number of events we did not experience. Reality as reflected in knowledge of the world is, in the final analysis, not objective but is the compilation of the knowledge gained from the inherently subjective social process of communication.

perceived as representing a broader reality (Drechsel, 1983). In other words, news sources forward an interpretation of issues that presents the view of the world they wish to have accepted. The reporter "beat" system—under which reporters cover specific subject areas within specific locales (for example, state politics or downtown crime)—further restricts a journalist's sources and perspectives so that, in general, news journalists report on those at or near the top of the social hierarchy and those who threaten them—particularly those at the bottom—to an audience mostly located in the middle (Gans, 1979, p. 284). The gathering of crime news can be described as fundamentally the product of the coupling of two information-processing machines—news organizations and government (Drechsel, 1983, pp. 12, 49, citing Sigal, 1973, pp. 4–5). This means that in news of crime and justice we normally hear criminal justice system and government officials talking about individual criminals and street crimes (Graber, 1980). Which crimes get reported is determined by each crime's "newsworthiness" in comparison with other crimes and other potential news.

Newsworthiness, Routinization, and Gatekeeping

Newsworthiness—that is, the value of any particular item to a news organization—is operationally defined by two components: "periodicity" and "consonance" (Cohen & Young, 1981, p. 22; see also Gelles & Faulkner, 1978). Periodicity refers to the time cycle of events. If an event's cycle is similar to the publication cycle of a medium and thereby better matches its organizational scheduling needs, that event is more likely to be reported as news. Thus, in daily news, preference is given to short, day-length events or to longer events that can be easily segmented into a set of day-length cycles. Consonance refers to how an event ties in with prior news themes and accepted public images and explanations. Unexpected or unusual events will be selected, but they will be presented in terms of previously established stories and explanations (Cohen & Young, 1981, pp. 22–23). Events that better fit established themes are more likely to be selected. Other, more specific criteria for news selection include the seriousness of the event, whimsical circumstances, sentimental or dramatic elements, and the involvement of high-status persons (Roshier, 1981). The reason that periodicity and consonance become important to news agencies is that, as organizations, they need to routinize their work to plan and schedule the use of their resources. But news organizations are in the unique organizational position of dealing with a commodity, news, that by definition is supposed to be unique and unpredictable. Their task, then, is to routinize the processing of nonroutine events. To do so, news media personnel must become active co-creators of the news. They cannot be totally reactive, as the market model implies, nor can they be totally proactive, as the manipulative model would have. In practice, they are somewhere in between—reactive to truly unexpected events, proactive and part of the creation process for much of the rest of the news. Westin (1982), for example, has described the television news agency practice of stocking and maintaining "story banks"—fully taped news stories that can be pulled and aired as needed. In contrast to the manipulative model, however, even when proactive, news agencies are not, as a rule, driven by political ideologies but by organizational pressures (Cohen & Young, 1981, p. 23; Westin, 1982). The more aspects of a social event that a news organization recognizes as newsworthy, the more likely that organization is to treat the event as news. Some news organizations value gossip and personal detail; some focus on financial or political themes; some prefer crime and violence.

In their efforts to routinize the creation of news, news agencies come to rely on standing social institutions from government and business as sources of news. The news media favor these institutions because their personnel can be cited as credible official sources and they represent an easy means of getting news. From this reliance, a cyclic pattern develops. The media and these institutions develop a working relationship, each fulfilling organizational needs of the other—the business and governmental institutions providing the news agencies regular, ready news in exchange for publicity and enhanced credibility. The result is news dominated by information and interpretations that tend to support these institutions (Cohen & Young, 1981). Because both the market and the manipulative models ignore these organizational constraints on the creation of news, they are both inadequate. News is neither a pure picture of society nor a fully controlled propaganda message but is instead an organizational product.

In regard to crime news, the process has the following results. Crime news makes up a large part of the total news, because, being prepackaged (suggesting the manipulative model) and popular (suggesting the market model), it helps news organizations in their routinization task (Chibnall, 1981; Tuchman, 1973, 1978). And because crime news tends to come largely from information supplied by the police, it can be gathered at little cost to the organization (Gordon & Heath, 1981; Roshier, 1981; Sherizen, 1978, p. 212).

The key "gatekeeper" in the crime news process—the one who decides the news—is the crime reporter. A crime reporter must develop reliable police sources and maintain their access and trust (Sherizen, 1978). The successful crime reporter develops a relationship with the police that benefits both. Over time, the two sides tend to develop similar work experiences and outlooks. Crime reporters don't gather news in the manner commonly assumed; rather, they are delivered information from sources with whom

The term *gatekeeper* was first introduced by White (1950). A subject of much review, police and crime reporters are said to undergo a process of "professional socialization" in which, because of their low status in news media organizations and lack of alternative sources of information, they come to reflect official police positions and hold values similar to the police concerning crime (see Chibnall, 1981; Isaacs, 1961; Sherizen, 1978; Terry, 1984).

they share values and on which they are professionally dependent. From these official sources they construct accounts of crime (Chibnall, 1981). The police benefit by having crime news reflect their perspectives, and crime reporters benefit by having a steady, reliable, credible, and flexible source of news that is unlikely to later need retraction or to raise charges of subjectivity (see Chibnall, 1981; Gordon & Heath, 1981; Sherizen, 1978). The end result is a reliance on the police for information about crime and crime news that largely reflects official police viewpoints (Sherizen, 1978, pp. 209–212).[4] This gatekeeping process results in the developmental sequence shown in Figure 3-1.

Figure 3-1 shows the seven processing points between the commission of a crime and the public's receipt of news about crime. At each step in the sequence is a gatekeeper, an individual who receives information on crimes from the previous step, discards some, and passes some on to the next step. These filtering steps make any correspondence between crime news and actual crime difficult. They also make ever achieving such a correspondence unlikely. The socialization of the police to pass along newsworthy crime of interest to the media and of the media to present the interpretations of the police results in a biased selection of the crimes that become the news of crime.[5]

Crime News Case Studies

Two case studies of the creation of crime news describe this process in detail. In the first, Stuart Hall and his associates studied the reporting of muggings in the British press:

> Mugging breaks as a news story because of its extra-ordinariness, its novelty. This fits with [the] notion of the extra-ordinary as the cardinal news value: most stories seem to require some novel element in order to lift them into news visibility in the first instance; mugging was no exception. The Waterloo Bridge killing, defined by the police as a "mugging gone wrong," was located and signified

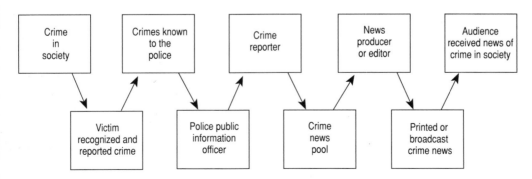

FIGURE 3-1 Gatekeeping points in the creation of crime news

Source: Adapted from "Social Creation of Crime News: All the News Fitted to Print," by S. Sherizen, p. 205. In C. Winick (ed.), Deviance and Mass Media. Copyright © 1978 by Sage Publications, Inc. Reprinted by permission.

to its audience as a "frightening new strain of crime." What lifts this particular murder out of the category of the "run of the mill" is the attribution of a "new" label. Importantly, this event is mediated by the police investigating it; they provide the mugging label, and hence the legitimization for its use by the press. The journalist then builds on this skeletal definition. He frames and contextualizes the details of the story in line with the operating logic. . . . He emphasizes its novelty.

However, the news value of "novelty" is eventually expended; through repetition the extra-ordinary eventually becomes ordinary. Indeed, in relation to any one particular news story, "novelty" clearly has the most limited life span. At this point in the "cycle" of a news story, other, more enduring news values are needed in order to supplement [its] declining newsworthiness, and so sustain its "news-life." Two in particular seemed to play such an augmenting role in relation to mugging; those of the "bizarre" and "violence." In respect to both of these news values, we find a growth in the number of mugging reports, throughout our sample period, which seemed to gain news visibility primarily because of the presence of such supplementary news values.*

A cycle of newsworthiness is thus created in which once a type of crime is defined as news, it will continue to be news for some time because of the actions of both criminal justice and media organizations: "The relationship between primary definers [the police] and the media serves to define 'mugging' as a public issue, as a matter of public concern, and to effect an ideological closure of the topic" (Hall et al., 1981, p. 358; see also Galtung & Ruge, 1981).

In a second case study, Mark Fishman (1978) reported on a similar process in the United States in which crimes against the elderly, after becoming the focus of media coverage, became the impetus for a media-generated perception of a crime wave in New York City. Here, as in Britain, the initial adoption of a crime theme by one news organization led to that theme's domination of crime news selection within the news industry over a significant period, which in turn came to influence the activities of criminal justice agencies. Fishman described crime news selection as a process in which news assignment editors use themes to organize and assign reporters and give structure to the presentation of the news:

This procedure requires that an incident be stripped of the actual context of its occurrence so that it may be relocated in a new, symbolic context: the news theme. Because newsworthiness is based on [current] themes, the attention devoted to an event may exceed its importance, relevance, or timeliness were these qualities determined with reference to some theory of society. In place of any such theoretical understanding of the phenomena they report, news workers make incidents meaningful only as instances of themes—themes which are generated within the news production process. Thus, something becomes a "serious type of crime" on the basis of what is going on inside news rooms, not outside them. (Fishman, 1978, p. 536)

---

*From "The Social Production of News," by S. Hall et al., pp. 335–367. In S. Cohen and J. Young, *The Manufacture of News.* Copyright © 1981 by Sage Publications, Inc. Reprinted by permission.

Because of the high level of internal monitoring and copying in the news industry, once one news organization adopts a crime theme, others will likely pick it up as well (Fishman, 1978, p. 537). If the focus becomes industrywide, a media crime wave results. The crimes chosen as news during this span in effect become the typical "atypical" event (the most frequently seen news of a set of unusual, newsworthy crimes) for that period.

In the views of both Hall and his colleagues and Fishman, the news media focus public attention on particular crimes without any evidence of an actual increase in victimization rates. The media thus create their own reality by selectively highlighting certain types of crimes from among the large, constantly available pool of known crimes. In doing this, the media create the perception of a crime wave. Media crime waves normally arise around safe crime themes: The media launch anticrime crusades that will have broad public and political acceptance, for example, against crimes against the elderly, street crime, or child abuse. Less frequently do the media focus on controversial topics such as illegal business practices.

The social importance of these media crusades is twofold. First, they enable the media to influence criminal justice policies by raising public concern about a particular offense or set of offenders, affecting sentencing and enforcement practices, and encouraging the application of public resources to address the newly created crime problem (Fishman, 1978). Second, because the media tend to operate around themes, a number of socially significant events will not become news, because they do not fit the current themes. For practical public purposes, such events therefore do not exist and are less likely to receive public attention or resources.[6] Driven by their unique organizational relationships, tasks, and deadlines, news agencies generate crime news from a relatively narrow and distinct information channel, a channel that gives preference to information from other organizational sources and to certain types of crimes and that the media sustain and rely on because it is reliable and easy to use. Because of the idiosyncrasies in the creation of crime and justice news, questions regarding the resulting content arise.

CRIME AND JUSTICE CONTENT OF CONTEMPORARY NEWS

The Content and Relative Prominence of Crime News

As with entertainment programming, examination of the content of crime news reveals a similarly distorted, inverted image. Numerous studies, using various methods and measures have established that crime news is a popular, significant, and constant component of the total news.[7] Within newspapers, crime news accounts for from 4 to 28 percent of all the news reported, averaging about 7 percent overall.[8] Crime news constitutes newspapers' third largest subject category (Sherizen, 1978, p. 208). For national television, Cirino (1972) found about 13 percent of its total news was crime news; Lowry (1971), about 10 percent; Graber (1980), 12.5 percent. For local television, Graber (1980) found 20 percent. This range of about 5 percent to 25 percent appears to hold true for different time periods, different localities, and different media (television, newspapers, and radio).[9]

Besides making up a significant portion of the news, crime news is well attended. For example, in newspapers, crime news is read consistently by a greater percentage of subscribers (24 to 26 percent) than other types of news items.[10]

Besides overemphasizing violent crime, crime news focuses heavily on the details of specific individual crimes. Graber (1980, p. 63), for example, found that nearly 56 percent of crime news dealt with crime details, whereas only 1.4 percent dealt with the personality of the criminal or victim. Coverage of individual crimes has in fact been found to rank as the single most common news item for both newspapers and television (Graber, 1980, p. 52).

The traditional definition of news is that which is new or uncommon. Following this maxim, violent crime is seen as more newsworthy precisely because it occurs less frequently. It also follows that the rarest type of violent crime, murder, is reported the most often (Esterle, 1986, p. 5). Crime news has been found to focus largely on violent personal street crimes such as murder, rape and assault, with more common offenses such as burglary and theft often ignored.[11] According to one study, murder and robbery alone account for approximately 45 percent of newspaper crime news and 80 percent of television crime news (Sheley & Ashkins, 1981, pp. 499–500). Graber (1980, pp. 39–40) reported that murder constituted 0.2 percent of the crime known to the police but was the subject of 26.2 percent of crime news, whereas nonviolent crime accounted for 47 percent of known crime but 4 percent of crime news stories. A number of criminologists have stated that the media's ignoring of certain types of crimes and criminal cases is as damaging as what is actually reported. Corporate crime, for example, is seldom reported as crime news.[12] Journalists, too, have criticized the myopic focus of crime reporting (see Shaw, 1990a, 1990b, 1990c; Sneed, 1985, p. 56). The paradox is that violent crime's relative infrequency in the real world heightens its newsworthiness and leads to its frequent appearance in crime news. Crime news thus takes the rare crime event and turns it into the common crime image. Gottfredson and Hirschi (1990, p. 35) have cited this media emphasis on publicizing the atypical crime as a serious source of misinformation about and false perceptions of the true nature of crime for both criminologists and the public. Additionally, just as crime in entertainment minimally reflects reported crime, variations that do occur over time in the amount of crime news that is reported have little relationship to variations in measures of reported crime.[13] Neither the content nor the total amount of crime news reflects changes in the crime rate.

The Criminal in the News

The image of the criminal that the news media propagate is similar to that found in the entertainment media. Criminals tend to be of two types in the news media: violent predators, or professional businessmen or bureaucrats (cf. Graber, 1980, pp. 57–58). Furthermore, as in entertainment programming, they tend to be slightly older (twenty to thirty years old) than reflected in official arrest statistics. (Graber did find close correspondence between the racial and sexual characteristics of criminals in newspapers and official FBI arrest statistics.) In general, the news media underplay criminals' youth and to some degree their poverty, while overplaying their violence (Terry, 1984, p. 36; see also Roshier, 1981; Sheley & Ashkins, 1981).

Additionally, many times crimes are reported without any description of the perpetrator and the public is left to fill in the image (Sheley & Ashkins, 1981). It follows that since most crime news is about violent interpersonal crime, the image that is filled in is that of a faceless predator. Thus, Graber (1980) found that the public's image of criminals reflected the stereotypical street criminal—a young, unemployed, black male. The significance of this is that the public's image of crime reflects but does not exactly match the news media's image. Even though the news reports a number of white-collar, terrorist, drug-related, and business crimes, and, when it identifies offenders, describes them as somewhat older and of higher status, the public appears to focus on the violent interpersonal street crimes that are reported, ignoring those characterizations that do not fit the stereotypical street criminal (Graber, 1980, p. 58). Although other crimes and criminals are shown, the violent and predatory street criminal dominates the news and the public's image of criminality (Gorelick, 1989).

The Criminal Justice System in the News

The criminal justice system and its component parts are seldom in themselves the subject of news reports. The criminal justice system serves as a background setting for a news story much more often than it appears as the subject of a story. Graber, for example, found in her study that less than 4 percent of all crime news explicitly assessed any part of the criminal justice system. When the justice system is explicitly referred to, it is usually the courts that are portrayed. The courts are not shown as institutions, however, but as settings for individual cases. According to Graber, reports on specific crimes or on the processing of specific criminal cases in the courts comprised 69 percent of all crime and justice news coverage.[14] In essence, the news supplies a large amount of information about specific crimes and conveys the impression that criminals threaten the social system and its institutions, but provides little explicit systemwide information to help the public evaluate or comprehend the information about individual crimes and cases (Graber, 1980, pp. 46, 74; cf. Terry, 1984, p. 36). Rare is interpretive analysis that places criminal justice information in historical, sociological, or political perspective (Gorelick, 1989; Graber, 1980, p. 45). In the absence of news media evaluations of the police, the courts, and the correctional system, the public is left to build its own general picture of the effectiveness of the criminal justice system (Graber, 1980; Terry, 1984).

Most media evaluations of the criminal justice system are thus implicit, conveyed through references to the ability or inability of the system to apprehend criminals, to convict and punish them when they are apprehended, and to return them to society reformed. In Graber's assessment, the news media implicitly portrayed the police as doing a fair job, comparatively speaking, but the courts and the correctional system as doing poor jobs. When she queried a sample of the public, the system's components did only slightly better in the same order—police being rated as good to fair, the courts as fair to poor, and corrections as poor. The public's largely negative evaluation of the criminal justice system thus reflects overall the information and impressions conveyed by the news (Graber, 1980, pp. 74–75, 80, 83).

Although the courts are the most frequently shown component of the criminal justice system, the police are the most often cited employees of the system, usually as sources of information regarding the basic facts of a crime. As noted earlier, this results from the news media's desire to attribute statements and information to authoritative, credible spokespersons (cf. Chibnall, 1981; Gordon & Heath, 1981; Sherizen, 1978). Police officers'

BOX 3-1 Negative Coverage of the Judicial System

role as quotable spokespersons is further heightened by the news media's emphasis on the beginning stages of the criminal justice system—another similarity between the news and entertainment media (see Bortner, 1984, p. 18; Garofalo, 1981). According to Sherizen (1978, pp. 216–217), more than two-thirds of crime news coverage relates to the beginning stages of the justice system, and postarrest stages are seldom mentioned except in trial reports.

Regarding corrections, the news media, like the entertainment media, mostly ignore it. Indeed, corrections is mentioned directly so infrequently in the news that content analysis studies discussing corrections are practi-

BOX 3-2   Negative Coverage of the Correctional System

cally nonexistent. When corrections is the subject of a news story, it is nearly always reported in a negative light.[15] Hence, Schwartz (1989, p. 40) has reported that the last long-running national story in the media about corrections was about the 1987 taking of hostages at the U. S. Penitentiary in Atlanta, Georgia, and the Federal Detention Center in Oakdale, Louisiana. The only other recent national media exposure occurred during the 1988 presidential campaign, during which prison furlough programs were attacked, with the implication that long, inflexible sentences are the only acceptable alternative.

"Info-tainment"

Another feature of present-day news coverage is the exploitation of crime news in tabloid-style "info-tainment" television programs that mix news and entertainment formats. These shows entertain by sensationalizing stories about crime and justice. They present crime in a realistic light, sometimes in reenactments, sometimes as dramatized stories based on real crimes and criminal cases, and sometimes in documentary-style stories. In their tendency to sensationalize, these programs are electronic versions of the supermarket tabloid newspapers. They are significant in denoting the final phase of a long trend noted in 1979 by Altheide and Snow (1979) toward merging the once distinct news and entertainment functions of the mass media.[16] As we enter the 1990s, more crime-focused entertainment–news shows are being broadcast than at any previous time. Among them are the following, listed with the year they were first broadcast:

> "Cops," 1989
> "Eye on Crime," 1989
> "Hard Copy," 1989
> "Trial by Jury," 1989
> "America's Most Wanted," 1988
> "Unsolved Mysteries," 1988
> "A Current Affair," 1987
> "The Judge," 1986
> "Divorce Court," 1984
> "The People's Court," 1981

The development of these info-tainment shows parallels another phenomenon, one that co-opts and usurps the criminal courts entirely.

Court News as Miniseries

As noted earlier, the police appear most often on the news as spokespersons regarding specific crimes, and corrections is largely ignored and when covered is shown negatively. It is the courts then that the news media most often show as system institutions. They therefore represent the criminal justice system as the social institutions charged with processing offenders and dispensing justice, and their portrayal in the phenomenon of "media trials" illustrates both the past development and possible future of crime and justice news.

A "media trial" is defined as a regional or national news event in which the media co-opt the criminal justice system as a source of high drama and entertainment (see Surette, 1989). It is, in effect, a dramatic miniseries built around a real criminal case. One of the primary factors behind the development of media trials is that news organizations competing over ratings increasingly structured the news along entertainment lines, presenting it within themes, formats, and explanations originally found solely in entertainment programming (Comstock, 1980). Eventually fast-paced, dramatic, superficial presentations and simplistic explanations became the norm. As this trend developed, some criminal trials came to be covered more intensely, and organizations expanded their coverage from "hard" factual to "soft" human interest news to emphasize extralegal and human-interest elements. This process has culminated in the total mergence of news and entertainment in the "media trial."[17]

Trials packaged as media trials involve cases that contain the same elements popular in entertainment programming—human interest laced with mystery, sex, bizarre circumstances, and famous or powerful people (Roshier, 1981, p. 47). Media trials are distinguished by massive and intensive coverage that begins either with the discovery of the crime or the arrest of the accused (Harper, 1982, p. 78). The media cover all aspects of the case, often highlighting extralegal facts. Judges, lawyers, police, witnesses, jurors, and particularly defendants are interviewed, photographed, and frequently raised to celebrity status. Personalities, personal relationships, physical appearances, and idiosyncrasies are commented on regardless of legal relevancy. Coverage is live whenever possible, pictures are preferred over text, and text is characterized by conjecture and sensationalism (cf. Barber, 1987, pp. 112–114).[18]

In their coverage, the media offer explanations of crime that are direct and simple: lust, greed, immorality, jealousy, revenge, and insanity. As in the entertainment realm, recurrent themes have dominated media trial portraits of crime. Three in particular can be identified: "abuse of power and trust," "the sinful rich," and "evil strangers" (see Surette, 1989). These three themes help to understand the content of the coverage by structuring it to promote the perceptions that the rich are immoral in their use of sex, drugs, or violence; that people in power are evil and greedy; that the authorities should not be trusted (an image and message that corresponds with the entertainment portrayal of businesspeople and high government officials [see Chapter 2; Bortner, 1984; Lichter & Lichter, 1983]); and that strangers and those with different lifestyles or values are inherently dangerous.

Media trials represent the final step in a long process of merging the news and entertainment—a process that has often resulted in multimedia and commercial news exploitation of these cases (see Figure 3-2). That the source of media trials is the judicial system eases the merger, for media trials allow the news industry to attract and entertain a large general audience

FIGURE 3-2 Cases such as serial murderer Ted Bundy's often result in print and visual productions by several media, in both the news and entertainment industries. The photos at upper right show Bundy's many guises; the photo at lower left is of Mark Harmon in the NBC film "The Deliberate Stranger," based on Bundy's story.

Source: (Top) AP/Wide World Photos; (center) photo courtesy of The National Broadcasting Company, Inc.; (bottom) from THE STRANGER BESIDE ME by Ann Rule. Copyright © 1981 by New American Library for book cover. Used by permission of New American Library, a division of Penguin Books USA Inc. Photo by Jeff Bender.

BOX 3-3   Examples of Media Trial Coverage

Headline:

The following lead from a *Miami Herald* article titled "Benson Is Hottest Show in Town" exemplifies the use of an entertainment format in dramatized coverage of a media trial:

> Ladies and gentlemen, welcome to the wild side of the Benson pipe-bomb murder trial. Step right up and see the contortionist. See the country-boy prosecutors who rock their swivel chairs in sync, and see the defendant the jailers call "Boom Boom." Sometime within the next few days, a jury will begin deliberations in what is a humdinger of a courtroom spectacle underlying a terrible tragedy. (Freedberg & Holzman, August 4, 1986, p. A-1. Reprinted with permission of *The Miami Herald).*

Regarding the coverage of the von Bulow trial in Rhode Island, Barber (1987, p. 113) noted:

> The von Bulow trial took on the proportions of an international television drama, with participants who resembled characters in a soap opera. WPRI-TV produced a 30-minute special called "The von Bulows of Newport" and aired this documentary at the close of the trial. During the trial itself, there was live coverage by Cable News Network. Thames Television from London covered the trial for about 4 weeks, and also aired a half-hour special on American "aristocracy" based on the von Bulows of Newport.

Murder defendant Claus von Bulow, leaving Providence, Rhode Island, Superior Court following a court session
Source: UPI/Bettmann

Media trials that fit the "abuse of power and trust" theme include those cases in which the defendant occupies a position of trust, prestige, or authority. The general rule is the higher the rank, the more media interest in the case. Cases involving police corruption and justice system personnel in general are especially attractive to the media. "Sinful rich" media trials include cases in which socially prominent defendants are involved in a bizarre or sexually related crime. These trials have a voyeuristic appeal and are covered in such a way as to persuade the public that they are being given a rare glimpse into the backstage world of the upper class. Love triangles and inheritance-motivated killings among the jet set are primary examples. The category of "evil strangers" can be considered as comprising two subgroups: "non-Americans" and "psychotic killers." "Non-American evil stranger" media trials may involve, depending on the political climate, immigrants, blacks, Jews, socialists, union and labor leaders, anarchists, the poor, members of the counterculture, members of fringe religions, political activists, crusaders, or advocates of various unpopular causes. "Psychotic killer" media trials usually focus on bizarre murder cases in which the defendants are portrayed as maddened, dangerous killers. Recent examples in this category include the cases of Albert DeSalvo (the Boston Strangler), Richard Speck, and Ted Bundy.

Papke (1987, p. 22) reports that similar themes existed in the 1830s. Popular pamphlets portrayed crime within two long-standing themes—the "rogue" (a semi-hero who commits property fraud) and the "fiend" (a diabolical, frenzied villain). This period saw the creation of a new theme—the "fiendish rogue." An example from the early part of the century is the 1913 Leo Frank case. This case involved the strangulation of a fourteen-year-old female factory worker in Georgia. As was common in such cases, coverage was heavily biased against the defendant. An Atlanta paper was typical: "Our little girl— ours by the Eternal God! has been pursued to a hideous death and bloody grave by this filthy, perverted Jew of New York." The commutation of his sentence from death to life imprisonment led to the Georgia governor's being driven out of office. A year after his conviction, Frank was taken from a prison farm hospital by a band of men, driven 125 miles to the scene of the murder, and lynched.

while maintaining its preferred image as an objective and neutral reporter of news (Terry, 1984). Furthermore, the courts have been described as already being less in the business of producing decisions than engaged in giving a performance (Ball, 1981, p. 62).[19] The judicial system and its judges and attorneys thus sometimes assist the media in the co-optation. The end result is that in media trials, news as entertainment is fully achieved (cf. Comstock, 1980; Gerbner, 1980). Media trials provide the news media with ready-made entertainment-style themes that give shape and direction to their coverage, and that at the same time simplify the task of reporting, interpreting, and explaining a trial. They thus serve a function analogous to the crime news themes discussed earlier (see Fishman, 1978). Media trial themes provide the news media with a framework by which to measure, choose, and sometimes mold the various aspects of a trial that will be reported or highlighted.

Media trials, as indicated by their popularity and the resources that the media are willing to expend to cover them, are a prominent component of crime-related news. They are significant for understanding crime news in general in that they highlight the entertainment criteria that guide the selection of all crime news. They provide concise and simplistic explanations of crime within the authoritative and dramatic vehicle of a trial. Crime in these productions is nearly universally attributed to individual characteristics and failings rather than to social conditions. Nearly 66 percent of the cases reported in Graber's study were attributed to personal quarrels, greed, and the like, and the public appears to perceive crime as clearly caused by deficiencies in the offender (Graber, 1980, pp. 70–71).

BASIC CONCERNS ABOUT CRIME AND JUSTICE NEWS

The public's high readership and retention of crime news, the large percentage of total news that is crime related, and the skewed content of crime news have raised concerns about crime and justice news similar to those expressed about the entertainment media.[20] The news media's coverage of the criminal justice system leads the attending public to evaluate the system poorly while paradoxically supporting both law enforcement that is more oriented toward crime control, and punitive justice policies (Graber, 1980, p. 83; see also Chapter 4). This paradox can be attributed to the public's adherence to a stereotypical image of a street criminal and media depictions that show curable deficiencies in the justice system and personality defects in individuals as the main causes of apparently rampant crime (Graber, 1980). Not surprisingly, Graber (1980, p. 73) found that most people (55 percent) who pay regular attention to the media support as their first policy choice criminal justice reforms that would toughen and strengthen the existing system. This is true even though these same people place a large share of the blame for crime on the criminal justice system. Despite the presentation and perception of the criminal justice system as ineffective, the news media implicitly suggest that improving it, at least as a law enforcement and punitive system, is the best hope against the many violent crimes and predatory criminals that are portrayed (cf. Barrile, 1984; Gorelick, 1989). In the same vein, commenting on the effect of the media image of corrections, Avery (1989) blamed tabloid-style crime reporting and the depiction of prison riots and brutal attacks by assailants on parole for helping to heighten the public's fear of crime, for further eroding its confidence in the ability of corrections to deter or rehabilitate criminals, and for increasing its desire to make the system more punitive for all offenders regardless of their dangerousness. In the end, crime and justice news advances the status quo, system-enhancing crime control policies, and individual-based explanations of society (see Fishman, 1978; Graber, 1980; Hall et al., 1981).

The best known concern is that mass media news coverage leads to disruption of the criminal justice process and violation of due process protections (covered more extensively in Chapter 7). Participants in media trials, for example, are sometimes prodded by the news media into seriously compromising cases.[21] In addition, extensive media attention can create social panics and result in public crusades against types or classes of individuals (Cohen & Young, 1981). The mass media have been especially active in periodically creating and supporting crusades against particular types of crimes and they have been credited with affecting enforcement, prosecution, and sentencing policies (see Fishman, 1978; Hall et al., 1981; Pritchard, 1986). Further, an "echo" effect has been hypothesized in which, following a media trial, the processing and disposition of similar but nonpublicized cases is influenced. Echo effects usually increase the punitiveness of the criminal justice system. The implication is that media news can influence the disposition of a large number of cases, including ones that receive no coverage.[22]

Another concern involves the image of the criminal justice system that the media project and the public receives. Because news portraits are inherently more credible than other images, the image of justice that the news media project has serious implications for the public's understanding of the judicial system and its perception of the legitimacy and fairness of the entire criminal justice system (O'Keefe & Reid, 1990; Randall et al., 1988). Learning about the criminal justice system from the news media is analogous to

---

An echo effect was first described by Loften (1966, p. 138):

> But while the impact of the press is most direct on specific cases covered, there is good reason to believe that [their] sway extends considerably beyond the cases actually appearing. . . . From the cases that are covered, officials become conditioned to expect demands for stern treatment from the press, and in the unpublicized cases they probably act accordingly.

And again by Kaplan and Skolnick (1982, pp. 467–468):

> This unwillingness [to plea bargain] appears to occur relatively infrequently. It is most likely to occur when there is strong pressure upon the prosecution to obtain maximum sentences for a particular class of crime: for example, after a notorious case of child rape, the prosecutor may refuse to bargain, for a time, with those charged with sex offenses involving children; after a series of highly publicized drug arrests allegedly involving dealers or pushers, the prosecution may be unwilling, for a time, to engage in reduction of charges from sales to possession.

Greene and Loftus (1984) and Greene and Wade (1988) provide empirical evidence of such an effect. In two experiments dealing with the impact of general pretrial publicity on jurors, researchers found that exposure to publicity that questioned the accuracy of eyewitnesses influenced decisions in later nonpublicized cases, resulting, in their research, in a reduction in guilty pleas (see Kaplan & Skolnick, 1982; Loften, 1966; Radin, 1964; Surette, 1989).

learning geology from volcanic eruptions. You will surely be impressed and entertained, but the information you receive will not accurately reflect the common daily reality of volcanoes or the criminal justice system. The media trial reality of high-stakes trials, confrontations, oratory, and detailed deliberations contrasts starkly with the criminal justice system's daily reality of plea bargains, compromises, and assembly-line justice (Snow, 1984). Most news coverage appears to appeal to voyeuristic instincts more than it serves any educational service (Barber, 1987, p. 113; Gerbner, 1980). Journalists generally disagree, however, with the contention that their role is to educate the public. They more often argue that their function is to inform the public of particular events and developments. In this view, an emphasis on noteworthy cases and court problems is more appropriate than a comprehensive review of court operations (Cashman & Fetter, 1980). Journalists are correct in stating that educating the public is not their responsibility, but this does not free them from taking responsibility for currently miseducating the public. The fact remains that coverage does educate the public, and often the coverage is inaccurate. Both media and criminal justice personnel

---

BOX 3-4 The Politicizing of Crime and the Misuse of Crime News: The Case of Missing Children

---

The crime of abduction of children by strangers provides an excellent example of how the media can politicize crime and misuse crime data.

The [following] statements are phrased so that they may be true, even if the numbers given are false. This is a standard journalistic technique. At first glance, each of these statements seems to give the number of children involved in a particular social problem. But consider the way the statements are phrased. Each such statement attributes its number to someone. When a reporter writes "Expert A said X," the sentence is true, so long as Expert A did say X; it makes no difference whether X happens to be false. The fact that the media repeat a statistic does not mean that the statistic is accurate or even that reporters made any special effort to check its accuracy. It only means that the media have a source for the number.

More than a million children are victimized each year by abuse or neglect. . . . Authorities say that as many as 3,000 children were killed by their own parents last year in America (CBS, Dec. 1, 1975).

The National Center on Child Abuse estimates between 200,000 and 500,000 children are sexually molested each year (CBS, Apr. 26, 1984).

It's been estimated that as many as two million American youngsters are involved in the fast-growing, multi-million-dollar child pornography business (NBC, May 23, 1977).

Police say the number of boy prostitutes may be as high as a million (NBC, Oct. 25, 1977).

By conservative estimate, 50,000 children are abducted each year, not counting parental kidnappings and custody fights. Most are never found. Four to eight thousand a year are murdered (ABC, May 24, 1982).*

As shown in the following excerpts from a 1985 *Los Angeles Times* article and an editorial in the *Boston Globe,* in the case of missing children the perception of a massive problem came to be challenged in the media. This is not frequently the case, however.

(continued)

have called for educating journalists about the criminal justice system (Cash-man & Fetter, 1980, p. 26). And in at least one instance, the media's voyeur-istic emphasis caused a trial judge to refuse to allow televised coverage of a trial. The judge noted that past media coverage of the case had focused on sex and violence, and he expected that coverage of the trial would also. The trial judge wrote, "Focusing on these factors does not enhance public awareness of the judicial system and does not promote the intent of the [ex-perimental coverage]" ("Audio-Visual Coverage on Trial in States," *News Media and the Law,* 1988, 12(1), p. 49).

CONCLUSION: NEWS AND ENTERTAINMENT RECONSIDERED

The impact of the media on crime and justice follows from the media's por-trayal of crime and justice. This is true for both the entertainment and news elements of the media. It is no coincidence that similar crimes and crimi-nals are depicted in entertainment and news, for the goals and needs of both are to assemble the largest audience possible to maximize readers, rat-

---

BOX 3-4   (continued)

Law enforcement officials . . . caution that the problem of missing children may be overstated, largely because several missing children pro-grams have promoted fearsome statistics that may be unfounded. . . .

Pictures of missing children have been fea-tured on about 50 million grocery bags and more than 35 million milk cartons, as well as on countless egg cartons, flyers sent out by banks and other businesses, and advertisements in newspapers and on buses and billboards. . . .

The National Center for Missing and Ex-ploited Children in Washington has reported that 1.5 million children a year are reported missing. Conceding that their statistics are only estimates, they say about 1 million are runaways. Between 20,000 and 500,000, they say, are ab-ducted by parents locked in custody disputes. And 4,000 to 20,000 are abducted by strangers.

"Their figures don't match up with what we have here," FBI spokesman Bill Carter said. He said, for example, that the FBI investigated 67 kidnappings by strangers nationwide last year.

Child Find in upstate New York once esti-

mated that there were 50,000 stranger abduc-tions annually. But the agency has backed off from that estimate in the face of questioning by skeptical law enforcement officials. . . .

A spokeswoman for Child Find . . . said the agency has recently disavowed the estimate of 50,000 stranger abductions a year and is more comfortable with a figure of "1,000 — more or less." (Claire Spiegel. Copyright, 1985, *Los Ange-les Times.* Reprinted by permission.)

Over the past year or more, the alarm about the abduction of children has been raised everywhere. . . . The media rounded up the usual statistics: 1.5 million children missing, 50,000 a year abducted. . . .

Now, just now, we hear that there are not 50,000 children a year abducted by strangers. Child Find in New York has altered its estimate to 600 such kidnappings, and the FBI says 67 were reported in 1984. Nor are there 1.5 million missing children in this country. The FBI esti-mates, rather, 32,000. (Ellen Goodman. © 1985, The Boston Globe Newspaper Company/Wash-ington Post Writers Group.)

---

*Excerpted from Joel Best, "Dark Figures and Child Victims: Statistical Claims about Missing Children," in *Im-ages of Issues: Typifying Contemporary Social Problems,* ed. Joel Best (Hawthorne, NY: Aldine de Gruyter, 1989).

ings, and revenue. Therefore, the image of justice that the most people find most palatable and popular is the image that has historically been projected. This image is one that locates the causes of crime in the individual criminal and supports existing social arrangements and approaches to crime control (Bergman, 1971; Gorelick, 1989). Because the image is fragmentary and presented separately from other social problems and issues, politicians can and have manipulated the crime issue, ironically through the media.

The public is simultaneously shown that the traditional criminal justice system is not effective and that its improvement is the best solution to crime. These messages translate into support for law-and-order policies and existing criminal justice agencies. Entertainment and news portrayals that expound social change or structural causes of crime are rare (Bortner, 1984; Gorelick, 1989). The repeated message of the news and entertainment media is that crime is largely perpetrated by predatory individuals who are basically different from the rest of us, that criminality is the result of individual problems, and that crimes are freely committed acts. That both the news and entertainment components of the media present similarly distorted portraits of crime and justice has naturally led to concern over the impact of this distorted picture. Audience fear and expectation of crime, mystification of the criminal justice system, support for punitive criminal justice policies, and increased tolerance for illegal law enforcement practices have all been forwarded as potential effects.[23]

Long-term constant exposure to these media images lays the foundation for the most important potential impact of the mass media on justice in our society—their effect on our attitudes and beliefs about crime and justice, on the reality we accept as true with regard to crime. Many have argued that the media's portrait of America and its social structure tends to become the accepted version of social reality (see Altheide & Snow, 1976; Cohen & Young, 1981; Jowett & Linton, 1980, pp. 106–109). Over time people tend to perceive things the way the media portray them. The media thus play not only a reporting role but a defining role, establishing their audiences' sense of reality; prescribing society's accepted norms, behaviors, and boundaries; and forwarding the proper means of dealing with injustice (Bergman, 1971; Cohen & Young, 1981). Because of their popularity, pervasiveness, and prominence, and the relationship of their content to questions of good and evil, morality, and social justice, media that depict images of crime and justice play a central role in this defining process.

The mass media have historically emphasized crime and justice in their content and have used the popularity of these topics to meet their commercial needs. The media have focused on violent interpersonal crime and explain crime as the result of individual choices and deficiencies. The primary concern raised regarding these portrayals has to do with their effect on public attitudes toward and perceptions of justice.[24] The evidence regarding the manner in which and the extent to which the mass media actually influence public attitudes toward crime and justice is explored in Chapter 4.

Notes

1. In 1733, for example, Boston papers reported the arrest, charging, trial, and sentencing of a young woman who had killed her illegitimate newborn (Drechsel, 1983, p. 44).
2. See Chibnall, 1981; Isaacs, 1961; Sherizen, 1978; Terry, 1984.
3. This shift was aided by a number of court decisions and legislative actions that protected the privilege of reporting judicial proceedings without fear of contempt or libel actions.
4. The main exception is news of police crimes and corruption, although even in police malfeasance stories the media actively seek official police input.
5. See Fishman, 1978; Hall et al., 1981; Roshier, 1981; Sherizen, 1978.

6. See Bortner, 1984; Cohen & Young, 1981; Estep & Lauderdale, 1980; Gorelick, 1989; Humphries, 1981.
7. Measures include the percentage of total space or time allocated to coverage of individual crimes (Deutschmann, 1959; Otto, 1962; Stempl, 1962), summary coverage of an issue, and story placement or prominence (Cirino, 1972; Deutschmann, 1959; Dominick, 1978, pp. 110–112; Lowry, 1971; Otto, 1962; Roshier, 1973, p. 33; Sherizen, 1978, p. 208; Stempl, 1962).
8. (See Dominick, 1978, p. 108; Garofalo, 1981. Proportions range from 22 to 28 percent being reported for all justice-related topics (Graber, 1980, p. 24).
9. See Bortner, 1984; Cirino, 1972; Garofalo, 1981; Lowry, 1971; Terry, 1984.

10. Graber, 1980; J. Haskins, 1969; Sherizen, 1978, p. 208; Swanson, 1953.

11. See Bortner, 1984, p. 16; Cirino, 1974; Ditton & Duffy, 1983; Dominick, 1978, p. 108; Fishman, 1978; Graber, 1980; Roshier, 1973, p. 32; Sheley & Ashkins, 1981.

12. See Coleman, 1974; Evans & Lundman, 1983; Molotch & Lester, 1981; Quinney, 1970.

13. Davis, 1951; Fishman, 1978; Graber, 1980, pp. 38–42; Jones, 1976; Roshier, 1981; Sheley & Ashkins, 1981.

14. Sentences reported in the media have been found to be equally atypical of actual practice. Roberts and Doob (1990, p. 453, citing the Canadian Sentencing Commission, 1988) reported that 70 percent of Canadian newspaper stories containing sentencing information report on a prison term. Fines appeared in less than 10 percent of the stories. In reality, imprisonment is rarely imposed in Canada, whereas fines comprise about half of all sentences. Alternate sentences, such as restitution or community service, almost never appeared in newspaper stories. Similarly, the researchers found that crime prevention stories are rare, relative to stories of individual violent crimes; and when crime prevention is covered, the coverage is usually negative.

15. This negative news image is exacerbated by the frequent problems reporters encounter when they seek access to inmates and correctional institutions (see Schwartz, 1989, and "Problems Frequent when Seeking Access to Inmates," *News Media and the Law,* 1989, 13(4), p. 6).

16. A concrete example of the continuing blurring of news and entertainment is ABC's contract with Barbara Walters. ABC gave Barbara Walters a $1-million-per-year contract, with part of her salary to be paid by ABC News for anchor work and part to be paid by ABC Entertainment for her prime-time specials (see Westin, 1982).

17. Media trials are a specific subset within the "celebrity layer of cases" referred to by Samuel Walker (1985, citing Friedman & Percival, 1981; and Gottfredson & Gottfredson, 1980). Media trials, however, make up only a small portion of "celebrity cases,"

which include all cases that make the news, whether initially or later, because of subsequent appeals or court rulings. The latter are referred to as landmark cases and include such cases as *Miranda* and *Escobedo* (Walker, 1985, p. 17). Media trials involve only those cases that attract intense coverage either immediately at the time of discovery or at the time of arrest. The totality of celebrity cases represents a pool that can subsequently be tapped for possible media trials.

18. These media justice events have occurred at regular intervals throughout this century. Proto media trials can be found in the late nineteenth century. The best known is the Lizzy Borden ax murder trial. Trial reporting in the eighteenth century was frank, to the point, and reasonably detached, and even during and after the penny press days of the nineteenth century, reporters frequently interviewed sources on both sides of disputes (Drechsel, 1983, pp. 53–54).

19. Ball (1981) described courtroom action as a distinct type of theater, "judicial theater," comparing the courtroom to a stage, legal arguments to script, and a trial to a performance, with the trial itself embodying the theatrical format of protagonist and antagonist. According to Ball, judicial theater serves various functions for society, the primary one being the definition and legitimization of law. See also Simonett, 1966.

20. cf. Graber, 1980; S. Haskins, 1969; Sherizen, 1978; Swanson, 1953.

21. Rosenberg (1990) has recounted a recent child sexual abuse case involving a California day care center in which the media publicized and encouraged efforts by the parents of children who were at the day care center to pressure for the refiling of child molestation and conspiracy charges against an already tried defendant whose jury had deadlocked.

22. See Kaplan & Skolnick, 1982; Loften, 1966; Radin, 1964; Surette, 1989.

23. See Barrile, 1984; Gorelick, 1989; Hennigan et al., 1982; Reiner, 1985; Surette, 1985b.

24. See Gerbner, 1980; Randall et al., 1988; Reiner, 1985; Zucker, 1978.

4 The Media's Influence on Attitudes and Beliefs about Crime and Justice

OVERVIEW

Chapter 4 reviews the evidence concerning the effect of news and entertainment on crime- and justice-related attitudes, beliefs, and policies. The media effects discussed in this chapter may be less dramatic and more abstract than behavioral effects on crime and violence, but they are no less important. As a prelude to examining the research on the effects of the news and entertainment media, the chapter examines first planned, purposeful efforts by the media to influence attitudes and beliefs through "public information" or "public communication campaigns." Evaluations of these campaigns provide a sense of what to expect and not to expect regarding attitudinal effects from the relatively unplanned content of news and entertainment. Perceptions of the strength of the media's effects have periodically shifted between strong and negligible, but the current perception is that planned media campaigns can be a strong source of influence if carefully designed but only in specific situations. If we conceptualize news and entertainment as a long-running, continuous, but poorly designed public information campaign, we can reasonably hypothesize that the media have unplanned but significant effects. And the research suggests that such effects will interact with other social factors and will be difficult to discern, and difficult to counteract once established. The last three sections of the chapter analyze in turn media influences on agenda setting, beliefs and attitudes, and policy with regard to crime and justice.

Regarding the public agenda, the research indicates that the media have a haphazard effect. When effects occur, they appear highly sensitive to local factors, and no consistent, generalizable effects have been observed. The concept of "agenda setting," in which the order of issues on the public agenda is studied, has given way to "agenda building," a wider conceptual view of the public agenda that explicitly incorporates policy makers and social and political environmental conditions into a media effects model.

The effects of the media on beliefs and attitudes about crime and justice have received the most study. Most studies have built on or reacted to two concepts formulated by Gerbner—those of a "mean-world view" and "mainstreaming." Overall, researchers have found that the effects differ depending on the subjects, the medium, and the content communicated. The effects of newspapers and television, in particular, have been found to differ. Newspapers tend to affect beliefs about crime, whereas television more affects attitudes such as fear of crime. Within our general review of media effects on beliefs and attitudes, the chapter gives special attention to the area of pornography and attitudes about sexual crimes.

The final set of research involves the shaping by the media of public policies related to crime and justice. A number of studies have reported consistent positive correlations between media consumption and support for punitive criminal justice policies among the general public. In addition, a fair amount of anecdotal evidence exists describing media effects on policy decisions within the criminal justice system. Spurred by these reports and building on the earlier research on agenda setting, researchers are currently studying the media's effects on policy from an ecological approach, a method that combines case studies with data analysis. Presently, this research is still in an exploratory stage, but some have reported that causal relationships exist in some cases. No one has yet been able to specify the structure of the causal relationship, however—that is, to offer a general process by which the media influence policy.

The chapter ends with a discussion of the implications of the research. As a group, the findings indicate that the media do, to various degrees, influence the agendas, perceptions, and policies of their consumers with regard to crime and justice, but not directly or simply. Perceptions of crime and justice appear to be intertwined with other social perceptions and are not determined solely by a person's perception of the crime problem. In the end, the media can alter reality by affecting the way people perceive, interpret, and behave toward the world.

THE MEDIA AND OUR VIEW OF REALITY

People today live in two worlds: a real world and a med limited by direct experience; the second is bounded o of editors and producers (Zucker, 1978, p. 239). Link..... media world with beliefs, attitude formation, and policy effects in the real world has long been a tradition in mass communications research (see Stroman & Seltzer, 1985, p. 34). In accordance with this tradition, this chapter focuses on the news and entertainment's influence on attitudes toward crime and justice and on crime and justice policies.

To what extent the media actually influence people's attitudes, and how significantly, has been the subject of some argument. The origins of attitudes and opinions are diverse and idiosyncratic, ranging from internal psychological factors to sociological, environmental, and historical influences. It is no surprise that attempts to tie one possible source, in this case the media, to attitudes have reported mixed results. The findings regarding attitudes about crime and justice are likewise mixed.

Those asserting that the media significantly affect people's attitudes about crime commonly argue that the vast majority of our exposure to crime and violence comes from the media (Dominick, 1978, p. 106; Greenberg, 1969). Public surveys have reported that as many as 95 percent of the general population cite the mass media as their primary source of information about crime (Graber, 1979), and as discussed in Chapters 2 and 3, crime is an extensively covered, prominent topic in the media. And because most people have little direct experience with crime, it follows that the media should be a significant force in the public's formation of attitudes and perceptions about crime and justice (cf. Barber, 1987; Lewis, 1984; Stroman & Seltzer, 1985, p. 340). This reasoning gives rise to both a common belief in the importance of the media and a long-standing concern regarding the media's potential ability to influence and manipulate public opinion with regard to crime and justice.

Despite concerns and many studies, however, the question of the extent to which the news and entertainment media actually affect attitudes, beliefs, and policies with regard to crime and justice has not been fully resolved. But the available research does allow one to draw some basic conclusions and suggests some working suppositions regarding news and entertainment's role in the formation of attitudes and policies related to crime and justice.

Before considering the research on news and entertainment's effects, however, a useful first step is to examine the research on the purposeful use of the media to influence the attitudes of the general public through public information or communication campaigns. In general, these planned media information campaigns have been aimed at generating specific effects in a large number of individuals, through an organized set of media activities (O'Keefe & Reid, 1990, citing Rogers & Storey, 1987, p. 539). The research findings regarding such efforts suggests much about the possible effects of unplanned, unorganized general depictions of crime and justice.

⌐ INFORMATION AND COMMUNICATION CAMPAIGNS

Public communication campaigns have a long history in the United States. Early campaigns employed a series of papers and pamphlets focused on specific political issues. Through the nineteenth century, such campaigns were normally conducted by private interest groups or political parties. But by the end of the 1900s, as people became more and more accessible through mass circulation media, these campaigns had expanded beyond lo-

---

BOX 4-1 The Media as a Source of Information about the Courts

In 1983, an agency conducting a national survey for Hearst Newspapers concluded that the media are a much more important source of information about the judicial system than are lawyers, personal experience, schools, or libraries. In fact, TV dramas alone rank ahead of all nonmedia sources, and media sources occupy the top five positions.*

The Importance of The Media

Americans tend to obtain information about courts through the media rather than through personal contacts. Americans are twice as likely to get information about courts from television drama (19%) as they are from people they know who had been jurors (9%) or had other court experiences (10%).

Where Do You Get Information about the Courts? (*n* = 983)

Rank	Source	Frequently	Sometimes	Rarely/Never	Don't know/ No answer
		%	%	%	%
1	Television news	54	31	14	1
2	Newspapers	51	28	20	1
3	Radio news	28	37	34	1
4	Television drama	19	31	48	2
5	Magazines	18	32	49	1
6	People you know who are legal professionals	18	29	50	3
7	Having been a juror	6	12	80	2
8	Other personal court experiences	6	18	73	3
9	People you know who have been jurors	9	29	59	3
10	People you know who have had other court experiences	10	33	55	2
11	From your school or library	16	25	56	3

Source: From The American Public, the Media, and the Judicial System: A National Survey on Public Awareness and Personal Experience, *by F. Bennack. Copyright © 1983 by The Hearst Corporation. Reprinted by permission.*

(continued)

cal and regional efforts to encompass larger and larger populations.[1] After the turn of the century, the federal government became directly involved in campaigns involving various social reforms and legislation. Thus, as mass media technology improved and expanded during the 1920s and 1930s to include film and radio, furthering the media's reach, the idea of using the media as an agent of social change was already well established. Serious research into the effectiveness and impact of these campaigns did not begin until the 1930s, however. Until then, people simply assumed that the media's effects on attitudes and opinions were direct, universal, and immediate.

The initial research conducted in the 1930s and into the 1940s appeared to substantiate the perception that the media constituted an extremely powerful system for influencing the public. The mass media were conceived of as hypodermic needle–like mechanisms that could be used to inject infor-

---

BOX 4-1 (continued)

Yankelovich and his associates (1978) found that even direct experience with courts (whether as juror, witness, defendant, and so on) only partially diminished the impact of the media as a primary source of information. In their study, 27 percent of the respondents who had court experience still listed the media as their primary source of judicial information, greater than the percentage citing education (25 percent), and equal to the percentage citing court experience.

Principal Sources of Information about State/Local Courts for Those with Court Experience

	Any state court experience	
Sources from which learned most:	%	
School/Media		
School, formal education	25	
Newspapers, magazines, books	14	
TV news programs	9	27
TV entertainment programs	4	
Court		
In court as juror	11	
In court as party in civil case	8	
Court spectator, tour of court	3	27
In court as witness	3	
In court as party in criminal case	2	

Source: From "The Public Image of Courts: Highlights of a National Survey of the General Public, Judges, Lawyers, and Community Leaders," by Yankelovich, Skelly, and White, Inc. In T. J. Fetter (ed.), State Courts: A Blueprint for the Future. *Copyright © 1978 by the National Center for State Courts. Reprinted by permission.*

---

*See also Barber, 1987; Bennack, 1983; Graber, 1980; Yankelovich et al., 1978.

Prior to the 1950s, most studies of the impact of the mass media were tied to commercial advertising needs. The federal government did not direct much attention to media impact until the 1950s, even though the 1934 Communications Act created a federal regulatory role. The first major set of studies were the Payne Fund studies (1928–1933), which coincided with the increased use of public surveys and market research. These studies investigated the effect of movies on society. The concerns about movies then were similar to the concerns about television in the 1960s. In the Payne Fund study on the effect of film on children, *Movies, Delinquency and Crime* (1933), H. Blumer and P. Hauser concluded that movies played a direct role in criminal careers. Overall, the studies reinforced the belief that the media had great social power. In the 1950s, congressional committees (the Harris subcommittee, 1952; the Hendrickson–Kefauver subcommittee, 1954–1955, and the Dodd subcommittee, 1961–1964) established a pattern of Congress conducting periodic reviews, debates, and research concerning the effects of the mass media, followed by insignificant changes in policy and programming (see Willard & Rowlanel, 1983).

mation and attitudes into the public. Spurred by this perception, government propaganda efforts as well as academic and public concern about the mass media increased during this period (Atkin, 1979, p. 655; Lazarsfeld et al., 1948; Merton, 1946). In the 1950s and 1960s, however, a perceptual reversal occurred when new, more sophisticated research showed that the effects of public information campaigns were largely unpredictable and uncontrollable. A number of evaluations of these campaigns reported that they had no significant effects.[2] Apparently, the mass media could only reinforce attitudes already existing in an audience. The researchers blamed the media's lack of influence on inherent and apparently irreversible characteristics of the public. Rather than as "passive," the research view during the 1930s and 1940s, the public was now described as "obstinate" (Atkin, 1979, p. 656; Salcedo et al., 1974, p. 91). The resultant pessimism regarding the usefulness and effectiveness of media campaigns caused their general dismissal as a possible social tool. The prevalent view was "When the media hypodermic needle failed, the public was to blame" (Mendelsohn, 1973, p. 50). A seminal work published in 1947 declared that even if all the physical barriers to communication were removed, five basic barriers would still block effective use of the media to change public attitudes. To begin with, 10 to 20 percent of the audience are "chronic know-nothings"—irredeemably apathetic people who are unreachable by any media techniques. In addition, only motivated people will acquire significant amounts of information about a subject; people seek information compatible with their current attitudes, tastes, and biases; people interpret the same information differently; and new information does not necessarily change existing attitudes (Hyman & Sheatsley, 1947, p. 413). These negative views remained largely unchallenged into the 1970s (see Douglas et al., 1970, pp. 480–481).

It was a study of the presidential campaign of 1940 that dealt the death blow to theories about direct media power. That study, published in the 1950s in *The People's Choice,* showed that the media did activate some voters to follow their predispositions and reinforced the positions of other voters, but the media's ability to convert voters from one position to another was minimal. The "Decatur" studies, which traced informal opinion patterns in relation to marketing, fashion, public affairs, and movie attendance, further weakened the idea of direct media influence and showed social ties between people, and the social structure, to be more important than the quantity of media messages in determining the media's actual impact (see Katz & Lazarsfeld, 1955). Lastly, the Revere Project study, which studied message diffusion through leaflet distribution in the early 1950s, also showed that inaccurate transmission quickly blurred the message and that the proportion of a total population receiving a media message follows a law of diminishing returns. Therefore, increased spending and efforts are less and less effective, and a saturation level is quickly reached. All told, these studies suggested that the media were a rather weak, ineffective means of reaching and influencing the public.

In the 1970s, however, some people began to recognize in the media a limited potential for influence in specific, controlled circumstances.[3] This renewed perception of the media as influential can be partially credited to societal changes that had occurred since the 1940s. First, television had developed into a pervasive, dominant, and encompassing medium unavailable in earlier periods. Additionally, and perceived by some to be associated with the rise of television, (see McLuhan, 1962, 1964; Meyrowitz, 1985a), traditional social ties and values had weakened and people were more geographically and socially mobile. All of these factors combined to encourage more reliance on the media rather than on other people for social information, thereby increasing the media's potential ability to influence beliefs and attitudes. Lastly, the social sciences now had more sensitive statistical and computerized research techniques available, enabling researchers to search for and discern previously hidden, more complex relationships between the media and consumers' attitudes. Influenced by these developments, academics adopted the current view that mass media communication campaigns, if properly designed and employed, can be effective under certain conditions (Atkin, 1979, p. 655), and a new set of guiding principles regarding the media's influence on public attitudes emerged (O'Keefe, 1971, p. 243):

1. The mass media may help form attitudes toward new subjects where little prior opinion exists.
2. The mass media may influence attitudes that are weakly held.
3. The mass media may strengthen one attitude at the expense of a series of others when the strength of the several attitudes is evenly balanced.
4. The mass media can change even strongly held attitudes when they are able to report new facts.

5. The mass media may suggest new courses of action that appear to better satisfy wants and needs.
6. The mass media's strongest and most universally recognized effect remains the reinforcement or strengthening of predispositions.

Besides noting the media's potential usefulness and effects, these principles also highlight the difficulty of using the mass media effectively and the limited scope within which they can be used. Within planned applications, the mass media tend to be more effective at building citizen awareness of an issue, but for complex attitudinal or behavioral changes, they must be coupled with more-direct forms of citizen contact and intervention (O'Keefe & Reid, 1990, p. 215).

Associated with this current moderate perception of the media's influence is a revised theoretical model under which influence and information flow through multiple pathways between the media, interpersonal communication networks, and the individual members of the public developed (Page et al., 1987). Only in the case of socially isolated people do the media appear to have a primary influence on attitudes (see Katz & Lazarsfeld, 1955; J. Robinson, 1976). Paradoxically, because of the multiple paths and complex social networks lying between the public and the media, it is also generally accepted that the media's influence can reach even those that do not watch, read, or listen (Zucker, 1978, p. 226). Accordingly, mass media public communication campaigns are now recognized as a possible source of strong influence in specific situations, but only through careful design and implementation can their effects be directed and predicted.

Implications for Attitudes toward Crime and Justice

When discussing the impact of the news and entertainment mass media on attitudes concerning crime and justice, remember that, as a whole, media campaigns expressly designed to influence attitudes and perceptions have had rather limited success and, when successful, have been largely limited to health-related topics (Tyler, 1984).[4] These facts raise some doubt about the ability of the mass media to affect attitudes through the "unorganized, unplanned" content of news and entertainment.[5] If deliberately influencing attitudes is difficult, should the general crime and justice content of the mass media be a concern?

If the crime and justice content of news and entertainment were mixed, accurate, or ignored, the answer would be no. The research reviewed in Chapters 2 and 3, however, establishes that this is not the case. Unfortunately, the fact that planned media effects appear hard to elicit or control does not mean that unplanned media effects are necessarily absent or innocuous. But the research does imply that if unplanned effects are occurring, they will most likely be interacting with other factors, difficult to discern, and, most important, difficult to counteract once established. The repetitiveness and pervasiveness of the media's general crime and justice content increase the possibility that the media may have significant unplanned effects on attitudes, particularly in the area of crime and justice and especially for persons with limited alternative sources of information. And because of the media's emphasis on law enforcement and crime control, we can expect that any media effects would tend to promote crime control more than due process policies.

What evaluations of public communication campaigns establish is the existence of significant but ephemeral media effects. To the extent that the content of entertainment and news can be perceived as a continuous, long-running, but poorly designed public communication campaign about crime and justice, it is reasonable to hypothesize that unplanned and uncontrolled effects are occurring. The search for these effects has been in three areas: the rank of crime on the public agenda, the shaping of public beliefs and attitudes about crime and justice, and the shaping of public policies related to crime and justice.

CRIME AND JUSTICE ON THE PUBLIC AGENDA

Still unresolved are concerns regarding the ability of the media, particularly the news media, to affect the public agenda. The concept of agenda setting derives from the work of political scientists who explored how and why certain issues emerge from the pool of social issues vying for public attention (Doppelt & Manikas, 1990; see also McConnell, 1967; Schattschneider, 1960). Researchers found that in agenda research the media, by emphasizing or ignoring topics, may influence the list of issues that are important to the public—what the public thinks about, rather than what the public thinks (cf. Cohen, 1963). In the agenda-setting research, it was hypothesized that people tend to judge a social concern to be significant to the extent that it is emphasized in the media. In time, some argue, the media agenda becomes the public agenda (see McLeod et al., 1974). Few researchers have examined how the mass media's influence on the public agenda may affect subsequent policy making. Instead, most have concentrated on the media's effects on the public's ranking of issues in the belief that issues that receive governmental attention are chosen from among those issues (Doppelt & Manikas, 1990, p. 132). In accordance with this focus, Doppelt and Manikas (1990, p. 134; see also Erbing et al., 1980; Rogers & Dearing, 1988) have identified as a key assumption in the initial research on agenda setting that the media influence public policy through a linear process: A story appears, the issue increases in importance to the public, the public becomes alarmed, interest groups are mobilized, and policy makers respond. Evidence of a linear process has not emerged from the research, however. Linearity simply fails to capture the range of actions that media attention can set in motion (Molotch et al., 1987; see also Salwin, 1986).

From a practical standpoint, the presumption of linearity resulted in research that is still inconclusive regarding the media's ability to set—that is, to affect the content or order of—the public agenda. Some authors have reported that the media do not significantly affect the public agenda (see

Cumberbatch & Beardsworth, 1976; Sacco, 1982; Stroman & Seltzer, 1985). Other studies have reported only minimal media effects.[6] The most recent, however, have concluded, that the media do affect the public agenda but not directly or linearly.[7] At best the media's influence appears to be secondary to other factors such as age, sex, or income (see Shaw & McCombs, 1977) and mediated through multiple steps and social networks (Page et al., 1987, citing Katz & Lazarsfeld, 1955). Protess and his colleagues (1985, p. 30), for example, reported that the strongest agenda-setting effect they found in a Chicago area study was a cycle of effects from the media to the public and back, in their study of an area newspaper. Agenda-setting effects have also been noted in several other studies, but only for television.[8] Furthermore, secondary but important unresolved questions also remain about the strength, form, and extent of the relationship. It may be, for example, that individuals whose agendas already match the media's tend to seek out the media for confirmation of the correctness of their priorities, whereas those who disagree with the media tend to avoid them. If so, the greater match between the media and those who attend to the media more would be due not to the media's reordering of the public's agenda but to a selective exposure or retention on the part of the public.

Specifically regarding crime and justice, the media emphasis on crime has frequently been credited with raising the public's fear of being victimized to disproportionate levels and hence giving crime an inappropriately high ranking on the public agenda (Gordon & Heath, 1981, pp. 228–229). Whether crime's high ranking is appropriate or inappropriate is ultimately a subjective determination, but it does encourage the development of media-directed "moral crusades" against specific crime issues, heighten public anxiety about crime, and push or block other serious social problems such as hunger from the public agenda (Cohen & Young, 1981). The relationship between the media's agenda and the public agenda is rather gross, however, and far more needs to be known about the conditions that maximize and minimize their correspondence (Murray, 1980, pp. 48–49; see also Fishman, 1978; Hall et al., 1981).

In essence, the research indicates that media effects are variable; are more common for television than for newspapers; appear to increase with exposure (those who watch more match the media more closely); are more significant the less direct experience people have with an issue; are more significant for newer issues but diminish quickly; and are nonlinear, sometimes reciprocal, and highly interactive with other social and individual processes (see McCombs & Weaver, 1973; Rogers & Dearing, 1988; Weaver, 1980). The original conceptual framework of agenda setting allowed researchers to determine when specific issues depicted by the media became more salient to the public. A major deficiency, however, is that such research documents the media's effect on policy making only if one assumes that increases in an issue's salience among the public necessarily trigger policy actions, a conclusion that has been seriously challenged.[9]

In an effort to better comprehend the relationship between the media and social agendas, researchers have expanded their focus from the effects of agenda setting by the media to what they term *agenda building*. In that policy makers may act without public attention or may ignore public concerns, in agenda building researchers examine the media's relationship to policy makers' agendas. For example, research into the effects of investigative reporting has revealed that the most consistent factor in determining the impact of the media on policy is the relationship that forms between the media and local policy makers (see Cook et al., 1983b; Leff et al., 1986; Protess et al., 1987). In terms of actual policy effects, the largely passive public and its agenda can apparently be circumvented (Lang & Lang, 1983). Indeed, the interactive and often reciprocal influences between the media and policy makers help to determine the likely composition of the public agenda, hence the term *agenda building* (Doppelt & Manikas, 1990; Graber, 1989; Lang & Lang, 1983). As the situation now stands, a media effect on the public's agenda is generally acknowledged, but unless the effect also appears among policy makers, it is usually regarded as socially insignificant.

Despite its limitations and current status, the agenda-setting approach has been instrumental in changing the view held until the 1970s that the media had minimal effects (Doppelt & Manikas, 1990, p. 133, citing Noelle-Neumann, 1983; Roberts & Bachen, 1981). The approach invigorated the search for special cases in which the media had a significant effect and refocused attention on policy formation. And although most of the literature concerning agenda setting analyzes media effects in the political arenas, the findings are thought to be equally applicable to the criminal justice system (Doppelt & Manikas, 1990, p. 134, citing Graber, 1989; Gordon & Riger, 1989; Pritchard, 1986). Regarding the media–agenda relationship and crime's place on the agenda, the best hypothesis at this time is that the media, policy makers, and the public have a yet unspecified mutually reinforcing causal impact on one another. In some cases, the media do seem to heighten crime's significance as a social problem, and some individuals do appear to obtain their personal social agendas largely from what the media tell them to be concerned about. Not surprisingly, those who are exposed the most to the mass media are more likely to show this association. Because crime is so prevalent in the media, those exposed the most are also more likely to rank it higher on their agendas. However, effects on the rank of crime on the public agenda may not be as important as once believed. More important are effects on policy makers and on public attitudes and beliefs about crime and justice.

THE SHAPING OF PUBLIC ATTITUDES AND BELIEFS ABOUT CRIME AND JUSTICE

In examining the evidence of a relationship between exposure to the mass media and a person's beliefs and attitudes about crime—respectively, the statements about crime a person accepts as true, and the feelings about crime a person believes to be justified—a beginning point is the work of George Gerbner and his associates (see Gerbner & Gross, 1976, 1980;

Gerbner et al., 1978, 1979, 1980). Gerbner investigated the association between watching large amounts of television and the audience's general perceptions about the world, with the idea that the medium creates a social reality for its audience. This process, initially described as "worldview cultivation," was felt to be directly related to the number of hours of television viewed (Carlson, 1985, p. 7). The researchers hypothesized that through exposure to television's content most everyone comes to have a similar view of the world—a mainstream, media view. They tested this thesis by having viewers choose answers to a series of questions about world conditions. One set of answers reflected the media portrayal of reality and the other a real-world measure. One question, for example, asked, "What proportion of people are employed in law enforcement, 5% or 1%?" Gerbner and his associates found that heavy television viewers were significantly more likely to choose the television answers and also to view the world as "mean," an outlook characterized by suspicion, fear, alienation, distrust, cynicism, and a belief that the world is a violent, crime-ridden, dangerous place. They suggested that heavy television viewers fail to differentiate between the television world and the real world. The television world either supplants and distorts the viewer's conception of the real world or confirms and then magnifies the viewer's real-world experience. Thus, the violent world of television can both instill and intensify the fear that the real world is a mean and dangerous place (Murray, 1980, p. 50). Over time the repetitive themes and content of the mass media homogenize the viewpoints and perspectives of the public. People come to think like the media and, consequently, to think alike. Gerbner concluded that even the most sophisticated viewers may receive many facets of their personal knowledge of the real world from purely fictional media representations of that world (Gerbner & Gross, 1976, p. 179).

Prodded by critiques of his initial research (see, for example, Hirsch, 1980, 1981), Gerbner subsequently amended his hypothesis of worldview cultivation according to which all media viewers are affected, to one of "mainstreaming," which posits that the media affect some viewers more than others regardless of exposure level. Gerbner now argues that the media are homogenizing society, influencing those heavy television consumers who are currently not in the mainstream to move toward it, while not affecting those already in the mainstream.[10] By sending pervasive, uniform messages concerning the structure and operation of society, television streamlines and standardizes the perceptions of its more dedicated viewers (Gerbner & Gross, 1976, p. 176). Ultimately, the media, led by television, are felt to influence even isolated, light media consumers to more closely reflect the views of middle America (Gerbner & Gross, 1980, p. 156). Other research has revealed, however, that the extent of this influence on beliefs is not absolute and may be reduced substantially when social background and individual characteristics are simultaneously controlled. Some now argue that television's effects on worldviews are severely limited.[11] Carlson, for example, has reported that mainstreaming effects are haphazard and in certain groups appear to operate contrary to predictions, whereas other groups appear to be especially susceptible (Carlson, 1985, pp. 135, 191).[12]

Irrespective of the criticisms and narrowed applications, subsequent research has mostly substantiated the association between the media and mean-world attitudes at least for specific audience subsets.[13] At the least, heavy consumers of television do share certain beliefs about high societal crime and victimization levels. For Gerbner and his associates, a mean-world view translates into attitudes regarding who can employ violence against whom, who are appropriate victims of crime, and who are likely criminals. It posits a world in which it is appropriate for some to have power and some to not.

Although the bulk of the research has been on television, some additional research tying newspapers to crime and justice beliefs and attitudes also has been conducted.[14] One European study went so far as to offer a theoretical "newspaper→crime attitude" model of the relationship between newspapers and attitudes toward crime (see Figure 4-1).

Despite the apparent substance of such models and the total amount of research available, the exact nature of the relationship between the media and attitudes and beliefs about crime is far from resolved, and conflicting research abounds.

In an extensive study, for example, Doob and MacDonald (1979) examined television viewing and fear of crime while controlling for crime rates in four communities. They discovered that the association between television viewing and mean-world attitudes tends to diminish when actual neighborhood crime levels are taken into account. In essence, if one's world truly is mean, television has less effect on one's view of the world. This finding is consistent with the general proposition that media effects are most powerful for issues that are outside of a subject's personal experiences. Thus, the media would be expected to have less impact on beliefs about crime among those who have had direct neighborhood experience with crime (cf. Lich-

---

M. Robinson (1976), for example, using both experimental and survey results, reported that reliance on television news was associated with antiestablishment attitudes that included social distrust, political cynicism, and powerlessness. He termed this set of attitudes "videomalaise." The dramatic power of television to influence audience beliefs through a single specially designed thirty-minute program was reported by Ball-Rokeach and his associates (1984) in *The Great American Values Test: Influencing Behavior and Belief through Television.* During the program, which was broadcast to three test cities, and not to one control city, information about eighteen values was presented with special emphasis on four: freedom, equality, beauty, and a comfortable life. People who watched the complete program raised their rankings significantly on two of the three values and were more likely to respond to appeals from voluntary associations. The authors concluded that "a single 30-minute exposure to a TV program designed to conform to certain theoretical considerations can significantly affect the beliefs and behaviors of large numbers of people for at least several weeks or months" (p. xiv).

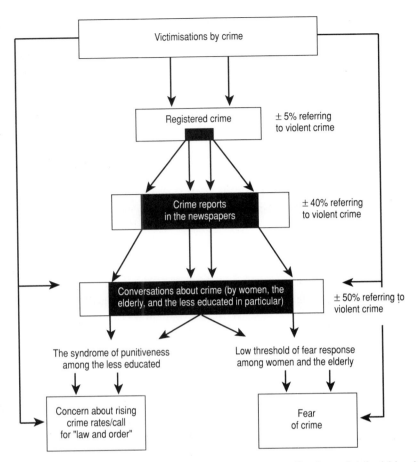

FIGURE 4-1 A graphic representation of a theoretical model that tries to explain the emergence of public attitudes toward crime. The different volumes of the blocks should not be interpreted to represent the exact ratio of the phenomena. Feedback loops have not been taken into account.

Source: From "The Extent of Public Information and the Nature of Public Attitudes Toward Crime," by J. van Dijk, p. 36. In A. Coenen and J. van Dijk (eds.), Public Opinion on Crime and Criminal Justice. Vol. XVII Collected Studies in Criminological Research. Copyright © 1978 by Council of Europe. Reprinted by permission.

ter, 1988, p. 38). Doob and MacDonald did not conclude that television has no effect on beliefs about crime and justice in high-crime neighborhoods, however. They reported consistent positive correlations between heavy television viewing and factual misperceptions about criminality and violence, and between television viewing and support for certain crime-related policies, such as higher spending on police or support for carrying a weapon. In addition to the Doob and MacDonald study, Sacco (1982) and Skogan and Maxfield (1981) have reported research that leads to similar conclusions.

Further support for the importance of consumers' perceptions of their immediate environmental conditions in determining the media's effects, in this case for the print media, is provided in a two-experiment study by Heath (1984) in which she reported that newspaper crime news affects readers' fear of crime differently depending on how the crime news is reported. Specifically, if a high proportion of crime news focuses on local crime and portrays it as predominantly sensationalistic or random, those papers' readers report fearing crime more. If, however, local crimes make up little of a paper's crime news, readers report less fear, regardless of how much crimes are portrayed. Heath concluded that the impact of crime news depends on whether the crime being read about is local or distant. Neither the total amount of crime news reported nor the style of coverage primarily determines its effect. Interestingly, the same factors that increase readers' fear when a crime is close at hand paradoxically reassure when the crime is distant (Heath, 1984, p. 274). Heath explained this unique finding by suggesting that people have an intrinsic need to control their environment and will engage in a process of "downward comparison" when assessing their immediate crime threat. News of distant, sensationalistic, random crime allows people to reduce their anxiety about local crime by allowing them to compare themselves with others who are worse off (Heath, 1984, pp. 264–265). Random crime is frightening when close because it suggests loss of control, but reassuring when distant because it suggests that conditions in other places are worse and one has less to fear in one's own immediate, apparently less dangerous environment. Liske and Baccaglini (1990), in a follow-up study that supports Heath's findings, suggested that readers' fear of crime is influenced by the type of murder coverage found in the first section of a newspaper. They reported that local coverage of murder is most related to fear of crime, while follow-up, nonlocal coverage of murder is related to decreased fear.

In addition to these studies, other significant, but mixed findings regarding the relationship of the electronic and print media to attitudes about crime have also been reported in a number of studies.[15] Overall, this research suggests that newspaper exposure tends to be associated with beliefs about the distribution and frequency of crime, whereas television exposure is associated with attitudes, such as fear of crime and victimization. However, some of the findings reported in these studies directly contradict findings reported in other research.

Pornography and Crime-Related Attitudes

As the foregoing indicates, the research picture concerning the media and beliefs and attitudes about crime and justice is indeed muddled. One area in which some consistent and clearer results are emerging, however, is that of the relationship between pornography and consumers' attitudes. Much research has been conducted in this area. On the basis of a series of experiments, depictions of sexual violence rather than of explicit sex per se appear to affect attitudes the most (Imrich et al., 1990; see also Linz, 1989). Specifically, studies that have compared subjects exposed to sexually aggressive material with subjects exposed to nonaggressive but sexually explicit material clearly indicate that nonviolent sexual material results in fewer antisocial attitudes and beliefs than sexually violent media (Imrich et al., 1990). Most consistently affected have been perceptions, judgments, and attitudes about rape and women who have been raped. Perceptions, judgments, and attitudes about males in general, and violent male sexual offenders in particular, have been unaffected, or the research results have been contradictory (Imrich et al., 1990). For example, Malamuth, Haber and Feshbach (1980) found that males who read a sexually violent passage were more punitive toward a rapist, whereas Weaver (1987) reported that 120 males and females exposed to depictions of male-coerced sex were less punitive toward a fictional rapist.[16]

Overall, the data do not show that exposure to nonviolent pornography significantly affects attitudes toward rape as a crime or more general assessments of female rape victims. In a review, Imrich and her associates (1990) concluded that

> Most consistently in both long [exposure greater than one hour] and short [exposure of less than one hour] term studies, negative effects such as lessened sensitivity toward rape victims and greater acceptance of force in sexual encounters emerge when media portrayals of violence against women or when sex is fused with aggression are used. This is especially true for "slasher" films. Every study that has included a "slasher" condition has found anti-social attitudinal effects. Anti-social effects arise either from exposure to violent pornography *or* from materials that are sexually violent but not sexually explicit. (p. 115)

Depictions of sexual violence foster antisocial attitudes about women and rape, such as the myth that women unconsciously want to be raped or somehow enjoy being raped. News portrayals of rape appear to contribute to distorted perceptions as well. In their study on rape, Gordon and Riger (1989) documented that rape is dramatically underreported in contrast to murder, which is overrepresented in the media, and that rape coverage is skewed in favor of sensationalized rapes by strangers.

Virtually none of the research, however, reveals direct main effects for pornography,[17] and even violent pornography does not negatively affect all male viewers. The research instead indicates an interplay between violent, sexual material and individual dispositions (Imrich et al., 1990). Many cultural and individual factors appear to mediate the effects of sexually violent material on attitudes. Malamuth and Briere (1986) described one indirect-effects model:

> Individual conditions and the broader social climate are postulated as the originating environmental influences on the individual. The mass media are considered one of many social forces that may, in interaction with a variety of many other cultural and individual factors, affect the development of intermediate attributes, such as thought patterns, sexual arousal patterns, motivations, and personality characteristics. These intermediate variables, in complex interactions

with each other and with situational circumstances, such as alcohol consumption or acute arousal, may precipitate [effects] ranging from passive [attitudinal] support to actual aggressive [behavior]. (p. 89)

A population identified as hypermasculine, or "macho" (termed "angry males" in earlier literature; see Gray, 1982), appears particularly likely to be influenced, especially by violent pornography. What is not clear is what effect the removal of pornography would have in society. There is no evidence that the number of sexual offenders would be reduced (Imrich et al., 1990), for the mechanism linking the media and sexual crime is thought to operate through the process illustrated in Figure 4-2. The key unresolved issue is the placement of the "hypermasculine" at-risk males. If they exist prior to exposure to sexually violent media content (in position 1) rather than following it (in position 2), then exposure to sexually violent media content is not as causally significant in the development of antisocial attitudes. In position 1, already-hypermasculine males would simply be seeking out sexually violent content, which would be reinforcing rather than creating their antisocial attitudes. In addition, it is not clear whether or not the third variable, "sexually coercive behavior," actually develops or can be predicted to develop as a result of any antisocial attitudes caused by exposure to sexually violent content. The sole link in the process that has been empirically established is that between sexually violent content and antisocial attitudes. This is no small result and lends strong credence to the argument that the media is influencing wider attitudes in regard to crime and justice.[18] But as with other aspects of crime and justice attitudes, neither a causal link to sexually coercive behavior nor the causal order of the variables have been established with regard to sexually violent content and antisocial attitudes.[19]

Summary

What does this research say about the media and people's beliefs and attitudes about crime? The evidence clearly remains mixed concerning news and entertainment's impact on people's perceptions of crime. The media has been found to be related to particular beliefs about crime but not straightforwardly or universally so. When effects do occur, the most com-

FIGURE 4-2   Hypermasculine males and sexually violent media content

*Increased support of aggression against women, increased belief in the rape myth (i.e., that women secretly want to be raped), higher likelihood of blaming rape victims, increased belief in general female promiscuity.

**Includes an increase in self-reports of the likelihood that a subject would commit rape.

mon are increased belief in the prevalence and spread of crime, victimization, and violence, and cynical, distrustful social attitudes. If nothing else, the research does indicate a strong, if not understood, interplay between media coverage of crime and public perceptions of it (O'Keefe & Reid, 1990, p. 220). Smith (1984; see also Warr, 1980) has concluded that the media's portrayal of crime creates and defines a broad public awareness of crime, but that many other factors, such as social and physical environmental conditions, have more to do with the final shaping of public beliefs. The media provide both a foundation for the public's various final images and the mortar with which the public construct its social reality. For example, Hughes (1987) and Roberts and Doob (1990) have concluded that the manner in which newspapers report criminal sentencing misleads the public into believing that sentences are more lenient than they are and encourages people to support harsher sentences. Hughes argues that the public combines this information with other perceptions to construct generally negative attitudes toward penal and judicial reforms. In such a process, it is not surprising that credibility has been found to be a primary factor in the generation of effects (see Hawkins & Pingree, 1981; O'Keefe, 1984; Slater & Elliott, 1982). It is especially true for television that the more real or credible a media source is perceived to be, the more it will influence perceptions (see Box 4-2).

A few definitive conclusions emerge. For one, an important distinction exists between the respective effects of print and visual electronic media. Television has been more related to fear of crime; print, to people's knowledge about crime and adoption of crime preventive actions (O'Keefe & Reid, 1990, p. 220). This difference may stem from the way in which crime is journalistically portrayed in each medium. Television, being more visceral and emotional in its content, would naturally tend to affect emotional attitudes such as fear and concern; print, being factual and analytical, naturally would tend to affect beliefs. Secondly, some individuals appear more susceptible to media effects than others—predisposed "hypermasculine" males to sexually violent content, socially isolated individuals to belief effects, and nonmainstream individuals who feel that news and entertainment is credible to attitudinal effects. The relationship between the media and beliefs and attitudes about crime ultimately depends on three factors: the medium being discussed; the medium's style of presentation and crime and justice content; and the experiences, predispositions, and immediate community of the consumer. Still remaining is the question of whether or not effects on beliefs and attitudes translate into support for specific crime and justice policies.

THE SHAPING OF PUBLIC POLICIES WITH REGARD TO CRIME AND JUSTICE

Do the media influence the formation of public policies with regard to crime and justice and the support specific policies receive? Effects in this area are considered the most important of the three types of effects (agenda setting, attitudes and beliefs, and policies) examined in this chapter, for effects here translate into the expenditure and allocation of social resources and define how society will react to crime. A way to begin answering the question is to look at the relationship between the media and general public policy. Recent research does suggest that the news media, at least, significantly affect policy preferences for general social issues. For example, Page and his colleagues (1987) examined the content of television news broadcasts in regard to a number of public policy issues and noted whether commentator comments and news coverage content were in favor or opposed to specific policies. They then noted whether public opinion consequently shifted in the same direction as the news coverage. In this way, they were able to explain on the basis of newscast factors nearly half of the variation in public opinion concerning the public policies under study. Their evidence suggests that both short- and medium-term changes in public support for particular policies are tied to television news content. A journalist's comment in favor of a policy, for example, was associated with an average opin-

---

BOX 4-2 The Methodology of Studying Media and Public Attitudes and Beliefs about Crime and Justice

As shown in the following table from Sheley and Ashkins (1981, p. 500), researchers typically measure news content, media preferences, or media consumption levels and then determine whether or not the public's beliefs have changed as a result (Stinchcombe et al., 1980). Using a similar strategy, others have contrasted the news media's depiction of particular crimes, criminals, and law enforcement with the facts contained in official statistical reports (Gordon & Riger, 1989; Reiner, 1985). Where the public's beliefs have more closely approximated the media coverage than the statistics, researchers have concluded that those beliefs have derived from the less accurate media portrayal (Doppelt & Manikas, 1990; see also Hughes, 1987).

Rankings of Relative Frequency of Index Offenses by Police, Media, and Public

Offense	Police	Times-Picayune	TV stations*	Public
Homicide	7	4	1	4
Robbery	3	1	2	1
Rape	6	6	5	3
Assault	5	3	3	5
Burglary	2	2	6	2
Larceny	1	5	4	7
Vehicle theft	4	7	7	6

Source: From "Crime, Crime News, and Crime Views," by J. Sheley and C. Ashkins, Public Opinion Quarterly, 1981, 45, 492–506. Copyright © 1981 by The University of Chicago Press. Reprinted by permission.
NOTE: $W = .397$; p = n.s. W signifies the Kendall Coefficient of Concordance for use in measuring the relations among several sets of rankings.

*All three television stations were so similar in rankings that they are reported here as one.

ion shift of more than 4 percent in the same direction. Although their study does not prove a causal linkage, and the public opinion shifts could simply reflect the impact of a preexisting consensus among opinion leaders that television news reflects first and the public later comes to agree with, Page and his colleagues interpret the association as part of a causal chain that results in real-world changes in public support for policies that are reported favorably in the media (Page et al., 1987, p. 31). Other research by Hallin (1984), McClosky and Zaller (1984), and Noelle-Neumann (1974, 1980) suggests a similar relationship.

Unfortunately, until just recently, in most of the studies in which a media effect on criminal justice policy is discussed, it is only alluded to as a "potential" result of media consumption and actual relationships are left unmeasured and unanalyzed. Pandiani (1978, p. 455), for example, asserted that "Television viewing elicits irrational policy support, heavily tilted toward a law and order punitive orientation," without, however, offering any empirical evidence of such. Gerbner (1976) and Culver and Knight (1979) have also hypothesized that heavy television viewing could lead to increased public acceptance of police violence. And Culver and Knight (1979) and Estep and MacDonald (1984) have stated that the incredible success rate of television entertainment crime fighters could unrealistically raise television viewers' expectations of police and the criminal justice system. In their view, such expectations would result in support for pro–law and order policies. Unfortunately, none of these statements is supported by data.

Furthermore, a good deal of the evidence that has been offered is of an anecdotal or correlational nature.[20] In addition to the work of Doob and MacDonald (discussed earlier), Carlson (1985), using survey data from 619 sixth- to twelfth-graders, identified those subjects holding views outside of the mainstream and then examined whether or not viewing television crime shows moved these groups toward mainstream views. He reported that adolescents who are heavy viewers of crime shows measure lower on knowledge of criminal justice processes, are disposed to support the law enforcement system, more highly value norm compliance, and favor crime control over due process (Carlson, 1985, p. 189). Carlson found that for certain groups the effects on support for criminal justice–related policies appear to be quite strong (p. 150). Even students who achieve high grades, are heavy readers, and are aware that television content is "unreal" come to devalue due process considerations such as the protection of civil liberties. And even among those already holding mainstream views, heavy crime show viewing promotes conventionality and heightened support for increased social control (Carlson, 1985, p. 189). More recently, Roberts and Doob (1990) and Roberts and Edwards (1989) have reported evidence that varying the content of a news story changes its effect on the public's support for crime control policies. Roberts and Doob reported that tabloid-style coverage creates the greatest support for harsher sentences, whereas summaries of court documents produced the least. Roberts and Edwards reported experimental evidence that newspaper stories about serious crimes cause subjects to be more punitive in sentencing recommendations. Other studies have also reported correlational evidence of a link between mass media consumption and support for particular public policies regarding crime (see Barrile, 1984; Marks, 1987; Stack, 1987; Surette, 1985b).

With evidence of a consistent positive correlation between media usage and public support for various policies, the search for evidence of a causal relationship between the media and policy makers commenced. This search has taken shape under an approach termed an ecological approach, which combines a case study methodology with public survey or justice system data analysis. In this approach the media are conceptualized not only as carriers of information and images but as direct actors in the politics of policy formation. In each local environment, the media are seen as helping to shape criminal justice policy by establishing ongoing relationships with local policy initiators, lobbyists, and decision makers (Doppelt & Manikas, 1990; Protess et al., 1985). This conceptualization recognizes the media's role in the "ecology" of public policy and the fact that journalists oftentimes collaborate with officials, sometimes to the point of "building official reaction into their stories" (Molotch et al., 1987, p. 39). The strength of this approach is its recognition of the overt role of the media in policy development and its simultaneous acknowledgment that differing local social, political, and historical conditions will make that role slightly different in each actual case.

The first study in this tradition, and one that revitalized the study of justice and the media, was by Fishman (1978). Fishman studied the role of the news media in creating the perception of a wave of crimes against the elderly in New York City. He reported that the end result of the news media theme coverage of crimes against the elderly was the creation of new enforcement squads, the reallocation of public resources, and the introduction of new legislation—all without any measurable increase in actual victimization of the elderly. A similar effect was noted in Britain by Hall and his associates (1981) regarding muggings.[21] John Hinckley, Jr.'s assassination attempt on President Reagan is another example of the media influencing public policy, in this instance by reporting on a single, ongoing, high-profile case. The demand for a revamping of the insanity plea following Hinckley's acquittal by reason of insanity was credited to the inflammatory manner in which the verdict for Hinckley was reported (see Snow, 1984). Analyzing the results of a mailed survey, Pritchard and his colleagues (1987) reported that Indiana prosecutors' perceptions of both public and press opinion were important factors in their deciding whether or not to prosecute pornography: The prosecutor's estimation of pornography's position on the local citizens' agenda and the local press's agenda were two of the most significant predictors of whether or not a prosecutor reported having filed formal obscenity charges within the prior year. This finding supports the contention that among criminal justice system personnel, prosecutors, at least, tend to respond to what they perceive to be local public and media opinion in determining their policy course (Pritchard et al., 1987, p. 396). Other research by Cook and his colleagues (Cook et al., 1983b) and Pritchard (1986) reported similar findings.

Researchers are still exploring the nature of the media–criminal justice policy relationship, but they have been able to report clear, positive associations between the two. The results of the ecological research, in particular, have established that the media can directly affect what actors in the criminal justice system do without having first changed the public's attitudes and agendas. Though establishing that causal relationships develop at least in some cases, the research has not been able to specify the causal nature or prevalence of the relationships. The idiosyncratic nature of the relationship makes predicting the direction and magnitude of influence in specific instances or specifying the mechanism through which the media's influence is

---

BOX 4-3   NRA Ads

Despite the lack of definite conclusions regarding the media's effects and mechanisms of influence, political and private lobby groups such as the National Rifle Association commonly use the media to try to influence the public's views on crime and justice.

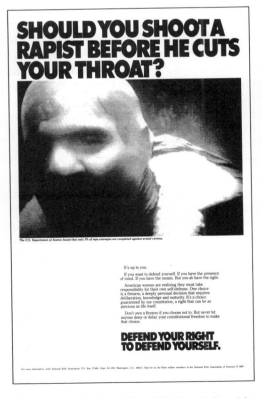

being exerted difficult. The difficulty arises because the media are most likely to affect criminal justice decision making indirectly rather than directly (Doppelt & Manikas, 1990; Jacob & Lineberry, 1982). Therefore, conclusions regarding the importance of the media for crime and justice policy must remain tentative.

However, knowledge has advanced far beyond the idea that the media have only "minimal effects" and the perception that the media's short attention span and the long-term development of most public policy preclude significant effects. Particularly in the criminal justice system, where the daily stream of case-by-case decisions means that policy is developed over both the long and short term, the media often significantly affect the policy process (Doppelt & Manikas, 1990, p. 139). The social and political "ecologies" in which the media exert their policy effects represent a complicated reality. At the level of the individual criminal justice policy maker, public policy is depicted as developing within an evolving environment. Effects are multidirectional, and the media's content, the timing of the presentation, and the characteristics of the general public and the criminal justice policy makers at any particular time interact to determine the media's influence on the criminal justice system's policies (see Ettema et al., 1989; Lang & Lang, 1983; Molotch et al., 1987).

Furthermore, among criminal justice system officials, response to the media can be either reactive or proactive in that they may react to what they have seen and heard in the media or act in anticipation of how they expect the media will respond (Doppelt & Manikas, 1990). Thus, even if the media ultimately pay no attention to an issue, an official may still act on the expectation that attention will be forthcoming. In effect, even if the media wished to eschew any policy-making role in the criminal justice system, that would be impossible (Drechsel, 1983, p. 14). The research indicates that among criminal justice officials, perhaps more than among the public, the media significantly influence both policy development and support for policies.[22] Effects have been shown to range from policy crusades, shield laws, and criminal legislation to influences on individual discretionary decisions within the criminal justice system. Indeed, media attention sometimes emerges as more important an influence than the legislation or policy initiative that its influence spurs.[23] Because agencies and decision makers mediate all of these effects, when only direct effects are sought, as in early research efforts, the media's influence appears sparse.

In the final analysis then, the media must be viewed as both messengers and actors in the criminal justice policy arena. Journalists, programmers, and editors are part of the policy-forming process, sometimes initiating and sometimes responding to changes in criminal justice policies. Although it is clear that media effects occur, the studies of these effects have not yet identified the characteristics of decision makers who are likely to be sensitive to media attention ("at-risk" criminal justice policy makers) or the situations in which criminal justice policy may be influenced. Because of the highly idiosyncratic and interactive nature of the relationship between the media and

Media attention results in an "announcement effect," a deterrent effect that follows the announcement of a new enforcement effort or investigative capability. Before a new policy can take effect, and sometimes even before a new policy is put into practice, media publicity stating that a new policy is in operation will result in measurable changes in offenses (see, for example, Nienstedt, 1990; Surette, 1985a). Publicizing a new DWI enforcement unit and stiffer penalties for drunken drivers, for example, can lead to an immediate decline in drunken driving—even if a new DWI unit is not put into operation and penalties are not increased. The announcement effect will decline and disappear, however, if such changes are not instituted, as the public eventually realizes that things are the same. The implications of the media announcement effect and efforts to use the media in crime control efforts are discussed in Chapter 6.

the decision-making process with regard to criminal justice policy, the effects of the media cannot yet be predicted with confidence at the individual level.

CONCLUSION

Many diverse factors influence attitudes, the public agenda, beliefs, and public policy with regard to criminality and criminal justice. On the basis of the existing evidence, the media cannot be forwarded as the primary factor determining developments in these areas, although its influence cannot be ignored. Given the limited media applications identified in the research on public communication campaigns, it is not surprising that strong and consistent relationships have not been found in the realm of crime and justice. Overall, the research findings indicate that the media do influence, to various degrees, the agendas, perceptions, and policies of its consumers with regard to crime and justice, but not directly or simply. In general the media appear to more directly influence factual perceptions of the world, such as consumers' estimations of the actual level of crime (especially when a consumer has few alternative sources of information about crime), than overall evaluations of social conditions or practices. The media also appear to affect people's perceptions of newer issues more than their perceptions of longstanding problems, and perceptions of the larger world more than perceptions of local community conditions (Cook et al., 1983b, p. 174). Thus, the research indicates that media may affect people's concern about crime as an issue without affecting their personal fear of victimization (see Gordon & Heath, 1981; Skogan & Maxfield, 1981; Tyler, 1984). And people's judgments about the world, such as whether the world is generally bad or good and what should be done about crime, remain more immediately influenced by personal experience, information from acquaintances, individual background, and local conditions.[24] Nonetheless, the media help construct social reality and to some degree influence the formation of the social policy that reflects the social reality.

Further complicating and obscuring the relationship between the media and crime and justice, perceptions of crime and justice appear to be intertwined with other social perceptions. Several researchers have pointed out that crime-related attitudes are not determined solely by one's perception of the crime problem.[25] And if perceptions of crime are intricately related to broader perceptions of the world, it is unrealistic to expect that they would change solely in accordance with media presentations of crime. Instead, perceptions of crime and justice are part of a larger conception of the nature and health of society and not a unique, separate component (Sacco, 1982, p. 490). The likelihood is that these broader media-influenced perceptions combine with previous attitudes and experiences to influence the public agenda with regard to crime control, which in turn translates into increased support from both the public and policy makers for particular public policies (Bortner, 1984, pp. 21–22; Lichter, 1988). These broader effects are generally considered to support the status quo and crime control. As Stark (1987, pp. 233, 268, 280) has stated:

> What these television depictions of zealous police tactics translate into is increased public support for both the weakening of constitutional protections, which impede prosecution, and the overall strengthening of law enforcement mechanisms. As public sentiment moves more in line with the "crime control" model of law enforcement and less in line with the "due process" model, largely due to the influence of television, it becomes less likely that extra-legal police actions directed against criminal suspects will draw censure or even disapproval from large segments of the American public. Television as a conservative, commercial medium has helped shape public opinion on questions concerning crime and law enforcement. . . . It is undeniable that in the 1970s, television helped solidify "crime control" values in the culture at large. Voters now overwhelmingly favored tougher crime-fighting measures, more freedom for the police, and less government spending on the social causes of crime. . . . As television moved to the right, the country and the courts moved with it.

A clear deficiency in the existing research lies in the concentration of past research on television and its effects. The cumulative and interactive effects of other types of media have yet to be explored. More attention should also be paid to how viewers interact with and use the media. Do people learn specific facts from the media that then influence what policies they will support, or do they notice and remember facts that agree with their already established preference for or predisposition toward particular policies? At present, the most plausible model of the relationship between the media and public perceptions is one in which causation is reciprocal and multidirectional.[26]

A slowly growing body of evidence suggests that the media can indirectly affect the way audiences perceive, interpret, and behave toward the world by influencing the social construction of reality. These effects may ultimately be of more significance than the relationship between media violence and behavior (Lichter, 1988, p. 40). For if we accept that the media influence the social construction of reality among the public, however haphazardly and indirectly, it is also a reasonable suspicion that the media influence behavior. Individuals behave in accordance with their perceptions of reality, so if the media are factors in the construction of people's reality with regard to crime and justice, it is a logical hypothesis that the media can influence behaviors related to crime and justice. Indeed, the enormous advertising and marketing industries are built on the premise that the media do influence a wide range of behaviors. The most worrisome potential behavioral effect is, of course, the possibility that the media may induce criminal behavior, the subject of Chapter 5.

Notes

1. Paisley (1981) identified three distinct phases in the historical development of communication campaigns. First, voluntary associations of private special-interest groups such as business associations, religions, or political parties conducted the campaigns. Second, the nature of the campaigns changed after the conclusion of the Civil War. Because of the emergence of large-circulation newspapers and magazines, the campaigns became more oriented toward the mass media. Third, with the completion of the national wire services, the shift to broad, modern mass appeals was set.

2. See Hyman & Sheatsley, 1947; Janis & Feshbach, 1953; Klapper, 1960; Star & Hughes, 1950.

3. See Mendelsohn, 1973; Robinson, 1972; Rogers, 1973; Zucker, 1978.

4. Communication campaigns have included general information campaigns, health campaigns, safe-driving campaigns, safe-sex campaigns, anti–drug abuse campaigns, and antismoking campaigns.

5. The issue of using the media in planned anticrime public communication campaigns is fully addressed in Chapter 6.

6. See Chaffee, 1975; Klapper, 1960; Kraus & Davis, 1976; McGuire, 1986.

7. See Doppelt & Manikas, 1990; Leff et al., 1986; Protess et al., 1985; Zucker, 1978.

8. Cook et al., 1983b; Leff et al., 1986; see also Cook et al., 1983a; Faunkhouser, 1973; Iyengar et al., 1982; MacKuen, 1981, 1984; McCombs & Shaw, 1972.

9. See Cook et al., 1983b; Graber, 1980, 1989; Protess et al., 1985; Swanson, 1988.

10. Gerbner also introduced the secondary concept of "resonance," which is the hypothesized heightened effect of television that is thought to result when the violent television world matches a real, violent world of heavy viewers. See Gerbner et al., 1980.

11. See Cook et al., 1983b; Hirsch, 1980, 1981; Hughes, 1980; Sacco, 1982.

12. Carlson also found that despite the fact that most people know little about the criminal justice system, television crime show viewers learn nothing about the criminal justice system, and television reinforces the ignorance of the mainstream (Carlson, 1985, pp. 116, 118).

13. See, for example, Barrile, 1984; Carlson, 1985; Marks, 1987; Sparks & Ogles, 1990; Surette, 1985b; and Tyler, 1980; cf. also Bennack, 1983; M. Robinson, 1976.

14. See Coenen & van Dijk, 1978; Gordon & Heath, 1981; Heath, 1984; Jaehnig et al., 1981; Sheley & Ashkins, 1981.

15. See Bandura, 1968; Drabman & Thomas, 1974; Gordon & Heath, 1981; Huesmann, 1982, p. 132; Jaehnig et al., 1981; O'Keefe, 1984; O'Keefe & Reid-Nash, 1987a; Sheley & Ashkins, 1981; Treevan & Hartnagel, 1976. For reviews see also NIMH, 1982, pp. 38–39; O'Keefe & Reid, 1990.

16. Other relevant research includes studies by Donnerstein, 1984; Krafka, 1985; Linz et al., 1988; Malamuth, 1981, 1983, 1986; Malamuth & Ceniti, 1986; Malamuth & Check, 1980, 1983, 1985; Malamuth, Check, & Briere, 1986; Malamuth & Donnerstein, 1982, 1984; Malamuth, Haber & Feshbach, 1980; Malamuth, Heim, & Feshbach, 1980; Malamuth & Spinner, 1980; Mohr & Zanna, in press; Padgett & Brislin-Slutz, 1987; Zillmann & Bryant, 1982.

17. *Main effects* is a term from statistics that denotes effects of a variable that are totally its own. Factors with main effects are felt to be particularly important, whereas those without main effects influence only through interactive effects or in combination with other variables.

18. In the only study to take this approach, Fisher (1989) explored the impact of the mass media on the attitudes about sex roles of men incarcerated in a maximum-security prison. He reported that increased radio and television exposure is associated with more egalitarian attitudes about sex roles. Fisher suggested that providing televisions in cells could have a rehabilitative effect.

19. In a review of the literature regarding media, crime prevention, and public opinion, Roberts and Grossman (1990) found little evidence of attitude change leading to behavior change. See also Chapter 6.

20. Stark (1987, pp. 257–258, 267) has listed a number of anecdotal references regarding specific effects from television entertainment on criminal justice policy. He lists increased jury acquittals, more-argumentative and hostile witnesses, influences on the way the police enforce the law and investigate crime, as well as influences on police recruits beginning their careers with false expectations and unrealistic attitudes about police work.

21. Both the Hall and the Fishman studies are further described in Chapter 3.

22. Cook et al., 1983b; Gilberg et al., 1980; Pritchard, 1986; Pritchard et al., 1987.

23. Nienstedt, 1990; see also Campbell, 1969; Campbell & Ross, 1968; Mayhew et al., 1979; Ross et al., 1970.

24. See Comstock, 1980; Doob & MacDonald, 1979; Sacco, 1982; Surette, 1984b.

25. See Furstenberg, 1971; Garofalo & Laub, 1978; Lotz, 1979; Sacco, 1982; Smith, 1984; Wilson, 1975.

26. See Cook et al., 1983b; Graber, 1980, pp. 119–122; Sacco, 1982; Smith, 1984. The media have also been described as a steering mechanism for long-term changes in attitudes (Graber, 1980). Whether the media do or do not have significant long-term effects is still unknown, and no empirical research addressing this possibility exists.

5 The Media as a Cause of Crime

OVERVIEW

Chapter 5 is a review of the research and ideas concerning the mass media as a cause of crime. Few people have actually directly examined the media as a cause of crime; the bulk of the research has focused on the media as a cause of social aggression and violence. Although narrowly focused and based on an unproven premise, this social aggression research has dominated discussion and received the most exposure. The evidence that violent media cause an increase in social aggression is clear in the laboratory but somewhat mixed in society. Though the idea that media depictions of violence have a cathartic effect has been discredited, a debate continues about the extent to which they may stimulate violence. Nonetheless, there is a rough consensus among researchers that, at least in the laboratory, televised or visual violence can elicit aggressive behavior in some viewers. There is no evidence of and little concern about a potential print media effect on social aggression. Overall, the research suggests, without proving conclusively, that we are a more aggressive society because of our mass media. Social aggression is not necessarily criminal, however, nor is most crime violent. Thus, irrespective of the media's effect on aggressive behavior, this set of research does not measure the media's effect on criminality.

Therefore, evidence of a criminogenic effect by the media is reviewed in the subsequent portion of the chapter. Media and aggregate crime rate studies suggest that the media's effect on crime might be independent of their violent content and their effect on aggressiveness. The research results implicate the visual media more than print media and point to increases in property crime rather than in violent crime. At least one exception to this generalization may exist, however, in sexually violent pornography. There is increasing evidence that even nonexplicit, non-X-rated depictions of sexual violence against women may evoke negative social effects such as trivializing rape and supporting aggression against women, and the potential influence of sexually violent material on predisposed males poses a clear danger.

A substantial review of the concept of copycat crime follows, exploring its nature, magnitude, and mechanisms of effect; its relationship to terrorism; and a theoretical model for its operation. In sum, copycat crime appears to be a persistent social phenomenon, common enough to influence the total crime picture—more by influencing offenders' choice of techniques than by criminalizing individuals. These effects appear to be especially apparent following a successful terrorist act using a novel approach.

On the basis of the total evidence available, which is admittedly less than perfect but considerable, the chapter concludes with the argument that the media is a factor in our crime rate. But though most reviewers accept that the media have an effect, the nature and the magnitude of that effect are undetermined. A criminogenic effect by the media is rare and highly interactive with variables external to the media such as the characteristics of the consumer, the setting, and the social context. The chapter closes with a general interactive model showing the interrelationships among these sets of variables.

STUDYING THE MEDIA AS A CAUSE OF CRIME

Crime is normally secret and hidden. Applying the concepts of front- and backstage behaviors, we can regard crime as one of the farthest backstage or even off-stage of social behaviors. Its surreptitious nature makes isolating, studying, and assessing individual factors such as the mass media's impact on crime difficult. Therefore, most conclusions about the influence of the media on crime have been extrapolated from studies of aggression and violence. And it is these studies that generate most of the concerns about the mass media's criminogenic potential. Underlying these concerns is a general belief in and focus on the following causal proposition:

Media depictions of violence → Increased social aggression →
Increased amount of crime

There are inherent problems with this proposition as a foundation for evaluating the media's effect on crime. Most seriously, it ignores the fact that much crime is nonviolent; the assumption that increased social aggression leads to more crime is unproven and largely uninvestigated; and the evidence that media depictions of violence cause an increase in social aggression is at best mixed. Furthermore, almost all of the research based on this proposition has been focused on the effects of the visual media. Despite these deficiencies in the research, the media are commonly cited as an exacerbating cause of crime—some have even advocated controversial public policies such as censorship as an effective means of reducing crime. Because crime encompasses a wide range of behavior from serious, predatory, violent crime to trivial, passive, victimless crime, however, it is not reasonable to expect to be able to describe the relationship between the media and crime in a single proposition or expect it to be manifested in a simple way. Nonetheless, researchers have not yet taken a broad, complex view of the relationship but have instead stuck closely to studying the proposition that depictions of violence lead to increased social aggression.

In examining how the mass media may affect criminality, note that the mass media were not created to affect the behavior of individuals, either positively or negatively, but exist simply to entertain or inform. Accordingly, media effects will probably not be consistent across all studies. Whether their effects are intended or not, however, the mass media have long been accused of influencing behavior; indeed, their financial base—advertising—rests on this firm belief. As early as 1908, journal and newspaper articles appeared expressing the worry that the mass media (then newspapers) were creating an atmosphere of tolerance for criminality and causing juvenile delinquency,[1] and with the advent of television in the 1950s, concern over negative media behavioral effects reached new heights. In 1955, a commissioner of the Federal Communications Commission (U.S. Senate Judiciary Committee on Juvenile Delinquency in the United States) expressed a still-common perception:

In the late 1940s and early 1950s, a New York psychiatrist, Frederick Wertham, led a public campaign against comic books as causes of crime and delinquency. Mostly ignored by social scientists but publishing in popular magazines and appearing on radio and television, Dr. Wertham aroused strong anticomic sentiments in the general public, convincing large portions of the public that all comics, but particularly crime-oriented comics such as the Batman series, had criminogenic and other negative effects (see Lowery & De-Fleur, 1983, Chap. 9; Wertham, 1954). Other than this episode and other isolated, sporadic incidents, the print media has been ignored as a serious cause of crime since the introduction of television. It is interesting to note that recent attacks against rock videos and rock lyrics are of the same tone as Wertham's earlier criticisms of comic books.

> Thirty-one million television receivers are pouring an unending stream of crime, violence, outright murder, brutality, unnatural suspense, and horror into the living rooms of America, where, in constantly increasing numbers, the children and youth of the country are found before the screen. The suggestions that there is no discernible relationship between these programs and the recent appalling increase in juvenile delinquency, in my opinion, flout common sense and rudimentary sound judgment. (1969, p. 7)

Spurred by this common concern, during the past thirty years numerous studies have examined the behavioral effects of the media on consumers, most focusing on children and television violence. Although this focus contributes little toward a full understanding of the media and crime, this area of research has received the most public exposure, and a review and assessment of the findings is a necessary first step in unraveling the relationship between the media and crime.

EVIDENCE OF MEDIA EFFECTS ON AGGRESSION

Driven by the folk logic of "Monkey see, monkey do," establishing whether "Child see, child do" holds true in terms of the media and aggression has proven more difficult than first expected. Research on the link between me-

---

The reason that television has been the focus of research is that three preconditions are considered necessary for the media to contribute significantly to societal violence: There must be a constant high level of violence portrayed in the media, the violence portrayed must be unique and unavailable elsewhere, and audience exposure to this media violence must be high. Television is felt to be the first mass media to meet all three conditions and has therefore generated the greatest concern and the most research. When other components of the mass media are added, the significance of the media to modern society is virtually unquestioned (Comstock, 1980, pp. 8–9). That television meets the first condition was established through the many media content studies discussed earlier. That it meets the second is indicated by surveys that show that few people ever observe the types of violent acts commonly portrayed in the media. For most Americans, life is relatively peaceful compared to life as shown on television. Thus, direct personal experience is not a source of learning about severe violence for most of the American population (NCCPV, 1969, vol. 9, p. 356). Regarding the third condition, the evidence is that television alone consumes on the average approximately 11 percent of every American's time. It is the third most time-consuming activity among Americans, second only to work and sleep. Young viewers often watch even greater amounts, and the total average amount of viewing time has steadily increased since television's introduction in the 1950s, while the portion of the public who are nonviewers has decreased toward zero.

dia depictions of violence and social aggression initially revolved around two competing hypotheses, one conjecturing a cathartic effect; the other, a stimulating effect. The cathartic-effect hypothesis can be stated thus:

> Exposure to properly presented violence acts as a therapeutic release for anger and self-hatred which are present in almost everybody. (Andison, 1977, citing Baldwin & Lewis, 1972, p. 349)

In contrast, the stimulating-effect hypothesis states that

> It is reasonable to conclude that a constant diet of violent behavior has an adverse effect on human character and attitudes. Violent [media content] encourages violent forms of behavior and fosters moral and social values about violence in daily life that are unacceptable in a civilized society. (National Commission on the Causes and Prevention of Violence [NCCPV], vol. 9, 1969, pp. 169–170)

Researchers positing a stimulating effect have explored a number of causal mechanisms by which the media could cause aggression. These include social "learning, imitation, and modeling" processes in which viewers learn values and norms supportive of aggression and violence, techniques to be aggressive and violent, and acceptable social situations and targets for aggression and violence (National Institute of Mental Health [NIMH], 1982, pp. 38–39). Advocates of a stimulating effect feel that through these processes children learn aggression the same way they learn cognitive and social skills—by watching parents, siblings, peers, teachers, and others. Accordingly, the more violence children see, the more accepting they become of aggressive behavior. Under this hypothesis, looking at violent scenes even briefly will make young children more willing to accept aggressive behavior from other children, and this acceptance of aggression will increase the likelihood that the children themselves will become more aggressive.[2]

What have more than seventy years of concern and thirty years of serious research yielded in evidence for or against the competing views on media-caused aggression? Most reviewers of a large body of relevant research agree that there is significant evidence that visual images of violence affect subsequent viewer aggression.[3] The cathartic-effect hypothesis has been discredited. Contrary to what the catharsis theory predicts, when viewing is combined with frustration or arousal, viewers are even more likely to behave aggressively.[4] The current debate revolves around the magnitude and significance of a stimulating effect. The research suggests that the relationship between visual media violence and audience aggression is clear, particularly for certain audiences, but the validity of extrapolating from that research evidence to a relationship between the media and crime remains questionable.

Periodic government assessments serve as mileposts in the history of research in this area. Two government commissions examined television violence in the late 1960s and early 1970s—the NCCPV in 1969 and the Surgeon General's Scientific Advisory Committee on Television and Social Behavior in 1972. Following a ten-year hiatus, in 1982 the NIMH released the report *Television and Behavior: Ten Years of Scientific Progress and Impli-*

cations for the Eighties. The conclusions stated in the 1969, 1972, and 1982 government reports reflect a consensus position. In the 1972 surgeon general's report, the advisory committee concluded that the convergence of evidence from both laboratory and field studies suggested that viewing violent television programs contributed to aggressive behavior. The 1982 NIMH commission report agreed with the authors adding that more recent research had significantly strengthened this conclusion. "Not only has the evidence been augmented," they said, "but the processes by which the aggressive behavior is produced have been further examined. For example, several important field studies have found that television violence results in aggressive behavior" (NIMH, 1982, pp. 36–37).

The research has also revealed, however, that media depictions of violence do not affect all viewers the same way, and it has indicated that a number of specific factors play into the media's effect. In other words, whether or not a particular depiction will cause a particular viewer to act more aggressively is not a straightforward issue and largely depends on the interaction between each individual viewer, the content of the portrayal, and the setting in which the portrayal is viewed. The total body of research shows that the media are not monolithic in their effects but contribute more or less to aggression in combination with other social and psychological factors (see Box 5-1).

In sum, the evidence indicates that a three-prong interactive model operates with regard to violent media images and their effects on individual aggressive behavior. The characteristics of the content of the portrayal, the setting in which it is viewed, and the viewer all interact to determine what effect, if any, a particular exposure to violent media images will have on the subsequent behavior of each viewer (see Figure 5-1). As Comstock (1983, pp. 255–256) has concluded, "Contrary results [should not be viewed] in the role of disconfirmation but in that of qualification. They simply demonstrate that in some circumstances a relationship does not occur, either because of attributes of the subjects, the particular portrayals involved, or the circumstances of exposure or subsequent behavior." At a practical social level, this gives the media significant aggregate effects but makes their effects difficult to predict on an individual level. The 1982 NIMH report conceded: "A distinction must be made, however, between groups and individuals. All the studies that support the causal relationships demonstrate group differences. None supports the case for particular individuals. . . . This distinction does not, of course, minimize the significance of the findings, even though it limits their applicability" (pp. 89–90). The sole individual-level effect that can be predicted is the absence of any cathartic effect leading to a reduction in aggression. This just does not occur: People do not become less violent from watching violence.

Some criticize the generally accepted conclusion that the relationship between media depictions of violence and viewer aggression is causal—that people become more violent because of exposure to violent images. Critics argue that it is premature to conclude from the available evidence that the media are causing the social aggression, rather than being simply correlated with it (see Box 5-2).

These criticisms are best summarized by Cook, Kendzierski, and Thomas (1983a), who after analyzing the 1982 NIMH report, concluded that the research was limited to examination of how the media's content influences

---

BOX 5-1   Factors Affecting the Impact of Media Depictions of Violence on Social Aggression

---

Researchers* have cited the following factors as interactive and important in determining the effect that a particular portrayal of violence by the media has on a particular viewer. Note that most of the factors relate to characteristics of the media, not of the viewers, a focus that reflects a deficiency in the general research.

1. Reward, or lack of punishment, for the perpetrator of violence (Bandura, 1965; Bandura et al., 1963; Rosekrans & Hartup, 1967)
2. Portrayal of the violence as justified by the behavior of the victim (Berkowitz & Rawlings, 1963; Meyer, 1972)
3. Similarity between details in the portrayal and the viewer's real-life circumstances, such as a victim in the portrayal with the same name as someone toward whom the viewer holds animosity (Berkowitz & Geen, 1966, 1967; Geen & Berkowitz, 1967)
4. Similarity between the perpetrator of violence and the viewer (Rosekrans, 1967)
5. Portrayal of violent behavior that is ambiguous in intent as motivated by the desire to inflict harm or injury (Berkowitz & Alioto, 1973; Geen & Stonner, 1972)
6. Portrayal of the consequences of violence in a way that does not stir distaste or arouse inhibitions over such behavior (Berkowitz & Rawlings, 1963)
7. Portrayal of the violence as representing real events rather than events concocted for a fictional film (Feshbach, 1972)

8. Portrayal of violence without critical commentary (Lefcourt et al., 1966)
9. Portrayal of violence whose commission particularly pleases the viewer (Ekman et al., 1972; Slife & Rychiak, 1976)
10. Portrayals, violent or otherwise, that leave the viewer in a state of unresolved excitement (Zillman, 1971; Zillman et al., 1973)
11. Viewers feeling angry or provoked before seeing a violent portrayal (Berkowitz & Geen, 1966; Geen, 1968)
12. Viewers experiencing frustration after viewing a violent portrayal (Geen, 1968; Geen & Berkowitz, 1967; Worchel et al., 1976)
13. The presence of live peer models of aggression (Murray et al., 1978)
14. The presence of sanctioning adults (Eisenberg, 1980)
15. Selective attention and emotional reactions on the part of the viewer (Ekman et al., 1972)
16. Low viewer self-esteem (Edgar, 1977)

Television violence has been linked to aggressive behavior whether portrayed by real or animated characters (Bandura, 1971, 1977; Ellis & Sekyra, 1972; Hanratty et al., 1972), and only unambiguous linking of violent behavior with undesirable consequences or motives appears to inhibit the viewer's subsequent aggression (Hennigan et al., 1982; Leifer & Roberts, 1972).

Source: From "Media Influences on Aggression," by G. Comstock. In A. Goldstein and L. Krasner (eds.), Prevention and Control of Aggression. *Copyright © 1983 by Pergamon Press. Reprinted by permission.*

---

*The first 12 factors were compiled by Comstock (1983, pp. 250–251) following his review of the relevant literature through 1982.

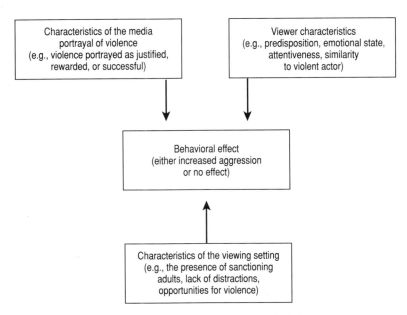

FIGURE 5-1 Conditions affecting the impact of violent media images on social aggression

viewers' perceptions and how these perceptions in turn affect viewers' attitudes and behavior. Referring to Himmelwitt's model of television and its influences (1980, reproduced in Figure 5-2), they noted that the research thus focuses on only part of the model, specifically parts E, F, and G (Cook et al., 1983a, p. 164). Institutions rarely come under study, and the NIMH report largely ignores the media industry, advertising, and government influences, in effect assuming that media influence audiences directly and solely through their programming content.

Cook and his colleagues further faulted the nature of the evidence gathered in the research. In their view, laboratory experiments contain a positive bias that exaggerates the link between exposure to violent images and social aggression. This bias arises, they argue, because aggression is a relatively rare event, so experiments have to be designed to (1) minimize subjects' internal inhibitions against aggression, (2) minimize external cues sanctioning aggression (to limit possible causes to media effects only), and (3) maximize the clarity and intensity of experimental treatments. The end results are unrealistic experiments and findings that have limited applicability to home and other social situations. Cook, Kendzierski, and Thomas felt that a positive bias is also likely in cross-sectional surveys and noted that field experiments produce little consistent evidence of effects, and that in the cases where an effect is claimed, the populations involved seem to be more aggressive to begin with (Cook et al., 1983a, pp. 180–182).

Another target of criticism has been researchers' ambiguity in defining and measuring the concept of aggression. For some, aggression is a broad

BOX 5-2 The Argument Against a Causal Link Between the Media and Aggression

A number of authors have argued that the media cannot be posited as a cause of aggression or violence based on the research currently available (see Brannigan, 1987; Brannigan & Kapardis, 1986; Feshbach & Singer, 1971; Freedman, 1984; Howitt & Cumberbatch, 1975; Mi- lavsky et al., 1982; Mould, 1988; Wurtzel & Lometti, 1984a, 1984b). They assert that to conclude that the media cause negative social behaviors is unjustified and premature. In their view, the true relationship between the media and aggression is as shown in the following figure:

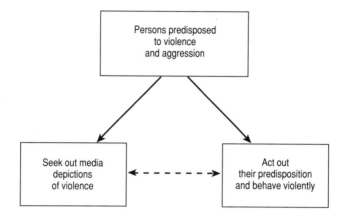

In this figure, exposure to violent content and violent behavior are linked but not causally. Rather, both are caused by the predispositions of some persons who seek out violent content and act violently because of their predisposition to aggression. Significantly for public policy, if the above figure is valid, eliminating portrayals of violence in the media will not reduce the level of violence in society. The number of individuals who are predisposed to violence will remain the same. Advocates of this model have correctly pointed out that the evidence of a link between violent content and social aggression supports the *noncausal* model just as well as it does a causal one.

Media critics ask how the media balance their assertion that advertising can influence viewers' behavior with their contention that violent content and images do not. Media proponents argue that the behavior portrayed in media advertising is socially acceptable whereas violence obviously is not; therefore, that people emulate behavior shown in advertising does not prove that they will emulate violent behavior. Society reinforces the behavior shown in commercials but generally does not reinforce violence. Proponents further argue that in contrast to the socially sanctioned behavior shown in media advertising, media depictions of violence often show it as undesirable and socially unacceptable (Wurtzel & Lometti, 1984a, 1984b).

In response to media critics who argue that the evidence of a link between violent content and social aggression is supplemented by laboratory research that substantiates a causal link, media proponents argue that the laboratory experiments conducted to determine the relationship between the media and violence are biased toward finding an effect. To isolate the effect of a single factor, the media, and observe a rare social behavior, violence, these laboratory experiments must exaggerate the link between the media and aggression and create a setting that will elicit violent behavior (Cook et

(continued)

BOX 5-2 (continued)

---

al., 1983a). In addition, the way those conducting the experiment operationalize aggression in the laboratory affects the likelihood that they will find a strong positive relationship between the media and aggression. Laboratory measures are the most consistent but because of their artificiality are not valid predictors of the real world. Thus, Andison (1977) reviewed sixtyseven studies dealing with the relationship between television violence and viewer aggression, studies conducted between 1956 and 1976 and involving more than thirty thousand subjects. He reported that studies employing "degree of shock administered" as their measure of aggression reported a consistent, more highly positive relationship than studies using overt physical aggression or responses to questionnaires as measures (Andison, 1977, p. 321). Critics argue that this laboratory operationalization of aggression is so flawed that it does not accurately reflect the watching of media violence and subsequent social aggression in situations outside of the laboratory. Many thus consider the effects that have been found in nonlaboratory, mostly correlational research trivial and substantively unimportant (Howitt & Cumberbatch, 1975; Milavsky et al., 1982; Wurtzel & Lometti, 1984a, 1984b). In their view, no study yet conclusively links the media as a cause of violent behavior.

The research regarding pornography exemplifies the difficulty in assigning a behavioral causal effect to the media (see Brannigan, 1987; Brannigan & Kapardis, 1986; Mould, 1988). Demare and his colleagues (1988), for example, assessed their subjects' exposure to violent and nonviolent sexually explicit media content, the supportiveness of their attitudes toward violence against women, and the self-reported likelihood of using sexual force if assured of not being caught. They report no significant associations between the amount of exposure to either violent or nonviolent pornography and the degree to which the subjects supported violence against women, but a significant correlation between the amount of exposure to sexually explicit violent images and the self-re-

ported likelihood of using sexual force. Demare and his colleagues (1988, p. 150) argued that it is the media's combination of sex and support for aggression that produces a tendency for sexual violence. However, in that it is equally likely that males with a predisposition toward sexual aggression are more likely to seek out sexually violent content, it cannot be concluded that the exposure causes a tendency for sexual violence. As with other research in this area, the reported correlations may be due to a third variable causing both consumption of sexually violent material and a proclivity toward sexual aggression (cf. Imrich et al., 1990).

Another study of individuals, this one examining actual sex offenders, was conducted by Marshall (1988). Contrary to earlier reports, Marshall found that rapists and child molesters whose victims were not related to them reported significantly greater use of sexually explicit materials than either incest perpetrators or nonoffender controls. More significant, rapists and child molesters also report frequent use of these materials while preparing to commit an offense. Because of the retrospective, self-reported nature of Marshall's data, however, it is impossible to determine whether exposure to sexually explicit materials contributes to sexually deviant behavior, or whether these offenders seek out this material after their deviant orientations are established.

Other research has attempted to predict aggression against women in laboratory settings and through self-reports (Malamuth, 1983, 1986). Malamuth (1986) concluded that the presence of any single factor is unlikely to result in high levels of sexual aggression. He argued, that though sexual arousal in response to aggression has been used in diagnosing and treating rapists (Quinsey, in press), this arousal pattern has also been found in a substantial portion of the general nonviolent male population (Malamuth, Check & Briere, 1986).

The research thus suggests but does not prove a causal connection, therefore a noncausal explanation of the research findings remains viable.

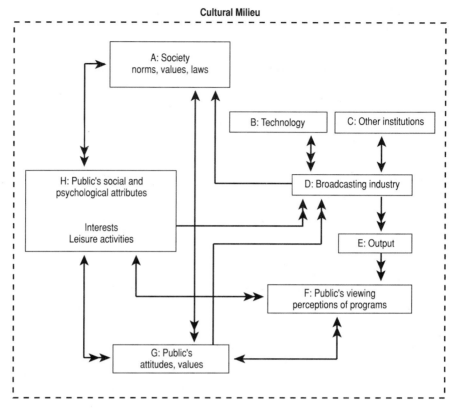

FIGURE 5-2 Model of the role of broadcasting. ↑ denotes direction of strong influences. ↑ denotes direction of some influence.

Source: From "Social Influence and Television," by H. Himmelweit, p. 142. In S. Withey and R. Abeles (eds.), Television and Social Behavior: Beyond Violence and Children. *Copyright © 1980 by Lawrence Erlbaum Associates, Inc. Reprinted by permission.*

concept that encompasses many types of social behaviors. Thus conceived, its relationship to the media cannot be separated from other antisocial but nonaggressive social behaviors (see Gottfredson & Hirschi, 1990, citing Eron, 1987, p. 440). Others narrowly operationalize aggression in the laboratory, reducing it to a single, obviously artificial behavioral response such as inflicting an electric shock. The relationship of these laboratory measures of aggression to real-world aggression is unclear and questionable.

Irrespective of all the flaws noted and the doubts and criticisms expressed, however, most reviewers do conclude that the research suggests a significant causal effect. Even Cook and his colleagues (1983a, pp. 191–192) finally concluded that

No effects emerge that are so large as to hit one between the eyes, but early measures of viewing violence add to the predictability of later aggression over and above the predictability afforded by earlier measures of aggression. These lagged effects are consistently positive, but not large, and they are rarely statistically significant, although no reliable lagged negative effects have been reported. The evidence indicates that a small association can regularly be found between viewing violence and later aggression when individual differences in aggression are controlled at one time. But is the association causal? If we were forced to render a judgment, probably yes. . . . There is strong evidence of causation in the wrong setting (the laboratory) with the right population (normal children) and in the right setting (outside of the lab) with the wrong population (abnormal adults). However, trivial proportions of variance in aggression are accounted for and there exists an exaggerated sense of confidence in the research supporting an important causal connection. . . . But the effects may aggregate when large numbers of children each are affected slightly, or a small number suffer much larger consequences.

The issue for most thus comes down not to the existence of an effect but to the magnitude and substantive importance of the effect. Despite clear laboratory evidence that media violence can lead to short-term imitation, researchers who have looked for an incorporation of violent behavior into the viewer's overall behavior pattern or a subsequent willingness among children to use violence as a problem-solving method have reported mixed results. Leifer and Roberts (1972), for example, reported that children who had viewed an aggressive program were clearly more likely to choose aggressive solutions; in another study, however, they found no effect on children's postviewing selection of violent resolutions to conflicts. Similarly, Collins (1973) also found no media effect on the choice of solutions to problems. Exactly how and to what extent the media cause long-term changes in aggressive behavior remains unknown, and so, despite the consensus that there is a positive relationship between violence in the visual media (particularly television) and viewer aggression, the substantive importance of this relationship is still under debate.

Not surprisingly, various descriptions of the causal impact of the media currently compete. Positing a significant impact, the NIMH report (1982, pp. 89–90) stated regarding television that

> recent studies have extended the age range in which the relationship between televised violence and aggressive behavior can be demonstrated . . . to include preschoolers and older adolescents . . . [and] suggests that the viewer learns more than aggressive behavior from televised violence. The viewer learns to be a victim and to identify with victims. As a result, many heavy viewers may exhibit fear and apprehension, while other heavy viewers may be influenced toward aggressive behavior. Thus, the effects of televised violence may be even more extensive than suggested by earlier studies, and they may be exhibited in more subtle forms of behavior than aggression.

Wilson and Herrnstein (1985, p. 346) have offered a conservative interactive model:

> Aggressive children, because they are not very popular, and low IQ children, because they have trouble with schoolwork, spend more time watching television than other children. These children identify with the television characters and may come to accept the apparently easy and sometimes violent solutions these characters have for the problems that confront them. To the extent they emulate this violence or further neglect their schoolwork, their reliance on tele-

vision may increase. Television provides for such children reinforcements that are not supplied by peers or schoolwork. . . . There is no doubt that aggressive boys, including those who grow up to acquire significant criminal records, spend a lot more time than other boys in front of the television, but we are not much closer to being able to say that these viewing habits cause much of the

---

BOX 5-3   The Substantive Importance of the Media

Researchers normally measured the substantive importance of the media in generating aggression in terms of the amount of "explained variance" in levels of aggression attributable to the media—in other words, the proportion of the changes in aggression that can be statistically associated with the media. When effects are present, the explained variance is usually between 5 and 10 percent. Though some have interpreted these levels as important (Andison, 1977; Comstock, 1980; Huesmann, 1982; Murray, 1980; NIMH, 1982), others have termed them slight or trivial (Cook et al., 1983a; Freed-

man, 1984; Lewis, 1984; Milavsky et al., 1982; Wilson & Herrnstein, 1985). Both Huesmann's (1982) and Milavsky and his colleagues' (1982) longitudinal panel studies, for example, were designed to test the cumulative effect of past exposure to media violence on aggressive behavior, and both attempted to determine the delayed effects of television violence by examining the "cross-correlations," or the associations between aggression and violent media at two points in time. The following figure from Eron and Huesmann (1980, p. 320) illustrates this approach:

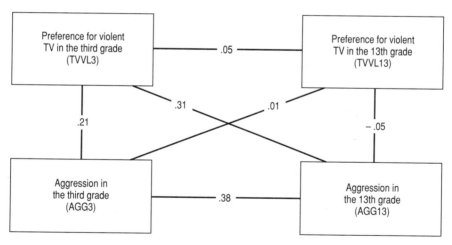

Correlations between a preference for violent television and peer-rated aggression for 211 boys over a 10-year lag

Source: From "Adolescent Aggression and Television," by L. D. Eron and L. R. Huesmann, p. 320. In F. Wright, C. Bahn, and R. Reiber (eds.), Forensic Psychology and Psychiatry. Copyright © 1980 by The Annals of the New York Academy of Sciences. Reprinted by permission.

As Cook and his colleagues (1983a) have noted, both studies found mostly positive relationships of low magnitude and low statistical significance. Huesmann, however, chose to interpret

the findings as evidence of an effect, whereas Milavsky and his colleagues chose to interpret their findings as evidence of no effect.

violence than we were twenty years ago . . . and even when all doubts are ignored, only trivial proportions of individual differences in aggression are accounted for.

Summary

Despite some contradiction (see Box 5-2), the research leads to the idea that in terms of magnitude, media violence correlates as strongly with and is as causally related to aggressive behavior as any other social behavioral variable that has been studied (Comstock, 1980, p. 258). This statement describes both the media's impact and our lack of knowledge about aggression. There is a consensus among social scientists that, at least in the laboratory, television or film violence can elicit aggressive behavior in some viewers (Phillips, 1982a, p. 388). Because of the many other individual and social factors that come into play in producing any social behavior, however, one should not expect more than a modest relationship between the media and aggression to emerge. In that the research has focused entirely on visual media, there is also no evidence of and apparently no concern about any effect by the print media on social aggression. How important the relationship between the media and aggression is to society and how much it influences our quality of life is still being researched and debated. Because aggression is perceived as a persistent problem, however, even those factors that only modestly contribute to it are considered socially significant. Accordingly, the media cannot be ignored regardless of the extent of their impact (cf. Rosenthal, 1986).

Regarding specific processes, the evidence supports the stimulation hypothesis, not the catharsis, and suggests that the media stimulate violence through a process of observation followed by imitation.[5] There is also evidence of a normative socialization process in which exposure to mass media portrayals of violence over a long period of time socializes audiences to norms, attitudes, and values supportive of violence. Thus, the more violence a person sees in the media, the more accepting of aggressive behavior he or she becomes (see Bandura, 1968; Drabman & Thomas, 1974; Huesmann, 1982, p. 132). Yet to be determined is whether media portrayals of violence increase the proportion of persons who assault others, encourage already-violent persons to use violence more often, or encourage violence-prone persons to use greater violence (Wilson & Herrnstein, 1985, p. 343). Who is most likely to be affected and under what conditions is not fully understood.

The research strongly suggests without conclusively proving that we are probably a more aggressive society because of our mass media. The media help to create a more violent social reality—though how much more violent is yet to be determined. As previously stated, however, social aggression is not necessarily criminal, nor is most crime violent. Consequently, whether or not the media foster aggressive behavior, it is still questionable whether or not their influence extends beyond aggressiveness to specifically increase criminal behavior—the central issue of this chapter.

EVIDENCE OF MEDIA EFFECTS ON CRIME

Aggregate Crime Rate Studies

There are inherent difficulties in researching and examining possible relationships between the media and criminal behavior. First, experiments are even more difficult to conduct in this area than in the area of social aggression; consequently most of the evidence consists of anecdotal reports rather than empirical studies. Second, the ways in which the media may be affecting crime are numerous. The media may be increasing the number of criminals by turning previously law-abiding persons into criminals. They may be helping already active criminals succeed more by teaching them better crime techniques. They may be increasing the seriousness or harmfulness of the crimes that are committed by making criminals more aggressive or violent. They may be fostering theft and other property crimes by cultivating in consumers the desire for certain things and encouraging instant gratification and impulsiveness. They may be making crime seem more exciting and satisfying (cf. Wilson & Herrnstein, 1985). Any of these processes would result in more crime, more criminals, and more costly crime. Third, research is made even more difficult because the pool of "at-risk" individuals who are likely to be criminally influenced by the media is probably quite small. This makes identifying them for research purposes problematic.

Because of these problems, there are few empirical studies in this area. In the best-designed empirical study of a medium's effect on recorded criminal behavior, Karen Hennigan and her colleagues (1982) examined aggregate crime rates in the United States prior to and following the introduction of television in the 1950s. Using both statewide and citywide data, they found that the introduction of commercial television is not associated with increases in the rates of violent crime but is associated with increases in the rates of certain property crimes, particularly larceny. They attributed this correlation to the materialistic focus of television programming and advertising, which promote a high-consumption, materialistic lifestyle. Hennigan and her colleagues felt this pervasive message of consumerism is the key through which the media affect crime, and that it is more important than the mechanisms of imitation or stimulation hypothesized in earlier research. They noted that violent programming is not constant and that viewers can avoid it by being selective about what they watch, but that images of a high-consumption lifestyle are constant and cannot be avoided except by not watching. In their view, television's criminogenic effect can thus ultimately be attributed to the arousal of feelings of relative deprivation and frustration in viewers, caused by constant exposure to high levels of consumption, rather than to the learning of larcenous values or robbery techniques from watching theft on television (Hennigan et al., 1982, p. 461).

Describing the process, they speculated:

> Lower classes and modest life-styles were rarely portrayed in a positive light on TV, yet the heaviest viewers have been and are poorer, less educated people. It is possible that in the 1950s television caused younger and poorer persons (the major perpetrators of theft) to compare their life-styles and possessions with (a)

Hennigan and her colleagues (1982) took advantage of the unique introduction of television in the United States:

> Television did not diffuse rapidly to all communities in the United States at the same time. Instead, the rapid spread of television broadcasting stations was artificially staggered between 1949 and mid-1952. Therefore, some communities gained access to television before the freeze while others had to wait until the freeze was lifted. If the introduction of television caused an increase in crime, the level of crime in the prefreeze communities should increase more than in postfreeze communities shortly after the prefreeze communities began to receive television signals. On the other hand, the level of crime in the postfreeze communities should increase relative to that in the prefreeze communities a few years later when the freeze was lifted and the postfreeze communities began receiving signals. To be convincing, an effect found at the earlier time in prefreeze communities must be replicated at the other time in the postfreeze communities.

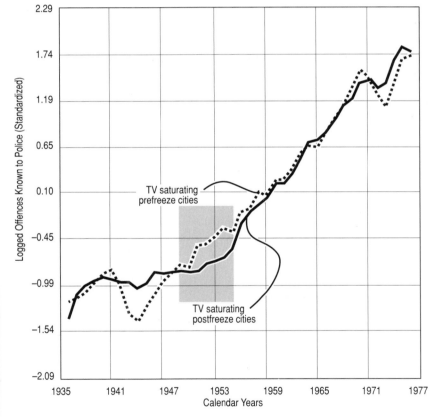

Larceny theft offenses known to police (logged and standardized) in prefreeze and postfreeze cities from 1936 through 1976 (the time series were standardized to aid visual inspection of the plots but they were not standardized in the analyses).

Source: From "Impact of the Introduction of Television on Crime in the United States," by K. Hennigan et al., Journal of Personality and Social Psychology, 1982, 42(3), 461–477. Copyright 1982 by the American Psychological Association. Reprinted by permission.

those of the wealthy television characters and (b) those portrayed in advertisements. Many of these viewers may have felt resentment and frustration over lacking the goods they could not afford, and some may have turned to crime as a way of obtaining the coveted goods and reducing any relative deprivation. (p. 474)

In terms of an overall aggregate effect on crime then, Hennigan's study first empirically forwarded the idea that television influences property rather than personal crime, at least initially. Whether this applies today is unknown, because we can no longer separate television's influence from other contemporary social processes. Hennigan and her colleagues, however, speculated that television still does contribute to an increase in property crime rates to some unknown degree (Hennigan et al., 1982, p. 475).

Berkowitz and Macaulay (1971) examined changes in the U.S. crime rate following the Kennedy assassination and two intensely covered mass murders. They discovered an unexpected increase in robberies but no increase in murder or manslaughter. Faced with what they saw as an anomaly, they offered the explanation that disruptions of the social norm and the legal system create the sense that the normal rules of society have been suspended. The effect is great enough to trigger robberies but not manslaughters. This argues against a wide-scale imitation of portrayals of violence and concurs with the conclusions of Hennigan and her colleagues that the media affect property crime more than violent crime. In regard to print media, as noted earlier, there is no evidence that newspapers have any general criminal effect, however. After reviewing the research through 1978 concerning whether or not the reporting of crime news encourages others to commit crimes, Joseph Dominick (1978) concluded that there was little evidence supporting such an effect, and the current consensus is that there is no rigorous evidence indicating a general relationship between the print media and crime (see also J. Haskins, 1969; Payne, 1974; Payne & Payne, 1970). In sum, the limited aggregate research suggests that the media may very well affect crime independently of their effect on aggressiveness or the violence of their content. The mixed results implicate the visual media as a contributor to property crime. One area of research, however, indicates that violent content in a particular context may indeed be criminogenic.

Pornography

Given that crime is normally considered aberrant behavior, an examination of aberrant media nearly suggests itself. It's commonly accepted that a link exists between pornography and criminal acts and that pornography has negative social effects. In 1972, however, the Commission on Obscenity and Pornography published findings contrary to these commonly held perceptions. In its report, the commission stated, first, that rapists reported significantly less exposure to pornography than the general public. Second, a higher percentage of male child molesters (when compared with the general public) reported never having been exposed to pornography. Third, in total, all types of sex deviants interviewed reported less than average exposure to pornographic materials than the general population (Goldstein et

> The theoretical positions regarding pornography are analogous to those held concerning the general media and viewer aggression. Two basic views compete: One posits a stimulating effect, hypothesizing that pornography encourages viewers to act violently toward women; the other, a cathartic effect, holding that pornography cannot change people's fundamental sexual natures but can help them resolve inner conflicts by releasing anger toward women without overt aggression (see Donnerstein, 1980; English, 1980; Eysenck & Nias, 1978; Gray, 1982; Malamuth & Donnerstein, 1984).

al., 1972). In addition, in reviewing Denmark's experiment with unrestricted legalized pornography, Kutchinsky (1972) noted that Denmark experienced a large decrease in minor sex crimes and a small decrease in rape and attempted rape. Finally, the commission report stated that only 2 percent of the general U.S. public considered pornography a serious problem. Because of these findings, the commission concluded in its 1972 report that pornography is generally harmless and that exposure to pornography is relatively innocuous and without lasting or detrimental effects.

Not surprisingly, given the morally laden nature of the topic, the conclusions of the 1972 report were not universally accepted. Court (1976, p. 153), for example, argued without empirical evidence that there was a causal link between the level of access to pornography and serious sexual crime. He cited the increased availability of material featuring sadomasochism and bestiality, reports of "snuff" films—sexually explicit films in which a person is actually murdered—the use of rape as an entertainment theme, and a wave of sadistic pornography as all evidencing a link between pornography and sex crimes. The feminist movement also spurred new research efforts, and in the years following the 1972 report, a number of contrary findings were reported (see Cline, 1974; Dienstbier, 1977; Wills, 1977).

Two subsequent federal reports—one authored by the U.S. Department of Health and Human Services and published in 1982, the other, *The Final Report of the Attorney General's Commission on Pornography,* published in 1986 by the U.S. Department of Justice—came to the opposite conclusion of the 1972 report. According to both reports, later intervening research indicated that pornography has sexually harmful effects in certain circumstances. Studies had shown, for example, that films that are both pornographic and violent can trigger aggression toward women (Donnerstein, 1980). In comparison to portrayals of nonpornographic aggression (a man hitting a woman) and nonaggressive pornographic material (sex between mutually consenting adults), "aggressive pornography" (forced, violent sex depicted as "pleasurable rape") increases male viewers' subsequent aggressiveness toward females, but not toward males (Donnerstein & Linz, 1986; Malamuth & Donnerstein, 1984). It has also been reported by Donnerstein and Linz (1984, 1986) that violent pornography increases the willingness of a man to say that he would rape a woman, increases aggressive behavior against women in a lab setting, strengthens the attitude that women

In one content review conducted in the 1970s, the "rape myth" was found to be a plot feature in one-third of adult books (see Smith, 1976). Typically, in these books, a woman would be forced to participate in an initially unwanted sexual act that begins with the woman protesting but ends with the woman pleading for more sex, her passion apparently unleashed by force (Donnerstein & Berkowitz, 1985; Malamuth, Heim & Feshbach, 1980).

want to be raped ("belief in the rape myth"), and decreases viewers' sensitivity to rape and sympathy for the rape victim. Sexually violent material has therefore been targeted as the most influential and socially harmful type of media content (Gray, 1982; Imrich et al., 1990; Malamuth & Donnerstein, 1984). As Comstock (1983, p. 254) has noted:

> At this point the recent research on the effects of violent pornography becomes relevant. It appears that the [1972] commission on obscenity and pornography may have been precipitous in its conclusions that exposure to pornography has no influence on antisocial behavior. More recent experiments indicate that pornography featuring violence against women stimulates subsequent aggression toward women, and especially so when the victim in the portrayal appears to gain some pleasure from the violence directed against her. The factor most clearly implicated as responsible is the portrayal of violence against a female in an erotic context. It is the presence of aggressive behavior [in the media] that results in the display of heightened aggressiveness [in male subjects].

In an attempt to determine whether or not these laboratory-elicited relationships have counterparts in the larger society, several recent aggregate studies have examined the relationship between pornography and rape rates. Studies by Baron and Straus (1984, 1985, 1986) compared state-by-state differences in rape rates with state-by-state differences in pornography consumption as measured by sales of eight sex-oriented over-the-counter male magazines. Their findings reveal a positive correlation between rape rates and sex-oriented magazine purchases. However, when they introduced a measure of "hypermasculinity,"[6] the relationship between magazine circulation and rape rate disappeared. Scott and Schwalm (1988, forthcoming), have reported similar findings that indicate that other factors may be more related to rape rates, including readership of outdoor-type magazines, such as *Field and Stream, Guns and Ammo,* and *The American Hunter.* All of this research suggests a noncausal relationship between sex-oriented magazine sales and rape rates. The researchers have suggested that the positive correlations may be explained by variations in the level of a "hypermasculine" culture. This underlying "macho" ethic, when strong, is suggested as accounting for both high pornography consumption and high rape rates (Imrich et al., 1990, p. 116).

Violent, sexual media depictions have thus been clearly associated with negative attitudes toward rape victims and an increased self-reported likelihood that subjects would use sexual force. We can therefore consider extending the hypothesis that exposure to media violence increases social aggression to the more specific "exposure to media depictions of sexual violence fosters antifemale attitudes, greater acceptance of violence toward women, and increased aggressiveness in a laboratory setting toward women by males" (see Chapter 4, Figure 4-42). As with media violence, however, it must be noted that most people are exposed to sexually explicit media (90 percent of males and 80 percent of females according to the 1972 commission report), and though most become aroused, few become sexually deviant in attitudes or behavior (Malamuth & Donnerstein, 1984, p. 4). There is little evidence that increased availability of pornography increases sexual crimes such as rapes, and some evidence that it may decrease some sexual crimes such as child molestation (Bowen, 1987; Kutchinsky, 1972, 1985). Hence, few are prepared to blame the media as the primary cause of sexual violence or callous attitudes toward women, but the media is identified as being among many contributors (see Donnerstein & Linz, 1986; Imrich et al., 1990). It is the linking of sex and violence in the media that is considered pernicious, not the explicitness of the sexual activity. Pornography's negative effects appear to operate not through sexual arousal of viewers but through heightening the aggressiveness of an unknown but apparently small number of males and negatively influencing the attitudes of a larger but also unknown number of males.

In sum, sexually violent pornography, because of its effects on angry hypermasculine males, presents the clearest and gravest danger,[7] though some still question even this link, and the methodology and generalizability of the research have been severely criticized (see Brannigan, 1987; Brannigan & Kapardis, 1986; Mould, 1988). Importantly, there is increasing evidence that sexual violence against women need not be portrayed in explicit sexual media to have negative effects (Donnerstein & Linz, 1986, p. 606, citing Donnerstein & Berkowitz, 1985 and Malamuth & Check, 1983). Of particular interest are the popular R-rated "slasher" films, which do not fit the general definition of pornography and whose social impact may be even more deleterious than X-rated films (see Donnerstein & Linz, 1986, p. 607; see also Imrich et al., 1990; Linz et al., 1984, 1988). Sexually violent images are thought to facilitate aggression by influencing cultural attitudes and beliefs regarding relationships and sex roles—specifically, by normalizing aggression toward women for some men in sexual and other interpersonal encounters and increasing the tolerance for aggression toward women in the larger culture (cf. Bowen, 1987; Weis & Borges, 1973). However, as stated in Chapter 3, whether or not the connection between sexually violent content and antisocial attitudes actually causes increases in sexually coercive behavior is yet unproven (Hawkins & Zimring, 1988). The opposing view is represented by the psychopathology model, in which sexual aggression is considered an individual emotional disorder, and the sexually violent material is sought out and correlates with sexual violence, but is not contributory or causal (see Brodsky, 1976).

If, for the moment, one accepts the premise that sexually violent content has negative behavioral effects, the immediate policy problem is what to do about the pernicious effects of sexually violent material on the few. Educational "debriefings" have been found to be useful in reversing the negative attitudinal effects, and some have suggested that society develop educational material to debunk the "pleasurable rape" myth and counter other attitudinal effects.[8] As in the recent campaign against child pornography, some also recommend that the curtailment and eventual elimination of sexually violent material (regardless of its industry rating) that portrays violence against women as pleasurable, rewarding, and acceptable be pursued as a public policy goal.

The general research findings on media violence and aggression, and pornography and sexual crimes, indicate that the media affect preexisting pools of at-risk individuals, some portion of whom will have the mix of characteristics that make them prone to display media-induced acts of aggression, sexual or otherwise. With sexually violent material there are clear links between the media and antisocial attitudes about sexual crime. Sexually violent material creates a social reality with a particular view of women and sex roles. Nonetheless, that these attitudes translate into an actual increase in the commission of sexual crimes, though suggested, has not yet been proven by the research. When combined with the research on media violence, the research on pornography indicates imitative modeling as the likely short-term mechanism through which the media influence individuals. This implication of modeling leads to the general concern over copycat crime—crime directly triggered by and emulated from media portrayals, another commonly acknowledged but poorly investigated media phenomenon.

COPYCAT CRIME

Its Nature and Reality

The first issue to be addressed concerning copycat crime is whether or not it actually occurs. Determining what seems a simple matter is complicated by the intrinsic nature of copycat crime. For a crime to be a copycat crime it must have been inspired by an earlier, publicized crime: There must be a pair of crimes linked by the media. The perpetrator of a copycat crime must have been exposed to the publicity about the original crime and must have incorporated major elements of that crime into his or her own. The choice of victim, the motivation, or the technique in a copycat crime must have been lifted from the earlier, publicized crime. These limits make identifying copycat crimes for study problematic, because two independent but similar crimes may easily be erroneously labeled a copycat pair, and true copycat crimes may easily go unrecognized and unidentified. Research is further complicated because the size of the "at-risk" pool of individuals who are likely to be criminally influenced by the media is unknown but probably small and therefore difficult to isolate. Moreover, not enough copycat criminals have been identified to allow for generalization or for scientifically adequate research.

> The courts have also had to address the existence of copycat crime. In a recent case, the producer of a violent movie and the theater that showed it were held not liable for the death of a youth in a gang fight after the assailant saw the film, *Warriors*, twice. The Massachusetts Supreme Court held that the film did not incite the attacker, rejecting a claim that the assailant was imitating a scene from the film during the attack and that the theater displayed negligence in showing the film after learning of violent incidents at other theaters. "Although the film is rife with violent scenes, it does not at any point exhort, urge, entreat, solicit, or overtly advocate or encourage unlawful or violent activity on the part of viewers," the court said (*Yakubowicz* v. *Paramount Pictures;* see also "Violent Movie Didn't Cause Youth's Death," *News Media and the Law,* 1989, 13(4), pp. 33–34).

Historically, references to possible copycat effects began appearing as soon as the mass media developed in the early 1800s. In 1828, for example, police court reporting was criticized on the grounds that "[it is] of little benefit to the cause of morals thus to familiarize the community, and especially the younger parts of it, to the details of misdemeanor and crime. . . . besides, it suggests to the novice in vice all the means of becoming expert in its devices" (Bleyer, 1927, p. 157, quoting the *New York Evening Post,* June 6, 1828). However, although the term *copycat crime* has appeared in the literature for many years,[9] few empirical studies touch on this phenomenon. Researchers have therefore relied on anecdotal evidence to argue the existence of a copycat crime phenomenon. The slowly growing file of compiled anecdotal reports does, in fact, indicate that criminal events that are rare in real life are sometimes committed soon after similar events are shown as part of a fictional show or a news story (Cook et al., 1983a). Collectively, this file provides significant and growing evidence of copycat crime.

Other research evidence that copycat crime is a real phenomenon and not just a linking of similar, sequential, but independent crimes originated in the laboratory research discussed earlier, in which viewers of media violence imitated the violence. The fact that people will mimic media behavior in the laboratory lends credence to the hypothesis that people are mimicking media-portrayed crimes in society. Evidence of copycat crime's significance would be established if a link could be found between the level of coverage of an event and the number of similar events occurring after this coverage. Evidence of such a link was found in a number of studies in which the suicide rate increased with the level of media coverage of a suicide.[10] The more publicity given, the greater the increase in suicides, with the increase in suicides greatest in the region where the story was most heavily publicized (Lesyna & Phillips, 1989). The link is particularly strong for stories aired on multiple TV stations and for teenagers (see Bollen & Phillips, 1982; Phillips & Bollen, 1985; Phillips & Carstensen, 1986). Although not without contradiction,[11] this set of research indicates that fictional and nonfictional stories widely publicized by the mass media can trig-

After reviewing U.S., Canadian, and European studies, Lesyna and Phillips (1989) concluded that suicides rise significantly following the front-page publicizing of a suicide. Similarly, television news stories of suicide are also followed by increases in suicides. Fictional television stories also appear to elicit imitative suicides (see Gould & Shaffer, 1986; Ostroff & Boyd, 1987; Ostroff et al., 1985; Phillips, 1982b; Phillips & Paight, 1987; Schmidtke & Hafner, 1988).

The effect is termed the Werther effect, after a fictional hero who committed suicide in a novel by Goethe. This fictional suicide was felt to have triggered imitative suicides throughout Europe in the nineteenth century. Similarly, Phillips (1974) calculated that within two months after the suicide of Marilyn Monroe in 1962 there were three hundred more suicides than would have occurred had she not died. The most disturbing finding is that media portrayals of suicide, whether in the news (Phillips & Carstensen, 1986) or within antisuicide programming (Gould & Shaffer, 1986), appear to trigger imitative suicides, particularly among teenagers.

ger fatal, imitative behavior. There is also some evidence of a link between the level of coverage and the number of similar subsequent events with regard to criminal, nonsuicidal acts. Phillips (1983) reported that just after the appearance of newspaper and television accounts of a heavyweight prize fight, the number of reported homicides increases by about one-eighth, with the increase greatest for the most highly publicized fights, and the homicides tending to involve victims of the same race as the loser of the fight.[12] The anecdotal cases in combination with the research on suicide and other cited studies establish reasonable grounds for concluding that copycat crimes occur regularly at an unknown but significant rate.[13]

Its Magnitude

The anecdotal cases broadly suggest that the copycat phenomenon may affect societal crime in two ways. First, the media coverage both triggers the occurrence of crime and shapes its form, creating crime that otherwise would not exist and turning formerly law-abiding individuals into criminals.

One now-dated study did examine the ability of the media to directly criminalize the law-abiding. Milgram and Shotland (1973) found no evidence of an immediate effect from a single portrayal of a crime followed by an opportunity to commit a similar crime a week later. The difficulty with this study is that an effect would have to be incredibly strong for a single show to affect a randomly selected group of subjects to steal or not to steal (Comstock, 1983, p. 252). The suicide studies are felt to measure the influence of the media on predisposed individuals who are not yet committed to suicide.

The result is an immediate increase in both the number of crimes and the number of criminals within a society. Second, the media coverage shapes the criminal behavior of already active criminals, molding the characteristics of crime without actually triggering it.

The scant evidence that is available concerning copycat crime does not support the first scenario (Comstock, 1980, p. 131). The copycat effect has not been found to be pervasive, and there is no empirical evidence that the media have a criminalizing effect (see Milgram & Shotland, 1973). The me-

---

BOX 5-4   Copycat Crimes

Anecdotal examples of copycat crimes include the following:

- A Canadian boy attempted to extort $50,000 from a local mayor after watching an episode of "Starsky and Hutch" (Nettler, 1982).
- A college student mailed letters to a bank president threatening his wife unless he was paid $5,000. After his arrest, the student reported that he got the idea from television.
- A nine-year-old girl was raped by several girls on a California beach a few days after a television movie was shown. In the movie a young female is raped in a similar fashion by three other teenagers in a juvenile reformatory (Pease & Love, 1984b).
- In Boston, a woman was doused with gasoline and set afire following a movie on television in which teenage boys roam Boston burning tramps for fun and amusement (Pease & Love, 1984b).
- The same evening that a television movie about a battered wife who pours gasoline on her sleeping husband was shown, a man poured gasoline on his sleeping wife and set her afire, saying he was trying to frighten her (Pease & Love, 1984b).
- An eleven-year-old boy murdered a postman in imitation of an adventure show (Pease & Love, 1984b).
- Another eleven-year-old boy, who became fascinated by strangulation scenes on TV, acted out his fascination by strangling a four-year-old girl (Toplin, 1975).
- Murders and the formation of delinquent gangs followed the showing of the movie *A Clockwork Orange* in England (Schmid & de Graaf, 1982, pp. 129–130).
- Following a television movie called *Doomsday Flight,* airlines reported a number of extortion calls making bomb threats (Schmid & de Graaf, 1982, pp. 131–132).
- A May 1981 bombing in New York City's Kennedy Airport was followed by more than six hundred bomb threats the next week (Mazur, 1982, p. 407).
- Alex Schmid and Janny de Graaf (1982, pp. 128–136) have listed a series of incidents following media news reports of crimes including kidnappings of corpses around the world for use in extortion of governments, bomb threats to televised government hearings, and twenty-seven parachute hijackings from 1971 to 1977.

And of course, two of the most infamous copycat crime episodes are

- The Extra-Strength Tylenol copycat poisonings, in which the initial murders occurred after the victims had purchased Extra-Strength Tylenol that had been laced with cyanide. The story received intense national coverage, and within a short time copycat poisonings and product tamperings were reported across the nation.
- And John Hinckley, Jr.'s assassination attempt on President Reagan. Hinckley was emulating the main character in the movie *Taxi Driver* (see also Box 5-5).

dia do appear to heighten the sophistication and brutality of criminals, espe-cially among those who rely heavily on the media for information about the world and for escape and who have a tenuous grasp on reality. For exam-ple, in the anecdotal case histories, most of the individuals who mimic me-dia crimes have prior criminal records or histories of violence, indicating that the effect of the media is more likely qualitative (affecting criminal be-havior) rather than quantitative (affecting the number of criminals).[14] The current perspective is that the media influence how people commit crimes to a greater extent than they influence whether or not people actually com-mit crimes (see Comstock, 1980, p. 138; Pease & Love, 1984b; Surette, 1990b). Hence, the media are important, but not as important as they would be if they were continually criminalizing individuals.

Nevertheless, it should be emphasized that most of the evidence sup-porting even this circumscribed view is anecdotal and that the empirical re-search is limited. A few researchers have examined offender populations to assess the proportion of copycat criminals and the role of the media in mo-tivating crime. In one study, Heller and Polsky (1976) interviewed 100 young male offenders and found that 22 percent reported trying criminal techniques they had seen on television, with only 3 of the 22 reporting fail-ure or arrest. Another 22 percent further disclosed that they had contem-plated committing crimes they had seen on television. In another interesting report, compiled by an offender serving a life term, Hendrick (1977) sur-veyed 208 of 688 inmates at Michigan's Marquette Prison regarding their use of television as a source of crime techniques. He reported that many prison-ers took notes while watching crime shows and that 9 out of 10 inmates said that they learned new tricks and increased their criminal expertise by watching crime programs. In addition, 4 out of 10 reported that they had attempted specific crimes they had seen on television. Pease and Love (1984a), after a random survey at the federal correctional institution at But-ner, North Carolina, reported similar findings.

All these results are interesting and suggestive, but because of the lim-ited samples and methodologies and because all three efforts examined only adult male offender populations, the results are inconclusive. Whether or not one can generalize from them to a wider population of offenders or to nonoffenders is unknown. In addition, none of the researchers examined for differences between the self-reported copycat criminals and noncopycat criminals. With these limitations in mind, the anecdotal evidence and the findings of the narrow, offender-focused research together indicate that the current best supposition is that copycat crimes are largely limited to but sig-nificant among the existing offender population (influencing somewhere between 20 and 40 percent), and rare but not unknown among the general noncriminal population. As Heller and Polsky stated (1976, pp. 151–152):

> A significant number of our subjects, already embarked on a criminal career, consciously recall and relate having imitated techniques of crimes. . . . For such men, detailed portrayals of criminal techniques must be viewed as a learn-ing process. None of our subjects ascribed any causative role to television view-ing. . . . They would, in all probability, have engaged in the same pursuits, but

A large body of printed matter detailing how to commit specific crimes is readily available through publishers such as Paladin Press. Paladin's 1986 catalog, for example, lists the following basic crime instruction manuals: *Gunrunning for Fun and Profit; Expedient Hand Grenades; Improvised Explosives: How to Make Your Own; New I.D. in America; The Complete Book of International Terrorism; How to Kill* (6 volumes); and *The Perfect Crime and How to Commit It.* These texts come complete with diagrams and directions to commit robberies, murder, and numerous acts of terrorism. Historically, such how-to manuals can be traced to the writings of Johann Most, who in his 1885 *Revolutionary War Science* published instructions for making nitroglycerin and dynamite, inflammable liquids, and poisons, and advocated their use in radical bombings and attacks. The 1886 Chicago Haymarket Square bombing is thought to have been a result (Papke, 1987, pp. 171–172).

their style was influenced to some degree by previously having watched skillful experts perform similar tasks on television.

Hendrick (1977) and Pease and Love (1984a) also reported that offenders seldom cite the media as a motivating source. Pease and Love reported that only about 12 percent of the inmates in their study named the media as a cause in their criminality, ranking them second to last behind all other possible factors except for "too much junk food." However, 21 percent of the inmates endorsed the media as a source of information about crime techniques, with books and magazines most often cited, followed closely by movies about crime. Overall, the media ranked fourth as a source of information about crime, behind "developed techniques by myself," "friends," and "fellow inmates."[15] Pease and Love concluded that except for isolated cases of mentally ill individuals, copycat offenders have the criminal intent to commit a particular crime before they copy a publicized technique. Few reports have suggested that copycat crime occurs because otherwise law-abiding people are influenced by the media to do so (cf. Schmid & de Graaf, 1982). The same holds true for terrorist acts. The scenario of the media triggering copycat crimes is not found to be pervasive or significant. But the shaping of the activities of existing criminals, though admittedly based on very limited research at this time, appears to be substantively important and may significantly affect overall crime. In regard to copycat crime, the media appear more capable of acting as a rudder than as a trigger for crime.

Cressey (1938), studying motion pictures in the 1930s as part of the Payne Fund studies, reached the same conclusion more than fifty years ago. In his view, young men, when suitably predisposed, sometimes utilize techniques of crime they have seen in the movies, but movies do not entice "good" boys into crime (p. 517, cited by Thrasher, 1949, p. 199).

Theory and Model

By what mechanism do the media generate copycat effects? Here again, direct research is limited. In that the concept implies the imitation of an initial crime, the most obvious starting point in discussing copycat crime is imitation. Gabriel Tarde (1912) in the beginning decades of this century was the first to offer a theoretical discussion of copycat crime. Focusing on violent crime and observing that sensational violent crime appears to prompt similar incidents, he coined the term "suggesto-imitative assaults" to describe the phenomena. In a pithy summation, he concluded that "Epidemics of crime follow the line of the telegraph." Tarde's line of research was largely ignored until the 1970s, however, when a surge of copycat crimes and media interest in them led to renewed attention to the role of imitation in the generation of crime. Picking up directly from Tarde's earlier perspective, researchers have most often attributed copycat crime to a process of simple and direct imitation (Bassiouni, 1981; Livingstone, 1982; Schmid & de Graaf, 1982). More recently, however, imitation has been critiqued as too simplistic a process to fully explain copycat crime.

Pease and Love (1984b) have faulted imitation theory as an adequate explanation of copycat crime because it fails to explain why most children imitate aggression within socially acceptable limits and only a few imitate aggression with a real gun. They have also noted that imitation theory focuses on the copycat criminal and tends to downplay other contextual social factors. Given these considerations, imitation is considered a necessary but insufficient factor in the generation of copycat crime. The primary flaw in the imitation theory is that it generally implies that the copycat behavior must physically resemble the portrayed behavior and therefore falls short in explaining any generalized effects or innovative applications (Berkowitz, 1984, p. 414). Note that Hennigan and her colleagues (1982) earlier dismissed imitation as an explanation for the aggregate criminal effects they discovered and that the studies of offenders found more links to general property crime than to specific violent crime (Heller & Polsky, 1976; Hendrick, 1977).

Partly in response, Berkowitz (1984) has posited another mechanism, more general than imitation, by which media portrayals may activate similar behaviors. Through this mechanism, termed a "priming" effect, the portrayals of certain behaviors by the media somehow activate a network of associated ideas and concepts within the viewer that increase the likelihood that he or she will behave similarly but not necessarily identically (Berkowitz, 1984, p. 414). Berkowitz felt that priming offers a conceptual explanation of both prosocial and antisocial media effects, as well as explaining the effects reported in the studies of suicide and aggregate crime effects discussed earlier. He concluded that priming occurs within a multifactor model incorporating media content, viewer interpretation, viewer characteristics, and the viewing setting. A study by Mazur (1982) offers some support for this process in the area of crime. Mazur reported that bomb threats directed at nuclear energy facilities increased significantly following increases in news coverage of nuclear power issues. Mazur's study is important in that it indicates that the media may initiate crimes even when they don't provide pre-

Priming is analogous to the "cognitive maps" Graber (1980) proposed to explain the effects of crime news on viewers. Priming is a concept also employed in research on agenda setting to explain the influence of previously received media content on viewers' interpretation of and attention to current media coverage. The mass media are perceived as "priming" consumers by giving salience to certain events, pushing the issues associated with these events to the forefront (Rogers & Dearing, 1988, p. 568; see also Fiske & Taylor, 1984, p. 231; Iyengar & Kinder, 1987). Priming can also be understood within the general perspective of this work as the forwarding of a set of ideas and beliefs that support a particular social reality—the perception that the world is such that a particular type of crime is appropriate, justified, and likely to be successful.

cise models to copy, as the bomb threats to nuclear facilities followed news stories that were not necessarily bomb-related. In Berkowitz's conceptualization, the news media coverage primed those who made the bomb threats but did not model the behavior.[16] The evidence that is available concerning copycat crime supports the view that predisposed at-risk individuals who have been primed by media characterizations of crime are the primary perpetrators of copycat crime (cf. Comstock, 1980, p. 131).

The above proposition suggests the model of copycat crime shown in Figure 5-3. Copycat crime is seen as a result of the interaction of four factors: the initial crime and criminal, the media coverage, the social context, and the characteristics of the copycat criminal. The reiterative model denotes a process in which select, usually successful, highly newsworthy crimes or crimes shown in popular entertainment media, after being publicized through media coverage, emerge as candidates for copying. The media coverage first affects individuals by inviting them to identify with the initial crime or criminal, and by generally priming a pool of potential copycat criminals. The size of this pool is affected by both the level of media coverage and other social context factors such as norms regarding deviance and violence; the preexistence of social conflicts; the number of opportunities available to the potential offender to copy a crime technique (there are more opportunities to copy a car theft technique, for example, than a bank robbery technique); the nature, credibility, and pervasiveness of the mass media; and the size of the preexisting criminal population. Media coverage and content and the social context are felt to mutually influence one another (Meyrowitz, 1985a). After the at-risk pool emerges, the first wave of copycat crimes results through a process of imitation, limited by and adapted to the criminal's opportunities (see Figure 5-3, Phase A).

Should these first-order copycat crimes receive further media attention, and particularly should they be incorporated into a news media crime theme, the likelihood of additional copycat crime increases (see Phase B of Figure 5-3). This extended reiterative process is regarded as much more likely to occur with violent crime because of the high news value of vio-

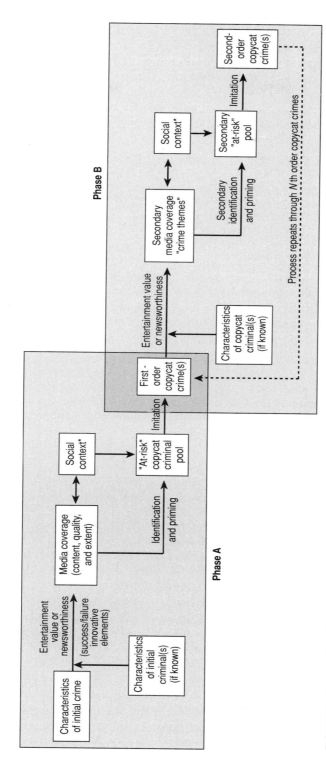

FIGURE 5-3 A reiterative model of copycat crime

*Social context includes social norms regarding crime, news reporting and entertainment; opportunities to copy; social tensions (racism, economic strife, and so forth); organization of mass media (state, private, profit, nonprofit, accessibility, regulation, audience size, and credibility).

Source: Adapted from Raymond Surette, The Media and Criminal Justice Policy, 1990. Courtesy of Charles C Thomas. Publisher, Springfield, Illinois.

lence. Thus, the model reflects a paradox. The process is more common for property crime and property offenders through first-order copycat crimes (Phase A). But violent copycat crime and offenders are most likely to generate second- and higher-order imitations (Phase B), as they are more likely to become the focus of intensive news coverage. Once more in regard to crime, the mass media are seen taking the rare real-world event and making it the more-significant, better-known event in the public's perception.

Copycat Crime and Terrorism

Terrorism's relationship to the media epitomizes the interplay between crime and the media and the dangers of copycat effects. Hickey (1976, p. 10) described the extent of the interrelationship: "If the mass media did not exist, terrorists would have to invent them. In turn, the mass media hanker after terroristic acts because they fit into their programming needs: namely, sudden acts of great excitement that are susceptible, presumably, of quick solution." The development of this symbiotic relationship can be traced to the fact that the news media and terrorists share several needs. Most fundamentally, both are trying to reach the greatest number of people possible.[17] For the news organization, terrorism is dramatic, often violent, visual, and timely and attracts high public interest.

> Unlike wars and most revolutions which are usually protracted and highly complex events . . . acts of terrorist violence normally have a beginning and an end, can be encompassed in a few minutes of air time, possess a large degree of drama, involve participants who are perceived by the viewing public as unambiguous, and are not so complex as to be unintelligible to those who tune in only briefly. (Livingstone, 1982, p. 62)

All of this transforms terrorism into high ratings and readership levels.

And as the media have pursued terrorists, terrorists have become "media-wise." They now understand the dynamics of newsworthiness and the benefits of news coverage: increased legitimacy and political status,

---

Carlos Marighella, in *Minimanual of the Urban Guerrilla* (n.d., cited by Alexander, 1979, p. 161) described the manipulation of the media by terrorists as follows:

> These actions, carried out with specific and determined objectives, inevitably become propaganda material for the mass communication system. . . . The war of nerves or psychological war is an aggressive technique, based on the direct or indirect use of mass means of communication and news in order to demoralize the government. In psychological warfare, the government is always at a disadvantage since it imposes censorship on the mass media and winds up in a defensive position by not allowing anything against it to filter through. At this point it becomes desperate, is involved in great contradictions and loss of prestige, and loses time and energy in an exhausting effort at control which is subject to being broken at any moment.

heightened perception of their strength and threat, and an increased ability to attract resources, support, and recruits. To the degree that a failed terrorist act is one that nobody notices, the media is an integral and manipulated component of successful terrorist crime. It is no longer uncommon or unexpected for terrorists to call a news conference soon after the initiation of a crime. Terrorists have come to focus especially on and manipulate television coverage (Schmid & de Graaf, 1982, p. 51), and electronic media publicity is now the sole objective in many terrorist acts (Crenshaw, 1981; Poland, 1988, p. 45). Like American politicians, terrorists, too, have learned to manipulate coverage to bypass the editing and contextual formatting of journalists and go directly to the public with their messages (Alter, 1985). In the process, terrorism has become a form of mass entertainment and public theater (Jenkins, 1975, p. 4; Schmid & de Graaf, 1982, p. 69).

Since terrorism sells so well and coverage of these episodes has become extensive, it is hardly surprising that negative effects have been cited, the primary one being a copycat effect.[18] Within the academic literature about terrorism, no doubts are expressed that the media motivate copycat terrorist acts (Poland, 1988, p. 47). Further, some argue that the media can provide the potential terrorist with all the ingredients needed to engage in terrorism. The media can reduce inhibitions against the use of violence. They can offer models and provide technical know-how. And though extra-media factors are probably equally important, the media are felt to provide sufficient impetus in themselves to lead to imitative acts in a number of instances (Bassiouni, 1981, p. 18; Schmid & de Graaf, 1982).

Additionally, competition for news coverage tends to cause terrorist violence to escalate (Poland, 1988). More-violent and more-dramatic acts are necessary to gain news coverage as the shock value of ordinary acts diminishes. As terrorist groups have learned to design their acts for the media and publicity, to the degree that violence is deemed newsworthy, terrorist acts have become more violent. Occupation of a building, for example, no longer garners world or even national coverage in most instances and without the potential of a confrontation will not receive even extensive local coverage in many cases. As long as news reporting is a commercial product whose content is influenced by sensationalism, excessive coverage will afford violent terrorist acts a disproportionate significance (Bassiouni, 1981, p. 25). The relationship between terrorism and the media is ultimately not qualitatively different from other criminogenic effects of the media on society. The relationship is clearer only because the links are more observable and because the two groups, terrorists and the media, so openly pursue each other.

Copycat Crime: A Summary

The available research suggests the following. Copycat crime appears to be a persistent social phenomenon, common enough to influence the total crime picture, mostly by influencing criminals' choice of crime techniques rather than by motivating criminal acts. Copycat criminals are more likely

The interplay between media coverage and copycat terrorist crime is dual. First, anecdotal evidence indicates that coverage of a terrorist crime encourages the making of false threats in pseudo copycat reactions. For example, a May 1981 bombing in New York City's Kennedy Airport was followed by more than six hundred bomb threats the next week (Mazur, 1982, p. 407). Secondly, real copycat events follow in significant numbers. As with general copycat crime, there is much anecdotal evidence that terrorist events such as the stealing of a corpse (of a national hero or leader) for ransom, bank robberies in which hostages are taken, kidnappings, plane hijackings, parachute hijackings (27 from 1971 to 1977), and the planting of altitude bombs on airplanes occur in clusters (Livingstone, 1982, p. 71; see also Schmid & de Graaf, 1982, pp. 128–136). These effects appear to be especially strong following a successful terrorist act using a novel approach (Bassiouni, 1979, p. 19). Although their number waxes and wanes, the historical pattern of these acts suggests that copycat terrorist crime has been and remains a persistent element of the total crime picture.

In addition, the blatant competition among the media for coverage—especially exclusive coverage—tends to degrade media news reporting and journalist behavior. Examples include a terrorist-staged interview of TWA passengers being held hostage at the Beirut airport. During this debacle, journalists had to be restrained by the terrorists, families of victims have been harassed for interviews, and terrorists have been offered payment for interviews or access to hostages. A hostage "press conference" situation that arose in the 1970s illuminates the dilemma the media face when deciding whether or not to curtail coverage (see Breman, 1977). During the incident one local television station switched back to its normal programming; two others carried the incident live and in its entirety. One letter captured the media's dilemma precisely: "Congratulations! You did the right thing. I switched over to another channel to see what would happen next—but you did the right thing." In an economically competitive environment where ratings determine livelihood, the media face choices that may be ethically correct but financially disastrous.

career criminals involved in property offenses rather than first or violent offenders (although a violent copycat episode will receive an immense amount of media coverage when identified). The specific relationship between media coverage and the generation of copycat crime remains unknown, as do the social context factors that are most important. The most likely mechanism behind copycat crime is a process of identification and priming leading to some degree of generalized imitation. There is no empirical evidence of a significant criminalizing media effect. The media influence how people commit crimes to a far greater extent than they influence whether or not people actually commit a crime.

Regarding public policies, the basic policy problem with regard to copycat crime is deciding when to publicize information about sensationalistic crimes. In such cases as the Tylenol poisonings (see Box 5-4), there is an obvious need to warn consumers, but in other types of crimes, such as bombings and hijackings, the issue may not be so clear-cut. The news media argue that the decision to publish is correct in nearly every case, but law enforcement and other public officials argue for restrictions. The confusion surrounding the best policy course in regard to copycat crime is exemplified by one commenator, who said, "There seems to be only one way to end the copycat tamperings. I think it will be short lived . . . before long, copycat tamperings will become so common that they will no longer provide thrill seekers with the excitement that they crave" (quoted by Church, 1982,

---

BOX 5-5   John Hinckley, Jr.'s Copycat Crime

The case of John Hinckley, Jr., a case in which news and entertainment merged, is a prime example of a copycat crime. Hinckley's assassination attempt on President Reagan and Hinckley's bizarre life fit the psychotic-killer theme popular in crime-related entertainment (see Chapter 2). Because of this overlap, the Hinckley story provided the media with both great entertainment material and great news material, having elements of drama, celebrities, money, and filmed violence. The entertainment media provided the role model and reality structure Hinckley followed in formulating his assassination attempt, which then provided the news media the frame they used to fit the resulting news story into an entertainment-style theme:

> Hinckley's story was perfect for news media, and television news in particular, as it went beyond the usual character of a major news story. . . .
> The Hinckley case not only had drama, a famous person, and filmed violence, it had an unexpected and fascinating twist. . . . [Hinckley] was motivated by an apparent irrational desire to impress a movie star. As reported by network television news, the Hinckley story was also framed within the typical prime-time television perspectives of simplicity and ideal norms. To this end, Hinckley was characterized much like the psychotic killer in a fictional television drama. (Snow, 1984, p. 217)

The Hinckley case thus displays the full range of possible effects by the media on crime and justice, from creating a tolerant atmosphere for violence, to providing criminal role models and techniques, to influencing the public reaction to the justice system's processing of the case (Hans & Slater, 1983; Snow, 1984). Snow summarized the multiple media effect as follows:

> First, since Hinckley's life prior to the shooting was lived largely through the media scenario of a Hollywood film and in vicarious involvement with a media personality, media may be understood as providing a cultural context for constructing and legitimizing bizarre and even criminal behavior. Second, an examination of how network television reported the verdict supports a contention that media plays a potentially significant role in the evaluation and administration of justice. In both points, the principal idea is not that the media inevitably produces particular effects, but that the media has become an important cultural arena for defining, enacting, and legitimizing a wide range of behavior, including crime and justice. (From "Crime and Justice in Prime-Time News: The John Hinckley, Jr., Case," by R. Snow. In R. Surette (ed.), *Justice and the Media,* 1984. Courtesy of Charles C Thomas, Publisher, Springfield, Illinois.)

In the final analysis, the news media's emphasis on drama, violence, and entertainment and the entertainment media's programming emphasis on themes of violent criminality appear to work together to foster copycat crimes such as Hinckley's simply for notoriety (Snow, 1984, p. 226).

p. 27). The paradoxical reasoning here is that, over time, a publicized copy-cat crime will become less newsworthy, receive less coverage, and therefore become less likely to recur—a plausible but unproven proposition. More proactive policies focus on the initial coverage given crimes. Suggested reforms include delaying coverage, avoiding live coverage, using screen crawl lines rather than interrupting programs, downplaying staged events, avoiding the portrayal of criminals as celebrities or heroes, avoiding crime coverage that reveals the techniques used, noting that most known copycat crimes are usually unsuccessful, and providing fuller, long-term reporting and follow-up stories that deal with prosecution and punishment. For the present, the best long-term policy course may lie in defining the characteristics of those at risk of committing copycat crimes and trying to limit their number through deterrence efforts. In the final analysis, however, some level of copycat crime may be an unavoidable part of the price of a free and private mass media.

CONCLUSION

The media do affect crime rates. Though imperfect, the evidence is extensive. Still, though most agree that the media have some effect, we don't know exactly what that effect is. Because of the nearly exclusive focus on violence generated by the media through modeling on an individual level, possible effects such as changes in people's willingness to delay gratification, in people's sense of equity and fairness, or in the deterrent effect of penalties for crimes have yet to be explored (Wilson & Herrnstein, 1985, p. 339). However, the existing research and literature from all of the areas (the media and social aggression, suicide, aggregate crime rates, copycat crime, and terrorism) suggest the model shown in Figure 5-4.

The evidence concerning the media as a criminogenic factor clearly supports the conclusion that the media have a significant short-term effect on some individuals. As shown, this effect depends on the combined influence of social context factors, the media context, and the media content interacting with characteristics of the audience. The more heavily the consumer relies on the media for information about the world and the greater his or her predisposition to criminal behavior, the greater the effect. Therefore, violence-prone children and the mentally unbalanced are especially at risk of emulating media violence. When sex and violence are linked, hypermasculine males are most influenced. When the news media sensationalize crime and make celebrities of criminals, the danger of imitation for notoriety increases. And when successful crime is detailed either in print or in a visual medium, some criminals will emulate it. The major unsolved question is the size of the at-risk populations—at present, only a small number appear to be significantly affected. But the media also slightly affect some larger portion of the general population, particularly in fostering attitudes that support crime. Both are therefore important potential influences on the total crime picture. The electronic media's pursuit of backstage social behav-

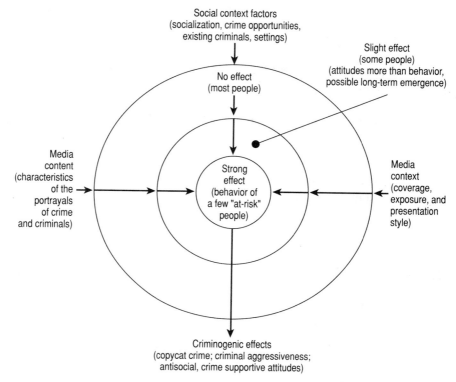

FIGURE 5-4 A general model of the media-crime relationship

ior they can portray as entertainment and report as news has inexorably driven crime from its backstage social position. In media-induced crimes committed for notoriety and publicity we now witness the paradoxical situation of backstage behavior being purposely performed for front-stage consumption. "Real" crime, particularly when committed by terrorists, is now sometimes a "pseudo-event" in the spirit of Daniel Boorstin's (1961) usage—created and contrived solely for the media. The media reality of crime thus sometimes becomes the social reality of crime.

The media are powerful but complex social agents whose effects need not be all negative. For if unplanned, haphazard media content fosters crime, perhaps planned applications of the media can help reduce it. Given the strong belief in the media's social power, it is not surprising that some have tried to use the media in positive, pro-social ways. Accordingly, Chapter 6 will examine the use of the media and media technology in reducing crime in society.

Notes

1. W. I. Thomas wrote in *American Magazine* in 1908:

   The condition of morality, as well as of mental life, in a community depends on the prevailing copies of the newspaper. A people is profoundly influenced by whatever is persistently brought to its attention. In the same way, advertising crime, vice, and vulgarity on a scale unheard of before in the annals of history has the same effect—it increases crime, vice, and vulgarity enormously. (cited by Fenton, 1910, p. 491)

2. Other mechanisms are mentioned in the 1982 NIMH report but lack convincing supportive evidence (see also Pearl, 1984). These mechanisms include:

   - Disinhibition processes, in which viewers become less inhibited about acting aggressively.
   - Desensitization processes, in which viewers become more tolerant and accepting of violence and aggression in others.
   - Psychological arousal processes. Physiological arousal is thought to have three possible consequences: (1) desensitization, (2) an increase in general arousal that may boost aggressiveness, and (3) desensitization that leads people to act

aggressively to raise their levels of arousal.

- Justification, in which people who are already aggressive look to depictions of violence to justify their own behavior. Watching violence is a result, rather than a cause.

3. See Andison, 1977; Comstock, 1983; Comstock & Fisher, 1975; Comstock & Lindsey, 1975; Comstock et al., 1978; Garofalo, 1981; Lewis, 1984; Murray, 1980; NIMH, 1982; Phillips, 1982a, 1982b.

4. See Andison, 1977; Berkowitz, 1964, 1969, 1970; Berkowitz, Corwin, & Heironimus, 1963; Berkowitz & Geene, 1966; Berkowitz & Rawlings, 1963; Garofalo, 1981; Greene & Bynum, 1982; Hennigan et al., 1982; Tannenbaum & Zillman, 1975; Watt & Krull, 1978.

5. See Comstock et al., 1978; Lewis, 1984; Liebert, Neale, & Davidson, 1973; NCCPV, vol. 9 & 9a, 1969, p. 276; Parke et al., 1977; Pearl et al., 1982, p. 6.

6. *Hypermasculinity culture* refers to the support for traditional, male-dominant, "masculine" attitudes and values; that is, that women shouldn't work, that husbands should make all decisions, that men shouldn't show emotions, exhibit pain, or discuss feelings, that women should please men, that women should be physically attractive. Sections of the population and ethnic groups that place value on these attitudes tend to have high rates of rape and use of pornography.

7. See Bowen, 1987; Donnerstein, 1984; Donnerstein & Linz, 1986; Gray, 1982; Imrich et al., 1990.

8. See Donnerstein & Linz, 1986, p. 611; Imrich et al., 1990, p. 120; Malamuth & Check, 1983. There is some evidence that the production of violent pornography increased during the 1970s (Malamuth & Spinner, 1980) and abated in the 1980s (Scott, 1985).

9. See Berkowitz et al., 1978; Eysenck & Nias, 1978; Siegel, 1974; Toplin, 1975.

10. See Bollen & Phillips, 1982; Gould & Shaffer, 1986; Phillips, 1974, 1977, 1978, 1979, 1980, 1982a, 1982b; Phillips & Carstensen, 1986, 1988; Phillips & Paight, 1987; Stack, 1987.

11. See Baron & Reiss, 1985; Berman, 1988; Kessler & Stipp. 1984; Kessler et al., 1988; Platt, 1987; Williams et al., 1987.

12. Phillips and Hensley (1984) subsequently reported evidence that homicide appears to increase when violence is rewarded in the media (for example, in prize fights) and decreases or is deterred when it is punished through stories of successful murder trials and executions. However, in a recent study that examined monthly homicide rates and television publicity, Bailey (1990) reported that homicide rates are not related to either the amount or type of execution publicity. Television news coverage, at least, was not found to deter future murders or, through a "brutalization" effect on society, to promote future killings. The issue of the media deterring crime is discussed in Chapter 6.

13. See Comstock, 1983; Pease & Love, 1984b; Schmid & de Graaf, 1982; Wilson & Herrnstein, 1985.

14. See also Comstock, 1980; Dominick, 1978; Greene & Bynum, 1982; Huesmann, 1982:132; Lewis, 1984; NCCPV, vol. 9, 1969, pp. 376–378.

15. These categories are similar to those used to identify the general information sources influencing people's attitudes. Personal experiences, family and friends, and peer groups rank before the media as general sources of influence.

16. John Hinckley, Jr.'s assassination attempt on President Reagan is a well-known anecdotal example of a crime where media priming appears to have occurred. See Box 5-5.

17. The basic theory of terrorism is similar to that of general deterrence in that both require extensive publicity to reach their objectives (Cooper, 1976).

18. Termed a contagion effect within the literature on media terrorism (Bassiouni, 1981, p. 18; Johnson, 1978; Schmid & de Graaf, 1982, pp. 117–119).

6 The Media as a Cure for Crime

OVERVIEW

Much has been written concerning the mass media as a cause of crime. Somewhat unusually then, this chapter deals with the increasing number of efforts to use the media to combat crime. These modern efforts are all conceptually rooted in the success and promise of the prosocial entertainment programs and public information campaigns of the 1960s. Those successes and subsequent advances in media technology spurred the development of a number of media-based anticrime programs in the 1970s and 1980s. These efforts have targeted two audience groups, criminals and citizens, with two basic program designs developed for each audience. Programs targeting criminals include mass media public information and communication campaigns geared to deter offenders and media-enhanced surveillance projects designed to reduce crime. Programs targeting citizens include mass media public information campaigns geared to reduce victimization by encouraging people to adopt crime preventive behaviors, and programs designed to solve crimes by encouraging citizen cooperation in law enforcement investigations. In that all four of these program types are designed to reduce crime levels, media anticrime programs in general emphasize crime control values, whereas critiques of them raise due process concerns.

Programs designed for deterrence are best exemplified by the now-common antidrug ad campaigns. To be effective they must arouse the concern of their target audience—in the case of the antidrug ads, either concern about being arrested or health-related concerns having to do with drug use. All three types of programs—surveillance, deterrence, and victimization reduction programs—must change their target audience's perception of social reality, in the hope that a perception change will result in a behavior change. The limited evaluations of these campaigns show that they are effective means of disseminating information and appear to influence attitudes. Not established, however, is their ability to significantly affect the behavior of their audience.

Advances in media technology have improved the surveillance capabilities of law enforcement agencies over the past decade. Taking advantage of a "surveillance effect"—the psychological effect of fearing that you might be under observation—surveillance programs have expanded the traditional police use of the stakeout and hidden camera to encompass more locations and conditions. Reduced costs have given more agencies these capabilities. Media technology has made constant surveillance of broad public areas possible, and cameras have begun to be permanently mounted on patrol cars and in police interrogation rooms. Not surprisingly, the use of this potentially powerful and intrusive technology has raised concerns at the same time that it has demonstrated clear benefits.

Programs designed to reduce victimization and those designed for deterrence both use the existing mass media distribution system to market anticrime information. As already noted, they differ in their intended audience—respectively, potential victims of crime and offenders. The goal of victimization reduction programs is a kind of self-executed "target hardening" (increasing the difficulty of or risk from committing a crime) by citizens to reduce the number of crime opportunities available to criminals. Evaluations suggest that such programs, like deterrence campaigns, are good means of disseminating information and appear to significantly influence attitudes but have not as yet been clearly shown to substantially affect citizen or criminal behavior.

The fourth type of program, designed to encourage citizen participation, is an updated electronic media version of the old West's "Most Wanted" poster. Best known as Crime Stoppers, these programs publicize unsolved crimes and wanted fugitives and pay rewards to anonymous citizens. Popular and positively evaluated, these programs still raise concerns regarding the practice of paying for information from anonymous tipsters, the news media's role in law enforcement, and the social reality these programs project with regard to crime. No means of resolving these concerns has yet been found, and given the nature of these programs, none is likely to be.

The chapter concludes with a discussion of the general usefulness of the media in combating crime. The media are not a panacea for crime, and though useful in specific areas, programs such as those discussed here have not proven able to reduce the overall crime rate. No program has empirically demonstrated a significant ability to reduce crime without displacing it. Because of their other demonstrated benefits, however—the ability to impart information and influence attitudes, and the short-term ability to suppress specific crimes in specific locations—the consensus is that such programs should be expanded but closely monitored and evaluated.

PROSOCIAL USES OF THE MEDIA

Programs that utilize the media to reduce or solve crimes are not new. The "Wanted Dead or Alive" posters used on the Western frontier and the FBI's "Most Wanted" list are two long-standing examples. What is new is the rapid increase in the number of media-based anticrime programs and the increased use of the electronic visual media by law enforcement agencies. In these recent developments, the media have been utilized in two ways—in the form of traditional advertising and entertainment, and in anticrime programs that directly incorporate the media's electronic and visual technology. In a sense, these applications use the media to try to construct a social reality with less crime. To better understand the expectations of the developers of these media anticrime programs, one must first review the literature on "prosocial" uses of the media—efforts designed to achieve positive social effects and teach values, attitudes, or skills through the media.[1]

Prosocial media applications are modern, tangential outgrowths of the public information and communication campaigns discussed in Chapter 4. As noted, public communication campaigns are media-based efforts at public persuasion and have a long history of use in the United States. Research on media campaigns can be traced to the Payne Fund studies of the 1930s. In one study in 1933, the film *Birth of a Nation,* a sympathetic and romantic portrayal of the creation of the Ku Klux Klan, was shown to 4,000 junior and senior high school students. Following the screening, students' attitudes toward blacks were found to be less favorable than prior to seeing the film. When a number of films with the same theme were shown, the change in attitudes was cumulative. Although the effects eventually wore off, they were found to persist for a significant period of time (up to eight months).

With the media's ability established to affect attitudes negatively, planners subsequently tried to utilize the media to effect planned, positive changes in attitude and perceptions. Perhaps the best known of such purposeful attempts were governmental propaganda efforts. During the 1950s, media campaigns aimed at changing general social practices became common. Then, for a time, negative research findings led to pessimism about the media's ability to influence their audience.[2] Not until the 1960s were attempts made to use the media to influence children positively. Based on evaluations of these efforts, in the 1970s researchers began recognizing a

Underlying prosocial uses of the media are the concepts of symbolic interactionism and social learning theory (see, for example, Bandura, 1973, 1977), which, in brief, state that social behavior is largely determined through a process of social interactions. Through these interactions, the meanings of words, gestures, and actions are established. Behavior is thus socially learned in the ongoing dynamic and evolving context of social situations. Extension of these ideas to the media came with the recognition that symbolic interactions can be vicarious and that social behavior can be acquired from interactions with the media. In prosocial uses of the media, for example, the norms and values presented through the "symbolic interactions" found in the content significantly influence children's social attitudes. Media-based behavioral learning has been reported for aggression, altruism, cognition, deviance, personality, and psychopathology (see Akers, 1977; Bandura, 1973; Mischel, 1981; Rosenthal & Zimmerman, 1978; Rushton, 1980; Wilson & O'Leary, 1980) and extends to the learning of norms and emotional responses (Bandura, 1969, 1973, 1977). Symbolic interactionism and social learning also provide theoretical explanations of the negative media effects discussed in Chapter 4.

limited media potential for influence, and some began forwarding the possibility that the media could be used to attain limited goals in specific controlled circumstances.[3] The current perspective is that the media can help form, change, and strengthen attitudes and actions in certain circumstances, but that persuasion efforts that ignore communication tenets in their design will fail. Enough campaigns have succeeded to encourage the emergence of planned media-based, advertising-style communication campaigns and entertainment-style programs designed for positive social effects.[4] Both approaches constitute prosocial media applications.

Whereas the earlier public information and communications campaigns had been aimed at various groups, entertainment-style prosocial media efforts initially targeted children, with the basic goal being to counteract the pervasive violent content of the entertainment media. Accordingly, most research on prosocial media applications has involved children's television programs. The PBS show "Mr. Rogers' Neighborhood," for example, has been the focus of a number of studies that found that children cooperate more, display more nurturing behavior, regulate themselves more, help others more, share more, persist longer in attempting tasks, and show more empathy, imaginativeness, and creativity after watching episodes of the show.[5] Encouraged by these findings, television programmers have designed and scheduled more prosocial programs, the best known and most successful being PBS's "Sesame Street."[6] Evaluations of these shows have revealed that programs of various types (animated, adventure, comedy, fantasy) all have the ability to elicit socially valued behaviors from children and adolescent viewers.[7] J. Philip Rushton (1982a) reported that television, for example, has been shown in more than thirty-six studies to be able to bring about improvement in four social areas: "friendly behavior," "altruistic behavior," "self-control," and "coping with fears." In contrast to the bulk of negative assessments of the medium, Rushton concluded (1982a, vol. 1, p. 51) that "television can have beneficial effects; it is a potential force for good." Some evidence has even been forwarded that prosocial media efforts can cancel out the negative effects of violent content (Heller & Polsky, 1976, p. 290). Spurred by these findings, there developed in the 1970s a new-found enthusiasm for utilizing the mass media, and an expectation that positive media effects could be elicited in a number of social arenas, that of crime included.

However, the research on prosocial uses of the media has focused on the short-term viewing of special programming under special viewing conditions and thus left unanswered the question of precisely how prosocial media efforts operate over the long term in a home setting (Cook et al., 1983a, p. 167). The 1982 report of the National Institute of Mental Health (NIMH, 1982, vol. 1, p. 90) summed up this limitation:

> Potentially, children and to some degree adults can learn constructive social behavior, for example, helpfulness, cooperation, friendliness, and imaginative play, from television viewing. It is less certain whether these positive benefits are actually being achieved. Such useful material is embedded in a complicated format and is viewed at home under circumstances not conducive to effective generalizations. Additional research is required to determine the conditions under which pro-social behavior is most likely to be learned.

Thus, although the research shows that positive effects are possible, longitudinal field studies are still needed to confirm that they appear in general social settings.[8] Despite the lack of definitive knowledge about the specific manner in which the media can best be used to influence people, acceptance of the media's ability to positively do so led to an extension of prosocial uses of the media into a variety of social areas, including that of fighting crime. Without clear direction and through trial and error, a variety of designs for anticrime programs have been developed. In practice these designs have borrowed media techniques from both entertainment- and news-style television shows and printed public communication campaigns. However, programs using the media to try to reduce crime have encountered unanticipated problems, and success has not proved as direct or as simple as first envisioned.

MEDIA-BASED ANTICRIME EFFORTS: AN OVERVIEW

With planners driven by the promise of positive effects and the reduced costs and increased capabilities of media technology, media-based anticrime programs have proliferated during the last decade. Collectively, they fall into two groups, each group having two basic designs. In the first group, deterrence programs and surveillance programs are both designed to directly deter offenders from committing crimes. Those designated deterrence programs use existing avenues for mass media advertising to convey anticrime messages to offenders. Surveillance programs use newly developed video technology to expand the surveillance capabilities of law enforcement agencies. Such programs either deter criminals from committing crimes out of fear of being observed or, if deterrence fails, provide visual evidence to assist in apprehension and conviction of the offender. In the second group of projects are victimization reduction and citizen participation programs, aimed not at offenders but at citizens. Similar to deterrence programs, they use existing mass media outlets to distribute information, communicate appeals, and solicit help. Programs designed to reduce victimization work to reduce opportunities for crime by inducing citizens to better protect themselves. Citizen participation programs are designed to increase solution and arrest rates by increasing citizen cooperation with law enforcement investigation efforts. The two groups and their basic designs are summarized in Table 6-1.

Anticrime programs that follow one of the four basic designs incorporate content and distribution elements from successful prosocial entertainment and public communication campaigns, as well as stylistic features from mainstream entertainment, news, and advertising. These projects are clearly crime control efforts, with only secondary consideration given to due process issues. And though some make use of print media, most have concentrated their resources in the electronic, visual medium of television. Except for citizen participation programs, they all also share an underlying reliance on fear as a motivating agent and a frequently questioned belief in the criminal justice system's ability to effectively retain, process, and punish criminals, once identified. Lastly, each of the four basic types of programs has

TABLE 6-1   The Four Basic Types of Media-Based Anticrime Programs

Basic type	Behavior change sought	Mechanism	Example
Programs targeting offenders			
Deterrence programs	Voluntary reduction of criminal behavior by criminals	Deterrence	Antidrug public service ad campaigns
Surveillance programs	Voluntary reduction of criminal behavior by criminals or increased apprehension of offenders	Deterrence Target hardening Reduction of opportunities for crime	Police hidden-camera "sting" operations
Programs targeting citizens			
Victimization reduction programs	Adoption of self-protective, crime preventive behavior by citizens	Target hardening Reduction of opportunities for crime	The McGruff "Take a Bite out of Crime" campaign
Citizen participation programs	Increased public cooperation with and involvement in law enforcement efforts	Monetary reward Anonymity	Crime Stoppers

Jeffery (1990) has argued that all media-based anticrime efforts are crime control efforts in the sense that most are designed to react to crimes after their occurrence. He argued that resources would be better used in developing programs that would prevent crime from occurring in the first place. Though some of the programs fitting the first three types are designed to prevent crime, he noted that there have been no empirical evaluations establishing that they actually have a preventive effect.

been forwarded as at least a partial cure for crime. To be judged a total success, such programs must ultimately change their audience's social behavior. But most are actually designed to influence attitudes and people's perceptions of the reality of crime, with the expectation that changes in attitudes and perceptions will lead to changes in behavior. Research on public information and communication campaigns, however, has established that the mass media do well in informing people about an issue, but that changing people's attitudes is more difficult, and changing behavior still more so. These programs thus rest on a set of questionable premises, and they have frequently not been able to reduce crime as intended.

PROGRAMS AIMED AT OFFENDERS

Deterrence Programs

Both the earliest and the most recent mass media efforts to reduce crime involve public communication campaigns about drug abuse. Evaluations of the early projects first revealed the difficulties in using the media to help reduce crime. Schmeling and Wotring (1976, 1980), for example, blamed the failure of early antidrug abuse campaigns on their inability to make drug abuse a salient social issue and the irrelevance of the campaign messages to any specific target audience. They reported that a 1976 campaign had no effect, whereas a 1980 effort with a specific, limited goal of increasing the salience of the issue of drug abuse for a specific targeted audience (upper-class white males) resulted in better-informed subjects whose attitudes and behavior, however, did not change. According to Hanneman and McEwen

Antidrug media campaigns have a historical tie to the *Reefer Madness* films produced by the Federal Bureau of Narcotics in the 1930s under the direction of Commissioner of Narcotics Harry Anslinger. Although marketed as deterrence films, in their effect and purpose they appear to have had more to do with program funding and legislation. These films greatly facilitated criminalization of marijuana and the expansion of the Federal Bureau of Narcotics (see Lindesmith, 1965).

(1973, p. 329), the prevalence of pro-drug messages in the media creates another problem in using the mass media to try to reduce drug abuse.

The propensity of media campaigns to ignore basic marketing and communication research design tenets continued into the 1980s. To be effective, a media campaign must tailor its content for a specific population, and that population should not be simultaneously receiving conflicting or competing information. In that these early campaigns were diffuse efforts and general mass media content was rife with pro-drug images, these projects were fatally flawed. In recognition of the effects of competing information, there has been a series of successful lobbying efforts to reduce the levels of pro-

---

BOX 6-1   Antidrug Ads

My brother's friend, Rick, wanted to do something special for him for his birthday.

He bought him some crack.

Maybe it was bad stuff. Maybe they just couldn't handle it.

That was two years ago...today. Sometimes I think Rick was the lucky one. He died.

Happy Birthday, Buddy.

Partnership for a Drug-Free America

Source: Courtesy of Partnership for a Drug-Free America   *(continued)*

drug information in the media. In addition, more-recent media antidrug campaigns—for example, the "Media–Advertising Partnership for a Drug-Free America"—are better designed and marketed. Evaluations of these recent efforts indicate that a media campaign can affect attitudes toward drugs among preteens, teenagers, and adults (see Black, 1988). Whether or not behavioral changes and reduced drug use follow as a result has yet to be substantiated, although the correlational evidence suggests they do (see American Association of Advertising Agencies, 1990).

A different approach to using the mass media to deter criminals, in this case through a shock incarceration program encapsulated in an Oscar-winning film, was reported by Cavender (1981). The film *Scared Straight!*, about a deterrence program for juvenile offenders, was first distributed in 1978. The original project was the Juvenile Awareness Project, begun by a "lifers" group at Rahway Prison, New Jersey, in 1976. The project consisted of bringing groups of teenagers into the maximum-security state prison for a short group session with convicts sentenced to life. The convicts would graphically describe the worst aspects of prison life while intimidating the teenagers. *Scared Straight!* consisted of a session that was filmed and syndicated in 1978 and televised nationally in 1979 as a docu-

---

BOX 6-1 (continued)

Examples of recent antidrug advertising—one for television, one for print—targeted at distinct audiences, such as teenagers and psychiatrists

Source: Courtesy of Partnership for a Drug-Free America/Photo by Bernard Lawrence

mentary. A highly polished, dramatically presented portrayal of prisoners and prison life, the film was an immense success and became a media phenomenon. The public was enticed to watch it through publicity efforts akin to "previews of coming attractions" promising a shocking and graphic film that contained a solution to the crime problem (see Box 6-2). Extensive media publicity resulted in a massive, national trend in which thirty-eight states initiated proposals to create similar programs (Cavender, 1981, p. 434). The documentary itself became so popular that it was shown to groups of youths in lieu of a real shock incarceration program. If you didn't have a real prison and convicts handy, a media image of one would apparently suffice.

However, the film forwarded a punishment-oriented solution to crime within the theme that traditional correctional treatment and rehabilitation are total failures.[9] The film's underlying premise is that only the shock of prison life can deter delinquency (Cavender, 1981, p. 436). Crime and criminality are presented as a matter of individual choice that have little relation-

---

BOX 6-2   The Opening Comments from *"Scared Straight!"*

Peter Falk: These teenagers are going to prison. Nothing, from arrest to rehabilitation, has worked to stop them from breaking the law. So now, at age 15, 16 and 17, they're going behind bars. Their sentence will be short — only three hours.

But during that time these juvenile offenders will come into direct confrontation with these hardened criminals. They call themselves the lifers. Together they're serving nearly 1,000 years. But the lifers are through taking lives. They're now saving them in a unique crime-prevention program created and run by the convicts.

Their goal is ambitious — make juvenile delinquents go straight.

A three-hour prison sentence that somehow reforms juvenile delinquents. It sounds too good to be true. But just intriguing enough to make me enter this world of thieves, rapists and killers.

But a word of caution — some of the language is plenty rough. It's crude and it's brutal. But there's simply no way to edit out certain words and descriptions and still preserve the true impact of the pro-

gram, the realities of prison life and prison language. In fact, the whole point of this program would be lost by censoring what we filmed.

So if you're not offended by bad language, then welcome to Rahway Prison. And some prison sounds you've never heard.

[Cut to prisoners and teenagers]

Prisoner 1: I'm here for murder, kidnapping, robbery, armed robbery and conspiracy . . .

Prisoner 2: When we got sexual desires, who do you think we get? And don't tell me each other. See 'cause I don't like nothin' in the first place and I don't like you!

Prisoner 3: You got your best shot, man. One punch. Punch me in my face. Then it's my turn. Your punch.

Prisoner 4: Man, get that fuckin' camera off my face. I'm telling you to cut it off!

[Cut and Title]

Source: "Scared Straight!" dialogue is reprinted by permission of Arnold Shapiro Productions.

ship to social conditions. The film's criminals are shown as inherently amoral and vicious. The documentary was popularly embraced because these images of crime and criminals conform to the stereotypes found in the entertainment and news media (see Chapter 2). Through these images, the film and subsequent news coverage of it marketed a simplistic solution to crime compatible with the entertainment presentation of the crime problem, promoting crime control while devaluing due process protections (Cavender, 1981, p. 431). Unfortunately, a subsequent evaluation of the original, real-world, nonmedia-filtered Scared Straight program in the New Jersey prison showed no reduction in recidivism (Finchenauer, 1979, pp. 8–9).[10]

Two lessons are taught by the *Scared Straight!* episode. First, the film's run as the basis for a popular anticrime policy demonstrates the power of the media to influence and shape reality and public policy with regard to crime and justice. Good media does not equal good policy. Second, the lack of effects found in the real project demonstrates the difficulty of using fear to induce behavioral changes. Given that media-generated fear of punishment underlies all anticrime deterrence campaigns and surveillance and victimization reduction programs, understanding the difficulty of using fear in media campaigns is important. Research has shown that using fear as a marketing technique and a means of influence is problematic and sometimes counterproductive (see Box 6-3). In essence, media-generated fear and concern, if not carefully managed, can result in exactly the opposite effects from those planned. If the fear that is generated is not balanced with viable and realistic choices, the audience may reject and ignore the campaign and take a fatalistic attitude toward crime or drug abuse. This suggests that media campaigns aimed at offenders must raise offenders' fear of apprehension and punishment or concern for their health, while offering viable alternatives to pursuing criminal activities.

Because of the mixed results of the anti–drug abuse campaigns, the problems with the *Scared Straight!* documentary, the volatile nature of fear as a campaign base, and the difficulty in identifying and reaching offender populations, use of the mass media for crime deterrence campaigns has generally declined, despite a recent resurgence in anti–drug abuse campaigns. Another approach to using the media to deter crime has not waned, however—that being media-enhanced surveillance.

Surveillance Programs

Camera surveillance programs are used to visually monitor, deter, and detect crime. Specific-site programs such as the use of surveillance cameras in banks, subways, and department stores have been in use for a number of years. These established uses differ from newer applications in that the areas surveyed were small and areas of public domain were not involved. In contrast, the new programs use electronic media technology (electronic audiovisual communication equipment) (see Chapter 1, p. 12) to directly prevent crime in geographically large public areas. The programs are also often mobile. In the field, camera surveillance programs take one of two basic forms: completely hidden systems that give potential offenders no indication that they are being observed and clearly marked, open systems (Surette, 1988). Although the first form functions more as a means of gathering evidence and aiding in apprehension, both forms take advantage of a "surveillance effect," using the psychological impact of the belief that one might be under surveillance to deter crime. Generally, rapid improvement in the technology has encouraged the use of surveillance systems, but a general lack of research regarding the most useful applications has hampered it.

BOX 6-3   Fear as a Marketing Technique

The use of fear as a means of marketing anticrime products is logical; after all, evaluations of victimization reduction programs show that unless some fear and concern over crime is generated, campaigns aimed at the public fail. However, the use of fear as a motivating mechanism is not simple and has been found to be less effective and predictable than expected. Janis and Feshbach first examined the use of fear as a marketing concept in 1953 and reported that strong appeals to fear were less effective than moderate or mild appeals to fear in motivating people to alter their behavior (in their study, dental hygiene). The discovery of this negative relationship—the greater the fear, the less the effect—led for many years to a rejection of fear as a marketing technique. However, subsequent studies reported that the use of fear was effective in certain circumstances. The antismoking campaigns of the late 1960s followed, with a significant drop in smoking. More-recent research has indicated that both very strong and very mild appeals to fear are ineffective: Too mild an appeal fails to attract attention, whereas too strong an appeal causes people to avoid the message (see Higbee, 1969, for a review of the research from 1953 to 1968). Accordingly, a curvilinear relationship has been postulated (Higbee, 1969, p. 440; Ray & Wilkie, 1970). Optimally, a message arouses sufficient fear to attract the audience's attention and compel its acceptance of the message and its recommendations but not so much fear that the audience avoids the message and rejects its recommendations as being inadequate to deal with the fear. In addition, in product marketing, portraying the intended purchaser as the victim of some type of physical harm in an appeal to fear actually works against the appeal. Burnett and Oliver (1979) have suggested that marketers instead portray the harm as directed toward a surrogate target (such as a spouse or child) or as consisting of threatening social consequences (Kohn et al., 1982; see also Berkowitz & Cummingham, 1966). Fear appears to also be an effective motivator among those who have not seen themselves as part of the market for the recommended product or brand (Wheatley, 1971). A good example of this technique can be found in the marketing of canned mace, a long-time popular product among police and mail carriers, to new market segments. To increase sales, smaller, key-chain-size vials were manufactured and advertised to women as a means of stopping would-be rapists.

The research on the use of fear in marketing efforts suggests that anticrime messages aimed at the occasional criminal or drug user and focusing on the negative social consequences of discovery and arrest, particularly to loved ones, will be the most effective. Recent survey research has supported this conclusion (see Black, 1988). Unfortunately, the research also suggests that, as with the antismoking campaign, such efforts will not influence a core of chronic, committed career criminals or drug abusers.

Several issues arise in examining surveillance programs. The most obvious issue is the effectiveness of these programs: Do they reduce crime? A second issue is the trade-off of privacy for security. The criminal justice system, often in response to prodding by the public, has begun to turn increasingly to media-based technology for more innovative countermeasures against crime (Marx, 1985, p. 23; Surette, 1985a). Because of their nature, however, such programs inevitably encroach on people's privacy, invading social realms and exposing and recording behavior that were previously considered backstage. Another basic question is how the social costs of these programs compare to their benefits (Surette, 1985a, p. 79). Lastly, surreptitious camera surveillance invariably raises the specter of *1984*, with its connotations of governmental abuses reducing support for the legitimacy of law enforcement agencies.

Interest in the use of surveillance as a crime reduction aid is not new and is based on the idea that surveillance heightens the perceived risk of committing crime (Mayhew et al., 1979). Research based largely on interviews with offenders does suggest that criminals do take into account the apparent level of surveillance and likelihood of intervention when deciding whether or not to commit certain crimes (Reppetto, 1974). Nonetheless, projects to increase surveillance on the part of the general public appear to be the least effective approach to using surveillance to deter crime. On the other hand, increasing (or appearing to increase) the surveillance capability of law enforcement officers, local residents, and employees, in that order, does have promise (Mayhew et al., 1979). Lastly, the limited literature that is available suggests that the impact of surveillance is related to the actual threat of intervention; that is, unless the surveillance actually leads to intervention, the deterrent effect will soon wane (see Box 6-4).

Though media-based surveillance programs do not introduce new law enforcement practices, the new technology greatly enhances the reach of law enforcement agencies' surveillance capability. The practical goals of using media-enhanced surveillance include reduction of the number of officers needed for patrol; an increased ability to provide full, twenty-four-hour-a-day coverage of an area; a reduction in citizens' fear of victimization; improved deterrence of street crime; an increased ability to apprehend and convict street criminals; decreased response time; and, for supervisors, an improved ability to oversee and direct line personnel and review field decisions.

The idea of increasing community surveillance to deter crime gained prominence in the early 1970s through the work of Oscar Newman, whose concepts of defensible space are based on the premise that community and building designs that increase the sense of community and that eliminate conditions favorable to the commission of crimes (such as inadequate lighting) can minimize the likelihood of crime (Newman, 1972, 1975, 1976; see also Jacobs, 1961).

On the other hand, critics have raised concerns that such programs will be difficult to control. Even when ineffective, these systems and their associated surveillance effect have been criticized as psychologically too powerful and therefore dangerous: "Agents are clearly limited in the surveillance and coercion they can carry out, but they are free to create the impression of police omnipresence and omnipotence. What they cannot do by force or by the actual power of their technology, they may attempt to do by creating a 'myth of surveillance'" (Marx, 1985, p. 21). Such projects have also been questioned regarding their cost and the reliability of the equipment, the community image that using such systems projects, and the likelihood that their use will merely displace rather than reduce crime (Surette, 1985a).

Despite these advantages and concerns and the increasing use of camera surveillance by law enforcement agencies, there are no definitive studies of surveillance systems' actual impact on crime. The best-known study in this area focused on the installation of closed-circuit television cameras in the London subway system in the 1970s. Cameras were placed in four London stations, with transmissions sent to a central monitoring site. The cameras allowed viewing of all principal station areas, were conspicuously mounted, and were accompanied by notices stating that the closed-circuit television was in use. Monitor operators could contact the station staff or nearest police station, make a public address announcement, or contact train drivers. Evaluation of the system showed that the cameras reduced the incidence of both theft and robbery, though there was some evidence that thefts had been displaced to adjacent stations without cameras. The evaluators cautioned, however, that the novelty of the system might have contributed to its effectiveness and that in time offenders might discover that the system is less to be feared than they had imagined. They warned that, as is true of the announcement effect that accompanies highly publicized increases in traditional law enforcement efforts (see Box 6-4), the initial deterrent effect of installing cameras would not last without actual intervention to apprehend lawbreakers (Mayhew et al., 1979, pp. 25–26, 28).

Only one surveillance effort covering a large outside public area has been studied. The project involved the placing of television cameras linked by microwave atop traffic lights in a downtown shopping district in Miami Beach, Florida (see Surette, 1985a, 1988). By allowing the police to monitor the retail area through television surveillance, this camera "patrol" program

---

More than a decade ago Mayhew and his colleagues (1979, p. 12) offered a prophetic assessment of the difficulties of using surveillance programs to prevent crime:

> The use of surveillance to reduce crime shares some of the usual problems of methods which attempt to reduce opportunities of crime; they do not tackle underlying factors that may motivate offenders; they can appear negatively "defensive"; and they cannot guarantee that crime is not merely displaced in time, place, or method.

It is unknown how many police departments have video capabilities, but most likely the number is quite high. The Indianapolis Police Department for example, makes extensive use of video technology, using a mobile van to supply video surveillance as needed. The van has been used to tape crowd and people movement in predominantly gay areas in an attempt to solve gay-related murders, and is periodically used in areas of high prostitution to deter both prostitutes and their customers (interview with a representative of the Indianapolis P. D. Public Information Office, June 30, 1987).

was designed to give the police department a significantly greater presence in the city's prime retail shopping district without adding patrol officers (Miami Beach, 1982). The stated goals of the program were "to accomplish a reduction in elderly fear of street crime and to create anxiety and a sense of paranoia among the criminal element in that they [will] fear that their activities may be televised and recorded by the police" (Wooldridge, 1981, p. 6). Thus, the project was expected to drastically lower fear of crime among the elderly and simultaneously deter street crime.

An assessment of this project reported that crime did decline in the monitored area, with the average number of strong-arm robberies falling from 4.83 per month before the program to 3.09 per month afterward (sig.

BOX 6-4   The Announcement Effect

The surveillance effect is similar to the "announcement effect," which follows extensive publicizing of changes in law enforcement and judicial policy aimed at offenders (see also Chapter 4). For example, significant behavior changes occurred in Massachusetts following heavy publicity about the introduction of a mandatory prison term for gun-related crimes (Pierce & Bowers, 1979).* Evaluation indicated that gun assaults fell significantly immediately following introduction of the law, with a displacement effect increasing the use of other weapons (knives, bats, and so forth). Initially, gun use in robberies also declined, though it later appeared to increase (Pierce & Bowers, 1979, p. 92). Other, better-known examples include the British use of breathalyser tests to curb drunken driving (Ross et al., 1970). The planned policy change was heavily publicized,

and evaluation showed a marked drop in alcohol-related accidents with the introduction of the law, followed by a slow return to prior levels. The authors reasoned that as enforcement waned and this became known, the deterrent effect followed suit. They concluded, "A breathalyser will help reduce serious traffic accidents when it is used to restrict drunken driving, but it will have this effect only if the courts enforce the law about drinking and driving." A third example with similar results involved an announcement by the state of Connecticut of plans to drastically increase its enforcement of speeding laws. Speeding fell initially but slowly returned to prior levels as drivers realized that enforcement had not changed (Campbell & Ross, 1968). See also Nienstedt (1990) and West et al. (1989) for recent studies that provide empirical evidence of announcement effects.

---

*The Barlet-Fox law, passed in 1975, mandated a one-year minimum prison term for the unlicensed carrying of a firearm.

BOX 6-5 Miami Beach's Surveillance System

The specifics of the project included the strategic placing of one hundred video camera housings along approximately two miles of the two retail shopping avenues of the city.

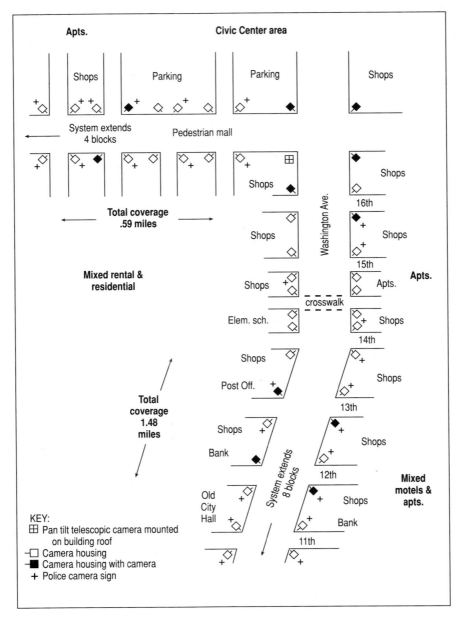

The street video patrol system used in Miami Beach

Source: From "Video Street Patrol," by R. Surette, Journal of Police Science and Administration, *1985, vol. 13, no. 1, p. 80. Reprinted by permission.*

(continued)

.026). It is possible, however, that the decline was part of a general decline in crime in the city or that the cameras had a displacement effect, reducing crime in the immediate area but increasing it in adjacent areas (Surette, 1985a, p. 83). Of special interest in the Miami Beach project is that the decline in street crime coincided with the installation of the camera housings, weeks before the actual cameras were available, clear evidence of the strength of the surveillance effect.

Designed as an open, fully publicized deterrence system, the Miami Beach system nevertheless came to be faulted by the police department for not functioning as a crime detection and apprehension system,[11] even though at the end of its first year of operation the department was crediting the system with contributing to a 70 percent decrease in area crime.[12] Some have argued that this program was attacked more for its political liabilities than for any lack of effect on crime. Such general public surveillance systems are likely to be sensitive political issues wherever they are employed (Surette, 1985a).

Cameras mounted on patrol cars represent an expanded, mobile use of video technology for surveillance. Cameras are mounted on the windshields of patrol cars and record on trunk-mounted videotape recorders for later administrative review and use as evidence. The mobility of the patrol car extends the practice of general law enforcement surveillance to virtually the

---

BOX 6-5 (continued)

A prominent sign stating "Police Television" was mounted with each camera housing. Of the 100 video housings located in the target area, 21 were to actually contain a movable camera at any given time; thus, "at no time [would] a criminal be able to determine which of the 100 housings actually contained a camera" (Miami Beach Police Dept., 1983, p. 1).

The entire assembled system consisted of the following:

1. A portable, wireless TV camera that could be controlled from a remote site. The unit had a self-contained power source and received TV images that were then transferred via microwave to a monitor.
2. A portable transmitter was contained at the same location as the camera. It transformed the TV images into microwaves and sent them to a receiver.
3. A micro-video receiver translated the micro-

waves into television signals and transmitted them to a monitoring screen located in a central command center.
4. Also located at the main intersection was one manually operated pan-and-tilt camera that could move vertically and horizontally and had a telescopic lens.

The focus of deterrence in Miami was a specific class of crimes: strong-arm robberies, muggings, purse snatchings, and other street crime. After installation, the microwave equipment was found to be highly sensitive to wind and weather and could not be operated for significant amounts of time. The central pan-and-tilt camera was not operating 80 percent of the time, and often as few as three of the traffic light cameras were working. Technical problems with the equipment most certainly had an impact on the success of the project.

The Supreme Court has stated that an invasion of privacy cannot result unless there is a reasonable expectation of privacy. Because there is no expectation of privacy in a traffic stop, the use of cameras by police on patrol appears to be allowed under almost all circumstances (see *New York* v. *Class,* U. S. 106 S. Ct., 960 [1986]). In a 1990 decision, *Penn* v. *Muniz* (110 S. Ct., 2714 [1990]), the Supreme Court concluded that the *Miranda* ruling allows the courtroom use of videotaped responses to routine booking questions asked before the Miranda warning has been given.

entire society (Sechrest et al., 1990, citing Rubinstein, 1973, p. 20). In this case, it can be argued that the police are as much under surveillance as the public, however, for the car camera transforms the relationships between line police officers, the administration, and the public by providing a reviewable record of officers' street interactions. The benefits of having an audiovisual record of a patrol are obvious: Administrators and the courts can later review officers' and suspects' actions; determine liability, voluntary search consent, and misconduct claims; and obtain more-credible, objective evidence of behavior and statements for DUI and drug cases. The cameras also deter the resisting of arrest by suspects, and mistreatment of suspects and other nonprofessional acts on the part of officers (Sechrest et al., 1990). The use of patrol car cameras has not been legally challenged, and as its benefits, especially to officers, are obvious, its spread is predictable. Indeed, in a recent review, Sechrest and his colleagues (1990) could suggest no disadvantages to using the technology.

A final use of media technology in law enforcement involves the recording of police interrogations on camera.[13] As with patrol car cameras, here again the cameras provide more objective, fuller records of interactions between police and citizens, as well as of the voluntariness of statements, suspects' understanding of their rights, police coercion and interrogation practices, and the physical and mental condition of suspects. A two-year evaluation by Grant (1987, 1990) of a Canadian experiment in videotaping police interrogations showed that the expected advantages of protection against unwarranted allegations of misconduct, the introduction of accountability in interrogation procedures, and the reduction in challenges to the admissibility of suspect statements were all realized.[14] Grant also reported that suspects did not appear inhibited by the cameras and that the confession rate remained the same. In fact, Grant reported that police, prosecutors, and defense counsel all came to support continuation and expansion of the project—the police because it relieves them of the need to take written notes during interrogations and reduces their court appearances, prosecutors because it usually disposes of all legal questions surrounding the police–suspect interview, and defense counsel because it ensures that police more strictly follow legal procedures and because the defense often can use the tapes to demonstrate their client's intent and remorse for sentencing purposes. The interrogation tapes provide a record of the frame of mind and emotional reaction of a suspect much nearer in time to the actual commission of a crime than has been previously available. Grant did not measure the opinions of those actually interviewed, so their perceptions are unknown.

Summary: Media Technology and Surveillance

The evaluations indicate that programs like these will have a significant immediate deterrent effect simply by having a well-publicized start. In fact, an announcement effect is normally the strongest effect found for deterrence and surveillance programs; indeed, their primary difficulty is maintaining these immediate gains over a longer period of time. An initial deterrent effect is lost over time if offenders realize that the law is not being enforced and that punishments are not being imposed. Surveillance and announcement effects are so psychologically powerful that planners can effect a quick but short-term behavioral change by convincing people that things are different—either that they are under observation or that transgressions, if discovered, will be more harshly punished. But if no actual change persists, when people discover that punishments are not harsher or that the cameras do not work or that no one responds, then the deterrent effect disappears. Effective use of the media and its technology thus dictates that sufficient resources and effort be allocated to ensuring and maintaining actual social policy changes as well as to initially publicizing the planned change.

The use of media technology is in most cases efficient, and legal questions of admissibility, privacy, and due process have been answered in favor of continued use of the technology in the United States.[15] Resistance to even greater adoption within law enforcement agencies appears to arise because law enforcement officers perceive the cameras as administrative tools, installed to watch them, more than as law enforcement tools, installed to increase convictions. In reality the cameras are both, and though their use originates in efforts to achieve crime control goals, they also generate enough due process benefits to have gained relatively broad-based support. In effect, these programs appear to protect police officers from frivolous charges of abuse and misconduct while protecting the public from actual abuse and misconduct by officers. Not surprisingly, where they have been experimentally employed they have, to date, been permanently adopted.

Beyond technical feasibility, all of the surveillance programs mentioned raise issues concerning the use of media technology in the daily policing of our society. Surprisingly, in the literature evaluating these projects, concerns over "Big Brother" and *1984* were raised only by the news media, law enforcement officers, and external observers, not by citizens, who appeared quite ready to trade off a measure of personal privacy for a potential reduction in victimization and fear. The acceptance of surveillance is thought to be associated with the acceptance of the increased media exposure of private, backstage behaviors: If privacy is already rare, then surveillance becomes less offensive. Such acceptance could encourage applications of media technology that undermine civil liberties. Another concern over the use of this technology is the prospect that it displaces crime. Thus, one eventual result could be the isolation of crime in poor neighborhoods that cannot afford such systems, permanently polarizing society into crime-free and crime-ridden zones (Surette, 1988, 1990a).

Further unresolved questions concern the perceived legitimacy of the police to enforce laws, the depersonalization of the criminal justice process, and effects on established work groups within the system. What is lost in legitimacy, symbolic impact, and the public image of justice when media technology is employed? The justice system is a mechanism for adjudicating guilt and administering punishment. It is also a means of legitimizing the whole social system. Accordingly, the police have a symbolic value. On the street, both the presence of a live police officer and the assurance of knowing when one is being observed affirm the values of voluntary consent and involvement, privacy, and public control of law enforcement. Loss of these symbols may diminish the aura of legitimacy sustaining the entire system and undermine an otherwise successful program (Surette, 1988).

The basic problem these programs present is how to balance police intervention and public safety—how much safety is gained at what cost? The equation seems clearly to be that increased fear of crime results in increased tolerance for intervention. Citizens fearful of crime are willing to open more backstage social areas to observation, even when the observers are hidden. Orwell's scenario in his book *1984* of total surveillance is less feared than a local mugger, and the danger is that fear will drive citizens to glibly surrender personal privacy for an unknown measure of personal security. Whether or not these crime control programs actually reduce crime enough to warrant the reduction in privacy is still an open question. The media and media technology do seem capable of producing short-term effects through purely psychological means, but whether the programs themselves can maintain these effects over the long-term or not remains an issue.

PROGRAMS AIMED AT CITIZENS

Victimization Reduction Programs

Programs aimed at reducing victimization differ from deterrence programs in that the target audience comprises crime victims rather than offenders. However, both types of programs share the goal of trying to change individual behavior, a heavy reliance on fear as motivation, and difficulties in empirically demonstrating success.

What victimization reduction campaigns strive to accomplish is the increased use of personal crime prevention techniques by citizens. Crime prevention falls under the umbrella of self-protective behaviors, which include avoiding health risks and other hazards. Weinstein (1987) has identified as key variables in triggering self-protective behaviors people's beliefs about the likelihood that they will be harmed and the severity of that harm if they do not act, the efficacy of the precautionary actions, and the costs of taking action. In general, persuading people to adopt more self-protective behaviors is difficult because of complex interactions among the above factors. Also, as Rogers and Storey (1987) have noted, programs advocating the adoption of behaviors to help "prevent" possible unpleasant future events (for example, crime) tend to be less successful than those that encourage actions that have an immediate, recognizable return, such as an increase in health from exercising or dieting. Encouraging crime prevention poses special problems. For one, perceptions of the importance of crime and the effectiveness of preventive behavior vary considerably among groups, so messages must be carefully matched to subpopulations to have an effect (O'Keefe & Reid, 1990).[16] Adding to the difficulty of determining which campaigns actually work, victimization reduction programs in general have rarely been adequately evaluated (O'Keefe & Reid, 1990). Only two campaigns have been seriously evaluated. One is the "McGruff—Take a Bite Out of Crime" campaign in the United States; the second is a "Let's Not Give Crime a Chance" campaign in Canada.[17]

The McGruff campaign, which began in 1979 and is still continuing, uses national public service ads (PSAs) to encourage the use of crime prevention techniques. The desired behaviors can be divided into individual actions to reduce personal risk of victimization, such as locking cars and doors, and community actions, such as forming crime-watch groups.

Despite lack of control over the placement of the PSA announcements, the campaign's evaluators have reported that the campaign has at least partially succeeded. Overall, 52 percent of a national sample had heard of the

---

BOX 6-6   Print Ad from the McGruff Campaign

Source: A message from the Crime Prevention Coalition, the U. S. Department of Justice, and the Advertising Council. © 1989 National Crime Prevention Council. For current information about the McGruff Campaign write to McGruff, One Prevention Way, Washington, D. C. 20539.

It should be noted that the McGruff campaign did show a slight behavioral impact, without any accompanying attitude or information changes, on citizens who saw themselves as more threatened by crime (O'Keefe, 1985a, p. 173). Thus, for a small number of citizens a behavioral change might be brought about directly through simple media "reminders" of anticrime actions that can be taken, without the need of a campaign focusing on the normal intervening factors of knowledge, increased salience, and a change in attitudes (see Figure 6-1; see also O'Keefe, 1985b; O'Keefe & Reid, 1990; Riley & Mayhew, 1980; Tyler & Cook, 1984; Tyler & Lavrakas, 1985).

campaign (O'Keefe & Mendelsohn, 1984).[18] Furthermore, of those exposed, 25 percent reported change in their attitudes. In general, there is consistent evidence of positive changes in people's knowledge about and attitudes toward crime prevention. But there is limited evidence that the McGruff media campaigns modify the behavior of potential crime victims. Only 8 percent reported actually changing their behavior (Tyler, 1984). To date, the McGruff campaign has shown a significant ability to impart information about crime prevention and influence attitudes, but it has not demonstrated an ability to substantially affect the level of crime preventive action taken in a community.

The Canadian program consisted of a two-stage media campaign in the province of Alberta in 1978. The goal of the program was to decrease the level of several specific offenses: vandalism, house break-ins, theft from automobiles, hitchhiking-related assaults and rapes, and auto theft. During the first stage, the aim was to increase general public awareness of crime prevention and the new program. The second stage consisted of messages promoting actual preventive behaviors and included radio and television announcements and newspaper and billboard advertisements. An analysis of pre- and postcampaign surveys showed that, as in the U. S. campaign, many people recognized the campaign messages. But in contrast to the McGruff program, the Canadian project reported little impact on respondents' attitudes toward crime prevention and, incredibly, found a slight decrease in crime preventive behaviors after the campaign. The evaluators, Sacco and Silverman (1981, p. 198), concluded that though a large number of Albertans were exposed to the campaign, a considerably smaller number saw the campaign themes and messages as salient, and only a negligible number altered their behavior in response—apparently in the wrong direction. On the basis of these two programs, media campaigns appear able to affect people's attitudes toward crime prevention more easily than their behavior.

Underlying these campaigns and deterrence and surveillance programs is a belief in the causal relationship shown in Figure 6-1. Thus, these programs are predicated on the belief that they will cause citizens to learn more about the risks of arrest and crime and the means to prevent it. This new information, in turn, is expected to cause a change in attitude—

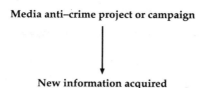

Media anti–crime project or campaign

New information acquired

(knowledge of surveillance cameras, punishments and high
risk of arrest or illness, crime prevention techniques)

New attitudes formed

(increased belief in the effectiveness of campaign suggestions
to reduce crime or stop drug abuse, increased salience of
crime and victimization, increased belief in the ability of
the criminal justice system to catch and punish criminals)

New behaviors shown

(offenders commit less crime, citizens
take more crime prevention measures)

FIGURE 6-1 The causal premise underlying
media anticrime programs

increasing citizens' sense of the importance of crime prevention and increasing offenders' fear of apprehension or, in the case of drugs, of death or illness. These new attitudes should finally result in the adoption of self-protective actions—citizens' taking on new crime preventive behaviors, offenders' committing less crime and abusing drugs less often. Unfortunately, program evaluations and communications research in general do not strongly support the validity of this premise (Roberts & Grossman, 1990). Behavior changes do not appear to follow readily from media campaigns.

Sacco and Silverman (1982) have pointed out some general difficulties with efforts to use the media to reduce victimization. As one would predict, based on the research on public communication campaigns, using the media to change crime-related attitudes and behaviors is a complex process. Simple audience exposure to media campaigns is not enough to ensure results, because media content does not directly affect audience actions with regard to crime or crime prevention. Unless carefully designed, the mass media are more likely to reinforce people's current behavior than they are to change it (Sacco & Silverman, 1982, p. 258, citing Klapper, 1960). Success is further complicated because a significant portion of the public does not believe that anticrime information reduces crime or that preventive actions are worth the effort. Anyone planning a media-based anticrime program

Sacco and Silverman (1982) offer five guiding principles necessary for successful mass media anticrime campaigns.

First, the information must be effectively disseminated, particularly in campaigns aimed at deterring crime.

Second, the relevance of campaign information must be gauged and the varying importance of crime to different segments of the public recognized. Often creating an interest in crime as an issue is a necessary first step.

Third, optimally, no contradictory information concerning the danger of crime or the effectiveness of anticrime measures would be presented. With so much information about crime being projected in entertainment, advertising, and news, however, anticrime campaigns are unlikely to be able to gain a monopoly over information. Crime campaigns must therefore take the nature and sources of these counter images into account in their design.

Fourth, goals must be realistically defined to allow for both evaluation of the program and efficient use of resources.

Fifth, to minimize the counterproductive effects of heightening the salience of crime as a social issue by making the public believe that they are likely to be victimized, the campaign must clearly communicate what anticrime behavior it is encouraging.

must consider that a significant proportion of the population does not perceive crime as an important personal concern (as opposed to an important social concern), that the salience of crime varies across categories of individuals and communities, that the relationship between exposure to mass media and perceptions of crime is indirect and ambiguous, and that the perception of crime as threatening can have counterproductive, even harmful consequences. Mass media anticrime programs must be designed so as to balance the need to overcome audience apathy against the consequences of scaring the audience too much. Sacco and Silverman concluded, "The mass media is not a panacea for crime control problems. . . . [Mass media campaigns] are likely to prove effective [only] if their design is informed by established communication principles and pre-campaign research" (p. 266).

To date, victimization reduction campaigns are considered useful means of disseminating anticrime information to the public and sometimes influencing related attitudes, but they appear to affect behavior only marginally, and more significant effects may be beyond their reach. To be effective, programs should tailor their messages to their audience; focus their efforts on television, which seems to have the greatest impact; stay simple; and directly and clearly instruct audiences on crime preventive behavior. Most important, additional local community follow-up and the creation of community support organizations such as citizen crime watch groups are necessary to achieve lasting effects. A dilemma revealed by the research is that the better the neighborhood, the less concern there is about crime but the greater the involvement in crime prevention activities and the more likely people are to report keeping watch on behalf of their neighbors. Interestingly, there is also a correlation between increased knowledge of crime prevention and increased viewing of crime-related shows, indicating a general interest in crime in at least one segment of the population. Recent ads in the McGruff campaign show that its developers have responded to the communications research; the linking of the campaign to the creation of neighborhood anticrime groups is a specific current goal of the McGruff effort (McGruff Campaign Team, n.d.). Unfortunately, no subsequent evaluation has been conducted to assess what behavioral impact, if any, these efforts are having (cf. O'Keefe & Reid, 1990).

Participation Programs

Programs of this last type aim to increase the level of crime-related information available to police from the public. Such programs, most commonly known as Crime Stoppers, use television reenactments of crimes and radio and newspaper items to obtain information on crimes ("tips") through anonymous phone calls.[19] Money is paid for useful information. The logic behind this approach is the same as that behind the "Most Wanted" reward posters of the nineteenth-century West and the FBI's "10 Most Wanted" posters displayed in post offices. Getting the image and a description of wanted suspects and unsolved crimes to as many people as possible and enticing reluctant citizens with rewards increases the possibility of solving crimes and apprehending suspects. The innovation here is using the modern print and electronic mass media as "electronic" and mass-distributed posters, thereby increasing enormously the number of people contacted and the potential amount of information received.

Although such programs will normally accept information concerning any felony, specific crimes are usually selected and highlighted as "crimes of the week." Reenactments of these crimes are televised as a weekly feature and descriptions of the crimes and any suspects are carried by radio stations and newspapers (Rosenbaum et al., 1986, p. 110). Many programs also include a "most wanted" component, printing the pictures and descriptions of fugitives in newspapers and broadcasting them on television and radio. The first Crime Stoppers program was started in 1976 in Albuquerque, New Mexico, and currently there are more than 850 similar programs worldwide, increasing at the rate of about 100 programs per year.

The development of Crime Stoppers programs raises a number of issues. The first and most obvious is the effectiveness of these programs: Do they result in more arrests and solutions of crimes, and are they an efficient means of gathering information? Second, there is a question of the image of criminality that such programs project. Do they perpetuate stereotypes of criminals, victims, and crime? In publicizing crimes of the week and appealing for information through other programs, the media depict crime as a serious, constant, and dramatic community problem. This image of crime is felt to be the most crucial issue concerning these programs, the subjects of these crime ads are presented as the "real" local crimes—as the important, unsolved cases in the community—and the suspects are presented as typi-

BOX 6-7   Crime Stoppers

The structure of a typical Crime Stoppers program is as follows. The program is under the supervision of a private nonprofit corporation. This corporation and its operating committees oversee the policy and distribution of reward money and coordinate information collection with the local law enforcement agencies. Crimes for the program are usually referred by participating law enforcement agencies; for example, detectives forward unsolved cases to Crime Stoppers for consideration. A review committee selects from those cases a number which are actually reenacted for television spots or described in newspapers or on the radio. The review committee reserves a veto over the acceptance of any particular crime. In addition to a description of the crime, the media coverage stresses the fact that a reward will be paid for information leading to an arrest and prosecution, the fact that the informant will remain anonymous, and the telephone number of the local Crime Stoppers program tips line. When information does lead to an arrest and felony indictment, a rewards committee reviews the case and decides on the amount of reward money (up to $1,000) to be paid.

Source: Courtesy of San Diego Crime Stoppers, Inc.

THERE ARE THREE ESSENTIAL ELEMENTS:

The Community

The Police

The Media

CRIME STOPPERS INTERNATIONAL, INC. (CSI)

as the world headquarters, is the central clearinghouse for Crime Stoppers materials, and the main source of problem-solving for individual programs. There is a minimal charge for information needed to start a Crime Stoppers program.

A 30-member Board of Directors establishes CSI policy and represents the Members.

From its Albuquerque, New Mexico, World Headquarters, the CSI staff:
- Distributes a comprehensive *Crime Stoppers Manual* and video tapes describing the operation of Crime Stoppers;
- Produces training, public relations and promotional tools;

- Processes hundreds of inquiries each month concerning statistics, legal issues, fundraising, publicity, promotion, insurance; and media, board and police relations.
- Sponsors, with a host program, the Annual Crime Stoppers International Conference, where law enforcement, community and media representatives from around the world exchange information and participate in professional training; and where CSI awards are presented;
- Publishes *The Caller,* a monthly magazine containing statistical information, instruction, and accounts of Crime Stoppers successes;
- Provides a Crime Stoppers *Directory;*
- Develops resources for the headquarters operations;
- Makes on-site visits.
- Provides a toll-free line for incoming calls.

Crime Stoppers International, Inc.
3736 Eubank Boulevard N.E. / Suite B-4
Albuquerque, New Mexico 87111
1-800/245-0009   505/294-2300   FAX 505/294-6479

Reprinted by permission.

cal and dangerous. In essence, because the crime ads are presented as representative of the actual crime in a community, the image they portray has great potential impact on social attitudes and perceptions of criminality. This potential leads to the third and final issue: What is the proper role of the news media in law enforcement efforts? These programs shift the media from their traditional roles as observers and reporters to being active participants in investigating crimes and hunting fugitives. In this new role are the media rendering an acceptable public service or compromising their traditional function?

Whether or not these programs affect the crime rate is not known. The number of cases cleared by Crime Stoppers is not great enough to expect an effect on the overall crime rate in a community unless one assumes a general deterrent effect from the mass media coverage. Neither effect has been reported. But anecdotal evidence does suggest that the programs are solving many felony cases that are unlikely to be solved otherwise (Rosenbaum et al., 1986, p. 34; 1989, p. 417). As of April 1990, the 645 programs reported by Crime Stoppers International claim responsibility for the solving of more than 282,000 felony cases, the conviction of more than 53,000 defendants, and the recovery of more than 1.5 billion dollars' worth of stolen property. The high visibility of these programs increases their effectiveness by attracting secondary tips for unadvertised crimes.[20] They also appear especially effective in solving cases involving fugitives, bank robberies, and narcotics (Nelson, 1989). The perception of nearly half of the program coordinators is that their programs have reduced the crime rate for specific types of crimes (Rosenbaum & Lurigio, 1985; Rosenbaum et al., 1986, p. 36). Because of these results and their relatively low operational cost, Crime Stoppers is generally viewed as a cost-effective program and its continuance is currently assured (Rosenbaum et al., 1986, p. 34; 1989). Despite the support it enjoys and its numerical successes, however, critics argue that the program's gains against crime are marginal and possibly outweighed by other, negative effects.

One possible negative effect is that paying rewards and providing anonymity for informants will reduce voluntary cooperation and encourage retributive "snitching" by citizens on their neighbors, family, and friends, thereby fostering a police-state mentality. There is also fear that reenactments of crimes will encourage false testimony and prejudice witnesses' testimony and trial juries (Rosenbaum & Lurigio, 1985, p. 61). In addition, there is concern that the media could become dependent on the criminal justice system and eventually become a base for a mass surveillance and informant system.[21] As Marx (1985, p. 21) has noted:

> Yet there are also potential dangers in institutionalizing such systems. They may encourage paranoia, suspiciousness, and vigilantism. They can weaken trust and offer a vehicle for malicious reporting from anonymous sources. In a different political climate, [they] would lend themselves equally well to informing on those who are merely different or unpopular rather than criminal.

Paying for information is at the crux of the uneasiness felt toward these programs. Program advocates argue that the programs are targeted at people unlikely to cooperate or become involved without a monetary incentive. Nationally, 25 percent of callers are estimated to be actual criminals and another 40 percent people active at the fringes of crime (Rosenbaum et al., 1986, p. 29). Program developers recognize this potential problem and are concerned that the programs will be used as a means of financially supporting regular police informants.

As for the effect on the public of the images of criminality projected through these programs, an assessment of one program, based on a review of its "crime of the week" and "most wanted" cases for the first two years of operation, revealed that in terms of the types of crime portrayed, violent crime dominated (Surette, 1984b, 1986). Robbery, assault, rape, and homicide accounted for 95.3 percent of the crimes of the week and had been committed by 75.3 percent of the most wanted criminals. Nonviolent crimes were rarely portrayed, and homicide was the most popular single crime shown. In addition, the crimes portrayed commonly involved the use of weapons, with handguns the weapon of choice. Only 10.6 percent of all of the combined incidents did not involve weapons, whereas 71.6 percent involved handguns. Further, only 10.9 percent of the victims were uninjured, whereas 68.3 percent died. On the whole, the program portrayed criminality as an attribute of a young, violent, dangerous class of criminals composed mostly of minorities. Crime was portrayed as largely stranger-to-stranger, injurious or fatal encounters in which handguns play a dominant role. The image portrayed in this program is thought to be representative of that portrayed nationally, which raises concerns about the probable effects of these crime spots on the public's perceptions of crime and justice (Rosenbaum & Lurigio, 1985).

The fears raised by participation programs become most clear when defense and public defenders are queried. Even among detractors, however, no one has questioned these programs' effectiveness in soliciting information about unsolved crimes (Owens, 1983):

"It seems that many of the tips are called in out of revenge. It's subject to abuse. If the police go out and investigate people based on anonymous tips, it can cause problems. The right to be secure in your home is not a technicality; it's an important right. It's what keeps the police off our backs. We're overreacting to the crime problem."

Former assistant public defender

"It's frightening, chilling. It induces me to rat on my neighbor. I think it's dangerous and dumb."

University law professor

"People who give tips for money are inherently suspect. People will take a suspicion and elevate it into a fact."

Defense attorney

The image of criminality forwarded by Crime Stoppers is similar to that portrayed in the general entertainment media—of a dangerous and crime-ridden world where murderous attacks are common (see Chapter 2). Such a portrait of the world has been associated with the creation of a "mean-world view" of reality and feelings of fear, isolation, and suspicion. Crime Stoppers programs, by adding similar realistic, credible, and official images of crime, contribute to this negative worldview. The effects on society include the polarization of society along ethic and economic lines as people isolate themselves and grow more wary of strangers (Bortner, 1984; Rosenbaum & Lurigio, 1985, p. 61). Further, by emphasizing violent crimes that appear to be due to greed or irrationality, Crime Stoppers forward individual explanations for crime and downplay broader structural, social, and economic factors (Bortner, 1984). The final consequence of this image is felt to be an unsubstantiated, undue support for law and order and crime control–based punitive public policies (see Culver & Knight, 1979; Dominick, 1978; Estep & MacDonald, 1984). Given that media programming marketed purely as entertainment has the same effect, many believe that Crime Stoppers programs, with their presentation of selected slices of real-life crime, are likely to have even more effect on viewers' attitudes about crime and their perceptions of reality and the criminal justice policies they support.

The possibility of negative social consequences from these programs leads to the third issue, concerning the proper role of the mass media in law enforcement efforts. Should the media restrict themselves to basic reporting of events or become involved in their resolution? On the involvement side is the argument made by program advocates that the media should cooperate and become involved as a civic duty. They feel that Crime Stoppers is a natural extension of the practice of public service announcements. Nationally, most media executives appear to agree with this view (Lavrakas et al., 1990; Rosenbaum et al., 1986, p. 109).[22] The media are not always cooperative, however, apparently because some in the media perceive involvement as contrary to the philosophy of separation of press and government, particularly separation from law enforcement agencies. This reluctance is found more often within print media than within broadcast media. The print media more than the electronic media have long had an adversarial, "watchdog" relationship with law enforcement that conflicts with their involvement in Crime Stoppers projects. They also gain less from cooperating in terms of increased readership (Lavrakas et al., 1990). In essence, some within the media feel that cooperating makes them uncomfortably close to being information-gathering subsidiaries of local law enforcement, rather than autonomous news agents. This is perceived as counter to their traditional adversarial relationship with the entire criminal justice system, and ultimately jeopardizing to their credibility as news journalists. When this journalistic concern is not counterbalanced by a pragmatic business benefit, media cooperation declines.

How all these concerns are to be resolved is unclear; indeed, the nature of these programs makes a resolution unlikely. Unfortunately, little indepen-

Most Crime Stoppers cases have also held up under judicial review ("Case Reviews Support Crime Stoppers," *The Caller*, May 1986, p. 7). Three Crime Stoppers cases have been reviewed by U. S. courts of appeal: In *United States* v. *Briley* (726 F.2d 1301 [8th Cir. 1984]) the court allowed anonymous tips corroborated by other information; in *United States* v. *Debango* (780 F.2d 81 [D.C. Cir. 1986]) and *United States* v. *Zamora* (784 F.2d 1025 [10th Cir. 1986]) the court ruled that the identity of Crime Stoppers informants need not be disclosed. Most recently, in a decision that will make using information from Crime Stoppers easier for law enforcement agencies, the U. S. Supreme Court in *Alabama* v. *White* (110 S. Ct. 2412 [1990]) ruled that anonymous tips backed with a "reasonable suspicion of criminal activity" are sufficient for a valid investigatory stop. The more stringent criteria of "probable cause" is not necessary.

dent data exist to support or lay to rest the expressed fears. We simply do not know at this time if the hypothesized negative consequences of Crime Stoppers–style programs counteract their positive and anticrime effects. First, we don't know how much positive, anticrime effect they actually have. Second, to determine whether or not the negative effects are in fact occurring and to what degree, community attitude surveys examining the relationship between viewing the Crime Stoppers ads, perceptions of criminality, and sources of support for crime-related public policies are needed but currently unavailable. In the interim, because people's reservations are all unsubstantiated, the low cost, apparent success, and popularity of the programs argue for and assure their continuance.

CONCLUSION

The media can be used prosocially to influence people's attitudes about crime and make more crime-related information available to the police. Such use can speed the processing of criminal cases. The media can be used to videotape police patrols, vehicle stops, and interrogations. And they can be useful in the investigation, surveillance, and deterrence of crime. The administrative, mostly crime control, benefits associated with these programs follow quickly, and the programs have consistently been assessed as efficient and cost-effective. Their increased use will be hastened by technological advances that make the equipment more economical, more flexible with greater capabilities, and less obtrusive. However, there are concerns about potential social costs and infringements on due process that do not emerge quickly and are difficult to quantify. The difficulty is that, should evidence of negative effects be found, curtailing established programs could well be impossible.

Despite their popularity, no program has empirically demonstrated a significant reduction of the crime rate without displacement. Regarding the existing programs, deterrence programs that did not include surveillance have not shown any behavioral effects, and it appears doubtful that the mass media can by themselves deter criminal behavior—much as it is unlikely that they alone can criminalize an individual (see Chapter 5). Media surveillance programs have shown short-term deterrence effects similar to the announcement effect observed for heavily publicized law enforcement changes, but their long-term ability to deter crime without simply displacing it remains unproven (cf. Dinitz, 1987). Media efforts to reduce victimization by teaching crime preventive behaviors have had mixed results. These campaigns aimed at potential victims have shown an ability to attain high recognition levels among the general public and have increased the public's knowledge and changed some attitudes. But they have not been shown to significantly change behavior. Programs designed to increase public involvement by advertising crimes appear effective in gathering information and in solving specific types of crimes. Their effect on the overall crime rate is not known but is likely negligible.

And all of these anticrime programs have potential costs that include increased depersonalization of the criminal justice system, isolation of the police from the policed, increased citizen fear and suspicion of surveillance, the polarization of society due to the creation of affluent, technologically secured "garrison" communities, and decreased citizen support for and legitimization of the criminal justice system. A final problem has to do with media coverage of these programs that conveys the impression that these efforts are working to reduce overall crime rates and that such media-based programs are indeed panaceas for the general crime problem. To the extent that the public believes this, resources for other, ultimately more beneficial avenues will be drained away (cf. Jeffery, 1990). The media and their technology are not panaceas for the crime problem.

To solve crimes and deter criminals the government must intervene in its citizens' lives. The media provide a means to do so in new ways, ways that are felt to be both more efficient and less obviously intrusive. In practice, however, such applications cannot avoid opening up for view areas of public life, of the criminal justice system, and of police–citizen interactions that are even further backstage. In certain instances such as in the use of patrol car cameras, where police actions are recorded as much as citizen actions, this is clearly seen as a positive course. In other instances such as in the use of hidden police surveillance systems, the desirability of doing so is not so clear. Still, these programs provide unique opportunities to study the interaction of media and justice from a new perspective. They let us look at the media as part of a solution to crime rather than as part of its cause. In addition, in using the media and media technology, and in being "news" themselves, these programs increase the dimensions of interaction between the media and justice. Study of this expanded interaction, in particular of the community dynamics that develop in support of and in opposition to these programs, would improve our knowledge of the influence of the media on crime and justice in our society. The impact of these programs on citizens' perceptions of criminality and criminal justice still needs to be assessed. Do they increase the fear of crime, perpetuate or exacerbate the stereotypes promoted by the entertainment media, and create support for or opposition to specific criminal justice policies? It's hoped that future research will provide answers to these questions. For now, the mass media and their technology are an additional, potentially positive, but limited resource to be used in reducing crime.

The expanded capabilities of the media made possible by its technological advances have also affected how the news media operate and how they report on the criminal justice system. The potential of the media to extensively cover live all aspects of the daily procedures of the criminal justice system have increased the long-standing tension between the news media and the judicial system. The next chapter will review the history and current status of this relationship.

Notes

1. See Himmelwitt, 1980; Murray & Clarke, 1980; Rushton, 1976a, 1976b.
2. See Hovland et al., 1949; Hyman & Sheatsley, 1947; Janis & Feshbach, 1953; Klapper, 1960; Star & Hughes, 1950.
3. See Mendelsohn, 1973; Robinson, 1972; Rogers, 1973; Rosenstock, 1960.
4. See, for example, Salcedo and his associates' 1974 "A Successful Information Campaign on Pesticides." The expectation that these programs will succeed is further bolstered by the fact that billions of dollars are spent annually by advertisers who believe correctly that brief, thirty-second exposures, repeated over and over, significantly affect the public's behavior (Rushton, 1982b, p. 255).

5. See Collins, 1973, 1975; Cosgrove & McIntyre, 1974; Fox et al., 1977; Friedrich & Stein, 1975; Stein & Friedrich, 1972; Stein et al., 1973.
6. See Ball & Bogatz, 1970; Coates et al., 1976; Lesser, 1974; Palmer, 1973.
7. Ball & Bogatz, 1970; CBS, 1974; Coates et al., 1976; Lesser, 1974; Noble, 1983; Palmer, 1973; Roberts et al., 1974; Rubinstein et al., 1974; Rushton, 1982a; Sprafkin et al., 1975; Teuchman & Orme, 1981.
8. Another question is whether or not prosocial media efforts are commercially viable. Probably not. "Sesame Street," "Mister Roger's Neighborhood," and "The Electric Company" have not been copied by any commercial networks and many of the

commercial prosocial programs developed in the seventies have been dropped.

9. There has been only one reported attempt to use prosocial television programming to improve the social behavior of institutionalized children and its evaluation reported some evidence of success (see Sprafkin & Rubinstein, 1982).

10. Contradicting the Finchenauer evaluation, Langer (1980) analyzed a sample of sixty-six juvenile offenders before and after their participation in the Scared Straight program and compared them with a similar nonparticipating control group of sixty-five juveniles. He reported that over a follow-up period averaging twenty-two months, the Scared Straight juveniles' delinquent activity was relatively constant after their participation in the program, while the control group's delinquency increased substantially. Also, the severity of the offenses was greater for the control group. Langer concluded that the Scared Straight program is a valuable contribution to the prevention and control of delinquency. In a final statement in the project's defense, it has continued to remain popular and is still supported and run at Rahway Prison. See also Cohn, 1980; Finchenauer, 1980; Maguire, 1980; Mos, 1980 for an overview of the *Scared Straight!* controversy.

11. One police officer was quoted as saying, "The system has failed totally. In the two years of operation, not one crime was recorded by the cameras" ("Miami Beach Gives Up on Street Anti-Crime Cameras," *Crime Control Digest*, Aug. 27, 1984, pp. 2–3).

12. "Police Take Shots at Street Crime" (*Security World*, vol. 20, no. 9, 1983, pp. 13, 15).

13. Some overlap exists between the media-based law enforcement programs discussed here and the judicial applications described in Chapter 8. In truth, criminal justice is a single continuous process that extends from field stops through the courts, and given that video from a patrol car camera often winds up being shown in court, the distinction between law enforcement and judicial applications is somewhat artificial. Out of necessity more than logic, the iden-

tification of a suspect-defendant is chosen as the break point. Police field stops, patrols, and interrogations are discussed here in Chapter 6 as part of anticrime law enforcement efforts, whereas booking, line-ups, arraignments, and all other judicial steps are discussed in Chapter 8.

14. The videotaping of 946 police interviews with suspects and accused persons was tested over a two-year period as a substitute for the traditional method of police taking written notes while questioning suspects and submitting written accounts to the court. The videotape of the interview became the official report and copies were supplied to judges, state attorneys, and defense counsel on request.

15. For example, appeals courts have dismissed a suit against ABC and Geraldo Rivera for broadcasting a portion of an interview that Rivera had secretly recorded with a hidden microphone and camera (see *Broddie* v. *ABC*, 881 F.2d 1318 [11th Cir. 1989]).

16. Citing Bureau of Justice Statistics, 1986; Greenberg, 1987; O'Keefe & Reid-Nash, 1987b; Sacco & Silverman, 1981; Skogan & Maxfield, 1981.

17. Previous programs include a 1978 anti–auto theft program in Spokane, Washington, that used television to teach theft prevention techniques to the public. Another program, associated with a Minnesota Crime Watch effort, was aimed at general crime prevention and a limited evaluation reported some success (see White et al., 1975). This program was more extensive than the Spokane program in that newspaper advertisements, television and radio commercials, movie theater ads, bus cards, and bumper stickers were all used to convey information throughout Minnesota.

18. The evaluation consisted of a one-time national survey of 1,200 adults and a pre- and postcampaign survey of three U. S. cities—Buffalo, Denver, and Milwaukee.

19. Also known as Crime Alert, Crime Solvers, Silent Witness, or Crime Line (see Lavrakas et al., 1990; Rosenbaum et al., 1989).

20. Indeed, given the large amount of unsolicited information received regarding unadvertised crimes, some argue that the adver-

tised crimes are more important as vehicles for obtaining tips regarding other crimes than as a means of solving the crimes actually publicized (author's interview with the chair of the Crime Stoppers, Media Relations Committee, Dade County, Fla., February 5, 1983).

21. See Marx, 1985; Paulin, 1988; Rosenbaum & Lurigio, 1985, pp. 60–61; Rosenbaum et al., 1989; Surette, 1986.

22. Nationally, program coordinators report high levels of media cooperation, with less than 10 percent reporting uncooperative local media (Lavrakas et al., 1990).

7 Media Coverage and the Courts

OVERVIEW

Chapter 7 examines the interplay and issues that arise when the media interact with the judicial system. Conflicts arise when the First Amendment rights of the media clash with the Fifth and Sixth Amendments responsibilities of the courts to ensure due process protections. Supposedly, though they are frequently at odds, the media and the courts have similar goals and reactions to criminal events. Both want to gather information, control access to this information, and present it to a specific audience. In addition, both have been pressed by the same social forces to be more open and accessible, to reveal their backstage news-gathering or case-processing procedures, and to provide information to the other. (Ironically, their disputes are often resolved in the courts, frequently by the Supreme Court.) Despite the enormous amount of case law, journal articles, and research that has focused on the media and the courts, these commonalities allow us to discuss their interaction within two broad topic areas. The first and largest encompasses news coverage and publicity issues. The second concerns the strategies the judiciary and the media use to control information and deal with each other.

First discussed is due process and publicity. Reviewing the difficulty the courts face in defining and identifying prejudicial coverage, the research on publicity and juries supports the surprising conclusion that the media may actually more frequently affect not highly publicized but nonpublicized cases. The chapter then discusses an additional group of publicity related issues, privacy, media access to information, and televised trials. In all of these areas the media have continually striven to increase their ability to ac-quire and reveal information while the courts have attempted to balance the media's rights against concerns over violation of privacy, access to govern-ment files, and the presence of television in the courtroom. Though both appeal courts and legislatures have attempted to resolve some of the ques-tions raised, these areas remain contentious. Only with regard to courtroom television has anything approaching a consensus emerged: In a reversal of the view held only twenty-five years ago, today live television is not only al-lowed in the courtroom but usually welcomed, and in at least one appellate case was actually demanded by a defendant.

The chapter continues with a discussion of efforts by the justice system and the media to maintain control of their information. The courts can adopt either a proactive strategy and seek to stop prejudicial information from being published, or a reactive strategy and seek to limit the prejudicial effects of information that the media have already published. Not surpris-ingly, the proactive strategy, which includes closing proceedings and issuing restrictive and protective orders, and which directly constrains the media, has aroused the strongest opposition from the media. But though the reac-tive, less restrictive mechanisms of the second strategy are more commonly employed, it is not clear when they should be used or how effective they are. On the other side, the media have worked to control their information by arguing on appeals that journalists have a constitutional right of "privi-leged conversation" with news sources and by lobbying for the passage of "shield" laws to legislatively ensure this right. These efforts have become more intense as the media have been pressed more often for information and reporters have been forced to testify. Though the media have had suc-cesses on both fronts, their ability to avoid opening their news files or testi-fying varies considerably from state to state and case to case.

Concluding the chapter is a comment on the factors that have encour-aged the opening of the judicial system to the media and the reforms that have been recommended to improve the relationship between the media and the judiciary. The trends all point toward greater access and exposure in the future, but both the criminal justice system and the mass media re-main among a handful of social institutions that still aggressively resist the easing of outside access and continue to struggle to keep their backstage realms closed.

THE NEWS MEDIA AND THE COURTS

The relationship between the news media and the courts in the United States is an area of primary concern for the judiciary. As evidenced in earlier chapters, these concerns have a long history and arise from direct conflict between the First and the Fifth and Sixth Amendments and the continuing struggle to define and balance the rights delineated under each amendment. Early in the Republic, Aaron Burr's attorney claimed that jurors could not properly decide his client's case because of prejudicial newspaper articles (*United States* v. *Burr,* 25 F. Cas. 49, 49 [C.C.D. Va. 1807] [No. 14692g], cited by Marcus, 1982, p. 237). Only in the last seventy years, however, coinciding with the development of the modern mass media, have the provisions of the First Amendment been meaningfully defined as a legal concept (Blasi, 1971, p. 233). More recently, the issues of reporters' privilege and shield laws, sunshine laws, media access to government files, and the live televising of criminal trials have exacerbated the conflicts between the news media and the judicial system. Ironically, despite their adversarial history and contentious interactions, the media and the judicial system normally react to criminal events in much the same manner, concentrating their resources on investigating the facts for later presentation to a specific audience—jurors, viewers, or readers. Their relationship is sometimes cooperative, but more often each jealously guards its information while attempting to discover what the other knows (Salas, 1984). This competition is exemplified by the media's attempts to protect their information through shield laws, and the courts attempt to control and protect their information through closed proceedings and restrictive access rules.

Beyond the constitutional questions and issues regarding control of information, an additional concern arises because of the unique function that courts play in society. Besides being an institution in which legal disputes are resolved, the courtroom is also a social arena in which the significance and value of social behaviors are determined. The courtroom thus functions not only as a mechanism for resolving individual disputes but also as a mechanism for legitimizing society's laws and government. Accordingly, anything that influences the public image of the courts invariably influences its legitimizing function. And without question the news media are crucial in the formation of the public image of the courts (Yankelovich et al., 1978). Of concern therefore is whether or not the courts are reacting to the news media by altering their traditional practices to better match media-dictated formats. The fear is that courtroom participants will alter the way they testify and argue to fit the needs of the media rather than those of the courtroom. Such changes have already been noted in religion, sports, and politics (Altheide, 1984).

The relationship between the media and the justice system is further strained because different considerations and values govern the means by which each obtains information and evaluates its worth. Whereas the criminal justice system is guided by legislative and constitutional mandates and the courts have the task of separating relevant from legally irrelevant information, the media respond primarily to newsworthiness and entertainment considerations. Each side's considerations dictate what facts are presented as well as when and how they are disclosed. Traditionally, in the courtroom, information is imparted in a form and process quite different from that preferred by the news media. Courtroom information is extracted point by point in long story lines by lawyers following legal procedures and rules of evidence. Moreover, the information is specially prepared for a limited audience comprising a judge or jury (Altheide, 1984; Bennett et al., 1983). In contrast, news stories are outwardly directed and developed in accordance with entertainment value rather than legal relevance. They are brief, time- or space-limited stories that must make their points quickly, and they are built around whatever film or dramatic elements are available (Altheide, 1984; see also Chapter 4). Whereas the courts have traditionally presented internally controlled, front-stage events to a specific audience, court news tends to present dramatic backstage information to an external, general audience. Indeed, the news media can delegitimize the whole judicial system by revealing previously shielded information regarding case negotiations and the significant role extralegal factors play in the judicial decision-making process. Another fear is that close media coverage will cripple the judicial system by forcing everyone to rigidly adhere to the formal legal rules and procedures and forego the discretion and bargaining common in case processing. In the end, the news media and the judiciary are often adversaries, with, ironically the courts frequently called on to resolve their disputes. Because their disputes generally involve clashes between fundamental constitutional provisions, the Supreme Court often acts as final arbiter.

On first examination, the interactions of the mass media and the judicial system appear to give rise to a morass of complex and seemingly disparate issues. All of them, however, can be subsumed within two broad subject areas. The larger of the two involves news media coverage of the courts and encompasses such issues as invasion of privacy and the effects of pretrial and trial publicity on due process. A basic judicial concern is that the media undermine the fairness of a trial and that media publicity violates due process protections. This concern is at the crux of the conflicts arising from media coverage of the criminal justice system. A corollary concern is that publicity destroys privacy and that media coverage may harm or embarrass innocent persons swept up in the coverage of heavily publicized cases. The second subject area involves judicial and media strategies for dealing with each other and controlling information. The courts gear their efforts toward minimizing the negative effects of news media coverage by closing trials, imposing prior restraints, granting continuances and changes of venue, and taking other judicial actions. The media gear their efforts toward both countering judicial actions that limit their activities and access, and limiting police and court access to information they hold.

ISSUES RELATED TO NEWS COVERAGE AND PUBLICITY

Due Process and Pretrial Publicity

Publicity before and during a trial may so affect a community and its courts that a fair trial becomes impossible. In effect, due process protections such as the presumption of innocence constitutionally afforded to defendants are destroyed. The media especially create problems when they publish information that is inadmissible in the courtroom and create a community atmosphere in which finding and impaneling impartial jurors is difficult (Box 7-1).

Unfortunately it is not always clear when particular coverage is prejudicial, and the Supreme Court has employed such ambiguous phrases as "fundamentally fair," "huge wave of public passions," and "flagrant" to distinguish biased from unbiased coverage. It has not, however, operationally defined these terms for the lower courts. The resulting dilemma for trial courts is twofold. The first problem is determining when media activities infringe on a defendant's right to a fair trial. When exactly is coverage prejudicial? At what point does a news story become inflammatory rather than just colorful? The second problem is deciding how to balance media access to court proceedings with defendants' right to fair and unbiased proceedings. How should prejudicial media coverage be dealt with? The problem is especially acute when the media's coverage precedes any formal judicial proceedings and there are as yet no accused defendants to protect.

Faced with these ambiguous problems and forced to render largely subjective determinations, both trial and appellate courts have focused on jurors and potential influences on them as the key to determining the fairness of a trial. If a jury is considered impartial and uninfluenced by media coverage, then the proceedings are normally considered fair. The assumption is that judges, lawyers, and other judicial personnel are able to insulate themselves from media influence because of their professional ethics and legal training and experience. Jurors, being the amateurs in the proceedings, are considered the most susceptible to media coverage. If they are unaffected, the reasoning goes, the trial also should be. The difficulty has been

It should be noted that the media are not always the originators of the publicity but are often sought out by attorneys or other parties. For example, Wise (1986) reported that the New York City Bar Association sought sanctions against attorneys for a number of abuses committed in dealing with the news media. These abuses included the "announcement" of indictments for publicity purposes and press conferences at which evidence was displayed; the alerting of TV camera crews to allow them to film suspects entering station houses to surrender, sometimes in handcuffs; and almost weekly examples of lawyers in public office expressing their opinions concerning the guilt or innocence of persons not yet tried and sometimes not even accused.

BOX 7-1   Prejudicial Information

Prejudicial information takes two forms: factual information that bears on the guilt of a defendant and emotional information—information aimed at arousing the emotions of an audience—that has no evidentiary relevance (Hoiberg & Stires, 1973; Kramer et al., 1990; Simon, 1966). Factual information includes the content of confessions or allusions to confessions, performances on polygraph or other tests (usually inadmissible as evidence) and refusals to take such tests, and past criminal records and convictions. Emotional information includes stories that question the credibility of witnesses or present the personal feelings of witnesses about prosecutors, police, victims, or judges;

stories about the defendant's character (he hates children and dogs), associates (she hangs around with known syndicate gunmen), or personality (he attacks people on the slightest provocation); and stories that inflame the general public (cf. Pember, 1987, pp. 364–366). When queried, judges have reported that publication of criminal records, performances on tests, and information about confessions are the most damaging (American Bar Association, 1978; Siebert et al., 1970). Information that a defendant has been released from custody has been reported to be inversely related to prejudice against that defendant (Eisenstein & Jacobs, 1977; Tans & Chaffee, 1966).

---

deciding when jurors are indeed impartial and what proof is necessary to establish prejudice (Apfel, 1980, p. 446). In practice, the operational definition of an impartial juror is derived from the Aaron Burr case, heard in 1807: "An impartial juror is one free from the dominant influence of knowledge acquired outside the courtroom, free from strong and deep impressions which close the mind" (*United States* v. *Burr,* 25 F. Cas. 49, 49 [C.C.D. Va. 1807] [No. 14692g]). Though not a precise rule, this definition does eliminate ignorance of a case or a total lack of exposure to media coverage as a requirement for impartiality. A reading of the case law in this area shows, however, that applying this definition has proven to be a haphazard task for the Supreme Court.

Following a set of piecemeal and not always clarifying Supreme Court decisions from the 1950s into the 1970s (detailed in Box 7-2), the current judicial position is that certain extreme but unspecified circumstances can be so prejudicial as to require judicial remedies without requiring that prejudice actually be shown (cf. Jaffe, 1965, p. 519; see also next margin note). It is left to the trial courts to determine on a case-by-case basis whether the circumstances are inherently or only potentially prejudicial. If potentially

---

Some jurisdictions allow testimony or affidavits, expert testimony, public opinion polls, and various "tests" to establish prejudice. The best known test is a content analysis of coverage measuring fact versus opinion. Reporting facts is perceived as nonprejudicial; reporting opinions is seen as prejudicial (Tanick & Shields, 1985).

BOX 7-2 Supreme Court Decisions Concerning Pretrial Publicity

The first modern Supreme Court case regarding pretrial publicity was *Sheppard* v. *Florida* (341 U. S. 50 [1951], 71 S. Ct. 549 [per curiam]), in which the Court reversed the conviction of two blacks for the rape of a young white woman. Contributing to the decision to reverse was the publication of a sheriff's statement that the defendants had confessed to the rape, though no confession was produced at the trial. The Court stated that the inherent difficulties of blacks in obtaining fair trials when accused of raping whites was compounded by the actions of the local press and law enforcement officers. The importance of this decision is that the Court implied that certain circumstances such as the publication of information about a confession are inherently prejudicial; that is, no actual evidence of juror prejudice had to be provided. In the Court's view, "The trial was but a legal gesture to register a verdict already dictated by the press and the public opinion which it generated" (341 U. S. 50 [1951]). The Court did not clearly state what conditions were necessary for inherent prejudice to exist, however, and over the following decade it was reluctant to accept unsubstantiated coverage effects as grounds for reversal (Jaffe, 1965, p. 514). The Supreme Court has been reluctant to extend its position in *Sheppard* to consider other circumstances inherently prejudicial.

For example, *Stroble* v. *California* (343 U. S. 310 [1952]) involved the murder of a child to which the defendant initially confessed but subsequently pled innocent and went to trial. Details of the confession were released to the media and resulted in widespread publicity. Unlike in *Sheppard* in 1951, the confession was introduced in court as evidence. The Supreme Court refused to reverse this conviction, arguing that the defendant failed to prove prejudicial results from the publication of the information and that his claim of press-generated bias was thus unsubstantiated. In contrast to *Sheppard*, in which prejudice was presumed, in this case actual proof of prejudice was required (Dubnoff, 1977, p. 93). In a similar decision in

1956, the Supreme Court in *United States ex rel. Darcy* v. *Handy, Warden* (351 U. S. 454 [1956]) declined to reverse the murder conviction of a defendant in a case where the trial judge was quoted in the local newspaper as saying that he couldn't see how the jury could have reached any decision but the one they had, for conviction and a sentence of death. He went on to comment that such decisions are the only hope of stemming the tide of crime (351 U. S. 454, 458). Again the Court ruled that the defense had failed to prove actual prejudice. A key in both cases for the Court is that the defense had failed to aggressively pursue the legal avenues available to mitigate prejudice, such as asking for changes of venue, using peremptory challenges, or requesting continuances (see Box 7-7). These decisions placed the onus on the defense in the 1950s not only to establish that the media had caused prejudice but to suggest and pursue remedies.

In *Marshall* v. *United States* (360 U. S. 310 [1959]), however, the Supreme Court abandoned the *Stroble* position for federal courts when it ruled that evidence or information that has been ruled inadmissible in court but that reaches the jury can be presumed to be prejudicial. The *Marshall* case involved the revelation to jurors that a defendant charged with unlawfully dispensing amphetamines had previously been found to be practicing medicine without a license. The trial judge had ruled the information inadmissible as evidence, but the jury had access to newspaper stories containing the information. The Supreme Court reversed, despite the fact that when queried by the trial judge, the jurors stated that they could reach a verdict solely on the evidence presented in court. The Court thus seemed to have established its first general rule regarding what is prejudicial and what is not in terms of media publicity: If the information is inadmissible as evidence and it reaches the jury, prejudice can be assumed to exist.

Since *Marshall*, the Court has held to its

(continued)

BOX 7-2 (continued)

---

position that under certain circumstances the defense need not provide evidence of prejudice. It has not, however, provided clearer guidelines for recognizing such cases, stating only that in extreme or flagrant cases, prejudice is inherent, without defining *extreme* or *flagrant*. For example, in 1961, the Court reversed in *Irvin* v. *Dowd* (366 U. S. 717 [1961]), a case that it deemed had flagrant circumstances of prejudicial media pretrial publicity. The prosecutor announced to the press that the defendant had confessed, and there were press reports of prior convictions, confessions to other crimes, and an attempt to plead guilty. Ninety percent of the prospective jurors admitted holding an opinion concerning Irvin's guilt, Irvin used all his peremptory challenges, and, finally, of the seated jurors, eight admitted prior to the trial to believing that Irvin was guilty (Dubnoff, 1977, pp. 94–95). A change of venue was granted but was limited by state statute to the next county, which had been exposed to the same coverage. The Court ruled that "such extraneous influences, in violation of the decencies guaranteed by our Constitution, are sometimes so powerful that an accused is forced, as a practical matter, to forego trial by jury. . . . It is not requiring too much that petitioner be tried in an atmosphere undisturbed by so huge a wave of public passion (366 U. S. at 730, 727–728). The Court did not specify which of the above factors were most important or what combination of factors would establish inherent prejudice but did establish in this case that review of voir dire (see Box 7-7) is an acceptable method of determining if prejudice exists (Jaffe, 1965, p. 515). In reaching this decision, the Court rejected, however, the argument that a jury must be totally uninformed of a case and that because the public had received a large amount of information about a case, a conviction should be automatically reversed.*

Subsequently, in *Rideau* v. *Louisiana* (373 U. S. 723, [1963]) the Court introduced the condition of "a fundamental fairness test" in reversing a conviction. Following his arrest, Rideau was filmed at the local jail in an "interview" with the local sheriff, during which Rideau confessed to a robbery, kidnapping, and murder. According to the Court, the television broadcast of the interview–confession was prejudicial enough to require a change of venue order, and failure to move the trial made "any subsequent proceedings in the community so overwhelmingly prejudicial as to require a reversal." The Court considered Rideau's televised confessions—at which he pled guilty to murder—in a very real sense to constitute his trial (373 U. S. 726). In its decision, the Supreme Court attempted to help trial judges identify inherently prejudicial situations, mentioning "the truthfulness of news reporting," "if the accused is a prominent person in the community," or "if the case by its nature attracts attention," as factors useful for determining bias. Responsibility for protecting a defendant from prejudicial publicity remained the defense attorney's, however. The Court held that defense attorneys should seek gag or protective orders, should introduce proof of the danger of prejudice and focus attention on offending media, and in any appeals should establish the inherent prejudice of the publicity.

In 1966, in perhaps the best known case in this area because of the coverage it received and the movies and books produced about it, as well as the subsequent fame of the defense lawyer, F. Lee Bailey, the Court in *Sheppard* v. *Maxwell* (384 U. S. 333 [1966]) shifted the onus of requesting protection from prejudicial coverage and establishing prejudicial effects from defense attorneys to the trial judge (Carroll et al., 1986, p. 188). The Court declared the judge re-

(continued)

---

* "It is not required, however, that the jurors be totally ignorant of the facts and issues involved. In these days of swift, widespread and diverse methods of communication, an important case can be expected to arouse the interest of the public in the vicinity, and scarcely any of those best qualified to serve as jurors will not have formed some impression or opinion as to the merits of the case" (366 U. S. at 722).

BOX 7-2 (continued)

sponsible for recognizing media-generated prejudice and pursuing means of controlling it. The *Sheppard* case involved a prominent Cleveland doctor who was accused of bludgeoning his pregnant wife to death. The coverage was intense and pervasive, beginning prior to an indictment and continuing through the trial. In its review, the Supreme Court not only reversed the conviction, but suggested for the first time specific actions that trial judges should follow in controlling the effects of publicity. It also reaffirmed, however, that it is not the amount of publicity per se that results in reversal in a particular case, but whether or not the defendant in that case received a fair and impartial trial (see also *People* v. *Speck*, 41 Ill. 2d 177, 183, N. E. 2d 208, 212 [1968]). Therefore, massive coverage alone would not automatically be interpreted as prejudicial or ensure a reversal. The Court still refrained from stating a general rule for determining prejudice and left that determination to trial judges, only suggesting specific factors that the judges should be sensitive to. The *Sheppard* decision thus clearly signaled judges that measures have to be taken in certain cases whether counsel requests them or not, but did not indicate exactly when they should be taken. The Court's precise directions read as follows:

> When there is a reasonable likelihood that prejudicial news prior to trial will prevent a fair trial, the judge should continue the case until the threat abates, or transfer it to another county

not so permeated with publicity. In addition, sequestration of the jury was something the judge should have raised sua sponte with counsel. If publicity during the proceedings threatens the fairness of the trial, a new trial should be ordered. . . . Neither prosecutors, counsel for the defense, the accused, court staff nor enforcement officers coming under the jurisdiction of the court should be permitted to frustrate its function. Collaboration between counsel and the press as to information affecting the fairness of a criminal trial is not only subject to regulation, but is highly censurable and worthy of disciplinary measures. (Sheppard, 384 U. S. 363 [1966])

Determining when a "reasonable likelihood" exists is left to each trial judge. In 1975, however, in *Murphy* v. *Florida* (421 U. S. 794 [1975]), the Court reaffirmed that only in extreme cases will inherent prejudice be accorded and returned to its position that the burden of showing inherent prejudice usually falls on the defendant. In its ruling, the Court concluded that the "petitioner has failed to show that the setting of the trial was inherently prejudicial or that the jury selection process of which he complains permits an inference of actual prejudice." Having established the trial court judge's responsibility for recognizing and controlling the effects of publicity, the Supreme Court in the 1980s declined to review a number of trial court decisions and has consistently supported trial judges' assessments and decisions in this area.

prejudicial, the defendant must prove actual prejudice. If inherently prejudicial, the trial judge must intervene of his or her own accord to stem and prevent prejudicial effects. There is no set formula to look to, however, and the Supreme Court has provided scant guidelines to determine whether a particular case falls in the first or second category (Dubnoff, 1977, p. 97). Having declined to clarify remaining questions during the 1980s, the Supreme Court is unlikely to be delineating more specific rules in the near future. The response of most state courts to this ambiguity has been to demand proof of actual prejudice by the defendant and to formulate their own

This posture was recently reaffirmed in a 1984 Supreme Court decision, *Patton* v. *Yount* (104 S. Ct. 2885), in which the Court stated that a trial court's findings of impartiality may be overturned only for manifest error and when there is evidence that a "wave of public passion" existed that would have made a fair trial unlikely.

series of standards, rejecting the concept of inherent prejudice. In most cases, all that is constitutionally required is that a juror be able to state under oath that he or she can render a fair and impartial verdict based on the evidence presented in court. Given that the Supreme Court has tended to reverse state court convictions only where it finds the lower court proceedings to be "outrageous" and the error of the trial judge "manifest" (Dubnoff, 1977, p. 98), the safe course for the defense is to assume that the burden of proving media-generated prejudice is theirs (Apfel, 1980, pp. 445, 449).

Social Science Research Concerning Publicity and Trials

Given the persistence of the judicial struggle over news coverage, it is appropriate to ask what social scientists studying the effects of media coverage on trial participants have discovered. How does news coverage actually influence jurors?

One research approach emphasizes anecdotal references and case studies of an actual trial.[1] Unfortunately, though interesting reading, because of their limitation to single cases these studies do not reveal much about the general effects of media publicity.

A second approach has been to create and study mock juries in pseudoexperimental situations. However, these mock laboratory or field jury studies, summarized in Box 7-3 and Box 7-4, also have deficiencies. Laboratory studies of mock juries, for example, normally draw mock jurors from a variety of sources, including actual jury pools, general community members, registered voters, high school students, undergraduate psychology students, and law school students. These subjects review the transcripts or hear tapes of cases with and without accompanying media accounts and decide guilt or recommend sentences. These "laboratory" studies generally support the conclusions that publicized confessions are especially influential on jurors, that biased news is more influential if it is the sole source of information, and that many potential jurors are able to recognize and set aside their own biases. The generalizability of these laboratory studies is weakened, however, because of the artificiality of the publicity presented and the lack of variation in the types of media used (all but the most recent used printed or audio material); the short, unrealistic time lags between exposure to the publicity and the rendering of verdicts; the questionable match between subjects and actual jurors; and the differences between deciding a verdict in the laboratory setting and doing so in an actual courtroom (see Pember, 1987, p. 366; Rollings & Blascovich, 1977, p. 60; Simon, 1977, pp. 520–521).

BOX 7-3 Laboratory Studies of Mock Juries

Klein and Jess (1966) selected 48 male university sophomores and formed eight six-man juries to be exposed to prejudicial and nonprejudicial news stories a few days prior to a simulated trial. Jurors were sent a copy of a newspaper with a story planted on page one and were asked to listen to a radio news tape including a story on the case. Following the trials and a reading of the standard jury instruction, the juries were surreptitiously observed during their deliberations. The results indicated that the judge's instructions to disregard external material influenced three of the four juries with regard to considering evidence encountered outside the courtroom. However, in all the jury deliberations involving jurors exposed to prejudicial information, reference was made to such information, and one jury used that information despite the judge's instructions.

Simon (1966) had 97 subjects drawn from a voter registration list listen to a forty-five-minute edited tape of a murder trial. The subjects were divided into two groups, one of which also read three sensational stories containing information about the defendant's prior record and the second of which read conservatively written stories. Simon reported that subjects who were exposed to the sensational stories were more likely to reach guilty verdicts, but that judicial instructions remedied these effects. However, the study did not include a no-instruction control, and participants were informed that the study regarded "the problem of trial publicity."

Tans and Chaffee (1966) used newspaper stories about crimes that differed in the severity of the crime reported and the type of prejudicial information disclosed. One hundred fifty subjects from various groups were asked to evaluate the suspects on 7-point scales measuring qualities including good–bad, guilty–innocent, young–old, dumb–smart, and honest–dishonest. Groups included a university extension class, a steel workers' wives' auxiliary, clerical and professional state Capitol workers, participants in a conference on home care of the ill, attendees at a conference for publicity chairpeople of the League of Women Voters, and attendees at a PTA meeting. Analyzing the results for the guilty–innocent scale, the authors reported that a police report of a confession was the single most damaging piece of information and that there was a clear relationship between unfavorable news articles and average guilty ratings.

Wilcox (1970), in association with McCombs,* studied 120 subjects selected from a voter registration list and divided them into eight groups. Each group was provided a newspaper story concerning the arrest of a murder suspect containing various combinations of information about confessions, evidence, or a prior criminal record. Reporting of a confession was the most prejudicial item, especially in combination with disclosure of a criminal record.

Hoiberg and Stires (1973) tested the response of 337 high school students to four pretrial publicity conditions, labeled high and low prejudgmental publicity and high and low heinous-crime publicity, with prejudgmental publicity implying guilt and heinous-crime publicity presenting vivid and dramatic descriptions of the crime. The subjects were randomly presented different versions of newspaper stories reflecting one of the four conditions of pretrial publicity and a fifteen-minute tape recording of a trial. They were then asked to rate on a 1-to-10 scale their certainty as to the guilt of the defendant. Only female students were found to be affected by the publicity: Those exposed to publicity that dramatized the heinousness of the crime were more certain of the defendant's guilt. Also, female students with low IQs who had been exposed to high prejudgmental publicity gave higher guilty scores than female students exposed to low prejudgmental publicity. Hoiberg and Stires concluded that pretrial pub-

(continued)

---

*Based on a study by W. Wilcox and M. McCombs, "Crime Story Elements and Fair Trial/Free Press." Unpublished report, University of California at Los Angeles, 1967.

BOX 7-3 (continued)

licity does not necessarily infringe on the right to a fair trial, but that certain types of information can influence certain jurors.

Sue and his colleagues (1974) sampled two groups—102 psychology undergraduates and 100 nonstudents—to examine the influence of pretrial publicity on verdicts and on the perceived strength of the prosecution and defense cases. Pretrial publicity was of two types—either damaging and relevant or damaging but irrelevant to the trial. Four factors were isolated: sex, the two types of pretrial publicity, and the judge's instructions to disregard. Subjects were given transcripts of the trial and newspaper accounts of the crime. The authors found that exposure to inadmissible evidence (the information that a gun found in the apartment had been identified by ballistics as having been used in the robbery) resulted in higher evaluations of the strength of the prosecutor's case and more guilty verdicts, but suggested that less damaging information had less effect. They concluded that relevant and damaging information has an adverse effect even when ruled inadmissible and even when the jurors are directed to disregard such evidence.

Padawer-Singer and Barton (1975) used jurors from regular jury pools and found initial evidence that prejudicial newspaper clippings may compromise a juror's impartiality. However, in a follow-up study, Rottenberg (1976) reported that voir dire examinations—examinations to determine the competence of potential jurors—apparently reduce the effect of prejudicial reports on jurors.

Sohn (1976) had twenty-four subjects who were chosen to conform to juror characteristics sort forty-eight news stories typed on $3'' \times 5''$ cards into piles forming a continuum from most guilty to most innocent. The stories manipulated three variables: (1) the kind of crime—a felony or a misdemeanor; (2) the name of the accused—common or uncommon; and (3) the penalty for conviction—high or low. The only effect they found for the three variables was that some people tended to as-

sume that suspects described in pretrial news stories were guilty if they were charged with committing a felony rather than a misdemeanor.

Greene and Loftus (1984) have discussed two experiments examining the impact of highly publicized news events on decision making by mock jurors. In their first, serendipitous experiment, 168 students rendered verdicts after reading about a trial that involved eyewitness testimony. In the middle of the experiment, the local newspaper ran a prominent news story about a mistakenly identified innocent man as the offender in a serious crime. Those students who decided after this story ran were less likely to convict a hypothetical defendant. In the second experiment, seventy-two citizens grouped according to whether or not they had read a *Reader's Digest* story about a mistakenly identified defendant were also asked to render verdicts in a hypothetical case. Those who had read the article were significantly less likely to convict than those who had not.

Davis (1986) studied twenty simulated juries (comprising undergraduate students enrolled in introductory psychology courses) that were exposed to either neutral or negative publicity about a case and then shown a videotape of the criminal trial either immediately or one week later. Analysis of the juries' verdicts showed no significant difference in conviction rates or in deliberation factors, and there was no evidence of damaging effects from prejudicial pretrial publicity. Davis concluded that the jury verdicts and individual juror measures revealed considerable resistance to the influence of prejudicial news, supporting earlier studies that found that juries are able and willing to put aside extraneous information and base their decisions on the evidence (p. 601).

Greene and Wade (1988; see also Greene, 1990) reported two other experiments exploring the impact of general pretrial publicity on juror decision making in unrelated cases. Using sets of 120 and 140 undergraduate psychology

(continued)

BOX 7-3   (continued)

students as mock jurors, Greene and Wade reported that in their first experiment, jurors who had read about a defendant who had been mistakenly identified and convicted were less likely to convict a defendant in an unrelated case than a control group or a group that had read about a series of heinous crimes. In their second experiment, they found a stronger effect when the pretrial publicity concerned a case that closely resembled the one being decided than when the two cases differed. They concluded that student–jurors who are exposed to news stories about certain crimes and trials may use that information to decide wholly unrelated cases (1988, p. 132) and that attorneys involved in nonpublicized cases similar to ones receiving publicity should be concerned about possible biasing caused by the general pretrial publicity (1984, p. 219).

Dexter and Cutler (1991) used sixty-eight college undergraduates in mock juries for a videotaped murder trial. They found that exposure to case-specific pretrial publicity increased conviction rates and that an extended voir dire did not reduce the effects of the pretrial publicity.

Kramer and his colleagues (1990) tested the remedial effects of deliberation, continuance, and judicial instructions with regard to two types of pretrial publicity—emotional and factual—on 617 residents chosen from a circuit court's jury rolls, with one group receiving judicial instructions regarding pretrial publicity and a control group not. Following a simulated written voir dire to identify biased jurors, juries were formed and a fifty-one minute videotape of a trial watched. Kramer and his colleagues report that the instructions had no effect, that deliberation exacerbated the effect, and that continuances remedied the effect of factual but not of emotional publicity.

In an attempt to correct the inherent artificiality of the laboratory studies, "field" mock jury studies have surveyed community members and involved real cases. These studies, summarized in Box 7-4, have unfortunately also reported mixed results.

The results of the field research suggest that juries can act fairly even when exposed to large amounts of information about a case prior to a trial (cf. Buddenbaum et al., 1981, p. 5; Pember, 1987, p. 367), and there are a number of examples of heavily publicized trials of notable defendants that ended in acquittals.[2] On the other hand, the question of the effects of pretrial publicity is far from settled, for the data clearly suggest that prejudicial effects sometimes persist despite the employment of the more common counteractive mechanisms of juror instructions from judges and expanded voir dire—proceedings to determine the competency of potential jurors (Carroll et al., 1986, pp. 194–195; Kramer et al., 1990). Reports of confessions, and media-fueled waves of public sentiment against a defendant, appear to be particularly dangerous (Buddenbaum et al., 1981, p. 2). In addition, a set of experiments with mock jurors by Greene and Loftus (1984) and Greene and Wade (1988) suggests that general publicity about events in the criminal justice system can influence jurors sitting on nonpublicized, totally unrelated cases that are similar to the publicized ones. There thus exists some evidence of a potential generalized "echo" effect, in which news coverage influences cases receiving no direct coverage (see also Surette, 1989, Chapter 3).

In the end a paradox emerges. The courts and social science researchers have focused nearly exclusively on cases that receive news coverage, but the evidence suggests that the effects of coverage in such cases can be re-

---

BOX 7-4   Field Studies of Mock Juries

Simon and Eimermann (1971) surveyed by telephone 130 registered voters a week prior to an actual murder trial. They found high levels of recognition and knowledge of the case (80 percent of the 130 respondents indicated that they had heard or read about the case) and pretrial sentiments favoring the prosecution (65 percent of those who had heard of the trial said that they favored the prosecution). However, approximately two-thirds of the respondents stated that evidence could change their views, that they could sit on a jury with an open mind, and that the defendants could receive a fair trial. In the actual case, one defendant pled guilty, and after a voir dire of 118 jurors and a two-week trial, a jury found the second defendant not guilty, indicating that real jurors can for the most part put aside extraneous information and base their decisions on the evidence presented at trial.

Riley (1973) surveyed by telephone people in three North Carolina cities regarding the murder of the family of a Green Beret. The cities included that of the scene of the crime and two probable change of venue sites. Riley found that approximately 23 percent of the 183 respondents across all three cities had prejudged the defendant guilty. He thus concluded that a change of venue or venire (the pool from which the jury would be drawn) would not be effective in reducing the influence of the media. In his view, "merely to publicize the fact that a person is suspected of a crime is enough to produce bias and prejudgment on the part of a great many people" (p. 17). But he also reported that roughly 70 percent of the respondents did not admit to prejudging the captain, indicating that despite heavy media publicity, the selection of an impartial jury would have been possible.

Robinson (1974) surveyed by telephone 103 subjects drawn from the phone directories of Oregon on the first day and again during the final week of the Watergate hearings, thereby providing a pre- and posthearing measurement of the influence of the publicity surrounding the hearings. The reported effect of publicity was to significantly increase knowledge and awareness of the Watergate case (nearly doubling in some categories); opinions regarding the guilt or involvement of the president however, changed little. There was an increase in the negative perception of politicians in general, though. Robinson concluded that even massive media coverage does not necessarily make for negative public attitudes.

Rollings and Blascovich (1977) sampled through written questionnaires prior to and following the arrest of Patty Hearst the opinions of 438 introductory psychology students as to her guilt and probable sentence if convicted, and the likelihood of conviction and probable sentence if the respondent were in Hearst's position. The authors found little influence from the pretrial publicity surrounding her arrest, in that responses to both surveys were similar.

Moran and Cutler (in press) surveyed first 604 community members regarding a marijuana smuggling case and second 100 community members about a police officer's murder. In both surveys, knowledge of the case correlated with perceived guilt, but knowledge was not associated with a willingness to admit bias. The authors concluded that even moderate publicity can deprive a defendant of the presumption of innocence and that juror bias may not be revealed or admitted during normal jury selection procedures.

duced through a properly used combination of available judicial mechanisms (although the ones most frequently used do not appear to be the most effective). Meanwhile, pervasive systematic media effects on a large number of nonpublicized cases are indicated but have not been sufficiently studied, nor are judges likely to consider taking mitigative measures in these nonpublicized cases. For now, the sole problems acknowledged within the judicial system are ensuring that those seated as jurors in directly publicized cases have not been influenced, and when prejudicial coverage occurs, recognizing what cases will need extra protection against the potential negative media effects. In the past, the courts and researchers have rightly focused on effects in the publicized cases, but in the future, they need to expand their focus to encompass more general, systematic effects.

Privacy, Media Access to Information, and Televised Trials

In a limited number of cases, news coverage of a criminal case has given rise to concerns about privacy and "media punishment" (Kaplan & Skolnick, 1982, p. 563). In relation to criminal cases, issues of privacy normally involve the reporting of embarrassing but truthful information, usually about either victims or defendants.[3] The Supreme Court has argued that a balance between, on the one hand, the gathering and dissemination of information by the media and, on the other, the preservation of privacy and a chance for rehabilitation is a valid goal and has not extended protections to shield the press from lawsuits based on truthful, but embarrassing publications (see Box 7-5). It has not detailed, however, where the balance between news making and the goals of the criminal justice system should be struck. But though there are few certain rules, there are some guidelines. In general, information of the following type is private and should not be subject to

Legally speaking, violations of privacy take any of four forms: (1) an unreasonable intrusion upon the seclusion of another, (2) appropriation of another's name or likeness, (3) unreasonable publicity given to another's private life, and (4) publicity that unreasonably places another in a false light before the public (Levine & Bussian, 1987, p. 1). Factors determining whether or not a person's privacy has been violated include whether or not the material published was legally obtained, the subject matter was newsworthy and of legitimate public interest, the publication would offend a reasonable person, the information was timely, consent was obtained, and the reported event or action was plainly in the public view. Invasion of privacy is a relatively new legal concept and can be traced to a *Harvard Law Review* article by Warren and Brandeis published in 1890. Writing before the era of electronic eavesdropping and other modern technology, Warren and Brandeis were remarkably prophetic in predicting that "mechanical devices threaten to make good the prediction that 'what is whispered in the closet shall be proclaimed from the housetops'" (cited by Levine, 1987, pp. 17–18, n.2).

In the pursuit of stories the press has sometimes, although not often, interfered with ongoing law enforcement efforts, usually by seeking access to information that the police wished to protect (Salas, 1984). News coverage of ongoing terrorist events epitomizes these clashes between the media and law enforcement agencies (Bassiouni, 1981; Salas, 1984; Schmid & de Graaf, 1982). In one 1977 case, for example, hostages were seized in Washington, D. C. Live coverage of the police efforts to free the hostages endangered the lives of the hostages, as the terrorists were monitoring news reports, which detailed police plans and strategies. In addition, continual phone conversations between the terrorists and the media prevented the police from communicating with the terrorists and the large amount of media equipment on the scene hindered their movements (see Poland, 1988, p. 62).

publication: sexual relations, family quarrels, humiliating illnesses, intimate personal letters, details of home life, photographs taken in private places, photographs stolen from a person's home, and contents of income tax returns. On the other hand, matters of public record are not generally considered private facts and may be published freely (Levine, 1987, p. 11). At present, the courts will discount privacy claims if doing so will further an important public policy interest ("Privacy Exemption Surmountable," 1985, pp. 33–35). One aspect of the continuing confusion is ambiguity about what constitutes a public record and a public interest. Legislative and court efforts to resolve the dilemma have not been greatly successful.

In response to growing difficulties in obtaining information held by the government, the media lobbied for the federal Freedom of Information Act, which was adopted in 1966. This act opened up numerous government files to the media and the public. An associated act is the Government in Sunshine Act, passed in 1976, which prohibits secret government meetings on policy. Both of these efforts have been duplicated in numerous states and have had mixed results in easing the news media's access to government files and information. The Sunshine Act, for example, applies only to bodies whose members are directly appointed by the President—and many of those are exempted. Under the Freedom of Information Act (FOIA), agencies or persons who want information about themselves withheld must list the exemption on which the denial is based, describe the materials being withheld, and relate the exemption to the withheld materials (Spaniolo & Terilli, 1987, p. 10). However, despite the FOIA's intention being to place the burden of proof on those denying access, in a few instances those requesting information have been forced to show an overriding public interest in order to obtain it (see "Privacy Exemption Surmountable," 1985, pp. 34–35). The primary criticisms of the FOIA concern the cumbersome procedures instituted to request information, the number of exceptions to the laws, and the often long delay in rulings and obtaining information.

To balance the effects of the FOIA and Government in Sunshine acts, Congress also passed the Privacy Act in 1974 to control the misuse of government information and to restrict access to certain information in criminal files and judicial records. Information required to be disclosed under the FOIA cannot be withheld under the auspices of the Privacy Act, but the boundary between the two acts is blurred (Pember, 1987, p. 304). As there are greater penalties for incorrectly disclosing private information than for incorrectly withholding FOIA information, less rather than more openness

---

BOX 7-5   Supreme Court Cases Concerning Privacy and Criminal Proceedings

In *Melvin* v. *Reed* (112 Cal. App. 285 [1975]) the plaintiff was a former prostitute who had been tried for murder, acquitted, and thereafter reformed. Seven years later, a movie revealing her identity and detailing the facts of her story was released. The California Supreme Court allowed a civil suit to continue and supported the defendant's view that her privacy had been unnecessarily invaded. The court cited the passage of time and the lack of relevancy in identifying the defendant for the movie.* However, in *Cox Broadcasting Corp.* v. *Cohn* (420 U. S. 469 [1975]), the U. S. Supreme Court ruled that the broadcasting corporation was not wrong in publishing the identity of the victim of a recent rape–murder, because the information was available to the public prior to the broadcast. The Court stated that although there is no broad media right under the First Amendment to the identities of crime victims, in this case, where the information was available in public court records, there was no invasion of privacy.

Subsequently, in 1977, in *Oklahoma Publishing Co.* v. *District Court* (555 P.2d 1286 [Okla. 1976], rev'd 97 S. Ct. 1045 [1977], per curiam), the Supreme Court again emphasized that information legally obtained in open court proceedings could be published. The case involved the publishing of the name and picture of an eleven-year-old murder suspect, both of which had been obtained during an open detention petition hearing. The judge moved to prohibit publication, but the Court held that the judge could not prohibit the publication of widely disseminated information obtained at court proceedings that are open to the public.

In regard to camera access, the Florida Supreme Court discussed the privacy issue in 1979 and ruled that Florida courts can allow cameras without defendants' consent. The court argued that a judicial proceeding is a public event that by its nature denies certain aspects of privacy and that there is no constitutionally recognized right to privacy in the context of courtroom proceedings (In re Petition of Post–Newsweek Stations, Florida, 370 So. 2d 764 at 799 [Fla.], app'l dismissed, 444 U. S. 976 [1979]). This position appears to be the one currently favored by the Supreme Court, which has deemed privacy only an interest and not an absolute right in judicial proceedings.

The question of prison inmates' right to privacy is still clouded. In 1978, in *Houchins* v. *KQED, Inc.* (438 U. S. 1, 5 n.2), Justice Warren Burger wrote that inmates in jails, prisons, or mental institutions retain certain fundamental rights of privacy. The limitations on this right for inmates has not been fully determined however. Another criminal justice issue that touches on privacy, the courts, and the media is that of "postverdict interviews" with jurors (see Bacharach, 1985; Sharp, 1983). At issue is the proper scope of press interviews of jurors following a trial and verdict. The concern is that intensive interviews will undermine the integrity of the deliberation process and invade the personal privacy of the individual jurors. The courts have the right to prohibit the interrogation of jurors regarding their deliberations or reasons for a particular verdict; however, when such prohibitions are proper is not clear (Sharp, 1983, p. 14).

---

* In 1971, in *Briscoe* v. *Reader's Digest Association* (4 Cal. 3d 529, 483 P.2d 34 [1971]), the California Supreme Court ruled on a similar case involving a plaintiff convicted in 1956 of truck hijacking and thereafter rehabilitated. The court acknowledged the importance of reporting crimes and judicial proceeding and even of identifying persons currently charged with crimes but ruled that reports of past crimes and past defendants were qualitatively different and that publicizing them served little independent public purpose.

is encouraged (Spaniolo & Terilli, 1987, p. 23). Hence, as in other areas regarding the media, the courts operate without absolute rules in determining when privacy supersedes public interests, and decisions are rendered on a case-by-case basis, with the currency or timeliness of the information and the means by which the information was attained crucial factors ("Privacy Exemption Surmountable," 1985, p. 33). In practice, the overall effect of the access legislation is more symbolic than significant (Spaniolo & Terilli, 1987, p. 22–23).

Nonetheless, because it denies the media access to newsworthy information, limiting media access to government files has become a highly litigated issue. Since 1979, the courts have held that the media cannot claim special privilege or right of access—that news gathering is not entitled to an extended First Amendment protection but is limited to information and access given to the general public (Apfel, 1980, p. 439). For example, in *Pell* v. *Procunier* (94 S. Ct. 2800 [1974]) and *Saxbe* v. *Washington Post* (94 S. Ct. 2811 [1974]), the Supreme Court stated that a way to determine whether or not the media have a right to interview prison inmates is to examine the public's level of access. In *United States* v. *Gurney* (558 F.2d 1202 [5th Cir. 1977], cert. denied sub nom. *United States* v. *Gurney et al.,* Miami Herald Pub. Co. et al.), the media were denied access to trial evidence including exhibits not yet admitted into evidence, transcripts of bench conferences held "in camera"—that is, in private—written communication between the jury and the judge, lists of names and addresses of jurors, and grand jury testimony. The Court also let stand a ruling that the judge could refuse access to documents not a matter of public record. This limitation of the press's access—to being equal to but not superior to the general public's— was more recently upheld in *Nixon* v. *Warner Communications* (435 U. S. 591 [1978]), in which the media sought access to Richard Nixon's Oval Office tapes. The Court refused the media access stating, "The First Amendment generally grants the press no right to information about a trial superior to that of the general public" (435 U. S. at 609).

Having established the equality of the media and the public with regard to access, the courts have yet to directly address the effect of disclosing the identity of victims and witnesses, particularly in sexual offense cases. It has been strongly argued that public identification can needlessly add to the pain of the victim and is likely to deter other victims from reporting crimes and witnesses from testifying (DeSilva, 1984, p. 43). There is reason to believe, for example, that rape witnesses fear the publicity they will receive if they testify more than they fear testifying (Barber, 1987, p. 35).

Paralleling this issue is the concern that media publicity will cause social harm to a defendant. The courts have not responded much to this concern, and they have thus far not recognized media coverage as a mitigating factor in subsequent sentencing decisions. A statement by Judge Frankel of New York summarizes the current judicial position:

> Public humiliation is the frequently heard contention that he should not be incarcerated because he "has been punished enough." Defendant's notoriety should not in the last analysis serve to lighten, any more than it may be permit-

ted to aggravate a sentence. It is not possible to justify the notion that this mode of non-judicial punishment should be an occasion for leniency not given to a defendant who never basked in such an admiring light at all. The quest for both the appearance and the substance of equal justice prompts the court to discount the thought that the public humiliation serves the function of imprisonment. (Quoted by Kaplan & Skolnick, 1982, pp. 563–564)

Left unaddressed are cases in which the defendant is found innocent of criminal charges but has his or her career or reputation permanently ruined by publicity. The consequence of publicity has been described in relation to government officials who have been investigated, as follows:

Once again the tendency to portray public officials accused of criminal or un-ethical activities as guilty [is displayed]. . . . We find it appalling that long after many of these individuals have been found innocent of the accusations against them, the disproven accusations continue to be repeated as almost a permanent addendum to their name in news stories. ("Trial by Media," 1984, p. 4)

Some have further suggested that live television coverage incites such negative feelings against defendants that, even if they are later acquitted, the feelings are irreversible (Barber, 1987, p. 115). The modern mass media has established a "legally innocent but proven guilty" social category for defendants that is beyond the control of the judicial system. Media coverage has great potential to confound for the public the separate concepts of legal guilt (is the defendant legally responsible for a crime?) and factual guilt (did the defendant actually commit the criminal behavior?). Factual guilt is not always equivalent to legal guilt, and the general public little understands and is poorly instructed by the media in the differences between the two. If defendants who have been found innocent are subsequently "punished" in a real sense by losing their careers or reputation because of publicity, then the system and society are flawed. And as the John Hinckley, Jr., case revealed (see Box 5-5), sensational and narrow coverage of a case that is ultimately decided on not factual but legal guilt can result in serious loss of credibility and legitimacy for the entire judicial system and in media-driven pushes for poorly considered changes in criminal justice public policy (Snow, 1984). Despite these implications, to date neither the courts nor the legislatures have addressed this problem.

Live televised proceedings represent the epitome of news media access to the judicial system. Televised proceedings raise unique and myriad questions about the impact of the modern, visually dominated electronic media in the courtroom. Of concern are possible effects from the televising of proceedings (see Table 1-1) and the widespread exposure of hitherto hidden backstage judicial processes and behaviors. For example, a Manhattan trial judge recently refused to permit television coverage of a widely publicized trial. The judge said that the case was an inappropriate subject for television coverage and noted that past media coverage of the case had focused on sex and violence and he expected coverage of the trial would emphasize the same. "Focusing on these factors," he said, "does not enhance public awareness of the judicial system" (cited in "Audio-Visual Coverage on Trial in States," 1988, pp. 48–50).

The judiciary has long been skeptical about visual coverage of trials. Recognition of its unique potential for disruption can be traced to Bruno Hauptmann's trial for the kidnapping and murder of the Lindbergh baby in the 1930s (see Marcus, 1982, p. 276; see also *State* v. *Hauptmann,* 115 N.J.L. 412 [1935] cert. denied, 296 U. S. 649 [1935]). In response to problems that arose during this trial, in 1937 the American Bar Association issued a new rule regarding the use of photographic equipment at trials: "The taking of photographs in the court room, during sessions of the court or recesses between sessions, . . . detract from the essential dignity of the proceedings, degrade the court and create misconceptions with respect thereto in the mind of the public and should not be permitted" (ABA Canons of Judicial Ethics No. 35). This ban of still cameras from the courtroom was widely adopted and was extended in 1952 to include television cameras as well. As recently as 1979, a clear majority of lawyers were opposed to allowing television cameras to broadcast court proceedings, with 75 percent feeling that television would tend to distract witnesses and would only be used to show the more sensational aspects of a trial ("Lawyers Aren't Convinced that TV Belongs in Courtroom," 1979, cited in Marcus, 1982, p. 278).

The Supreme Court first reviewed the question of television access to courtrooms in *Estes* v. *Texas* (381 U. S. 532) in 1965. As described in Chapter 1, the *Estes* trial received intense television coverage with nightly news reports broadcast from the scene. Television equipment caused a significant disruption in the courtroom, with camera operators moving about and cables and wires snaking across the floor (381 U. S. at 535–536). The Court reversed Estes's conviction without clearly stating why television should be excluded but indicating that television was unavoidably disruptive and should be banned from the courtroom: "Television in its present state and by its very nature, reaches into a variety of areas in which it may cause prejudice to an accused. . . . The televising of criminal trials is inherently a denial of due process" (381 U. S. at 538 and 544). Most states subsequently severely limited television's access to their courts, and many simply banned all coverage.

However, encouraged by the development of less obtrusive equipment, various states continued to experiment with televising proceedings.[4] In 1979, the Florida Supreme Court allowed television reporting from trial courts, subject to coverage guidelines. The permission of the defendant was not required. Florida's procedures were challenged and were reviewed by the Supreme Court in 1981 in *Chandler* v. *Florida* (101 S. Ct. 802 [1981]), in which the Court rejected many of the assumptions about television it had forwarded sixteen years earlier in *Estes* v. *Texas* (381 U. S. 532 [1965]). The most significant assumption it rejected was that televising a criminal trial without the defendant's consent is a per se denial of due process. Emphasizing the modernization of the medium, the lack of substantiation of a psychological impact from televised coverage on trial participants, and an increase in the public acceptance of television as a fact of everyday life, the Court upheld the *Chandler* conviction, placing the burden of establishing a prejudicial effect from television on the defendant. The *Chandler* decision is seen

Present-day camera coverage of a court proceeding
Source: James L. Shaffer/PhotoEdit

as a broad victory for the electronic media in that since *Chandler,* to prohibit broadcasting the defendant must show material, prejudicial effects and interference with due process (Marcus, 1982, p. 286).

The *Chandler* decision marks a remarkable shift in the attitude of the judicial system toward the presence of television. As recently as 1976 all but two states prohibited cameras in courtrooms, but as of 1990, forty-four states allowed cameras in their courts at either the appellate or trial level or both. Criminal trials are regularly televised in thirty-four states, twenty-seven of which have established permanent court programs ("Judges Deny Court Camera Use," 1990, pp. 40–42). Attitudes regarding television news coverage have changed to such an extent that an ironic reversed appeal to the *Estes* case has been argued. In *United States* v. *Hastings,* a defendant demanded live television coverage of his federal trial.[5] The defendant, federal judge Alcee Hastings, asserted that he was entitled to television coverage as part of his right to a public trial and that television coverage was necessary to restore his reputation as an effective judge. The news media argued that recent access to criminal proceedings also gave the media the right to broadcast federal criminal trials ("First, Sixth Amendments Permit Ban on Televising Federal Trials," 1983, pp. 2339–2340). The appeals court disagreed, however, stating that recent decisions stated only that television coverage is not constitutionally prohibited, not that it is constitutionally mandated.

Regarding the concerns first raised in the *Estes* decision about the inherent biasing effects of televised coverage, social science researchers since *Chandler* have not noted negative results and have been generally positive toward continued coverage. Lancaster (1984), for example, comparing two trials in Indiana, one having television cameras present and the other not, reported that the public claimed to have learned more about trials and the working of the criminal justice system when television cameras were present. He also found that it was the presence of the reporters, not the equipment, that signaled trial participants that the trial had attracted the attention of the media. Half of the jurors claimed they would find television cameras distracting in a future trial, but most did not recognize the small cameras present at their trial as being television cameras. Similarly, Paddon (1985) reported that television coverage of criminal trials enhanced viewers' information about the trial but caused no negative attitude changes. Along the same lines, in a review of state experiments with courtroom television coverage, Haas (1988) reported generally favorable findings from evaluations in Florida, Washington, California, Nevada, Arizona, Minnesota, Iowa, and Louisiana. For the most part, surveys of trial participants indicate that they do not perceive serious negative effects from television coverage of court proceedings. Indeed, the sole negative reaction to courtroom cameras was reported in a 1982 Michigan State Bar report of the results of a national survey of 600 attorneys. Disapproval of cameras was greatest among lawyers who had had the least experience with them and among older lawyers, indicating that experience and familiarity with television significantly reduce opposition (Haas, 1988).

So it is that Barber (1987), in an extensive review of nineteen separate court experiments with cameras, concluded that one by one the early concerns about and arguments against televising courtroom proceedings have fallen. Concerns about physical disruption have declined as smaller, better equipment has become available; as judges have shown themselves able to maintain the dignity and decorum of a courtroom; and as effects on trial participants (judges, prosecutors, witnesses, and jurors) have usually been found to be slight and attitudes toward television's presence supportive. As a group, public defenders have been found to be the sole exception to this supportive attitude.

The presumption of openness of the courts has been extended to the news media, television included, as public surrogates and instructors. The courts have come to accept television. Still at issue, however, are the impact of televised trials on the general society and the potential negative effects arising from the types of cases chosen for television coverage and the style of this coverage.[6] Specific unresolved issues include the deterring of crime victims from reporting crimes or testifying to avoid embarrassing coverage, the exacerbation of the negative social effects from the entertainment media such as heightening viewers' fear of crime, the furthering of a distorted view of the judicial system, the encouraging of copycat crimes, and the pillorying by publicity of defendants found innocent. As can be seen, the focus of the issues that remain regarding televised trials is no longer on internal effects, but has shifted to possible external effects, particularly attitudinal effects on the viewing public (see Barber, 1987; Surette, 1989). However, none of the above negative effects has proven severe enough to warrant curtailment of televised coverage, and televising trials is now seen as having the potential to further both due process and crime control through education of the public about the judicial process, enhancement of the deterrence effect of trials, and promotion of the public's confidence in the courts (see Chapter 1).

Intensive and sometimes intrusive news coverage is accepted as a fact of life in the judiciary. The courts have come to an unsteady acceptance of the media in most cases but are still uneasy about the media's presence and actively resist it in certain circumstances. Future clashes between the two are to be expected as the media seek access to other backstage judicial activities and as surveillance technology makes observing and recording them easier. These clashes will continue to revolve around the control of information. The courts will need to control the information juries consider in reaching verdicts, government agencies will continue to try to control access to their files, and the media will strive to gain broader access to judicial proceedings and government files while trying to maintain control over and limit access to their own news files and information. The media are aided in this process by the societywide effects of the mass media over the last forty years, which have persistently discouraged closed social institutions and information. Ironically, these same forces undermine the media's arguments for secrecy regarding their own information. In response to the increasing number of requests for information, both the media and the judicial system have developed strategies and mechanisms to limit access to their information and to minimize the negative effects from the access that does occur.

EFFORTS BY THE JUDICIARY AND THE MEDIA TO CONTROL INFORMATION

Efforts by the Judiciary

The courts have two strategies they can pursue in dealing with problems resulting from news media coverage. One is proactive and seeks to limit the availability of potentially prejudicial material to the media. The second is reactive and seeks to limit the effects of the material after it has been disseminated by the media (Dubnoff, 1977, p. 91). Under the first strategy, if a court deems information to be prejudicial then it acts to restrict either media access to the information or, if the material is already in the media's possession, the publication of the information. This approach directly clashes with the First Amendment protection of freedom of the press and has been most vigorously resisted by the media. It has also not been a favored strategy of the courts, as shown in test cases in which the Supreme Court has been more stringent in reviewing appeals where the proactive strategy has been used. The courts have had more success using the proactive strategy when they have been able to prevent media access to information than when they have attempted to keep the media from publishing.

On the other hand, appeals by the media have been less successful when the courts employ the reactive strategy, for this strategy allows the news media access and publication, and attempts to compensate for the resulting publicity and protect the due process rights of defendants through various judicial mechanisms. Some feel, however, that given the pervasiveness and intrusiveness of the mass media, these "after-the-fact" attempts to compensate are costly, disruptive, and, most important, ineffective, especially in massively covered cases. They accordingly call for greater support for the proactive restricting of media access to prejudicial information (cf. Carroll et al., 1986). However, the proactive strategy tends to close off the judicial system and thus runs counter to the societywide, media-driven trend toward open social institutions and realms (Foucault, 1977; cf. Meyrowitz, 1985a). Therefore, although still utilized, the mechanisms of the first strategy are likely to continue to decline in popularity in the future, being reserved only for the rare and unusual case and challenged whenever they are used.

Court Mechanisms to Limit Prejudicial Materials

Under this first strategy of limiting the availability of prejudicial information, the courts have three mechanisms they can employ. Each mechanism utilizes a court order restraining to varying degrees the ability of the media to report a criminal case. And all three—closure, restrictive orders, and protective orders—have been vigorously opposed and decried by the media.

Closure. Closure involves isolating a judicial proceeding from outside (public and press) attendance. Given that information is kept directly from the media, closure is felt to be a very effective means of preventing prejudicial coverage once a proceeding has begun, as there can be no prejudice if there is no coverage. Though logical, closure encroaches directly on the freedom of the press to observe government proceedings and violates the long-standing tenet of open, public trials. Furthermore, a number of assumptions underlie the logic of the need for closure in a specific case:

> First, that prejudicial information will be revealed during a proceeding;
> Second, that the media will report the information;

Closure of court proceedings, media access to government files, and citizen access to media resources are all linked by similar legal arguments. The media react similarly when government files are closed to the press and when a judicial proceeding is closed. And in an interesting counterpoint to *United States* v. *Hastings,* the public's right to access to space in the media was rejected in *Miami Herald Publishing Co.* v. *Tornillo* (418 U. S. 241 [1974]). In that case the Supreme Court unanimously ruled that decisions as to newsworthiness and public interest should be made by editors; citizens have no inherent right to expression in the mass media, in the same way that defendants have no inherent right to news coverage or reporters an inherent right to access beyond that of the general citizenry.

Third, that the public will take notice of this information from the media;

Fourth, that prejudice will actually result;

Fifth, that enough people will be prejudicially influenced to make it impossible to empanel an unbiased jury (Pember, 1987, p. 358).

In opposing closure, the media argue that these assumptions seldom if ever are true and that when they will be cannot be predicted. They further argue that the media are proxies for the general public and therefore have an inherent right of access to the courts. Proponents respond that the media have no inherent right of access and no special claim to court information, particularly information that would be inadmissible at a trial, and that the defendant's right to a fair trial supersedes any public or media interests. Proponents have also argued that precisely because predicting when prejudice may be generated is difficult, a conservative approach of closing a proceeding when there is any doubt is necessary. In the appeals that have arisen, the main subject of contention has been the closing of pretrial proceedings and hearings. Judges frequently close such proceedings to keep evidence and other information that might be revealed in the pretrial sessions but ruled inadmissible for the trial from reaching prospective jurors through the press.

During the seventies, as the mass media advanced technologically and broadened their scope of influence, trial judges began to close proceedings at an increasing rate (new additional closures increasing 141 from 1979 to 1981), encouraged by the ambiguity and tone of the *Gannett Co.* v. *DePasquale* ruling (443 U. S. 368 [1979]; see Box 7-6). Trials, preindictments, pretrial hearings, and posttrial proceedings were all subject to closure (Apfel, 1980, p. 467; Pember, 1987, p. 390; "Secret Court Watch," 1979, pp. 17–23).

Within a year of *Gannett,* however, the Supreme Court, in *Richmond Newspapers* v. *Virginia* (448 U. S. 555 [1980]), moved to reaffirm the presumption of open access to criminal trials. Then in 1986, in *Press-Enterprise* v. *Riverside Superior Court* (Sup. Ct. 106 S. Ct. 2735 [1984]; see also 106 S. Ct. 2735 [1986]), the Court extended its negative posture toward closure and ruled that the press and public have a qualified privilege to attend a preliminary criminal hearing, stating that "criminal proceedings cannot be closed unless there is a substantial probability that the defendant's right to a fair trial will be prejudiced by publicity." This ruling established a clear presumption of openness and access, and suddenly closing even pretrial hearings was extremely difficult (Pember, 1987, p. 395).

At present, judges can still close pretrial proceedings and criminal trials but must show cause. Thus, voir dire, depositions, suppression hearings, and other pretrial proceedings have all been closed, and their closures upheld by the Supreme Court. A number of lower appeal courts have established various burdens of proof that must be overcome before state trial judges can issue a closure order. Most courts agree that closure orders should be preceded by a hearing to examine the necessity of closure; that requesting counsel should demonstrate that there is a substantial chance that unreliable, untrustworthy, or inflammatory information will reach pro-

BOX 7-6   Supreme Court Decisions Regarding Closure, Restrictive and Protective Orders

Closure Orders

The increase in closure orders ultimately resulted in the Supreme Court's decision in *Gannett Co.* v. *DePasquale* in 1979.[a] After a fair amount of publicity regarding the case, all major parties agreed to closure of a pretrial hearing. The media claimed a public right of access to criminal proceedings based on the right to a public trial provided in the Sixth Amendment. The Supreme Court, however, held that the public trial provision of the Sixth Amendment exists solely for the benefit of the defendant and does not confer any constitutional right of access on the media or the general public (Bell, 1983, p. 1299). Even though the justices ruled against the media in this case, they did not clearly address the general issue of closure and failed to specify standards for the use of closure (Apfel, 1980, pp. 461–467).[b] A majority accepted the media's claim that members of the general public, and, by extension, the media, have a constitutional right to attend a pretrial hearing but did not agree that the right had precedent in this case.

The Court addressed the rank of the right to trial access relative to a defendant's right to a fair trial in *Richmond Newspapers* v. *Virginia* (448 U. S. 555 [1980]). The *Richmond* case involved a defendant who was tried for murder four times over two years. At the fourth trial, the defense counsel moved that the trial be closed to the public. The prosecution did not oppose the motion, and the trial judge granted it. The judge's closure of the trial was seen as particularly significant, for it represented a break with prior Supreme Court rulings in which clear distinctions between pretrial and

trial proceedings had been made (Apfel, 1980, p. 472). Reviewing the closure, the Court ruled that the media and the public have a right of access to trials and that access cannot be closed arbitrarily and without cause (Bell, 1983, p. 1300). The Court did not, however, give the media's right of access supremacy over the defendant's right to a fair trial (Marcus, 1982, p. 262). Furthermore, the Court placed the burden of showing compelling evidence that media access would result in the loss of Sixth Amendment due process protections squarely on the party seeking closure. Also specified in the *Richmond Newspapers* decision was the rule that before a trial judge can exclude the public and press from a trial, he or she must determine that alternative means will not meet the goal of assuring the accused a fair trial. In reversing, the Court noted that "the trial judge made no findings to support closure; no inquiry was made as to whether alternative solutions would have met the need to ensure fairness" (448 U. S. 580–581 [1980]).

Restrictive Orders

In *Nebraska Press Association* v. *Stuart* (427 U. S. 539 [1976]), the judge presiding over a preliminary hearing for a sensational small-town murder trial ordered that no information concerning confessions or statements "strongly implicative" of the defendant could be published until a jury had been impaneled. The Supreme Court reversed the ban in this specific

(continued)

---

[a] 443 U. S. 368 (1979). The case involved the investigation of the disappearance of a Rochester, New York, man who appeared to have met a violent death.

[b] See also "Secret Court Watch," 1979, p. 17. A majority of the justices disagreed that the trial judge must conduct a hearing before issuing a closure order. Rehnquist stated that if the parties agree to a closed proceeding the trial court need not advance any reason for declining to open a hearing to the public. Powell stated that the public and the media have a First Amendment right to be present at a pretrial suppression hearing and concluded that the trial judge must make specific findings of fact in a hearing attended by all interested parties before closing a courtroom (Apfel, 1980, p. 470).

BOX 7-6 (continued)

---

case but left open the possibility that future restrictive orders might be upheld in cases of "clear and present danger" and if alternative actions to neutralize pretrial publicity were ineffective or not feasible. The Court ruled that in this case the state had not shown that alternatives to a restrictive order would have failed to protect the defendant's rights.

The position that restrictive orders are acceptable only in rare circumstances was soon reinforced in *Landmark Communications* v. *Virginia* (435 U. S. 829 [1978]) and in *Smith* v. *Daily Mail Publishing Co.* (443 U. S. 97 [1979]). Both Supreme Court decisions overturned lower court restrictive orders because of a lack of clear overriding need for such orders.

Protective Orders

The seminal case in this area is *Central South Carolina* v. *Martin* (431 F. Supp. 1182 [D. S. C.], modified, 556 F.2d 706 [4th Cir. 1977], cert. denied, 431 U. S. 928 [1978]), in which the trial court in 1978 prohibited any statements that might divulge prejudicial material not a matter of the public record. Upholding the order, a federal appeals court (the Supreme Court declined to review the case) ruled that protective orders are to be judged by the less strict standards of closure and are not equivalent to restrictive orders (Apfel, 1980, p. 477). The current standard governing the proper use of protective orders is the perception of a "reasonable likelihood" that prejudicial effects will result from statements by participants. The Supreme Court has resisted applying the stricter standards of closure orders, which require that "clear and present danger" be established (Apfel, 1980, p. 478) and has specified one significant limitation to the use of protective orders. In *U. S.* v. *Mandel* (408 F. Supp. 673 [D. Md. 1975]), the government petitioned for a protective order that would have included the defendant, Governor Mandel of Maryland. The Supreme Court ruled that the accused cannot be denied his right of free speech, even though other trial participants may be denied this right.

---

spective jurors; and that the media should have an opportunity to argue that alternative methods of ensuring due process are available.[7] The Supreme Court, however, has not endorsed any definitive rules. With the exception of juvenile proceedings and juvenile testimony in sexual cases, the Court appears to wish to make closure rare and a choice of last resort for trial judges. It will, however, support closure in properly documented situations, and once closed, reopening a court proceeding through appeal has not often been successful ("Secret Court Watch," 1979, pp. 17–23).

Restrictive Orders. Second only to closure, the next most effective court mechanism available to control prejudicial materials with regard to the media is the use of restrictive orders (also sometimes termed prior restraint or gag orders). Restrictive orders prevent the media from printing or broadcasting information. Obviously, if information is not published it cannot cause bias. Not surprisingly, the media have argued vigorously for the right to publish what they have already discovered, and this right has generally been recognized (Jacobs, 1980, p. 685). A form of censorship, the granting of restrictive orders against the press is a potent and chilling action and

Juvenile proceedings have traditionally been recognized as unique within the system of justice. Confidentiality is arguably essential to the rehabilitative function of the juvenile court. However, the Supreme Court has sided with media access and publication rights in two cases referring to juvenile decisions. In *Oklahoma Publishing Co.* v. *District Court* (555 P.2d 1286 [Okla. 1976], rev'd 97 S. Ct. 1045 [1977], per curiam), the Court reversed a ban on dissemination of information obtained at a pretrial detention hearing about an eleven-year-old, holding that once information is made public, prior restraints may not be employed. In *Smith* v. *Daily Mail Publishing Co.* (443 U. S. 97 [1979]), the Court held that criminal penalties may not be applied to the publication without prior court approval of lawfully obtained information, in this case publication of the names of juvenile offenders.

has been acknowledged as such by the Supreme Court (*Nebraska Press Association* v. *Stuart,* 427 U. S. 539 [1976]; see also Jacobs, 1980, p. 686). However, such orders may be upheld if essential to safeguard other constitutional rights.

The current judicial support for restrictive orders originated in the Sam Sheppard case (*Sheppard* v. *Maxwell,* 384 U. S. 333 [1966]), in which the Supreme Court made trial judges directly responsible for controlling the media during proceedings. In criticizing the trial judge in the *Sheppard* case, the Supreme Court listed possible countermeasures that could have been taken, including restricting media publications. Later, in 1968, the American Bar Association recommended that judges use contempt rulings to back restrictive orders. The combined result was an increase in the number of restrictive orders, starting in the late sixties. The increasing tendency of judges to issue restrictive orders climaxed in *Nebraska Press Association* v. *Stuart* in 1976. Besides reversing the restrictive order in *Nebraska Press,* the Supreme Court established some guidelines for issuing them. To justify a request for an order under the standards of *Nebraska Press,* the accused must show a clear and present danger that unchecked news reporting will prejudice his or her right to a fair trial. If, however, alternative methods can be used, they should be, and the inadequacies of each alternative must be explained. The judge must examine the nature and extent of the publicity and find that unrestrained publicity is certain and would prevent the court from finding unbiased jurors. The judge must also consider the practical limitations of restrictive orders: As the Court noted in this case, courts have jurisdiction only over persons in their jurisdiction. Therefore, national press coverage is largely beyond the reach of restrictive orders by local courts. Finally, if the trial judge feels that prospective jurors may receive information from other sources besides the media, such as through word of mouth, prior restraint requests should be denied (Apfel, 1980, pp. 456–459). Clearly, the free use of restrictive orders was not encouraged. Currently, recognizing that restrictive orders are frequently overturned and that the Supreme Court favors the media in generally opposing this method, lower courts seeking to deal with media effects have looked more to closure of proceedings and to the less contentious reactive mechanisms, which are aimed at limiting the effects of information already reported.

Protective Orders. The third judicial mechanism that can be used to limit the availability of prejudicial materials is the protective order. Trial participants are a common source of prejudicial information, and these orders, in which a trial judge proscribes statements made outside the courtroom, are most effective in the early stages of a case (Apfel, 1980, p. 449; see also Dulaney, 1968, pp. 51–52, 59). Problems arise because protective orders restrict trial participants' freedom of speech. The legal rationale for allowing their speech to be restricted is that they possess privileged information regarding a criminal case and no longer have the same First Amendment right to speak as the public at large. Though the Supreme Court views protective orders in a better light than restrictive orders, uncertainty remains as to whether or not a trial court must first exhaust other, less contentious measures before resorting to a protective order. It is currently easier for a trial judge to restrict the speech of a trial's participants, excluding the defendant, than to close a proceeding or to restrain the media from publicizing information and statements they have obtained.

Court Mechanisms to Limit the Effects of Published Prejudicial Material

Failing to limit access to and dissemination of prejudicial material, courts can invoke a number of reactive mechanisms to limit the potential negative effects of information reported by the media. These mechanisms are generally preferred over closure, restrictive orders, and protective orders, as they do not directly limit the activities of the media and thus do not directly undermine First Amendment freedom of the press. They rest on the premise that even if most of the public may be influenced and biased by information in the news, an unbiased jury can still be assembled and an unbiased trial conducted (Apfel, 1980, p. 483; Carroll et al., 1986, pp. 187–189). Within this second, reactive strategy, judges can expand the voir dire, grant continuances, grant changes of venue, sequester jurors, and give special instructions to the jury to counteract the effects of publicity (see Box 7-7). However, current case law and legislation provide little direction concerning the appropriate use of these mechanisms, and little empirical research is available regarding their relative effectiveness (Kramer et al.,

---

In a rare and now-dated empirical piece that examined trial participants as sources of prejudicial information, Dulaney (1968) found that police, particularly local police, were the main providers of such information. Contrary to popular lore, defense attorneys were rarely implicated. Dulaney also found evidence that protective orders significantly reduced disclosures of prejudicial information by the police.

BOX 7-7   Judicial Mechanisms to Limits the Effects of Publicity

Voir dire ("to speak the truth") is a process in which prospective jurors are queried regarding prejudice. Attorneys can prevent jurors from serving either through challenges for cause, where they must state a valid reason for eliminating a juror, or peremptory challenges (normally limited in number) that do not have to be supported by a reason. Voir dire will only identify those jurors who admit knowledge and prejudice about a case and is based on the premise that jurors will recognize themselves as biased and truthfully admit it. The proportion of potential jurors who have detailed knowledge and prejudice about a case is often used as a measure of the level of prejudice in the general community (Apfel, 1980, p. 452). Despite its limitations, judges and lawyers generally feel that the process is an effective means of choosing an impartial jury (Carroll et al., 1986, p. 192; Siebert et al., 1970). Although Buddenbaum and his colleagues concluded in 1981 that voir dire is a more certain remedy for the effects of publicity than a change of venue, more-recent research questions the effectiveness of voir dire as a means of identifying biased jurors and thus of countering the effects of prejudicial publicity (Carroll et al., 1986, p. 194; see also Dexter & Cutler, 1991; Kerr et al., 1990; Krauss & Bonora, 1983; Zeisel & Diamond, 1978).

A *continuance* is simply a delay in the start of a trial until the coverage and its effects are thought to have subsided enough to allow an unbiased trial. The practice is based on the premises that media interest in the case will wane and that jurors will forget details of past media reports (Apfel, 1980, p. 451; Pember, 1987, p. 373). Disadvantages include its inconsistency with the defendant's right to a speedy trial, and the possibility that witnesses and evidence may not be available at a later time. Also, the reality is that highly newsworthy trials are not normally helped by continuances. Kramer and his colleagues (1990) found that continuances appear to help mitigate the effects of factual publicity but not of emotional publicity.

A *change of venue* occurs when a trial is moved from a location in which the case has received heavy media coverage to one in which it has received less coverage and is of less interest, and where residents, therefore, are assumed to be less biased. However, even twenty years ago, a change of place was not often found to mean less bias (see Dulaney, 1968, p. 93), as prejudicial news items tend to be widely disseminated and coverage outside the community where the crime occurred is often similar to that within it (see also Tanick & Shields, 1985). Thus, the basic premise underlying changes of venue is questionable, and the effectiveness of the practice appears to depend on the second community's having less interest in a case and therefore having given less attention to the coverage. However, no studies examining this question are available.

Although costly and questionable in effectiveness, venue changes are deemed necessary in certain cases—for example, in rural areas where the jury pool is limited and a major crime is likely to be the dominant news story for a long time. Thus, in *People v. Taylor* (Ill. Sup. Ct., No. 58258 [1984]),* the Illinois Supreme Court ruled that a change of venue should have been granted a thirteen-year-old murder defendant when evidence showed that a large proportion of the general population and half of the jury knew of the release of a co-defendant due to insufficient evidence and of the results of a lie detector test. The court noted that the volume of publicity, although great, was not the deciding factor, but the type of prejudicial information, an inadmissible test result, was. Once information of this type reaches a jury pool, a change of venue is required. That the amount of publicity is not crucial was again emphasized in *United States v. Faul* (8th Cir. 1984), in which the U. S. Court of

(continued)

---

*Cited in "Jurors' Knowledge of Lie Detector Test Raises Presumption of Partiality." (1984). *Criminal Law Reporter* 35, no. 5: 2082–2084.

BOX 7-7 (continued)

Appeals upheld a denial of a change of venue after reviewing the nature of the publicity. The court found that, though widespread, the publicity was mostly objective rather than inflammatory, and the trial judge had instituted other corrective measures by expanding the voir dire and increasing the number of peremptory challenges. Unless publicity is pervasive *and* prejudicial, whatever its magnitude, it is not deemed to be in and of itself grounds for a change of venue ("Publicity Didn't Require Venue Change for Federal Defendants," 1984, pp. 2140–2141). Change of venue requests are routinely denied (Cotsirilos & Philipsborn, 1986).

Sequestration is the isolation of a jury to control the information that reaches it. This practice can be very effective if the jury has not been exposed to prejudicial information prior to being impaneled. However, it is extremely costly and disruptive to jurors and is felt to generate animosity toward the accused (Pember, 1987, p. 375). Its actual effectiveness has not been empirically established, but judges commonly consider it effective (Jaffe, 1965; Pember, 1987).

Jury instructions are probably the simplest

and least expensive judicial mechanism that can be invoked, as they comprise only the directions the trial judge gives to the jury. They fundamentally consist of telling jurors to ignore media reports of the trial and not to discuss the case with anyone. Trial judges and other judicial participants believe that such instructions are effective with most juries (Ebbesen, 1987; Horowitz & Willging, 1984; Pember, 1987, p. 374; van Dyke, 1977). Therefore, standard warnings concerning the media and outside sources of information are now commonly given as a matter of course in most trials that receive any media coverage. The empirical studies that have examined this mechanism suggest for the most part, however, that standard jury warnings do not completely eliminate publicity bias (see Carroll et al., 1986, p. 184). How much bias remains is undetermined, but studies have indicated that juries do discuss prejudicial information despite instructions not to (see Jones, 1987; Klein & Jess, 1966; Kramer et al., 1990; Marshall, 1983; Padawer-Singer & Barton, 1975; Padawer-Singer et al., 1974; Sue et al., 1974; Tans & Chaffee, 1966; Thompson et al., 1981; for a review, see Hans & Vidmar, 1986).

1990). Therefore, although each mechanism has recognized strengths and weaknesses, its application is based on unproven but commonly accepted assumptions concerning its effectiveness and appropriate use.

The primary difficulty for trial judges in using these various mechanisms is determining when action should be taken and which of the mechanisms to employ. Appeals courts have used various ambiguous terms to describe cases where a trial judge must intercede: "wave of public passion" (*Patton* v. *Yount,* 104 S. Ct. 2885 [1984]), "invidious or inflammatory" (*Murphy* v. *Florida,* 421 U. S. 794 [1975]), "highly inflammatory material" (*People* v. *Taylor,* Ill. Sup. Ct., No. 58258 [1984]), "pervasive and prejudicial" (*United States* v. *Faul,* 8th Cir. [1984]), and "a spectacle" (*Rideau* v. *Louisiana,* 373 U. S. 723 [1963]).[8] This ambiguity reflects a judicial preference for not spelling out specific rules: "We prefer to leave [the decision] to the trial judge's judgment and discretion, subject to his *[sic]* later review after verdict on appropriate motion, and our review on appeal . . . rather than invoke a standing inflexible rule" (*State* v. *Kirkland,* Mont. Sup. Ct. [1979]).[9]

These mechanisms interact with one another in complicated ways that make utilization of them by trial judges extremely problematic. At the most basic level, to enforce their decision, trial judges rely on contempt-of-court rulings to deter and punish the ignoring of their orders regarding media publicity. In practice, the threat of a contempt finding normally works better with local criminal justice system personnel, as they also have to consider future dealings with the court, and less well with jurors, witnesses, reporters (especially those from other jurisdictions), and other temporary participants (Jaffe, 1965, pp. 506–507, 524; Pember, 1987, p. 358). Like most deterrence mechanisms, contempt rulings function better when reserved as a threat than when frequently employed. Trial judges, therefore, most often rely on the reactive measures of voir dire and jury warnings, although there is little empirical evidence that these measures adequately attenuate media effects.[10] Their effectiveness remains an unsubstantiated hypothesis, and continued reliance on them is based largely on faith. Usually, only when a case has attracted widespread, adverse news coverage are more costly reactive and more intrusive proactive measures instituted to limit the prejudicial information. As a last resort, a mistrial can be declared and a retrial ordered if jurors are exposed to or admit to being influenced by prejudicial news once a trial has begun. A retrial can be thought of as the ultimate judicial remedy for media publicity—but it also represents an expensive failure of the system and does not prevent the recurrence of renewed massive coverage.

In dealing with the media, trial judges and attorneys face a maze. All must constantly monitor media coverage of a case and act expeditiously when it is apparent that prejudicial information will be released. Exactly what course is adequate or proper in any particular case is unfortunately still determined largely by the trial judge's past experience and best guess (cf. Hans & Vidmar, 1982; Kramer et al., 1990).

Efforts by the Media to Control Information

Reporter's Privilege and Shield Laws

On the opposite side of the information control issue, the media sometimes possess information that the courts or law enforcement want but that the media do not want to divulge. Controversy generally revolves around journalists' claim of the right to "privileged conversation" with news information sources. Journalists argue that they should be protected from having to divulge information or identify their sources to the same extent that communications between husbands and wives, priests and confessors, and psychiatrists and patients are protected. In each of the latter relationships the courts cannot compel disclosure. Journalists argue that to fulfill their function as watchdogs of government activities, protect their First Amendment rights, and guarantee the credibility of and access to future information, their news sources must be similarly protected (Gerald, 1983).

Opponents to the protection of media sources have argued that the media should have no more protections or privileges than the average citizen,

The subject of privileged communications is an old one. The right to confidentiality between a lawyer and client was recognized during the sixteenth century reign of Queen Elizabeth. At the same time, common law extended the privilege to husbands and wives. Today, communications between priests and penitents, physicians and patients, and informers and the government are recognized as privileged (Steigleman, 1971, pp. 196–197). Historically, Benjamin Franklin in his autobiography described the jailing of a publisher for not revealing his news source (Franklin, 1964, p. 69). Journalists began to seriously lobby for equal status in the 1890s, and the first reporters' shield law was passed in Baltimore, Maryland, in 1896.

whose duty to provide testimony in criminal matters has frequently been affirmed. Even within the media industry, opinions differ greatly as to when sources should be protected (cf. Blasi, 1971). Opinions range from the view expressed in Canon 5 of the American Newspaper Guild's Code of Ethics, which states that reporters shall always refuse to reveal confidences, to that spelled out in the Associated Press Managing Editors Association Code of Ethics, which recommends that sources be disclosed unless there is a clear and explicitly stated reason not to.

Most in the media industry, however, feel that journalists are not adequately protected by Supreme Court decisions that have failed to recognize a constitutional right of the media to privileged communication and feel that legislative protection in the form of shield laws is necessary. The media have lobbied successfully for shield laws, and currently more than half (twenty-six) of the states have enacted some form of shield law. Most qualify the privilege and provide a test for assessing whether or not the information is relevant and whether or not it can be obtained from other sources (Kirtley, 1990, p. 164). The effectiveness of shield laws has been questioned, though, and the protection they afford the media is subject to state court interpretation and procedural rulings. Often the degree to which reporters are shielded depends not on what a state's laws say, but on a judge's attitude toward the press (Kirtley, 1990; "State Shield Laws: Do They Work," 1982, pp. 31–33).[11] A second serious deficiency with state shield laws is that they operate only within each state, and contemporary news organizations are national in scope. Because of these deficiencies, few journalists believe their state's shield laws provide substantial help in protecting confidential files or preventing their forced testimony ("State Shield Laws: Do They Work," pp. 31–33). Some journalists believe that shield laws actually work against reporters in that for the laws to be upheld, an "uncomfortable distinction" must be made between journalists and the rest of the American people that may eventually lead to government regulation of the news business (Kennedy, 1985, pp. 44–45). Currently, the media are seldom asked to provide information. However, when they are, reporters may be forced to divulge it, especially if the information can be shown to be crucial to a case

BOX 7-8 Supreme Court Decisions Regarding Journalists' Right to Protect Their Sources

The seminal Supreme Court decision with regard to the protection of news sources' identities is *Branzburg* v. *Hayes* (408 U. S. 665 [1972]). In rendering this ambiguous decision, the Court reviewed three separate cases *(Branzburg, in re Pappas,* and *United States* v. *Caldwell),* all focusing on the right of journalists to maintain secrecy about the identity of sources before grand jury proceedings.[a] The media requested that a reporter be exempt from appearing before a judicial proceeding unless the desired information was not available from another source and the need for the information was great enough to overcome First Amendment considerations, similar to the clear-and-present-danger rule forwarded in *Nebraska Press* for restrictive orders. The Court, however, concluded that public interest in effective law enforcement was sufficient to override burdens on the press caused by testifying (*Branzburg* v. *Hayes,* 408 U. S. 690–691). In rejecting the media's argument, the Court did suggest that a three-prong, case-by-case test in which the interests of society in completing criminal investigations would be balanced against the need to maintain an independent press would not be overruled if adopted at the state level (Bohrer & Ovelmen, 1987).[b] First, the reporter must have the information and the information must be clearly relevant to a specific offense. Second, the information must not be available elsewhere. Third, there must be a compelling and overriding need for the information. Application of the *Branzburg* decision has been varied. Some courts have simply concluded that no privilege exists, and some have narrowly limited the decision to grand jury proceedings. Most jurisdictions, though, have defined a qualified privilege that gives reporters the right to

refuse to answer questions in situations that fail the three-part test outlined above (Kirtley, 1990, p. 164; Pember, 1987, p. 324). In practice, however, the privilege usually fails in criminal cases.

From the media's perspective, the situation became even graver with the *Zurcher* v. *Stanford Daily Press* decision in 1978 (426 U. S. 547, reh'g denied, 439 U. S. 885 [1978]). The case involved a police search of the offices of the Stanford University student newspaper for photographs of a clash between police and student demonstrators. The police obtained a search warrant prior to conducting the search, but the paper argued that they should have obtained a subpoena, which would have required a judicial review and ruling prior to a search. The Supreme Court disagreed with the media and ruled that legally warranted searches of press files and offices were allowable. The media feared that such searches would greatly reduce their access to news sources, in that, potentially, any information given to a reporter, not just that which is eventually published, could be given up in future police searches of news files. Furthermore, fulfilling the media's fears, the number of police searches of newsrooms dramatically increased during the following decade. In response and somewhat countering this trend, the media lobbied for passage of the Federal Privacy Protection Act, which was enacted in 1980 and has reduced the threat of arbitrary newsroom searches at both the state and the national level. The Privacy Protection Act requires subpoenas in most cases and limits situations in which searches based on a simple warrant are allowed (Kirtley, 1990, pp. 172–173; Pember, 1987, pp. 340–341).

---

[a] *Branzburg* v. *Hayes* (408 U. S. 665 [1972]) involved a reporter who, after assuring secrecy to sources, was subpoenaed to testify before a grand jury as to illegal drug activity. *In re Papas* dealt with a reporter who refused to divulge to a grand jury events that had transpired inside Black Panther headquarters. In *United States* v. *Caldwell,* a *New York Times* reporter refused to testify before a federal grand jury about Black Panther activities.

[b] Five justices agreed that a reporter must appear before a grand jury and, if a witness to a crime, must testify as to what was seen; four would have extended a First Amendment privilege to the press; and Justice Powell, while siding with a majority opinion, recognized a qualified privilege requiring a balancing of interests (Bohrer & Ovelmen, 1987, p. 5).

Steigleman (1971, pp. 201–202; see also Van Alstyn, 1977) summarized the arguments for and against shield laws:

For

1. Disclosure of sources chills further news information.
2. Disclosure of crimes aids justice.
3. Reporters can tap sources that are reluctant to talk to police or authorities.
4. Libel laws assure adequate protection against reckless publication.
5. A reporter's relationship with his source is equivalent to that of a lawyer with his client.

Opposed

1. Courts fear that their authority will be weakened if necessary evidence is excluded, and fair trials will be impossible.
2. Sensational press may extol criminals.
3. Public officials could be held up to ridicule and distrust by the press, which would not be responsible to remedy the situation it exposed.
4. Reporters would be turned into detectives or effect alliances with the underworld.
5. In all other classes of privilege, the identity of both parties is known, but shield laws conceal one party. Therefore, it could not be determined if such a relationship actually existed and [could] increase the use of irrefutable "blind quotes."

and unavailable elsewhere.[12] The media's efforts have made obtaining their information more difficult, and in that sense they have successfully increased control of their information. But like the courts themselves, the media are now more open to inspection and more often pressed for access and information.

CONCLUSION

In this world of frequent and increasing interaction between the media and the criminal justice system, the question remains as to what reforms in the media–judiciary relationship should be pursued. Most often suggested with regard to news media coverage of the courts is the development of mutual voluntary guidelines (see Wise, 1986); indeed, some have argued that voluntary cooperation between the courts and the press is the only real solution (Dulaney, 1968). Standards for coverage are also important, as judges' biggest complaint about news reporting is not that it interferes with fair trials but that it is inaccurate and incomplete (Drechsel, 1985, p. 389). Thus, surprisingly, judges do not so much want to bar the media from the courtroom as want them to be more thorough in their reporting. They also wish the media would select a more representative set of cases to cover and not emphasize those selected for their entertainment value.[13] Creating and applying effective voluntary standards acceptable to both sides has not been without problems, however.

For example, the national accreditation standards established in 1979 for police departments include standards for interacting with the media. Few journalists were included in the development of the standards, though, and many departments have not distributed the standards to local members of the media. Departments that have, not surprisingly, often find the media uninterested in adhering to standards they see as put together by outsiders ("Police Adopt Media Guidelines," 1985, pp. 31–32), and the historical pattern of the press and law enforcement agencies' interacting only when problems arise remains the norm. In contrast, guidelines mutually developed by members of the judiciary, the bar, and the news media have been more successful. An underlying reason the police and the media have had more difficulty agreeing to and following standards is that their relationship is more adversarial than that between the judiciary and the press. The police have more often been the focus of negative exposés and tend to see the press as a hindrance to crime control and cooperating with the media as of little benefit to them. Attorneys, in contrast, are generally more sensitive to due process values and thus more sensitive to both the need to accord the media their rights and the larger benefits of both a conscientious and a robust free press. Twenty-eight states currently have guidelines that suggest what kinds of information about a criminal suspect and a crime can be released and published with little danger to the trial process. Maintaining a cooperative relationship takes considerable effort, but in jurisdictions where guidelines work well and both sides cooperate, restrictive orders and closures are rare (Pember, 1987, p. 400).

Phrases such as "government in sunshine" and "freedom of information" reflect a larger, media-driven social trend toward greater openness of public institutions. The two dominant social institutions, the media and the criminal justice system, play critical roles in the continuing development of this trend. That the courts, as central players in these struggles, would be pressured by the media, especially the electronic media, to open their institutions to scrutiny was inevitable. Ironically, the media have also felt the pressure to open their institutions, processes, and files and have suffered through their own exposés of backstage activities (see, for example, *Newswatch* by Av Westin, 1982). In regard to the judicial system specifically, several other factors have further encouraged the movement toward greater media access. First, many perceived the public as distrustful and ignorant of the function of the courts and believed that media access would increase public understanding and support. Second, judges have come to accept the news media more and are more comfortable with the measures necessary to control media behavior during trials. Third, the constitutional importance given to defendants' rights has diminished, with the balance swinging toward general societal interests and thus toward increased media access (Salas, 1984). Fourth, more recently, there has been a shift in judicial attitudes toward the media with regard to due process and crime control. The media are no longer viewed as obstacles to due process, and crime control is now seen as an attainable and desirable role for the media, particularly television (Tajgman, 1981).

All of these developments can be understood as part of the general process of exposing more and more of the previously hidden, backstage areas of society to the public. In a society with a pervasive, multimedia mass media system, closed institutions and proceedings and secret sources of information are automatically viewed with suspicion and challenged. Nonetheless, the criminal justice system and the mass media remain among a handful of social institutions that still resist outside access and continue to struggle to keep their backstage realms closed.

One area in which the judiciary has not strongly resisted media input, however, is in the adoption of media technology to ease the courts' administrative burden—the subject of Chapter 8.

Notes

1. See Becker, 1971; Brady, 1983; Sullivan, 1961; Treuhaft, 1957. Using a single-case study approach, Brady, focusing on "political trials," reviewed the 1976 press coverage and trial of guerrilla bombers in Portland, Maine. From this single case and without reference to other specific trials, he concluded that the Portland case exemplified a historical trend toward biased trials for political defendants—a trend caused by sustained and hostile media coverage (Brady, 1983, p. 241).

2. For example, those of John Delorean, John Hinckley, Claus von Bulow, Maurice Stands, John Connally, and Angela Davis.

3. Generally, privacy concerns truthful articles. If the information published is false, the appropriate legal vehicle would be a libel action, in which the libeled individuals would sue the media for distributing false, defamatory information about them (Levine, 1987, p. 11). Defamation includes both libel (a written defamation) and slander (an oral defamation). The law of defamation can be traced back several centuries. Initially the law was an attempt by government to establish a forum for resolving disputes brought about by an insult or by what today is called a defamatory remark. Though protection of reputation still remains a primary objective of the law of defamation, the law is also seen as a means of ensuring that the press remain accountable. Although the laws against defamation are complex, certain basic principles prevail. Unlike criminal actions, civil libel suits lay

the burden of proof on the plaintiff, who must prove four elements: (1) that the libelous communication was published, (2) that the plaintiff was identified in the communication, (3) that the communication is defamatory in some way, and (4) that the libelous matter was published out of neglect or disregard or carelessness; that is, that its publication was not simply the result of an honest error. The last element is usually the hardest to prove. The plaintiff must prove that there was a real intent to print libelous, defamatory, or untrue material and not just to publish facts. For a full discussion of these issues with a review of cases, see Pember, 1987.

4. The first trial to receive television coverage took place in 1953 in Oklahoma City. The first to receive live coverage took place in 1955 in Waco, Texas. The Florida experiment with televising trials, which ran from July 1977 to June 1978, contributed the most to changing the Supreme Court's view of television and led to the *Chandler* v. *Florida* appeal.

5. *United States* v. *Hastings* 695 F.2d (11th Cir. [1983]), cert. denied, sub nom. *Post-Newsweek Stations* v. *United States,* 461 U. S. 931 (1983). An interesting sidelight to this development is the reluctance of the federal courts, normally leaders in innovation, to allow cameras (*CBS* v. *U. S. District Court,* 729 F.2d 1174 [9th Cir. 1984]; *Combined Communications Corp.* v. *Finesilver,* 672 F.2d 818 [10th Cir. 1982]). It is still federal court policy not to allow cameras in the courtroom. The reasons cited for the ban echo the fears first raised in the *Estes* case in 1965 ("Radio, TV," 1984). However, the new policy guidelines released by the U. S. Judicial Conference in September 1990 and a planned three-year experimental pilot program (in which coverage of criminal proceedings will remain prohibited) lead observers to expect that camera access will soon be expanded throughout the federal system (see "In Re Judicial Conference Guidelines," 1990).

6. See Barber, 1987; Borgida et al., 1990; Gerbner, 1980; Surette, 1989.

7. See Apfel, 1980, pp. 455–458; Bell, 1983, pp. 1310–1315; "Trial Court May Order Trial Proceedings Closed," 1985, p. 180, citing *In re* Knight Pub. Co., 743 F.2d 231 (4th Cir. 1984); and *Press-Enterprise* v. *Riverside Superior Court,* 104 S. Ct. 819 (1984).

8. Contributing to the ambiguity is the variety of rules directing judges. For example, a federal district judge can deny habeas corpus based on alleged pretrial publicity without having to review all the news articles and newscasts underlying the appeal claim. (Habeas corpus is a legal request to release an accused from unlawful imprisonment that is in violation of due process protections.) ("Pretrial Publicity—Habeas Corpus," 1984, p. 2366). A judge also does not have to immediately query jurors to determine whether or not they are aware of questionable publicity and, if so, the effect of such publicity every time a prejudicial news release is brought to his or her attention during the course of a trial (*State* v. *Kirkland,* Mont. Sup. Ct. [1979]).

9. *State* v. *Kirkland,* Mont. Sup. Ct., 11/21/79. Cited in "Fair Trial—Free Press—Exposure to Prejudicial News." *Criminal Law Reporter* 26, no. 13: 2279–2280.

10. See Carroll et al., 1986, p. 195; Kramer et al., 1990; Kerr et al., 1990; Moran & Cutler, in press; Thompson et al., 1981.

11. The questionable effectiveness of shield laws is shown in the case of *In re Farber* (394 A.2d 330 [1978]), in which the New Jersey high court ruled that the state's shield law must yield to the due process rights of a murder defendant. Farber, a *New York Times* reporter, was ordered to turn over his investigation notes and information about the case. The Supreme Court declined to review the case.

12. See "Fair Trial—Free Press—Reporter's Privilege," 1983, *Criminal Law Reporter* 32, no. 20.2428, citing *United States* v. *Burke,* 700 F. 2d [1983] cert. denied, 104 S. Ct. 72 [1983]; "Major Setback for the News Media," 1983, p. 9; "Confidential Sources and Information," 1989.

13. See Barber, 1987; Gerbner, 1980; Surette, 1989; see also Chapter 3.

III

8 Media Technology and the Judicial System

OVERVIEW

In this chapter the increasing application of media technology (audiovisual communication equipment) within the judicial system is reviewed and discussed. In these applications the technology is central to a proceeding and participants must interact through the equipment, often testifying directly into a camera or participating by watching a television screen. In contrast to the use of media equipment in news coverage, here the technology has changed from a tangential, temporary visitor to an indispensable, permanent tool of the judiciary.

Discussed in order from the longest standing and least controversial to the newest and most controversial, the uses of media technology by the courts include the presentation of physical evidence, the presentation of testimony, the creation of permanent records of proceedings, the linking of separated participants for live proceedings, and the prerecording of trials for later presentation to a jury. The chapter reviews the history, development, issues, and research associated with each of these five types of applications. Though the use of media technology has come to be widely accepted in the presentation of physical evidence and testimony, in the creation of permanent records and in live proceedings only limited uses are currently supported, and the prerecording of entire trials has generally been rejected.

The acceptability of an application seems to rest on whether or not a crucial element of justice is felt to be lost in the use of the technology. For preliminary and short procedural steps, most participants, including defendants, appear to feel that the integrity of the process is unaffected. With regard to longer, more-significant, and more-symbolic steps such as trials, concerns and resistance arise, especially among defense attorneys and public defenders. The technology, in most cases, enhances efficiency, and questions of admissibility and due process have been answered in favor of continued use. Though the use of media technology has been initially promising, however, its effects on participants and on courtroom atmosphere and decorum—and thereby, ultimately, on justice in our society—have not yet been fully assessed.

THE JUDICIAL USES OF MEDIA TECHNOLOGY

Like law enforcement agencies, the courts too have recently begun to incorporate media technology into their activities. Here, as in law enforcement, the basic incentives are the administrative benefits of increased speed and efficiency. The hope is that the technology will help the judicial system's crime control "assembly line" function better without damaging its due process "obstacle course." Because most of the benefits of this technology facilitate crime control, most of the concerns that have been raised involve due process. Historically, the impact of visually oriented media technology in the courts has long been of concern because of the effects of news photographic and television coverage (see *State* v. *Hauptmann,* 115 N. J. L. 412 [1935]; *Estes* v. *Texas,* 381 U. S. 532 [1965]; Chapter 7), but with the rapid development of mass media technology, especially within the areas of television and videotape, it was inevitable that media technology would find application within the courtroom. The key difference between the new in-house applications of media technology by the judiciary and news media camera coverage is that in news coverage the equipment is tangential to the judicial activity and the goal is to have the participants ignore the equipment. As visitors, the media and their technology are to be unobtrusive bystanders to the proceedings. But in these new applications, the participants must interact with the equipment, often speaking to a camera or watching a screen rather than interacting with a person. The equipment has thus become central to the activity and therefore cannot be ignored. No longer a temporary, passive visitor, the equipment is, rather, a permanent, active judicial tool.

The first recorded judicial use of television cameras was in 1962 in

Michigan, where a courtroom and a law school were linked to permit law students to view trials. From this simple beginning the use of media technology has expanded, and over the past decade courtroom use of media technology has increased markedly. Currently, many potential uses are available to the courts. Already traditional trials, first appearances, and misdemeanor arraignments have been videotaped to create a visual and audio record of courtroom proceedings. Physically separate locations have been linked through two-way networks, allowing defendants, attorneys, and judges to interact with one another across great distances. These sessions may be broadcast to a public audience; they may be electronically scrambled to prevent eavesdropping; and they may be videotaped for future use. Indeed, videotaped presentations have been used instead of the live testimony of witnesses, and videotape has been used to record confessions; physical evidence for courtroom presentation; recreations or simulations of a crime, accident, or other event; and even entire trials for presentation to a jury. Within the judicial system, applications of media technology fall into five categories. From the longest standing and least controversial to the newest and most controversial, these uses are:

1. to prerecord and present physical evidence,
2. to prerecord and present testimony,
3. to create permanent records of judicial proceedings,
4. to enable the live processing of cases with physically separated participants,
5. to prerecord trials for presentation to a jury.

The first use involves the presentation of evidence that for various reasons cannot otherwise be readily examined by the court. The second involves the prerecording and presentation of some of the individual testimony in an otherwise live, traditionally formatted trial. Both of these uses have become common and widely accepted in specific applications. The third use is using the technology as a neutral recorder in place of a stenographer and has not been universally accepted. The fourth involves the live processing of cases in which the defendants, witnesses, judges, or lawyers are in separate locations. Oftentimes, a defendant is in a correctional facility while the judge is in a distant courtroom. This application is fairly recent, and its effects have not been fully evaluated. The fifth use, in which an entire trial is prerecorded and later shown to a jury, has been adopted in only a single jurisdiction.

Despite the fact that many commentators have approved such efforts,[1] these applications raise a number of questions. How does the introduction of media equipment into the judicial process affect the relationships between judges, attorneys, and other court personnel? How does it affect the ability of defendants to interact with their attorneys and judges? How do defendants feel about its use? Are media-facilitated cases fair, just, and efficient when compared to traditionally processed ones? In essence, does crime control win at the expense of due process? These questions revolve around three interrelated issues: the efficiency in cost and time of using media technology versus using traditional courtroom methods, legal questions regarding the admissibility of evidence and due process, and the effects on participants and courtroom atmosphere and decorum. A review of each application in turn sheds light on these issues and suggests a general explanation for the acceptance or rejection of the technology in the judicial system.

PRESENTING PHYSICAL EVIDENCE

Utilizing media technology to present physical evidence in court has long been well received. Videotape is frequently used to record physical evidence and exhibits prior to their presentation in the courtroom. Where objects, such as machinery, airplanes, and automobiles, are too large to be brought into court, or where the geography of a crime scene, accident scene, or other location must be viewed, they can be videotaped for subsequent courtroom use (Benowitz, 1974, p. 86). Objects that are small or detailed may also be videotaped to highlight their features and ensure that they are seen clearly. Taping can preserve for the jury objects and conditions subject to change before the trial (for example, property destroyed in a condemnation case, the alleged nuisance in a nuisance action, or unsatisfactory goods in a contract case [Joseph, 1982]). The use of videotape in the presentation of evidence has increased markedly, and admission rules have been altered to further encourage its use (Coleman, 1977, p. 2; see also Joseph, 1986). In comparison with traditional methods, videotape has been found to yield more economical, more effective, and more comprehensive presentations because of the ease of editing it, its simple adaptability to multiple monitors, its elimination of the need for special lighting, and the general acceptance of television as a medium (Dombroff, 1981). Currently, the range of applications frequently seen in court in connection with the presenting of physical evidence include:

- Demonstrations and instructional tapes (for example, showing how machinery or a device operates)
- Accident reconstructions (the validity of which is sometimes challenged)
- Tests, experiments, methods, processes, or techniques (as an aid to expert testimony to illustrate scientific or technological principles)
- "Day in the life" tapes (to convey disability and evidence of pain and suffering)
- Surveillance tapes (showing evidence of covert activity)
- Inaccessible site visits (travelogues showing equipment or locations otherwise inaccessible or costly to visit) (Joseph, 1986; Salvan, 1975, p. 224)

Judicial concerns about videotaped evidence relate to admissibility and the production of good-quality evidence without misleading or irrelevant material. To be admissible, a videotape, like a photograph, must be a fair and accurate representation, must be relevant, and cannot be unfairly prejudicial or otherwise contain inadmissible evidence, such as hearsay. A narration will often prompt a hearsay objection, which may require that the narrator be present to testify or that the video be shown without sound (Joseph, 1986, p. 61). Doret (1974) identified two primary sources of prejudice as being camera angle (since the camera represents the juror's eye, the juror can watch only what is shown on the tape, and all off-camera, possibly crucial information is unavailable) and tape editing (choice of camera shots, timing and sequence, cutting of important footage or scenes). However, the courts have found these concerns no greater or less than those found with any photographic evidence. The presence of a judge during taping and editing or review of a tape by the judge and litigants prior to its showing to a jury has effectively minimized problems, and using videotape as a means of presenting evidence is no longer unusual (Joseph, 1986, p. 61).[2] The benign history and general untroubled acceptance of videotaped evidence established a positive foundation for subsequent expanded uses of media technology in the judiciary. The natural first extension was from physical evidence to verbal evidence—the videotaped presentation of testimony in lieu of written depositions.

PRESENTING TESTIMONY

The judicial acceptance of media technology as a substitute for the "live" testimony of witnesses is particularly important in regard to the expanded use of this technology in the courts. The resolution of the questions raised regarding videotaped testimony eased the development of the more controversial media-based communication and case-processing systems now found within many judicial systems. Though the videotaping of inanimate objects and external scenes was never seriously challenged and did not displace any traditional judicial practices except the costly one of site visits, the videotaping of testimony directly replaces the practice of having a live person in the courtroom either testifying or reading a written deposition. It therefore quickly met with close scrutiny and opposition.

In support of videotaped testimony, the National Center for State Courts has argued that the "most useful application of video recordings" is in place of an in-court reading of a typed deposition (cited by Greenwood et al., 1978, p. 27). A number of authors are also enthusiastic about the use of videotaped testimony, listing among its many advantages convenience, elimination of the problem of unavailable witnesses, and enhancement of the ability to hear and follow testimony.[3] In addition, videotape alleviates scheduling problems; reduces the likelihood of last-minute trial postponements and delays; allows more clearly ordered, comprehensible testimony; and limits jurors' exposure to inadmissible material, byplay, and other potentially prejudicial, irrelevant, or unnecessary material (Murray, 1978). In an evaluation of video depositions, Murray (1978, p. 261) stated:

> Videotaped depositions have become an indispensable part of most conventional trials in Erie County: this year for example, 261 videotaped depositions have already been filed [and] represent about one-third of all testimony in civil

trials. [The] result is a "multi-media" trial in which readily available witnesses usually testify live, perfunctory unavailable witnesses testify through a written deposition, and if demeanor evidence is important, or if visual evidence may enhance the persuasiveness of the oral testimony, a videotaped deposition [is used].

Spurred by these advantages, procedural barriers to recording the testimony of witnesses have steadily fallen, and a videotaped presentation is now generally preferred over the reading of a transcript of an unavailable witness's testimony (Coleman, 1977). First sanctioned in the federal courts in 1970, videotaped depositions are now accepted in all but a handful of jurisdictions.

Despite assurances by advocates of the benefits of expanded use of videotape in presenting testimony, its use has raised concerns. Specific early concerns involved the effects of video testimony on jurors and its admissibility when challenged. Regarding admissibility, it was argued that videotape should be admitted into evidence only when certain safeguards have been met (Salvan, 1975). These include establishing the authenticity and correctness of the recording; showing that no changes, additions, or deletions have been made to distort the substance; and showing the voluntariness of the speakers (especially in regard to confessions). As with physical evidence, questions regarding editing and its control arise, as certain courts allow testimony to be taped without the presence of a judge. The courts have not established generally accepted standards to ensure that these criteria are met, however, and admissibility remains the central concern of those seeking or opposing videotaping (Rypinski, 1982). Other procedural concerns relate to the handling of witnesses who do not want to be videotaped and the question of whose burden it is to demonstrate that videotaping should be allowed or not allowed. Some courts rely on the requester to demonstrate solid reasons for videotaping testimony. Other courts hold that motions should be granted unless the opponent argues convincingly that video would be prejudicial (Rypinski, 1982, p. 72). Challenges arguing the inherent inadmissibility of videotape have failed, however, and its future use, although not its admissibility in specific cases, is currently assured.

Beyond the issue of admissibility, in examining the effects of video on the processing of testimony by juries, Doret (1974) and Shutkin (1973) have cited a number of possible negative effects. First, unlike physical evidence, they noted a loss in the completeness of the verbal information communicated. This has both positive and negative implications in that it narrows the field of information offered the juror at any given moment during testimony but can also filter out extraneous events and preserve a crucial moment that a juror might otherwise miss in a lapse of attention. Second, they expressed the fear that video could not capture the total psychological and physical essence of a witness—that the electronic distortion of information would degrade the accuracy of the communication and limit its clarity, detail, and realism. Another source of concern is that video favors some witnesses—telegenic subjects—and not others, distorting viewers' perceptions. The fear is that the courtroom reality created by videotaped testimony will differ substantially from the reality of live testimony (Brakel, 1975, p. 957). "To the extent that television increases the degree to which credibility is assessed on the basis of the looks of the witness, it emphasizes a factor extraneous to the truth of the testimony, and renders the truth-finding process less objective" (Doret, 1974, p. 244). One of the chief problems associated with the use of videotaped depositions was that of boredom (Benowitz, 1974, p. 90), particularly when such presentations were compared with commercial television.[4]

All of these concerns involve a possible effect on the interaction between witness and jury. What are lost with videotaped testimony are in essence the elements of a two-way communication system with feedback. Video changes testimony from a total communication system to a unidirectional reality. Feedback from seeing witnesses' reactions to answers and questions is lost not only for juries but for attorneys, witnesses, and judges. No longer can a lawyer evaluate how well his or her questioning is being received and change tactics accordingly. This may make for less-effective counsel (Doret, 1974, p. 252).

With the courts pressured because of the administrative benefits to adopt the practice and spurred by the above concerns not to, researchers undertook the study of the effects of videotaped testimony. These evaluations focused on jurors' attention span and boredom and their ability to retain information, reach decisions, and detect lying when viewing videotaped testimony. The most extensive evaluations were conducted in the 1970s by Miller and his colleagues.[5] Miller and Fontes (1979a, 1979b) studied civil trial reenactments in actual courtrooms with real judges and jurors from a regular jury pool. Jurors were told that the video trials were actual cases and that their decisions would be binding. After various experiments, Miller and Fontes (1979b, p. 207) concluded that "within the confines of our research, there is no evidence to suggest that the use of videotape exerts any deleterious effects on the juror responses studied; in fact, as far as retention of trial related information is concerned, it appears that videotaped testimony sometimes results in higher retention levels."[6] Regarding the ability of jurors to discern lying, they reported, "our findings do not support the argument that videotape will curtail jurors' abilities to assess the demeanor of witnesses" (1979a, p. 100). In fact, nonverbal cues may hinder rather than help jurors make accurate judgments; Miller and Fontes found the highest percentage of correct judgments followed written transcripts. Additionally, Miller and Siebert (1974, 1975) found that jurors who watched live versus videotaped trials tested no different with respect to attribution of negligence, dollar award, attorney credibility, retention of information, and motivation and interest in the trial. In comparing live, color, black-and-white, audiotaped, and read transcripts they further reported that all three electronic methods were superior to the read-transcript method. Only one research effort, conducted in the 1970s, reported significant negative findings regarding the effect of video testimony. Junke and his colleagues (1979) presented a criminal trial to male and female undergraduates in one of four modes—video, audio, transcript, or summary. They reported significant differences in verdicts, with video more likely to produce guilty verdicts than a written transcript. They also found differences in jurors' perceptions of the effectiveness of attorneys' presentations, but no differences in perceptions of witnesses. Lacking a live-trial comparison, however, this study shed no light on questions regarding the substitution of video for live testimony. Its other findings have not been replicated.

Despite a number of initial concerns, the use of media technology in the courts had passed its first crucial test. In fact, video is now felt to be clearly superior in certain situations. The research supports the contention that videotaped testimony is better than written transcripts and in some ways surpasses live testimony (Brakel, 1975). Allaying concerns about the effect on judicial outcomes, the research indicates that the use of videotaped testimony does not significantly affect either juror verdicts or monetary awards. It should be noted, however, that this research focused on civil cases, not criminal concerns. That the effects of video testimony in criminal trials will be similarly benign and insignificant has simply been assumed (see Hartman, 1978).

Both videotaped testimony and videotaped evidence are thus now regularly accepted in the criminal justice system, and expanded uses are continually advocated. For example, the Supreme Court now supports the videotaping and closed-circuit televising of children's testimony in child abuse cases as a solution to maintaining press access to trials while protecting child witnesses from emotional or mental strain (see *Craig* v. *Maryland* (89 U. S. 478 [1990] [Md. Ct. App. 1989]; Shutkin, 1973, p. 391). Nonetheless, many still resist expanding the role of video, and even advocates of its use for depositions argue that presenting large portions of testimony by videotape is inappropriate.[7] Whereas using video for a small segment of the total testimony in a trial is quite acceptable, the idea of making it the dominant method of presenting testimony, and in the process drastically changing the traditional appearance, process, and nature of a trial, arouses sharp resistance. Another area where limited use of media technology has been accepted but expanded use has met resistance is as a replacement for a written stenographic record of a proceeding.

AS A PERMANENT COURT RECORD

Trials and other case-processing steps are now being videotaped as a means of creating a permanent visual and aural record of proceedings, replacing the stenographic notes of the court reporter and other paper files. Despite the potential financial merits of this use and its possible value in appellate procedures, its threat to the role and livelihood of court personnel has fueled opposition, not only from court reporters,[8] but also from appellate judges.[9] Because of this opposition and questions about the effectiveness of using such records in appellate cases, enthusiasm for this application has declined in recent years. Initially, court administrators felt that videotaped records would provide advantages over the traditional written transcripts.

Coleman (1977, citing Madden, 1969) listed as the main advantages expected from videotaping court sessions that videotape records gesture and facial expressions as well as words, the equipment is not obtrusive or disruptive to court proceedings, and the master tape can be readily copied, making a record available in much less time than is required to prepare a typed transcript.

However, contrary to the advantages initially expected from videotaped records, the practice of videotaping court proceedings for appeals was dropped after a thirty-month trial in Ohio. Attorneys found too much of the taped material inaudible and found reviewing the tapes time-consuming. Additionally, the Ohio court of appeals found that viewing the tapes took much longer than reading transcripts, and appellants were eventually required to attach a typed transcript of the portion of the videotape supporting the appeal with indexed references to the videotape included (Kosky, 1975). A second trial project in Tennessee ended after two years. The videotaped records again neither shortened the appellate process, nor reduced the expense of preparing a record for review (Coleman, 1977, pp. 13–14). Videotape had, in fact, the opposite effect to what was expected. Burt (1978, p. 63), referring to the Ohio test, said: "The use of videotapes in place of the printed transcripts have had the effect of slowing down the appeal process rather than accelerating it. From court reporters' point of view, it is more difficult, [more] time-consuming, and less accurate to produce a transcript from videotape than from a stenographer's notes." Kosky (1975, pp. 231, 235) summarized the criticisms of video as a trial court record as follows: "[Its] use as the sole official record in the courtroom is impractical for both trial purposes and subsequent appellate review. [There is] no savings of time especially when a transcript of the audio portion of the tape is required as is often the case." From appellate judges' point of view, the appellate process focuses primarily on issues of law rather than on issues of fact; therefore, what is needed is a written transcript of the lower court case rather than a videotape (Benowitz, 1974, p. 86). To date, the videotaping of trial proceedings has not proven an acceptable substitute for a traditional transcript prepared by a court reporter.[10] Other, less-ambitious video records have, however, shown themselves to be beneficial. Thus, videotape provides a useful record of the more-backstage hearings and procedural steps found early in the judicial process, which are simply dated and logged and otherwise not recorded. These early backstage steps include bookings, first appearances, arraignments, and bond and plea hearings.

An increasing number of police departments currently use the technology to record booking of all arrests. These video "mug shots" provide a pictorial record of arrestees that includes voice, accent, and a continuous front-to-profile view. The availability of these video records has also allowed changes in two other common practices—the traditional identification of a suspect from a lineup and the identification of a suspect from a set of photographs of known offenders (see O'Neill, 1990; Surette, 1988). In a video lineup, a crime witness is shown a series of video bookings selected for their similarity. The witness chooses from this video lineup the individual he or she feels is the offender. This process is felt to be fairer than the old practices in that the individuals in video lineups more closely resemble one another than the groups usually assembled for a live lineup and it provides a permanent record of the lineup for later review should questions of fairness arise. It also frees law enforcement personnel from having to serve in lineups. In video mugbooks, a computer searches the pictorial file for specific characteristics (for example, tattoo, bald, heavy, white male) and displays, and prints if desired, the pictures that match.

Video records of arraignments, first appearances, bond hearings, and pleas have also proven inexpensive and useful. A single videotape of hundreds of cases can be stored as a permanent record that can be consulted should the state of mind of a defendant, his or her comprehension of rights or instructions, or the voluntariness of a plea later be questioned. Thus, unlike videotaping trials, videotaping these short, nontrial procedural steps offers both crime control and due process benefits. Crime control proponents like the savings of time and money. Due process adherents feel that the knowledge that a permanent record is being created makes law enforcement and judicial personnel more conscientious in following proper procedures. Videotaping procedural steps also provides a means not previously available of resolving any subsequent due process concerns. In addition, a bit more of the backstage world of the criminal justice system is revealed for outside review. As was true regarding the videotaping of vehicle stops and interrogations by police (see Chapter 6), once instituted these systems gain support from both crime control and due process advocates. Furthermore, the same technology used in creating a video record also allows, if

BOX 8-1   Video Mug Shots

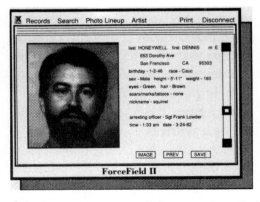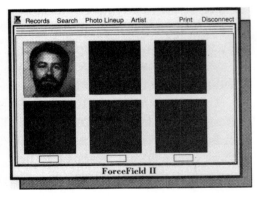

An example of a present-day use of media technology in the criminal justice system: a computer-enhanced booking and lineup photo system

Source: Courtesy of XImage Corporation

desired, the separation of the participants, thus allowing a judicial proceeding to be conducted in a completely new way—in live but media-linked sessions.

LIVE, VIDEO-FACILITATED PROCEEDINGS

This use of media technology electronically expands the traditional courtroom so that defendants, witnesses, judges, and lawyers who are physically separated can still communicate visually, aurally, and live. In a sense, the traditional courtroom is thus "diffused" to physically isolated but electronically linked locations. The available technology allows various configurations of the communication links; this flexibility in turn allows multiple applications. In practice, such systems primarily benefit not judges but other system personnel, who spend less time traveling and waiting for a judge to be available (Doret, 1974). As with videotaped depositions, the use of video in judicial systems to conduct live proceedings has increased. Likewise, using video to conduct live proceedings has raised concerns about the constitutionality of the proceedings, the creation of a new trial reality that differs significantly from the traditional trial, the possible restriction and distortion of communications, a loss of judicial legitimacy and decorum, and effects on the norms, values, and interpersonal relationships within the system.[11]

Live interactive video has been most extensively used in misdemeanor arraignments. Not only does the handling of misdemeanor cases comprise a large proportion of a judicial system's caseload, it also presents a number of logistical problems for the judicial system. Media-facilitated misdemeanor appearances were introduced to reduce the number of court and correctional personnel involved in first appearances, to reduce costs, to increase security, to alleviate courtroom crowding, and to speed up the handling of cases—all administrative benefits that further crime control goals.

A survey of the media-facilitated arraignment systems that have been publicized reveals both successful and unsuccessful programs. In 1974, the city of Philadelphia, for example, linked its nine police divisions, its twenty-two district police headquarters, its arraignment court, and its central police administration building through a closed-circuit multipurpose video system ("Philadelphia's Popular Police Station," 1979, p. 1). In an arraignment, the judge reads the charges to the defendant, asks about the assignment of counsel, sets bail, and schedules another court appearance date. No pleas are heard (New York City, 1983, p. 21). However, the Philadelphia police

In 1975 an appellate case was argued via picture-phone service between Washington, D. C., and New York (Weis, 1977). The first live video-facilitated proceeding was most likely a bail bond hearing in Cook County (Illinois) Circuit Court in 1972 (Surette & Terry, 1984).

Trial jurors prepare to view videotaped testimony
Source: AP/Wide World Photos

believe that the savings in transportation costs gained by the use of the video system are more than offset by the additional police staffing needed.[12] Although still in use, according to the city's Court Administrator's Office, the system will most likely be dropped in the near future, when a new court building becomes available. Phoenix, Arizona; Santa Barbara, California; Suffolk County, New York; Boise, Idaho; Las Vegas, Nevada; Los Angeles, California; and Miami, Florida, also have installed video systems through which live proceedings can be conducted.

The system in Phoenix, a videophone system that used existing telephone lines, was discontinued because of the expense involved (approximately $3,000 per month for phone service) (Rockwell, 1983). While in operation, however, this system encountered no serious opposition from participants and if a need for a remote site developed in the future a less expensive video system would be supported locally.[13]

Santa Barbara's system has been in operation since 1981 and is used primarily by probation officers and public defenders to communicate with their inmate-clients at the Santa Barbara County Jail (Court Vision Communications, n.d.). Since 1985, it has also been used in the Maricopa Superior Court to arraign defendants held in custody at the county jail who are pleading not guilty (Coleman, 1977, p. 17). Despite reports that this microwave system is down approximately half the time and that the Public Defender's Office opposes its use in any judicial proceedings, there are no plans to discontinue the system (author's interview with G. Maurer, Public Defender's Office, Santa Barbara, Calif., June 30, 1987).

In New York, Suffolk County's system was installed in 1982 and linked the police precinct headquarters with the courthouse, some twenty miles away (New York City, 1983, p. 9). This system also has been discontinued because of its expense and cost overruns.

Boise, Idaho's system went on-line in 1979 (Gilmore, 1980, p. 397). Boise judges, who, unlike judges in other jurisdictions, conduct the arraignments of both misdemeanor offenders and felony offenders, use the system in arraignments and first appearances. Public defenders use the system to interview clients, and prosecutors, to interview the sheriff and police. This system is still in operation and there are no plans to discontinue or limit its use.

Like Boise's, Las Vegas's system was fully operational in 1979 (Brown, 1980). An average of 2,300 hearings per month are processed by this system, and its use will probably be expanded in the near future (Las Vegas, 1978; author's interview with Judge Brown, City Municipal Court, June 30, 1987).

Los Angeles County has a pilot video arraignment system in use in its Glendale Municipal Court. Used for both felony and misdemeanor hearings, the system connects defendants and public defenders with judges and prosecutors one block away and is well accepted and thought reliable by judges and attorneys (Antonovich et al., 1987). Of the more than 3,000 defendants processed through the system so far, only three have refused arraignment via video. The report on the first year is positive and the project is expected to be continued (author's interviews with M. Judge, Public Defender's Office, and R. Mimura, Criminal Justice Committee, Glendale, Calif., June 30, 1987).

Lastly, a program begun in 1982 in Miami, Florida's Eleventh Circuit Court has been continued and expanded (Surette & Terry, 1984). When arraigned, Miami defendants are called to a podium in the county jail's chapel, where they are informed via video of the charges against them and their pleas are heard. To date, more than 100 thousand defendants have been thus arraigned in the Eleventh Circuit Court.

As is evident, the response to these programs has been mixed, with five jurisdictions satisfied with their use of video to facilitate live proceedings and three not. The expense of a system is the most often cited reason for discontinuation. Technical unreliability, even when a system appears to be down for significant amounts of time, has not been a common complaint. Also, despite criticism of video images as inadequate substitutes for live interaction, appeals based on a loss of due process protections and the inherent unfairness of a video-facilitated proceeding have all failed. However, early reviews have largely ignored questions of the effect of the technology on the attitudes of participants, concentrating instead on the efficiency and cost of the equipment. Therefore, little is understood regarding the dynamics of successful versus unsuccessful implementations of the technology or its systematic effects after installation. Conversations with personnel in the various cities suggest that to succeed over the long term, programs must be initiated by and receive the continued support of the judiciary[14] and that, at least in the systems surveyed, hard-wire setups perform better than microwave systems. The successful programs appear to have employed less-expensive approaches, to have had early on the support of the people who were to operate and use the systems, and to have limited the focus of their applications. More-complicated and -expensive systems seemed to lose support and encounter more difficulties, perhaps because expectations were higher or unrealistic.

The Eleventh Circuit Court program in Miami, Florida, has been more fully evaluated to determine the broader effects of using media technology (see Box 8-2). Judges and prosecutors like the system; public defenders do not. The public defenders' criticisms have to do with the loss of the normative reality of the courtroom. In the Miami system, public defenders are confined to the jail's chapel, whereas the judge and prosecutor remain in the

---

BOX 8-2 Media-Facilitated Arraignments in the Eleventh Circuit Court, Miami, Florida

---

Evaluation of the Eleventh Circuit Court's system was based on a survey of all of the judicial participants involved and a sample of the defendants with respect to the use of video equipment in a judicial setting (see Surette & Terry, 1984; Terry & Surette, 1985). The results revealed that of the four judges using the system, all agreed that it is an improvement over previous means of conducting arraignments and that less general disruption occurs during video arraignments. The judges also reported that the use of video either increases or has little effect on their ability to maintain control of proceedings, to evaluate defendants' demeanor, and to communicate with them. Furthermore, they all felt that video either increases or has little effect on the speed of the arraignments, the effectiveness of the defendant's legal representation, and the humaneness of the arraignment process. Judges' complaints focused on the quality of the video picture and the sound system, especially on feedback and echo problems. All of the judges felt that the system should be expanded. None felt that it should be restricted.

The four state prosecutors in Miami also viewed the video arraignment system favorably, but slightly less so than the judges. Two felt that the video system was an improvement over previous arraignment methods. Two did not. Nevertheless, they all felt that the use of video did not detract from the overall quality of legal representation and that the speed of arraignments and the sentences defendants received were unaffected. In criticism of the system, several prosecutors felt that the video system made it difficult for defendants to communicate. Regardless, all four prosecutors agreed that video arraignments are a good idea. In fact, they thought that more cameras should be added to the system and that it should be expanded. None felt that the system should be restricted or eliminated.

Unlike the judges and prosecutors, all seven of the public defenders involved in the video-facilitated arraignments felt that the use of video decreased the judge's ability to control the courtroom. Six felt that there was more general disruption during video arraignments

(continued)

more familiar surroundings of the courthouse. Consequently, they feel that the traditional courtroom atmosphere has been lost and that their ability to act as effective advocates for defendants has been diminished. Contrary to how the public defenders feel, however, Miami defendants largely support video arraignments.

In general, it is apparent from the comments of judges and prosecuting attorneys, as well as from the more critical comments of public defenders, that the video systems usually achieve their manifest objectives—namely, easing the logistics and reducing the cost of processing defendants. Reviews of this use of media technology in the courts have improved as the technology has improved. In the Las Vegas system, for example, public defenders remain in the courtroom with the judges and prosecutors, and, not surprisingly, according to developer Judge Brown, they are as supportive of the system there as their judicial counterparts. They are also allowed access to the system before the hearing to confer confidentially with their clients. Acceptance of this program is also aided because it does not involve a highly

---

BOX 8-2 (continued)

---

and that the quality and effectiveness of legal representation were diminished. They felt that video arraignments were less personal and less humane and that their defendants were nervous, intimidated, and more likely to plead guilty. In sum, none of the public defenders supported the idea of video arraignments, and none saw the practice as an improvement over previous methods of arraignment. The public defenders volunteered the following comments:

- "The video system presents only an image of the accused. The personal confrontation, which is essential, is effectively removed."
- "No courtroom atmosphere—the prison chapel with a TV screen on the altar beneath the crucifix totally lacks any courtroom atmosphere."
- "By having the arraignment in the chapel, judges can 'turn us off.' The state attorney, however, is five feet from the judge. It makes our positions very unequal."
- "It puts the judge and prosecutor on the same side and the public defender and the defen-

dants on the other—the good guys versus the bad guys."

Among the 352 video-arraigned defendants who were surveyed, most felt that their ability to argue their case was unhindered (64.3%), as was their ability to ask questions (78.4%). More than three-quarters of these defendants (79.1%) felt that they acted and spoke as they would have had they been in a "regular" courtroom. And 85.5% felt their plea was the same as it would have been had they pled in "regular" court. In short, 72.1% felt that using video for misdemeanor appearances is a good idea, and 78.5% were happy with their court appearance. A substantial proportion (24.9%) of these individuals were not happy with their arraignment; however, this proportion was found to be similar to the proportion of dissatisfied defendants found in a group of defendants who had been traditionally arraigned. Analysis of these findings indicates that negative perceptions are more related to the outcome of the arraignments (whether the defendants had been released or returned to jail) than to the use of video equipment.

The high-profile trial of the "Chicago 7" in the 1960s, during which disruptive defendants were bound and gagged in the courtroom, led to criticism of the use of restraints on defendants and to the practice of totally removing such defendants from the courtroom. The Supreme Court subsequently upheld this practice, stating that disruptive behavior on the part of a defendant constitutes a waiver of the right of confrontation (*Illinois* v. *Allen*, 90 S. Ct. 1057 [1970]). Closed-circuit television is commonly used in many jurisdictions to enable disruptive defendants who have been removed to at least watch their trials on television.

visible component of the judicial process such as a trial, and each individual hearing is short. Even at the trial level, however, live, media-linked sessions have been gaining favor. The use of closed-circuit television to allow disruptive defendants to witness their trials is now accepted as meeting a defendant's right to be present at his or her trial. The Supreme Court has also supported the live, one-way, televised testimony of children in child abuse cases, allowing the defendant and defense attorneys to view the child testifying but protecting the child from having to see the defendant. Currently thirty-two states permit sexually abused children to testify live via a media link. Of these, twenty-four allow one-way closed-circuit testimony, and eight permit two-way systems (Epstein, 1990). Though criticisms remain, expanded use is likely for the future.

However, live video-linked proceedings have led to the development of at least one latent, unintended consequence: disruption of the traditional courthouse culture. Such disruptions affect the judiciary's use of media technology in that they raise concerns about due process, increased depersonalization of the courtroom, and the public image of the judicial system. The public image of the courts is felt to be particularly significant, as it is interrelated with people's perceptions of the legitimacy of the entire criminal justice system, the general government, and in turn the total social structure. To the extent that media technology alters the reality and perception of justice, it has a potentially significant impact on the public image and legitimacy of justice. In no application is the format and appearance of justice more changed by media technology than in the recording and presentation of full trials using media technology.

The Supreme Court in *Craig* v. *Maryland* (89 U. S. 478 [1990] [Md. Ct. App. 1989]) ruled that in child abuse cases, a child witness may testify via one-way closed-circuit television where the child cannot see the defendant. Justice O'Connor, writing the majority opinion, stated that testimony on one-way television systems serves the major purpose of the confrontation clause by enabling the judge or jury to observe the demeanor of a witness being cross-examined under oath.

PRERECORDED, VIDEOTAPED TRIALS (PRVTTS)

In prerecorded videotaped trials, a videotape of an entire trial is presented to a jury after a judge has deleted all inadmissible questions, answers, and comments from the tape (see McCrystal, 1978, p. 251). The first such trial involved a 1971 Ohio civil suit that developed from an automobile accident. Between the lawyers' opening and closing arguments, which were presented in person to the jury, the jury watched two hours and forty minutes of prerecorded testimony, as opposed to an estimated five days of trial proceedings (Salvan, 1975, pp. 222, 224). From this tape, the judge had deleted all inadmissible material, avoiding, as much as possible, any "contamination" of the jury (McCrystal, 1978, pp. 253–254).

PRVTTs constitute a marked departure from traditional trials in that video becomes the exclusive means of presenting testimony without regard to the availability of the individual witnesses, all extraneous and objectionable statements are eliminated from the jurors' knowledge, and counsel, judge, and litigating parties need not be present while the testimony is being shown to the jury (Coleman, 1977). The main advantages are speed and cost savings. Although not a well-known application, as early as 1973 comments regarding the use of videotaped trials and noting the difference between live and videotaped testimony appeared:

> Although similar, the videotape trial is more than a procedural extension of videotape depositions. It is not incorporated in the normal trial framework but is the sole means by which evidence is introduced to the jury. . . . The essence of the videotape system is that it allows the trial to be subdivided into three units: testimony (involving lawyers and witnesses), rulings (involving trial judges and lawyers), and presentation (involving jurors). These units proceed chronologically but relatively independently, each impinging only slightly on the schedules of the others. (Shutkin, 1973, pp. 363–364)

According to proponents, prerecorded video trials have been very successful in reducing overloaded court dockets and have cut the amount of time needed to complete the hearing of a case.[15] Many other advantages of PRVTTs have been cited, including:

* more efficient utilization of participants' time
* minimized use of courtroom space
* fewer errors by judges in making rulings because they have longer to research and consider
* more-effective voir dire examinations by lawyers and opening and closing statements because they know all the testimony that will be presented
* more-relaxed witnesses
* more-attentive jurors because trials are shorter[16]

Irrespective of its apparent advantages, however, critics have argued against the expanded use of video to present entire trials, and PRVTTs have not been accepted outside of Ohio. Brakel (1975, p. 958), for example, strongly faulted the use of simulations in evaluating the effects of video because the real essence of trials, he said, cannot be simulated. And Kosky

The first criminal case, *State of Ohio* v. *Lange* (1982, case no. 9320 Erie County Court of Common Pleas) involved a crossbow killing and advanced to the point where all the testimony had been recorded. The case terminated when a plea bargain was struck and the defendant pled guilty to manslaughter. The second case, which involved a lesser charge, was pled prior to the recording of testimony. Therefore, the constitutionality of this procedure has not been tested through appeal. In both of the Ohio cases the defendants had requested the PRVTT and voluntarily waived the traditional trial process (author's interview with Judge McCrystal, August 16, 1990).

(1975) criticized the positive evaluation of videotaped trials in Ohio because they involved only simple, short, civil cases. Even among authors who support the use of video for depositions, many argue that presenting entire trials or even large portions of traditional trials by videotape is appropriate (see Surette, 1988). The objection is to making video the sole or primary method of presenting testimony in a trial. The use of PRVTTs is not expected to increase in the near future, even in seriously backlogged jurisdictions. The reluctance to adopt PRVTTs appears to revolve partly around constitutional questions. Among the problems foreseen in the extended use of videotape in the courtroom are the constitutional issues of the right of confrontation, the right of the accused to be present during the trial and the right to a public trial, and the requirement that the judge be present at the trial. Due process issues have not proven problematic in Ohio, however, and PRVTTs have been initiated in two criminal cases, one involving a capital crime. A more-significant source of resistance is the effect of videotaping trials on the traditional atmosphere and appearance of a trial.

Critics of this technology frequently mention the effect of videotape on juries and jury deliberations.[17] It is feared that jurors will bring their television experience to the viewing of PRVTTs, expecting entertaining, engaging sessions.

> Research has demonstrated that the whole juror comes to court: he *[sic]* brings to the courtroom his entire experience with the media. That experience includes watching soap operas, tv westerns and gangster movies, where actors may die ghastly deaths, but spring to life to play new roles again. Further research is necessary to tell us whether we can fully separate tv as reality from tv as entertainment. We don't know what unconscious forces might be at work affecting our judgment when we see a trial in the form of a television program. (Hartman, 1978, pp. 256–257; see also Doret, 1974, p. 245; Monteleone, 1982, p. 863)

According to Kosky, "Many authors embrace videotape as a panacea for all the infirmities of the judicial process. The literature of enthusiasm, however, 'has been excessively concerned with the advantage of the technique, but not concerned enough with its practical and normative difficulties' " (1975, p. 231, citing Doret, 1974).

Brakel (1975, p. 958) has argued that one is inescapably drawn to the conclusion that expanded use of video will drastically alter the trial process, its internal relationships and procedures, and, ultimately, verdicts (see also Doret, 1974; Shutkin, 1973), for the presumption behind the formal court setting and proceedings is that they have an impact on witnesses' performance and perceptions, as well as on the behavior of other trial participants and observers.

> The trial process itself will be altered as will the relationships between and among lawyers, parties, witnesses, and judge. From a drama directed and to various extents controlled by a professional and "impartial" judge, the trial will be transformed to a far more "partisan" event, directed and controlled by a larger variety of participants — lawyers in all their variety of competence, personality, and partisanship; cameramen of varying degrees of neutrality and proficiency; and witnesses who will be less readily surprised or otherwise made to lose their poise. (Brakel, 1975, pp. 957, 958; see also Shutkin, 1973, p. 391)

Doret (1974, p. 256) and Kosky (1975) have further noted the importance of the courtroom as a mechanism of legitimization. Its symbols and processes are important in and of themselves and by severing testimony from the courtroom a crucial function of the trial in the larger social community may be sacrificed. Kosky (1975, pp. 237–238) has concluded:

> A jury in a room with a witness will produce a much more sensitive human evaluation and clean video trials may be too sensitized. Perhaps some of the apparent disadvantages of present trial procedures are good in that they are educative and socializing. . . . Live judicial rulings and corrections convey a metacommunication that what the juror is viewing is an important and dignified social event.

Though other judicial adaptations of media technology have proved successful, PRVTTs do not appear to hold much promise as an accepted alternative for live courtroom trials (Burt, 1978, p. 66). Though the constitutional questions, at least for civil cases and in at least one criminal case, have been overcome, if PRVTTs are to be broadly accepted in the future, they must not undermine the symbolic functions of the trial process. Otherwise, the common expectation of what a trial should be must alter considerably. At present, few are convinced that either is possible.

UNRESOLVED CONCERNS OF THE JUDICIAL USE OF MEDIA TECHNOLOGY

Concerns about using the technology can be traced in part to questions regarding technical feasibility and constitutional due process,[18] but they are more deeply rooted in established social attitudes, perceptions, and expectations with respect to the judicial process, and trials in particular. Ultimately, judicial acceptance or rejection of the technology rests on whether or not its use leads to a perceived loss of a crucial symbolic element of justice. When the traditional, familiar reality of the judicial system is changed drastically, resistance to the new reality rises. For preliminary and short procedural steps, most participants, including defendants, appear to feel that the integrity of the process is unaffected by the use of the technology. Its use in longer, more significant, and more symbolic steps such as trials triggers greater concern and resistance.

From this symbolic alteration of the reality of the judicial system three concerns emerge, even for the now-common and accepted applications. These concerns are the technology's effects on the working relationships among courtroom personnel, its depersonalization of the criminal justice system, and its impact on the image and legitimacy of the judicial system. Though uses of the technology have been initially promising, questions regarding the effects of this technology on participants, on the judicial system, and on the public's perception of the criminal justice system as a whole, and thereby ultimately on justice, have not been fully answered.

Regarding the technology's effects on the relationships among courtroom personnel, comments from the attorneys (especially those from public defenders) and judges, indicate that the relationships among courtroom personnel can be upset by the introduction of media equipment. It is significant that in a number of the pilot projects public defenders remain largely skeptical of the technology's advantages even for short procedures. The question arises whether attorneys deliver equivalent representation if they feel legally and organizationally disadvantaged in media-constructed proceedings. If their morale suffers, does their subsequent effort also suffer?

An examination of case outcomes to address the question revealed no significant aggregate differences between cases conducted using media technology and those not using the technology in terms of case outcomes (see Surette & Terry, 1984). The possibility remains, however, that such an effect could be operating in other locales or develops only after a large number of cases over a significant period of time have been processed. (The realignment of communication channels and changes in behavior and attitudes seldom occur simultaneously [Lipetz, 1980]). These systems also have the potential to increase the administrative supervision of courtroom personnel and thereby decrease the substantial discretion they now have. What effect such a utilization would have on morale, effectiveness, and case outcomes, or whether it would have crime control or due process implications, is unknown.

A second concern is that expanded use of this technology within the judiciary will almost certainly lead to further depersonalization of criminal justice proceedings. Adjudication within the criminal justice system is based on face-to-face interaction, particularly on the premise that the accused are entitled to face their accusers. Extended use of media technology, however, will reduce live, face-to-face encounters between witnesses and defendants, police and the public, attorneys and their clients, judges and defendants, and jurors and all of the previous groups, thereby seriously altering the interpersonal structure of the system. This process will most likely be hastened by equipment advances that make this technology more economical, less obtrusive, and more approximate (but never equal) to live meetings. The full effects of these changes may become apparent only after such practices have been in place for a long time.

A third key unresolved concern is what is lost in legitimacy and the public image of justice when media technology is employed. The justice system is a means of adjudicating guilt and administering punishment. It is also a means of legitimizing the whole social system, its rules, laws, and government. Accordingly, the courtroom and its personnel have a symbolic value. The "majesty" and "mystery" of actions in the courtroom embody the sanctity and well-being of the larger society. Loss of these symbolic qualities may diminish the aura of legitimacy sustaining the entire system. If the structure and nature of the system are altered, will the system lose or gain public support? From this systematic perspective, how the system treats individuals is crucial (cf. Casper, 1978). If people become alienated from the system or if they feel intimidated or dehumanized by it, whatever benefits that result from the use of media technologies in the courtroom may cancel out. If these systems ultimately result in the further isolation and separation of the police from the policed, and the courts from the public, the social costs of such losses would outweigh any organizational benefits that might accrue from their use.

A crucial unexamined factor within this area is the technology's effect on courtroom visitors and friends and family of defendants. These external observers participate in the construction of reality with regard to the criminal justice system, affecting the legitimacy of the entire system. It is reasonable to expect that defendants, who are immediately threatened by punitive sanctions, would be more concerned with procedure outcomes than with the process itself. However, unthreatened observers may receive an image of the system that is unacceptable if they see the use of technology as a degrading means of keeping the defendant out of the courtroom. Inasmuch as these observers represent a larger part of society than the actual defendants, effects on them cannot be ignored. But to date, no information regarding the affects of the use of media technology on the perceptions of the larger public is available. As crime control values become more popular there is considerable desire, especially on the part of administrators, to make the court system more effective and efficient. Nevertheless, the system must remain moral in the public's eyes if it is to remain a legitimate and viable system of justice.[19]

CONCLUSION

Media technology has proven itself useful in the judicial system, especially as a substitute for personal, in-court testimony and as a means of presenting evidence and courtroom exhibits. There is less agreement, however, about its usefulness as a substitute for live proceedings and written records. In general, the use of media technology in the processing and recording of brief, nontrial procedural steps and small portions of a trial is accepted;

more extensive uses are not. In all of these projects the trend is for crime control benefits to emerge quickly and to overshadow the possibility that due process losses may emerge over the long term. As these systems are increasingly instituted, long-term studies are needed to address whether such effects do in fact develop. With this is mind, we may consider media technology an extremely useful tool, but not a panacea for the judicial system's problems. There are invariably costs that accompany its benefits.

Notes

1. See Benowitz, 1974, pp. 86–88; Brakel, 1974, p. 956; Burt, 1978, p. 66; Greenwood et al., 1978, p. 27; Kosky, 1975, p. 231; Lieberman, 1976, p. 89; Monteleone, 1982; Murray, 1978; Salvan, 1975, p. 225.

2. Further aiding the use of videotaped evidence is that any print of a videotape is considered an original, not a copy. It is thus outside the scope of the best-evidence rule, which would normally bar the use of a copy as not being the best available evidence (Joseph, 1986, p. 61).

3. See Benowitz, 1974, pp. 86–88; Brakel, 1975, p. 956; Burt, 1978, p. 66; Greenwood et al., 1978, p. 27; Kosky, 1975, p. 231; Lieberman, 1976, p. 89; Monteleone, 1982; Murray, 1978; Salvan, 1975, p. 225.

4. The arguments against videotaped testimony are similar to those listed in the Supreme Court's *Estes* decision, which in 1966 banned television cameras from trial courts.

5. See Boster et al., 1978; Hocking et al., 1978; Kaminski et al., 1978; Miller, 1976; Miller & Fontes, 1979a, 1979b; Miller & Siebert, 1974, 1975.

6. Miller and Fontes also found that jurors retain more information from black-and-white videos, but that color videotape enhances the credibility of a witness, raising an unresolved dilemma: Should the courts select a system that seems to enhance witness image (color) or one that enhances jurors' retention of information (black-and-white)? (1979a, p. 100). In practice, the ten-

dency has been to go with color, because it is felt to be more realistic and, despite the contrary evidence, better able to sustain jurors' attention.

7. See Brakel, 1975; Doret, 1974; Farmer et al., 1976; Kosky, 1975; Shutkin, 1973.

8. Burt, 1978; Kosky, 1975; Weiss, 1982, p. 64. Benowitz (1974, p. 86) has noted that court reporters are not unequivocally opposed to the use of videotape equipment in the courtroom: "Under the leadership of the National Shorthand Reporter's Association, they have examined objectively the possible applications of this new tool, have been pioneers in the use of videotape where applicable and desirable, and have arrived at the conclusion that in certain areas of litigation, a marriage between court reporters and VTR will better serve the judicial process."

9. Brakel, 1975, p. 957; Burt, 1978; Coleman, 1977; Greenwood et al., 1978, p. 27; Kosky, 1975, pp. 231, 232–235.

10. This use of videotape may be advantageous in actions subject to a trial de novo (new trial) on appeal, or to full appellate review of determinations of fact involved as opposed to questions of legal procedures (Coleman, 1977, p. 14).

11. These early complaints focused on the loss of a two-way communication system with feedback, a concern that remains valid with regard to videotaped testimony, but not so for live, media-facilitated proceedings, in which communication is restricted but remains two-way.

12. Two officers are needed to operate each console, which, on a twenty-four-hour basis, entails assigning eight officers to the operation of the CCTV (New York City, 1983, p. 18).

13. Transportation and prisoner security are not currently concerns in Phoenix and therefore there is no perceived need for a system (author's interview with G. Allison, Maricopa County Criminal Court Administrator's Office, June 30, 1987).

14. Ironically, as stated earlier, these programs primarily benefit not judges but other system personnel, who spend less time traveling and waiting for a judge to be available (Doret, 1974).

15. Kosky (1975) cited a 22 percent reduction of the docket in civil court in Ohio (see also McCrystal, 1976, 1978, pp. 253–254; Miller & Fontes, 1979a, p. 92; Murray, 1978, pp. 260–261). Acceptance of empirical evidence of positive effects from PRVTTs must be tempered, however, as PRVTTs have yet to be fully and rigorously evaluated.

16. See Coleman, 1977, citing Bermant et al., 1975; "How Jurors Feel about Videotaped Trials," 1980; Shutkin, 1973.

17. Benowitz, 1974; Brakel, 1975; Burt, 1978; Hartman, 1978; Kosky, 1975.

18. Field tests show the technology to be efficient, and legal questions of admissibility, privacy, and due process have been answered in favor of its continued use (see Rypinski, 1982; Shutkin, 1973).

19. It should be noted that the visuals created by these projects are used frequently in news reports and thereby contribute to the public's image of justice. They have thus changed the reality of justice and have opened previous backstage judicial activities to public review. Ironically, while still wary of the news media's intrusions, the courts simultaneously pursue the media's technology that will ultimately have many of the same effects of exposing backstage events that are feared from news coverage. The judicial process will become, for good or ill, a less arcane, more open and accessible system due to this technology, its processes becoming more visible.

9 Media Justice: From the Past, to the Future

FROM ENTERTAINMENT TO MEDIA TECHNOLOGY

In the preceding eight chapters, we have moved from the origins of news and entertainment to the recent uses of media technology in the judicial system. As we have seen, by the late nineteenth century the "pre-mass media" media contained the same criminal stereotypes and causal explanations of crime found in today's media. And crime-related themes have been the most common plot element throughout the ninety-plus-year existence of U.S. commercial media. The image of justice that is most palatable and popular to the most people is the image that has been historically projected. The messages of the entertainment media conform to a "law of opposites": The reality the media depict with regard to crime and justice is opposite to any objective measure of reality. Much the same is true of news: Crime constitutes a constant, significant portion of the total news; criminals are normally portrayed as either predatory street criminals or dishonest business-people and professionals; and the criminal justice system is shown as an ineffective, often counterproductive means of dealing with crime. In every category—crimes, criminals, crime fighters, the investigation of crime, arrests, case processing, and case dispositions—the media present a world of crime and justice that is not found in reality. The increased merging of the news and entertainment media means that the portraits of crime and justice in each will continue to be more alike than different. As a basic rule of thumb, both the news and entertainment media consistently take the least common crime or justice event and make it the most common crime or justice image.

The lack of realistic information in the media further mystifies and obscures criminality and the criminal justice system (Dominick, 1978; Estep & MacDonald, 1984). The media emphasize individual personality traits as the cause of crime and violent interdiction as its solution, showing a preference for crimes involving weapons or sophisticated technology (Culver & Knight, 1979, pp. 207–209; Garofalo, 1981). They present criminality as an individual choice and imply that other social, economic, or structural explanations are irrelevant. Their frequent use of a vocabulary of force and terms like "crime fighter" and "war on crime" suggests to the public that crime must be "fought" rather than "solved," "eliminated," or "prevented" (Gorelick, 1989, p. 429). Media portrayals further instruct the public to fear others, for the criminal is not easily recognizable and is often found among the rich, powerful, or seemingly trustworthy. These images are tilted toward law enforcement and crime control, for, ironically, although the criminal justice system is not shown favorably, the solutions to crime suggested involve expansion of the existing criminal justice system through harsher punishments and more law enforcement.

The media also appear to subtly but significantly affect attitudes about crime and justice. To varying degrees, they also influence the agendas, perceptions, and policies of their consumers with regard to crime and justice. These media effects interact with other factors, are difficult to discern, and are difficult to counteract. Perceptions of crime and justice appear to be intertwined with other, broader perceptions of social conditions; therefore, it is not surprising that consistent strong relationships have not been found between the media and crime and justice public attitudes. In general, media portrayals of crime and justice appear to influence most easily people's factual perceptions, such as the amount of crime they believe to be occurring, and to have less direct influence on overall evaluations of social conditions or ideas about what should be done (Cook et al., 1983a, p. 174).

The evidence of an increase in social aggression following exposure to violent visual media content is clear in the laboratory but mixed in society. Though a cathartic effect has been discredited, debate continues about the extent to which the media may stimulate violence and the significance of such an effect. The research suggests, without conclusively proving, that we are a more aggressive society because of our mass media. However, social aggression is not necessarily criminal, nor is most crime aggressive in nature, and the media's influence on criminality, independent of its effect on aggressive behavior, has not often or adequately been directly explored. Aggregate crime rate studies suggest that the media may very well affect crime independently of violent content. In addition, evidence has suggested that the visual media, more than print media, may have more of a copycat or stimulation effect on property crime than on violent crime. One important exception to this generalization concerns sexually violent media. There is increasing evidence that sexual violence against women need not be portrayed in explicit, X-rated media to have negative effects, and the influence of sexually violent media content on predisposed, "hypermasculine" males presents a clear danger.

The total available evidence suggests, and most reviewers agree, that the media do affect crime rates. But both the nature of the effect and its magnitude are undetermined. The research on media violence and pornography indicates that the media operate on pools of already-at-risk individuals, some unknown proportion of whom will have a mix of characteristics and circumstances that make them likely to respond with violence. The results are media-induced acts of aggression, sexual and otherwise, most likely induced through the short-term mechanism of modeling. The more heavily the consumer relies on the media for information about the world and the more predisposed the viewer is, the more likely the effect. Therefore, violence-prone children and the mentally unbalanced are especially at risk of aping media violence. When sex and violence are linked, hypermasculine males are most influenced. When the news media sensationalize crimes and make celebrities of criminals, people seeking notoriety imitate those crimes. And when successful crimes, in particular property crimes, are detailed either in print or in visuals, some criminals will emulate them. Only a small number of people appear to be significantly affected, but the media likely slightly affect a larger, unknown portion of the general population, in particular fostering attitudes that support crime. Both attitudinal and behavioral effects by the media are therefore important potential influences on the total crime picture.

Media-based anticrime efforts are aimed at two audiences, criminals and citizens. The available evaluations show these efforts to be effective means of disseminating information and to have an apparent ability to influence attitudes. However, their ability to significantly affect behavior has not been established. The media are not a panacea for crime, and though useful in specific areas, media-based anticrime programs are not likely to significantly reduce the overall crime rate. No program has empirically demonstrated a significant long-term effect without displacement of the crime rate. Still, the evaluations show that media-based anticrime programs can have significant immediate effects simply by having well-publicized starts. In fact, an "announcement effect" is normally the strongest effect found, and the prime difficulty for these programs is to maintain their immediate gains over a longer period of time. To use the media and media technology effectively to combat crime, planners must therefore allocate resources and effort to ensuring and maintaining real changes in social policy, such as changes in prosecution and sentencing practices, not just to publicizing and equipping a program. The media alone appear to be as unable to deter criminal behavior as they are to criminalize individuals singlehandedly.

Despite being frequently at odds, the media and the courts react similarly to criminal events. Both want to gather information, control access to this information, and present it to a specific audience. In addition, both have been pressured by the same social forces to be more open and accessible, to reveal their backstage news-gathering or case-processing procedures, and, sometimes reluctantly, to provide information to the other. Not surprisingly, when the courts use a proactive strategy such as closure to control their information and directly constrain the media, the media respond with vigorous opposition. But though reactive, less-restrictive mechanisms such as expanded voir dires are more popular, their effectiveness is questionable, and it is not clear when they should be used. On the media's part, they have worked to control their information by arguing that journalists have a constitutional right to "privileged conversation" with news sources and by lobbying for the passage of "shield" laws to legislatively ensure this protection. These efforts have intensified as the media have been more frequently pressed for information and reporters have been periodically forced to testify. Though the media have had successes, at this time their ability to avoid opening their news files or testifying varies considerably from state to state and case to case.

In regard to the use of the technology of the media in the courts, such use has become common in the presentation of physical evidence and testimony. But media technology has been used only in limited applications in creating permanent records and facilitating live proceedings. For most judicial personnel the processing and recording of brief, nontrial procedural steps and small portions of a regular trial is acceptable; anything more is not. Acceptance or rejection seems to depend on whether or not a crucial element of justice is felt to be lost because of the technology. For preliminary and short procedural steps, most participants feel that the integrity of the process is unaffected. With regard to longer, more-significant, and more-symbolic steps such as trials, concerns and resistance arise, especially among defense attorneys and public defenders. As a judicial tool, the technology is in most cases efficient, and its use has been judged not to violate due process protections. Though initially promising in restricted uses, however, the technology's long-term effects on participants, on the decorum of the judicial system, and, ultimately, on justice have not yet been fully assessed.

Overall, the mass media are constant, subtle, and unpredictable agents with regard to crime and justice—beneficial if carefully used, but neither the magic cure nor the potent demon they are sometimes presented as. They cannot be ignored, and they should not be seen as uncontrollable. Where then do we stand in terms of a broad understanding of media, crime, and justice?

TOWARD A BROAD UNDERSTANDING OF THE MEDIA, CRIME, AND JUSTICE

A beginning point for addressing the above question are the three most socially significant paradoxes that we have uncovered with regard to the media, crime, and justice.

- The media more often than not portray the criminal justice system and its people negatively and as ineffective. Yet the cumulative effect of these portraits is support for more police, more prisons, and more money for the criminal justice system.

The media message is that the system does not work but remains the best hope against crime.

- Despite being portrayed as objective and chosen for its newsworthiness, crime news is routinely created and prepackaged by and for news agencies, which then present the crime news within established, stereotypic themes.

The public is encouraged to believe that crime news is representative and reflects actual crime while receiving an organizationally created product.

- As the technical capability to cover crime news has expanded, media organizations have conversely increasingly blurred the news and entertainment media. In the process, crime stories have become the mainstay of new hybrid news-and-entertainment or "info-tainment" programs.

As the news media, led by the electronic media, have become more able and willing to cover backstage events and expose new information, they have also been spurred by industry competition to present these events and information in entertainment formats to maximize ratings.

All three of these paradoxes reflect the continuing disparity between the media-constructed reality of crime and justice and the actual reality. This disparity has come about because the media have converged on a single image of crime and justice, emphasizing it in news, entertainment, info-tainment, and anticrime programming—an image of rampant, predatory criminality ineffectively checked by current criminal justice system methods. And though the media have increased their capability to discover and deliver information about the world, both the print and the electronic media have moved instead toward greater reliance on created, prepackaged information, stereotypes, and entertainment-style content. As a result, the public receives an image of crime and justice that not only is unnecessarily distorted but supports basically one approach to anticrime policy. Crime control mechanisms are advanced ahead of due process protections.[1]

Commercial, organizational, and cultural forces drive the media to perpetuate this image. The media are commercial businesses and must show a profit. They therefore must compete for consumers while keeping their production costs low. This makes them conservative in two ways. They become reluctant to experiment with new content, and they become reluctant to explore controversy or challenge the status quo. The result is both news and entertainment dominated by standard styles, themes, plots, and content. In addition, media agencies are organizations and must respond to organizational constraints such as deadlines and the need to control resources and schedules (Scott & Hart, 1979). These factors pressure the media to apply their limited resources in established, "safe" ways. They thus continue to produce updated versions of what has been produced and found acceptable in the past. And it is in determining what is socially acceptable with regard to crime and violence that cultural forces come into play. As a culture, we embrace the crime and justice images that the media portray. Depictions of predatory criminals both entertain and comfort us—entertain because they scare us, and comfort because they relieve our social conscience by showing crime as clearly not due to social inequities, racism, or poverty—things society could be held responsible for and might address. The media's maddened, greedy predators are criminals out of their own fault, or maybe God's fault, but certainly not society's fault. Such criminals, and with them the crime problem, can therefore be guiltlessly eliminated. Together, the commercial, organizational, and cultural forces create a strong resistance to new, broader images of crime and justice in the media: the media resist because they cannot afford to seriously challenge it, and we resist as consumers because we are uncomfortable with the broader picture. The media continue applying old themes, but to new social areas.

Phrases such as "government in sunshine" and "freedom of information" reflect government responses to a larger, media-driven social trend toward more-open public institutions. The two dominant social institutions, the media and the criminal justice system, play critical roles in this process, which can be understood as part of the general process of exposing more and more of the previously hidden, backstage areas of society to the public. In a society with a pervasive, multimedia, mass media system, closed institutions and proceedings, and secret information and sources are automatically viewed with suspicion and challenged. The results of this trend toward greater access and the revealing of previously hidden, backstage events are apparent throughout the preceding chapters. Entertainment and news about crime are more graphic, the public is more tolerant of surveillance, more judicial steps and interactions between the police and citizens are being recorded, media trials are more common, and media technology and the media in general are accepted in more situations. Ironically, despite all of these developments, the criminal justice system and the mass media remain among a handful of social institutions that still resist full open access and struggle to keep their realms closed.

A consequence of the shift in attention to backstage behavior is that as the media have evolved, the distinction between front- and backstage coverage has blurred, and we now have only "on- and off-stage" behavior; that is, an event or an individual is either an object of media attention and subject to full exposure, or ignored by the media. Thus for the media the concepts of public and private are losing their meaning. Any aspect of anything that is the focus of media attention is now open to coverage, so, in today's media-saturated society, to ensure privacy, one must be ignored. Like the highly visible British royal family, participants in high-profile criminal cases forfeit broader and broader areas of their lives to media scrutiny. Our vicarious entrance into the backstage private lives of the famous and unfortunate has also led to pseudosocial, media-based relationships with "media friends" whom we feel we know intimately and whose life developments we follow with personal interest.[2] The nature of media coverage as currently practiced is to cover a subject intensively for a short period of time, slack off, and turn to something new (Altheide & Snow, 1979, p. 238). In doing so the modern media reveal the humanity, the ordinariness of almost everyone they expose. Though this exposure may reassure and comfort consumers in one sense, it also demystifies and can disappoint (Meyrowitz, 1985a, p. 155).

With regard to crime and justice, as well as other social concerns, the critical issue is ultimately the media's role in the social construction of reality. Evidence is building that the media alter reality by affecting the ways in which the audience perceives, interprets, and behaves toward it. The question is no longer whether the media have a substantial social impact or not, but how their impact will be felt. The most solid evidence indicates that their impact is indirect:

> Thus the media affects elections not so much by changing votes as by molding the images of reality that lead to vote decisions. They affect public policy not by forcing change but by channeling information that stimulates or stymies the efforts of political elites. They affect opinion not by changing minds but by shaping the political culture that makes certain opinions seem reasonable or defensible. They affect our social institutions not by calling for their preservation or destruction but by influencing our expectations and evaluations of their performance. (Lichter, 1988, p. 40)

The media influence the real world of crime and justice by projecting a multimedia image of crime and justice that makes increasing the punitiveness of the real criminal justice system appear to be the most reasonable course. And in a cyclic effect, the actions of the real criminal justice system are compared and evaluated against the expectations and desires raised by the media criminal justice system. Ironically, one reason for the resistance to the use of media technology by the judiciary is that such uses alter the traditional, media-supported image of a trial.

LOOKING TOWARD THE FUTURE

> We cannot have some of the media forces for social change without having all or most of the forces. We cannot select uses for new media that advance old goals without altering the social systems out of which the goals developed. Hence, we cannot use television to educate without altering the functions of reading and the structure of the family and the school. (Meyrowitz, 1985a, p. 319)

And by extension, we cannot use the media in crime reduction and case processing without also changing the functioning of the criminal justice system. Of concern for the immediate future are two areas: anticrime applications and negative attitudinal and behavioral effects of the general media.

To solve and prevent crimes the government must intervene in its citizens' lives. The media provide a means to do so in new ways, ways that are considered both more efficient and less obviously intrusive. In practice, however, such applications cannot avoid opening up for view further-backstage areas of public life, criminal justice system operations, and interactions between police and citizens. In certain instances, such as patrol car cameras, where police actions are recorded as much as citizen actions, this is seen as positive. In other instances, such as hidden police surveillance systems, it is not so clear. Future experimentation with media technology seems assured.[3] History demonstrates that once developed, a technology will be used. And the growing tolerance of surveillance as a fact of life is likely a by-product of our acceptance of the increasing exposure of back-stage behavior by the general media.

Planned expansions of these technology-based systems will further de-personalize criminal justice procedures. Adjudication within the criminal justice system is based on the principle of face-to-face interaction, particu-larly that an accused person is entitled to face his or her accusers. The ex-tended use of media technologies, however, will mean a decline in live, face-to-face encounters between witnesses and defendants, police and the public, attorneys and their clients, judges and defendants, and jurors and all of the previous groups. This process will be hastened as the technology be-comes more economical, less obtrusive, and more approximate (but never equal) to live personal meetings. As with surveillance, as the general media have become pervasive and common, the public has become more accept-ing of an impersonal criminal justice system and the substitution of media technology for live encounters. The full effects of these changes may be-come apparent only after such practices have been in place longer.

Regarding the negative effects of the general mass media and their con-tent, there is considerable doubt regarding an ability to institute effective counter public policy. Comstock (1983) has noted that of the three parties who could act—the federal government, the mass media industry, and the audience—the government is an unlikely and probably impotent source of change; the industry has an economic interest in continuing its violent, criminogenic portrayals; and audience groups' desire and ability to organize and create change are questionable, as they have failed to do so in the past. And those audiences that are attracted to such portrayals but susceptible to their influence cannot be expected to voluntarily abstain. In addition, more must be known about the form and nature of the relationship between me-dia and society before any effective broad-based policy initiatives can be de-veloped.

Future Research Needs

Media Technology

A basic unanswered question is how the social costs of judicial and law enforcement applications of media technology compare against their admin-istrative benefits. All of these applications change the nature of the interac-tions between citizens and the criminal justice system, making them less di-rect and less personal. By their pervasiveness, such applications also under-mine the expectation of privacy in society. These effects make research into the general social effects of both media coverage of crime and justice and the use of media technology in anticrime efforts imperative. Furthermore, the impact of these programs on citizens' perceptions of criminality and criminal justice must be assessed. Do they increase people's fear of crime and exacerbate the stereotypes found in the entertainment media? One crucial unexamined impact is the technology's effect on the general public's perception of the criminal justice system. Observers may gain an image of the justice system that is unacceptable if they see the use of technology as degrading. Inasmuch as these observers represent a larger proportion of society than the people actually involved, effects on them cannot be ignored. Future research will, it is hoped, provide answers to these questions. For now, the mass media and their technology are an additional, potentially positive, but limited resource to help reduce crime.

Attitudinal and Behavioral Effects

Those populations who are most susceptible to having their attitudes and behavior influenced by the media must be identified and described. At present, their relative size and demographic composition is largely unknown. Better knowledge of these media-susceptible consumers and the situations and content that most influence them would allow more-focused policies that specifically target these consumers. For example, educational counter "debriefings" have been found to be useful in reversing the negative attitudinal effects of pornography (see Malamuth & Check, 1983), and some have proposed the development of preemptive educational media to debunk the "pleasurable rape" myth and other attitudinal effects (Donnerstein & Linz, 1986, p. 611; Imrich et al., 1990). It is further recommended that the curtailment and eventual elimination of sexually violent material (regardless of its industry rating) that portrays violence against women as pleasurable, rewarding, and acceptable for either the perpetrator or the victim be pursued as a public policy goal.

Because most of our knowledge about the media and crime and justice is general rather than specific, existing public policies are also general, aimed largely at the general population rather than at specific at-risk groups. Identifying these groups will enable policy makers to develop policies that are more focused and more effective. But more research is also needed to identify precisely what content is at fault (Belson, 1978). Such research could help media industry programmers improve programming without losing their audience, whereas the current research leads to an economically unacceptable policy focus on violent versus nonviolent programming. The media industry is more likely to voluntarily cooperate with suggestions that will not compromise the size of program audiences.

Research into the long-term effects of violent, criminogenic, and pornographic media should also be pursued. The cumulative and interactive effects of television, print, and other types of media have yet to be explored. In addition, more attention to how consumers interact with and use the media is needed. For example, do people learn specific facts about crime and justice through the media and then apply these facts in deciding what public policies to support? Or does their preference for or predisposition toward particular policies determine which crime and justice facts they cull and retain from the media? Such questions illustrate the need for empirical testing and validation of the variables which comprise the underlying media models of the mechanisms involved in agenda setting, decision making, copycat effects, and echo effects relative to crime and justice. Although researchers agree that some media effects operate both at an individual level and at the level of the criminal justice system, they do not agree on how and through what mechanisms they operate. A basic question continually debated, is the causal position of the media. Does exposure to media precede or parallel certain behavior? Do the media cause changes in subjects or do predisposed individuals selectively seek out and attend to media content that supports their perceptions? (See Figure 9-1.)

If the simple direct causal models of Figure 9-1, rather than the noncausal, associative models, are true, then media-focused policies become more sensible and effective. At present, however, neither type of model is considered realistic; rather, reciprocal-feedback models, in which causal influences are multidirectional, are forwarded as the most plausible models of the relationship between the media and crime and justice (see Figure 9-2).[4]

Causal models		Associative models	
Violent pornography ⟶ Sexual crimes		Hypermasculine males ⟨	Exposure to sexually violent media content ⟋ Sexual crimes ⟍
Violent media content ⟶ Aggression		Predisposed persons ⟨	Exposure to violent media content ⟋ Aggressive behavior ⟍
Crime-related media content ⟶ Mean-world views and support for punitive policies		Persons holding mean-world attitudes ⟨	Exposure to crime-related media content ⟋ Support for punitive policies ⟍

FIGURE 9-1 Competing models of the media's relationship to sex crimes, aggression, and support for punitive policies

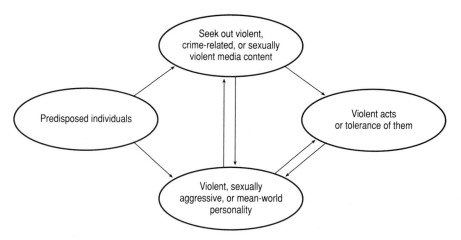

FIGURE 9-2 An example of a reciprocal-feedback model

Future Concerns

Media Technology

We don't know what impact emerging technologies will have over time. It appears safe to assume, however, that no technology will be without unforeseen consequences and that some of those consequences will spawn the social problems of tomorrow (Brody, 1990, p. 43). Like computer technology, media technology has been steadily declining in cost while increasing in capability. It is now technologically feasible to record virtually any criminal justice system act and, if desired, to have a live image, with sound, transmitted to another location. The technology not only works but has achieved most of the administrative crime control goals set for it, so we can expect a steady expansion of its uses and adoption of the technology throughout the criminal justice system. We must beware, however, of potential social costs that do not emerge quickly and are difficult to quantify. The difficulty is that should evidence of negative social costs emerge, programs and personnel may already be so entrenched that curtailment could well be impossible.

These potential social costs include increased depersonalization of the criminal justice system; isolation of the police from the policed and therefore increased fear of surveillance among citizens, and a polarization of society into affluent, technologically secured "garrison" communities and crime ghettos. Also possible are decreased citizen support for the criminal justice system and an overall loss of legitimacy. Finally, if people believe that media-based anticrime efforts are effectively combating crime and that such programs are panaceas for the general crime problem, resources may be drained from other, ultimately more beneficial policy avenues.

Attitudinal and Behavioral Effects

Of greatest concern regarding the general content of the media with regard to crime and justice and the media image of crime and justice are the manipulation of public policy and citizen paralysis. According to Lichter (1988, p. 38), continued journalistic criticism of social institutions leaves

---

BOX 9-1   I Was a Drug-Hype Junkie

. . . My editor called me in and offered me authorship of a story on drug abuse in America. He gave me the angle, told me the points we wanted to make and how he wanted it to conclude. Again, I tried to resist. This wasn't back-of-the-book recreational sensationalism. This was the hard stuff: a cover story.

I called the National Institute on Drug Abuse (NIDA) for their statistics, made some calls to well known doctors, and ordered clips up from the library. Everything I read and everybody I talked to made drugs sound really bad, and I began to become intoxicated by the overwhelmingly negative reputation they have. What I didn't realize was that I was losing track of the facts and slipping into a journalistic dream world where the writer is free to write almost anything he chooses because nobody is going to call him on it. Nobody, but nobody was going to defend drug abuse in America, least of all the people who use drugs every day. In a way, it was the perfect covert story: sensational, colorful, gruesome, alarmist, with a veneer of social responsibility. Unfortunately, it just wasn't true.

Let me say flat out that drug abuse in America is not a good thing, and that people who do drugs have become more messed up in recent years as drugs have become cheaper, more plentiful, and more potent. The problem is, the statistics do not show that more people are doing drugs. That doesn't mean drug abuse isn't a major problem. It is. But it is not, as *Newsweek* would have it, an epidemic "as pervasive and as dangerous in its way as the plagues of medieval times." Nor are drugs, as *U. S. News and World Report* puts it, "the nation's No. 1 menace." Not while we still have poverty, unemployment, illiteracy, malnutrition, murder and the Soviet Union.

But here's how it looked to you folks at home. The *Atlantic* was first and best, publishing a thorough, non-alarmist cover story about cocaine in January. Starting in March, *Newsweek* did three covers on

drug abuse within five months. *Time* used drugs on the cover twice, in March and September, and gave them a cover line in between. *U. S. News and World Report* devoted a cover to drugs on July 28. Ted Koppel chatted with his video monitors about it.

All of the network news shows covered it ad nauseum and reductio ad absurdum in their nightly reports. CBS iced the cake September 2 with a "news" documentary called "48 Hours on Crack Street." According to the Nielsen ratings, "Crack Street" earned the highest rating for any news documentary on any network in more than five-and-a-half years, delivering almost 15 million news addicts to its advertisers—three times the highest estimate for the number of regular cocaine users in America. Three days later, NBC ran its cocaine special, "Cocaine Country."

Now I'll make the call. Based on NIDA's figures for 1985, 17 percent of all high school seniors have tried cocaine at least once in their life. That's a whopping increase of one percent from 1984. Between 1982 and 1984, the percentage held steady at 16.

An upward trend? Sorry. In 1981, 17 percent said they had tried the white stuff. Yes, the percentage did go up in 1985, but it has been hovering around the 16 percent mark for almost seven years. Wouldn't it be more accurate to refer to the '84-to'85 increase as a fluctuation? If we were talking about the stock market, would a one percent increase four years after a one percent decrease and a three-year period of stability be cover-story material? Not on your life. Maybe that's the point. We're talking about human lives here, not meaningless statistics based on cold, hard cash. Fair enough. But it doesn't make for hot news. "Use of cocaine among high school seniors increased one percent in 1985, according to statistics released today by the National Institute on Drug Abuse. At a press conference in Washington, D. C., a spokesman for NIDA said . . ." Look for that item on page 23 of your local paper in the capsule news column."

Source: From "I Was a Drug-Hype Junkie," by A. Weisman, The New Republic, October 6, 1986, p. 15. Excerpted by permission of The New Republic, © 1986, The New Republic, Inc.

consumers feeling that they can neither comprehend nor control events. Thus, portrayal of the criminal justice system as ineffective may not only delegitimize the criminal justice system but also undermine the public's confidence in their ability to cope with the wider world as journalists and politicians manipulating the media lead the public from crime crisis to crisis.[5]

In the end, the media function as much as a means of avoiding reality as a means of constructing it:

> The ritual of crime and punishment—in newspaper headlines and on television screens—has become America's great reality avoidance mechanism, its all sufficient substitute for knowledge and thought: let a scapegoat be found, let a culprit be punished, and the public relaxes, confident that the crisis has been surmounted. (Powers, 1990, p. G8)

Notes

1. Not only have the electronic media influenced the criminal justice system, but their influence has cycled back through society to the other mass media. The print media has responded to a visually attuned society reared on sixty-second messages by becoming more like the visual media. Shorter articles and photographs are employed where possible. The superficial has become the norm.

2. It has also led to a new form of murder and a new type of murder motive. In addition to murders committed by persons who know the victim and murders committed by strangers, there are now murders committed by persons who know the victim only through the media—(John Lennon's murder by Mark Chapman, for example).

3. Other developing applications include the use of small, concealable, wireless video recorders and transmitter systems ("Video Transmission to Counter Hijacking," 1986, p. 18), and multisite, full-system networks linking jails, public defenders' offices, state attorneys' offices, courthouses, and police stations through fiber-optic lines. The new technologies are characterized by their interactivity—that is, the ability of users to interact with others through communication channels (Brody, 1990, p. 103).

4. See also Cook et al., 1983b; Graber, 1980, pp. 119–122; Sacco & Silverman, 1982;

Smith, 1984. The media have also been described as a steering mechanism for long-term attitude change (Graber, 1980). Whether they do or do not have significant long-term effects is still unknown, and no empirical research exists investigating this possibility.

5. The media have also undermined the status and legitimacy of many formal front-stage roles and reduced the need for them (Meyrowitz, 1985a). In that the role of judge is the epitome of a formal role, the undermining of this role, and of attorneys in general, was predictable. The increasing use of informal judicial procedures, dispute settlements, do-it-yourself divorces, and the like reflects the decline of formal legal roles.

References

AGREE, W., AULT, P., & EMERY, E. (1982) *Introduction to Mass Communications.* New York: Harper & Row.

AKERS, R. (1977) *Deviant Behavior: A Social Learning Approach.* Belmont, Calif.: Wadsworth.

ALEXANDER, Y. (1979) "Terrorism and the Media: Some Considerations." In *Terrorism: Theory and Practice,* edited by Y. Alexander, D. Carlton, and P. Wilkinson. Boulder, Colo.: Westview Press.

ALTER, J. (1985) "The Network Circus." *Newsweek,* July 8, p. 21.

ALTHEIDE, D. (1984) "TV News and the Social Construction of Justice: Research Issues and Policy." In *Justice and the Media,* edited by R. Surette, pp. 292–304. Springfield, Ill.: Charles C Thomas.

ALTHEIDE, D., & SNOW, R. (1979) *Media Logic.* Newbury Park, Calif.: Sage.

AMERICAN ASSOCIATION OF ADVERTISING AGENCIES (1990) *What We've Learned about Advertising from the Media-Advertising Partnership for a Drug-Free America.* Pamphlet. New York: Author.

AMERICAN BAR ASSOCIATION (1937) *Canons of Judicial Ethics,* no. 35. Reprinted in *ABA Reporter* 62: 1123, 1134–35.

AMERICAN BAR ASSOCIATION (1978) *Standards Relating to the Administration of Criminal Justice, Fair Trial and Free Press.* Chicago: Author.

ANDISON, F. (1977) "TV Violence and Viewer Aggression: A Review of Study Results, 1956–1976." *Public Opinion Quarterly* 41: 314–331.

ANTONOVICH, M., PROSPTER, R., OLSON, K., & KROTT, C. (1987) "Video Arraignment Pilot Project Glendale Municipal Court—Year End Report." Glendale, Calif.: The Municipal Court Glendale Judicial District.

ANTUNES, G., & HURLEY, P. (1977) "The Representation of Criminal Events in Houston's Two Daily Newspapers." *Journalism Quarterly* 54: 756–760.

APFEL, D. (1980) "Gag Orders, Exclusionary Orders, and Protective Orders: Expanding the Use of Preventive Remedies to Safeguard a Criminal Defendant's Right to a Fair Trial." *American University Law Review* 29: 439–484.

ARMOUR, R. (1980) *Film.* Westport, Conn.: Greenwood Press.

ARONS, S., & KATSH, E. (1977) "How TV Cops Flout the Law." *Saturday Review,* March 19, pp. 11–19.

ATKIN, C. (1979) "Research Evidence on Mass Mediated Health Communication Campaigns." In *Communication Yearbook, volume 3,* edited by D. Nimmo, pp. 655–668. New Brunswick, N.J.: Transaction Books.

"AUDIO-VISUAL COVERAGE ON TRIAL IN STATES" (1988) *News Media and the Law* 12, no. 1: 48–50.

AVERY, D. (1989) "Corrections: The Hard Sell." *Correction Today* 51: 6.

BACHARACH, R., (1985) "Posttrial Juror Interviews by the Press: The Fifth Circuit's Approach." *Washington University Law Quarterly* 62: 783–788.

BAILEY, W. (1990) "Murder, Capital Punishment and Television: Execution Publicity and Homicide Rates. *American Sociological Review* 55: 628–633.

BALDWIN, J., & LEWIS, C. (1972) "Violence in Television: The Industry Looks at Itself." In *Television and Social Behavior, vol. 1, Media Content and Control. Report of the Surgeon General's Scientific Advisory Committee on Television and Behavior,* edited by G. Comstock and E. Rubinstein, pp. 290–373. Washington, D. C.: National Institute of Mental Health.

BALL, J., & BOGATZ, G., (1970) *The First Year of "Sesame Street": An Evaluation.* Princeton, N.J.: Educational Testing Service.

BALL, M. (1981) *The Promise of American Law.* Athens: University of Georgia Press.

BALL-ROKEACH, S., ROKEACH, M., & GRUBE, J. (1984) *The Great American Values Test: Influencing Behavior and Belief through Television.* New York: Free Press.

BANDURA, A. (1965) "Influence of Models' Reinforcement Contingencies on the Acquisition of Imitative Responses." *Journal of Personality and Social Psychology* 1: 589–595.

BANDURA, A. (1968) "What TV Violence Can Do to Your Child." In *Violence and the Mass Media,* edited by O. M. Larson, pp. 123–130. New York: Harper & Row.

BANDURA, A. (1969) *Principles of Behavior Modification.* New York: Holt, Rinehart & Winston.

BANDURA, A. (1971) *Social Learning Theory.* Morristown, N.J.: General Learning Press.

BANDURA, A. (1973) *Aggression: A Social Learning Analysis.* Englewood Cliffs, N.J.: Prentice-Hall.

BANDURA, A. (1977) *Social Learning Theory.* Englewood Cliffs, N.J.: Prentice-Hall.

BANDURA, A., ROSS, D., & ROSS, S. A. (1963) "Imitation of Film: Mediated Aggressive Models." *Journal of Abnormal and Social Psychology* 66: 3–11.

BARBER, S. (1987) *News Cameras in the Courtroom.* Norwood, N.J.: Ablex.

BARON, J., & REISS, P. (1985) "Same Time Next Year: Aggregate Analyses of the Mass Media and Violent Behavior." *American Sociological Review* 47: 802–809.

BARON, L., & STRAUS, M. (1984) "Sexual Stratification, Pornography, and Rape in the United States." In *Pornography and Sexual Aggression,* edited by N. Malamuth and E. Donnerstein, pp. 185–209. New York: Academic Press.

BARON, L., & STRAUS, M. (1985) *Legitimate Violence, Pornography, and Sexual Inequality as Explanations for State and Regional Differences in Rape.* Unpublished manuscript, Yale University.

BARON, L., & STRAUS, M. (1986) *Rape and Its Relations to Social Disorganization, Pornography, and Sexual Inequality in the United States.* Unpublished manuscript, Yale University.

BARRILE, L. (1984) "Television and Attitudes about Crime: Do Heavy Viewers Distort Criminality and Support Retributive Justice?"

In *Justice and the Media,* edited by R. Surette, pp. 141–158. Springfield, Ill.: Charles C Thomas.

BASSIOUNI, M. (1979) "Prolegomenon to Terror Violence." *Creighton Law Review* 12: 745–752.

BASSIOUNI, M. (1981) "Terrorism, Law Enforcement, and the Mass Media: Perspectives, Problems, Proposals." *Journal of Criminal Law and Criminology* 72: 1–51.

BECKER, T. (1971) *Political Trials.* Indianapolis, Ind.: Bobbs-Merrill.

BELL, B. (1983) "Closure of Pretrial Suppression Hearings: Resolving the Fair Trial/Free Press Conflict." *Fordham Law Review* 51: 1297–1316.

BELSON, W. (1978) *Television Violence and the Adolescent Boy.* Westmead, England: Saxon House, Teakfield Limited.

BENNACK, F. (1983) *The American Public, the Media and the Judicial System: A National Survey on Public Awareness and Personal Experience.* New York: The Hearst Corporation.

BENNETT, W., FELDMAN, L., & FELDMAN, M. (1983) *Reconstructing Reality in the Courtroom.* New Brunswick, N.J.: Rutgers University Press.

BENOWITZ, H. A. (1974) "Legal Applications of Videotape." *Florida Bar Journal* 48, no. 2 (February): 86–91.

BERGMAN, A. (1971) *We're in the Money.* New York: Harper & Row.

BERKOWITZ, L. (1964) "Aggressive Cues in Aggressive Behavior and Hostility Catharsis." *Psychological Review* 71: 104–122.

BERKOWITZ, L. (1969) (ed.) *Roots of Aggression: A Re-Examination of the Frustration-Aggression Hypothesis.* New York: Atherton Press.

BERKOWITZ, L. (1970) "Experimental Investigations of Hostility Catharsis." *Journal of Consulting and Clinical Psychology* 31: 1–7.

BERKOWITZ, L. (1984) "Some Effects of Thoughts on Anti- and Prosocial Influences of Media Events: A Cognitive-Neoassociation Analysis." *Psychological Bulletin* 95: 410–417.

BERKOWITZ, L., & ALIOTO, J. (1973) "The Meaning of an Observed Event as a Determinant of Its Aggressive Consequences." *Journal of Personality and Social Psychology* 28: 206–217.

BERKOWITZ, L., CORWIN, R., & HIERONIMUS, M. (1963) "Film Violence and Subsequent Aggressive Tendencies." *Public Opinion Quarterly* 27: 217–229.

BERKOWITZ, L., & CUMMINGHAM, D. (1966) "The Interest Value and Reliance on Fear Arousing Communications." *Journal of Abnormal and Social Psychology* 4: 138–147.

BERKOWITZ, L., & GEEN, R. (1966) "Film Violence and the Cue Properties of Available Targets." *Journal of Personality and Social Psychology* 3: 525–530.

BERKOWITZ, L., & GEEN, R. (1967) "Stimulus Qualities of the Target of Aggression: A Further Study." *Journal of Personality and Social Psychology* 5: 364–368.

BERKOWITZ, L., & MACAULAY, J. (1971) "The Contagion of Criminal Violence." *Sociometry* 34: 238–260.

BERKOWITZ, L., PARKE, R., LEYENS, J., WEST, S., & SEBASTIAN, R. (1978) "Experiments on the Reactions of Juvenile Delinquents to Filmed Violence." In *Aggression and Antisocial Behavior in Childhood Adolescence,* edited by L. A. Hersov and M. Berger, pp. 59–72. Oxford: Pergamon Press.

BERKOWITZ, L., & RAWLINGS, E. (1963) "Effects of Film Violence on Inhibitions against Subsequent Aggression." *Journal of Abnormal and Social Psychology* 66: 405–412.

BERMAN, A. (1988) "Fictional Depiction of Suicide in Television Films and Imitation Effects." *American Journal of Psychiatry* 145: 982–986.

BERMAN, R. (1987) *How Television Sees Its Audience.* Newbury Park, Calif.: Sage.

BERMANT, G., CHAPPELL, D., CROCKETT, G., JACOUBOVITCH, M., & McGUIRE, M. (1975) "Jury Responses to Prerecorded Videotaped Trial Presentations in California and Ohio." *Hastings Law Journal* 26: 975.

BLACK, G. (1988) *Changing Attitudes toward Drug Use: Executive Summary and Statistical Report.* Rochester, N.Y.: Partnership for a Drug-Free America.

BLASI, V. (1971) "The Newsman's Privilege: An Empirical Study." *Michigan Law Review* 70: 229–284.

BLEYER, W. (1927) *Main Currents in the His-*

tory of American Journalism. Boston: Houghton Mifflin.

BLUMER, H. (1933) *The Movies and Conduct.* New York: Macmillan.

BLUMER, H., & HAUSER, P. (1933) *Movies, Delinquency, and Crime.* New York: Macmillan.

BOHRER, S., & OVELMEN, R. (1987) "Judicial Access: The Reporter's Right of Access to the Judicial System and Qualified Privilege from Compelled Testimony Relating to Newsgathering." In *The Reporter's Handbook.* Tallahassee: Florida Bar Association.

BOLLEN, K. A., & PHILLIPS, D. (1982) "Imitative Suicides: A National Study of the Effects of Television News Stories." *American Sociological Review* 47: 802–809.

BOORSTIN, D. (1961) *The Image.* New York: Harper & Row.

BORGIDA, E., De GONO, K., & BUCKMAN, L. (1990) "Cameras in the Courtroom: The Effects of Media Coverage on Witness Testimony and Juror Perceptions." *Law and Human Behavior* 14, no. 5: 489–509.

BORTNER, M. A. (1984) "Media Images and Public Attitudes toward Crime and Justice." In *Justice and the Media,* edited by R. Surette, pp. 15–30. Springfield, Ill.: Charles C Thomas.

BOSTER, J. F., MILLER, G. R., & FONTES, N. E. (1978) "Videotape in the Courtroom: Effects in Live Trials." *Trial* 14, no. 6 (June): 49–51, 59.

BOWEN, N. (1987) "Pornography: Research Review and Implications for Counseling." *Journal of Counseling and Development* 65: 345–350.

BRADY, J. (1983) "Fair and Impartial Railroad: The Jury, the Media and Political Trials." *Journal of Criminal Justice* 11: 241–263.

BRAKEL, S. J. (1975) "Videotape in Trial Proceedings: A Technological Obsession?" *American Bar Association Journal* 61 (August): 956–959.

BRANNIGAN, A. (1987) "Is Obscenity Criminogenic?" *Society* 24: 12–19.

BRANNIGAN, A., & KAPARDIS, A. (1986) "The Controversy over Pornography and Sex Crimes: The Criminological Evidence and Beyond." *Australian and New Zealand Journal of Criminology* 19: 259–284.

BREMAN, P. (1977) "Television's Dilemma: Stay on the Air or Bail Out?" *The Quill,* March, pp. 8–9.

BRENNER, L. (1989) "Attention, Arnie Becker: Your Motions in Courtrooms—Not Bedrooms—Would Be More Help." *TV Guide,* June 17, pp. 10–14.

BRODSKY, S. (1976) "Sexual Assault: Perspectives on Prevention and Assailants." In *Sexual Assault,* edited by M. Walker and S. Brodsky, pp. 1–7. Lexington, Mass.: D. C. Heath.

BRODY, E. (1990) *Communication Tomorrow.* New York: Praeger.

BROOKS, T., & MARSH, E. (1985) *Complete Directory to Prime Time Network TV Shows, 1946–Present.* 3rd ed. Cambridge, Mass.: Ballantine Press.

BROWN, S. H. (1980) "Video Arraignment Statistics." Interoffice memorandum from Judge Seymore Brown, chief municipal judge, to Lloyd W. Zook, court administrator, Las Vegas, Nev., March 21.

BUDDENBAUM, J., WEAVER, D., HOLSINGER, R., & BROWN, C. (1981) *Pretrial Publicity and Juries: A Review of Research.* Bloomington: Indiana University, Center for New Communications, Research Report no. 11.

BUREAU OF JUSTICE STATISTICS (1986) *Crime Prevention Measures.* Washington, D. C.: U. S. Department of Justice.

BURNETT, J., & OLIVER, R. (1979) "Fear Appeal Effects in the Field: A Segmentation Approach." *Journal of Marketing Research* 16: 181–190.

BURT, L. W. (1978) "The Case against Courtroom TV." *Trial* 12, no. 7 (July): 62–63, 66.

CAMPBELL, D. (1969) "Reforms as Experiments." *American Psychology* 24: 409–429.

CAMPBELL, D., & ROSS, L. (1968) "The Connecticut Crackdown on Speeding." *Law and Society Review* 3: 33–53.

CANADIAN SENTENCING COMMISSION (1988) "Sentencing in the Media: A Content Analysis of English-Language Newspapers in Canada." Research reports of the Canadian Sentencing Commission. Ottawa: Department of Justice, Canada.

CARLSON, J. (1985) *Prime Time Law Enforcement.* New York: Praeger.

CARROLL, J., KERR, N., ALFINI, J., WEAVER, F., MacCOUN, R., & FELDMAN, V. (1986) "Free Press and Fair Trial: The Role of Behavioral

Research." *Law and Human Behavior* 10: 187–201.

CASHMAN, V., & FETTER, T. (1980) *State Courts: Options for the Future.* Williamsburg, Va.: National Center for State Courts.

CASPER, J. (1978) *Criminal Courts: The Defendant's Perspective.* Washington, D. C.: Law Enforcement Assistance Administration, Department of Justice, National Institute of Law Enforcement and Criminal Justice.

CAVENDER, G. (1981) "Scared Straight: Ideology and the Media." *Journal of Criminal Justice* 34: 430–441.

CBS. See Columbia Broadcasting System.

CHAFFEE, S. (1975) *Political Communication: Enduring Issues for Research.* Newbury Park, Calif.: Sage.

CHARTER, W. (1933) *Motion Pictures and Youth: A Summary.* New York: Macmillan.

CHASE, A. (1986) "Lawyers and Popular Culture: A Review of Mass Media Portrayals of American Attorneys." *American Bar Association Research Journal* 2 (2): 281–300.

CHIBNALL, S. (1981) "The Production of Knowledge by Crime Reporters." In *The Manufacture of News,* edited by S. Cohen and J. Young, pp. 75–97. Newbury Park, Calif.: Sage.

CHURCH, G. (1982) "Copy Cats Are on the Prowl." *Time,* November, p. 27.

CIRINO, R. (1972) *Don't Blame the People.* New York: Vintage Books.

CIRINO, R. (1974) *Power to Persuade.* New York: Bantam Books.

CLINE, V. (ed.) (1974) *Where Do You Draw the Line?* Provo, Utah: Brigham Young University Press.

COATES, B., PUSSER, H., & GOODMAN, I. (1976) "The Influence of 'Sesame Street' and 'Mister Rogers' Neighborhood' on Children's Social Behavior in the Preschool." *Child Development* 47: 138–144.

COENEN, A., & VAN DIJK, J. (eds.) (1978) "Public Opinion on Crime and Criminal Justice." *Collected Studies in Criminological Research,* Vol. XVII. Strasbourg Cedex, France: Council of Europe.

COHEN, B. (1963) *The Press and Foreign Policy.* Princeton, N. J.: Princeton University Press.

COHEN, S., & YOUNG, J. (eds.) (1981) *The Manufacture of News.* Newbury Park, Calif.: Sage.

COHN, A. (1980) "A Social Psychologist Views 'Scared Straight!': Discussion." In F. Wright, C. Bahn, and R. Rieber, *Forensic Psychology and Psychiatry.* New York: Academy of Sciences.

COLEMAN, G. V. (1977) *The Impact of Video Use on Court Function: A Summary of Current Research and Practice.* Washington, D. C.: Federal Judicial Center.

COLEMAN, J. (1974) *Power and the Structure of Society.* New York: Norton.

COLLINS, W. A. (1973) "Effect of Temporal Separation between Motivation, Aggression, and Consequences: A Developmental Study." *Developmental Psychology* 8: 215–221.

COLLINS, W. A. (1975) "The Developing Child as a Viewer." *Journal of Communication* 25: 215–221.

COLUMBIA BROADCASTING SYSTEM (CBS) (1974) *A Study of Messages Received by Children Who Viewed an Episode of "Fat Albert and the Cosby Kids."* New York: CBS Office of Social Research.

COMSTOCK, G. (1980) *Television in America.* Newbury Park, Calif.: Sage.

COMSTOCK, G. (1983) "Media Influences on Aggression." In *Prevention and Control of Aggression,* edited by A. Goldstein and L. Krasner, pp. 241–272. Elmsford, N. Y.: Pergamon Press.

COMSTOCK, G., CHAFFEE, S., KATZMAN, N., McCOMBS, M., & ROBERTS, D. (1978) *Television and Human Behavior.* New York: Columbia University Press.

COMSTOCK, G., & FISHER, M. (1975) *Television and Human Behavior: A Guide to Pertinent Scientific Literature.* Santa Monica, Calif.: Rand Corp.

COMSTOCK, G., & LINDSEY, G. (1975) *TV and Human Behavior: The Research Horizon, Future and Present.* Santa Monica, Calif.: Rand Corp.

"CONFIDENTIAL SOURCES AND INFORMATION" (1989) Washington, D.C.: Reporters' Committee for Freedom of the Press.

COOK, T., KENDZIERSKI, D., & THOMAS, S. (1983a) "The Implicit Assumptions of Television Research: An Analysis of the 1982 NIMH Report on Television and Behavior." *Public Opinion Quarterly* 47: 161–201.

COOK, T., TYLER, T., GOETZ, E., GORDON, M., PROTESS, D., LEFF, D., & MOLOTCH, H. (1983b) "Media and Agenda Setting: Effects on the Public, Interest Group Leaders, Policy Makers, and Policy." *Public Opinion Quarterly* 47: 16–35.

COOPER, H. (1976) "Terrorism and the Media." *Chitty's Law Journal* 24: 226–232.

COSGROVE, M., & McINTYRE, C. (1974) "The Influence of 'Mister Rogers' Neighborhood' on Nursery School Children's Prosocial Behavior." Paper presented at the meeting of the Southeastern Regional Society for Research in Child Development, Chapel Hill, N. C.

COTSIRILOS, J., & PHILIPSBORN, J. (1986) "A Change of Venue Roadmap." *The Champion,* July, pp. 8–15.

COURT, H. (1976) "Pornography and Sex-Crimes: A Re-evaluation in the Light of Recent Trends around the World." *International Journal of Criminology and Penology* 5: 129–157.

COURT VISION COMMUNICATIONS, INC. (n.d.) Photocopied news release.

CRENSHAW, M. (1981) "The Causes of Terrorism." *Comparative Politics* 13: 374–396.

CRESSEY, P. (1938) "The Motion Picture Experience as Modified by Social Background and Personality." *American Sociological Review* 11: 517.

CULVER, J., & KNIGHT, K. (1979) "Evaluative TV Impressions of Law Enforcement Roles." In *Evaluating Alternative Law Enforcement Policies,* edited by R. Baker and F. Mayer, pp. 201–212. Lexington, Mass.: Lexington Books.

CUMBERBATCH, G., & BEARDSWORTH, A. (1976) "Criminals, Victims, and Mass Communications." In *Victims and Society,* edited by E. C. Viano, pp. 72–90. Washington, D. C.: Visage Press.

CURRAN, J., & SEATON, J. (1980) *Power without Responsibility.* London: Fontana.

DALE, E. (1935) *Children's Attendance at Motion Pictures.* New York: Macmillan.

DAVIS, F. (1951) "Crime News in Colorado Newspapers." *American Journal of Sociology* 57: 325–330.

DAVIS, R. (1986) "Pretrial Publicity, the Timing of the Trial, and Mock Jurors' Decision Processes." *Journal of Applied Social Psychology* 16: 590–607.

DeFLEUR, M., & BALL-ROKEACH, S. (1975) *Theories of Mass Communication.* 3rd ed. New York: D. McKay.

DeFLEUR, M., & DENNIS, E. (1985) *Understanding Mass Communication.* Boston: Houghton Mifflin.

DEMARE, D., BRIERE, J., & LIPS, H. (1988) "Violent Pornography and Self-Reported Likelihood of Sexual Aggression." *Journal of Res. in Personality* 22: 140–153.

De SILVA, B. (1984) "The Gang-Rape Story" *Columbia Journalism Review,* May–June, pp. 42–44.

DESMOND, R. (1978) *The Information Process: World News Reporting in the Twentieth Century.* Iowa City: University of Iowa Press.

DEUTSCHMANN, P. (1959) *Front Page Content of Twelve Metropolitan Dailies.* Cincinnati: Scrips-Howard Research Center.

DEXTER, H., & CUTLER, B. (1991) "In Search of the Fair Jury: Does Extended Voir Dire Remedy the Prejudicial Effects of Pretrial Publicity?" Paper presented at the American Psychological Association Meeting, August, San Francisco.

DIENSTBIER, R. (1977) "Sex and Violence: Can Research Have It Both Ways? *Journal of Communication* 27: 176–188.

DINITZ, S. (1987) "Coping with Deviant Behavior through Technology." *Criminal Justice Research Bulletin* 3, no. 2: 1–15.

DITTON, J., & DUFFY, J. (1983) "Bias in the Newspaper Reporting of Crime News." *British Journal of Criminology* 23: 159–165.

DOMBROFF, M. (1981) "Videotapes Enter the Picture as Demonstrative Evidence Tool." *National Law Journal,* November 23, pp. 24–25.

DOMINICK, J. (1973) "Crime and Law Enforcement on Prime-Time Television." *Public Opinion Quarterly* 37: 241–250.

DOMINICK, J. (1978) "Crime and Law Enforcement in the Mass Media." In *Deviance and Mass Media,* edited by C. Winick, pp. 105–128. Newbury Park, Calif.: Sage.

DONNERSTEIN, E. (1980) "Pornography and Violence Against Women." *Annals of the New York Academy of Science* 347: 277–288.

DONNERSTEIN, E. (1984) "Pornography: Its Effects on Violence against Women." In *Pornography and Sexual Aggression,* edited by N. Malamuth and E. Donnerstein, pp. 53–81. New York: Academic Press.

DONNERSTEIN, E., & BERKOWITZ, L. (1985) *Role of aggressive and sexual images in vio-*

lent pornography. Unpublished manuscript.

DONNERSTEIN, E., & LINZ, D. (1984) "Sexual Violence in the Media: A Warning." *Psychology Today,* January, pp. 14–15.

DONNERSTEIN, E., & LINZ, D. (1986) "Mass Media Sexual Violence and Male Viewers." *American Behavioral Scientist* 29: 601–618.

DOOB, A., & MACDONALD, G. (1979) "Television Viewing and Fear of Victimization: Is the Relationship Causal?" *Journal of Personality and Social Psychology* 37: 170–179.

DOPPELT, J., & MANIKAS, P. (1990) "Mass Media and Criminal Justice Decision Making." In *The Media and Criminal Justice Policy,* edited by R. Surette, pp. 129–142. Springfield, Ill.: Charles C Thomas.

DORET, D. M. (1974) "Trial by Videotape: Can Justice Be Seen to Be Done?" *Temple Law Quarterly* 47 (Winter): 228–268.

DOUGLAS, D., WESTLEY, B., & CHAFFEE, S. (1970) "An Information Campaign that Changed Community Attitudes." *Journalism Quarterly* 47: 479–487.

DRABMAN, R. S., & THOMAS, M. J. (1974) "Does Media Violence Increase Children's Toleration of Real-Life Aggression?" *Developmental Psychology* 10: 418–421.

DRECHSEL, R. (1983) *News Making in the Trial Courts.* New York: Longman.

DRECHSEL, R. (1985) "Judges' Perceptions of Fair Trial–Free Press Issue." *Journalism Quarterly* 62: 388–390.

DUBNOFF, C. (1977) "Pretrial Publicity and Due Process in Criminal Proceedings." *Political Science Quarterly* 92: 89–110.

DULANEY, W. (1968) *An Assessment of Some Assertions Made Relative to the Fair Trial and Free Press Controversy.* Ph.D. diss., Northwestern University.

DYE, T., & ZEIGLER, H. (1986) *American Politics in the Media Age.* Pacific Grove, Calif.: Brooks/Cole.

EBBESEN, E. (1987) Affidavit in *People* v. *Rubio,* Superior Court of the State of California, Solano County, No. C21691.

EDGAR, P. (1977) *Children and Screen Violence.* St. Lucia: University of Queensland Press.

EISENBERG, G. (1980) "Children and Aggression after Observed Film Aggression with Sanctioning Adults." In *Forensic Psychology and Psychiatry,* edited by F. Wright, C. Bahn,

and R. Rieber, pp. 304–317. New York: Academy of Sciences.

EISENSTEIN, J., & JACOBS, H. (1977) *Felony Justice: An Organizational Analysis of Criminal Courts.* Boston: Little, Brown.

EKMAN, P., LIEBERT, R., FRIESEN, W., HARRISON, R., ZLATCHIN, C., MALMSTROM, E., & BARON, R. (1972) "Facial Expressions of Emotion while Watching Televised Violence as Predictors of Subsequent Aggression." In *Television and Social Behavior, vol. 5, Television's Effects: Further Explorations,* edited by G. Comstock, E. Rubinstein, and J. Murray, pp. 22–58. Washington, D. C.: U. S. Government Printing Office. Report of the Surgeon General's Scientific Advisory Committee on Television and Behavior.

ELLIS, P., & SEKYRA, F. (1972) "The Effect of Aggressive Cartoons on the Behavior of First-Grade Children." *Journal of Psychology* 81: 37–43.

ENGLISH, D. (1980) "The Politics of Porn." *Mother Jones,* April, pp. 20–23.

EPSTEIN, A. (1990) "Ruling Allows TV Testimony in Child-Abuse Cases." *Tallahassee Democrat,* June 28, pp. 1A, 4A.

ERBRING, L., GOLDENBERG, E., & MILLER, A. (1980) "Front-Page News and Real-World Clues: A New Look at Agenda-Setting by the Media." *American Journal of Political Science* 24: 16–49.

ERON, L. (1987) "The Development of Aggressive Behavior from the Perspective of a Developing Behaviorism." *American Psychology* 42: 435–442.

ESTEP, R., & LAUDERDALE, P. (1980) "The Bicentennial Protest: An Examination of Hegemony in the Definition of Deviant Activity." In *A Political Analysis of Deviance,* edited by P. Lauderdale. Minneapolis: University of Minnesota Press.

ESTEP, R., & MACDONALD, P. (1984) "How Prime-Time Crime Evolved on TV, 1976–1983." In *Justice and the Media,* edited by R. Surette, pp. 110–123. Springfield, Ill.: Charles C Thomas.

ESTERLE, J. (1986) "Crime and the Media." *Jericho* 41: 5, 7.

ETTEMA, J., PROTESS, D., LEFF, D., MILLER, P., DOPPELT, J., & COOK, F. (1989) "Agenda-Setting as Politics: A Case Study of the Press–Public–Policy Connection at the Post-

Modern Moment." Paper presented at the Association for Education in Journalism and Mass Communication Convention, June, Washington, D. C.

EVANS, S., & LUNDMAN, R. (1983) "Newspaper Coverage of Corporate Price-Fixing." *Criminology* 21: 529–541.

EVERSON, W. (1964) *The Bad Guys: A Pictorial History of the Movie Villian.* New York: Citadel Press.

EVERSON, W. (1972) *The Detective in Film.* New York: Citadel Press.

EYSENCK, H., & NIAS, D. (1978) *Sex, Violence and the Media.* New York: Harper & Row.

"FAIR TRIAL FREE PRESS—REPORTER'S PRIVILEGE" (1983) *Criminal Law Reporter* 32, no. 20: 2428.

FARMER, L., WILLIAMS, G., LEE, R., CUNDICK, B., HOWEII, R., & ROOKER, C. (1976) "Juror Perceptions of Trial Testimony as a Function of the Method of Presentation." In *Psychology and the Law,* edited by C. Nemeth and N. Vidmar, pp. 209–238. Lexington, Mass.: D. C. Heath.

FAUNKHOUSER, G. (1973) "The Issues of the Sixties: An Exploratory Study in the Dynamics of Public Opinion." *Public Opinion Quarterly* 37: 63–75.

FENTON, F. (1910) "The Influence of Newspaper Presentations upon the Growth of Crime and Other Anti-Social Activity." *American Journal of Sociology* 7: 342–371, 538–564.

FESHBACH, S. (1972) "Reality and Fantasy in Filmed Violence." In *Television and Social Behavior, vol. 2, Television and Social Learning,* edited by J. Murray, G. Comstock, and E. Rubinstein, pp. 318–345. Washington, D. C.: U. S. Government Printing Office.

FESHBACH, S., & SINGER, R. D. (1971) *Television and Aggression: An Experimental Field Study.* San Francisco: Jossey-Bass.

FINCHENAUER, J. (1979) *Juvenile Awareness Project: An Evaluation Report.* New Brunswick, N. J.: Rutgers University School of Criminal Justice.

FINCHENAUER, J. (1980) "'Scared Straight!' and the Panacea Phenomenon: Discussion." In F. Wright, C. Bahn, and R. Rieber, *Forensic Psychology and Psychiatry.* New York: Academy of Sciences.

"FIRST, SIXTH AMENDMENTS PERMIT BAN ON

TELEVISING FEDERAL TRIALS" (1983) *Criminal Law Reporter* 32, no. 16: 2339–2240.

FISHER, G. (1989) "Mass Media Effects on Sex Role Attitudes of Incarcerated Men." *Sex Roles* 20, no. 3/4: 191–203.

FISHMAN, M. (1978) "Crime Waves as Ideology." *Social Problems* 25: 531–543.

FISKE, S., & TAYLOR, S. (1984) *Social Cognition.* Reading, Mass.: Addison-Wesley.

FOGELSON, R. (1977) *Big City Police.* Cambridge, Mass.: Harvard University Press.

FORREST, W. (1892) "Trial by Newspapers." *American Criminal Law Magazine* 14: 553.

FOUCAULT, M. (1977) *Discipline and Punish: The Birth of the Prison.* Trans. Alan Sheridan. New York: Vintage Books.

FOX, S., STEIN, A., FRIEDRICH, L., & KIPNIS, D. (1977) "Prosocial Television and Children's Fantasy." Paper presented at the Biennial Meeting of the Society for Research in Child Development, March, New Orleans.

FRANKLIN, B. (1964) *The Autobiography of Benjamin Franklin.* New Haven, Conn.: Yale University Press.

FREEDBERG, S., & HOLZMAN, T. (1984) "Benson is Hottest Show in Town." *Miami Herald,* August 4, pp. 1A, 5A.

FREEDMAN, J. (1984) "Effect of Television Violence on Aggressiveness." *Psychological Bulletin* 96: 227–246.

FRIEDMAN, L., & PERCIVAL, R. (1981) "The Roots of Justice: Crime and Punishment in Alameda County, California, 1870–1910." Durham: University of North Carolina Press.

FRIEDRICH, L., & STEIN, A. (1975) "Prosocial Television and Young Children: The Effects of Verbal Labeling and Role Playing on Learning and Behavior." *Child Development* 46: 27–38.

FURSTENBERG, F. (1971) "Public Reactions to Crime in the Streets." *American Scholar* 40: 601–610.

GALTUNG, J., & RUGE, M. (1981) "Structuring and Selecting News." In *The Manufacture of News,* edited by S. Cohen and J. Young, pp. 52–63. Newbury Park, Calif.: Sage.

GANS, H. (1979) *Deciding What's News.* New York: Pantheon.

GAROFALO, J. (1981) "Crime and the Mass Media: A Selective Review of Research." *Journal of Research in Crime and Delinquency* 18: 319–350.

GAROFALO, J., & LAUB, J. (1978) "The Fear of Crime: Broadening Our Perspective." *Victimology* 3: 242–253.

GEEN, R. (1968) "Effects of Frustration, Attack and Prior Training in Aggressiveness upon Aggressive Behavior." *Journal of Personality and Social Psychology* 9: 316–321.

GEEN, R., & BERKOWITZ, L. (1967) "Some Conditions Facilitating the Occurrence of Aggression After the Observation of Violence." *Journal of Personality* 35: 666–676.

GEEN, R., & STONNER, D. (1972) "Content Effects in Observed Violence." *Journal of Personality and Social Psychology* 25: 145–150.

GELLES, R., & FAULKNER, R. (1978) "Time and Television News Work." *Sociological Quarterly* 19: 89–102.

GERALD, E. J. (1983) *News of Crime, Courts, and Press in Conflict.* Westport, Conn.: Greenwood Press.

GERBNER, G. (1976) "Television and Its Viewers: What Social Science Sees." Rand Paper Series, Santa Monica, Calif.: The Rand Corp.

GERBNER, G. (1980) "Trial by Television: Are We at the Point of No Return?" *Judicature* 63, no. 9: 416–426.

GERBNER, G., & GROSS, L. (1976) "Living with Television: The Violence Profile." *Journal of Communication* 26: 173–199.

GERBNER, G., & GROSS, L. (1980) "The Violent Face of Television and Its Lessons." In *Children and the Faces of Television,* edited by E. Palmer and A. Dorr, pp. 149–162. New York: Academic Press.

GERBNER, G., GROSS, L., JACKSON-BEECK, M., JEFFRIES-FOX, S., & SIGNORIELLI, N. (1978) "Cultural Indicators: Violence Profile No. 9." *Journal of Communication* 29: 176–207.

GERBNER, G., GROSS, L., MORGAN, M., & SIGNORIELLI, N. (1980) "The Mainstreaming of America: Violence Profile No. 11." *Journal of Communication* 30: 10–29.

GERBNER, G., GROSS, L., SIGNORIELLI, N., MORGAN, M., & JACKSON-BEECK, M. (1979) "The Demonstration of Power: Violence Profile No. 10." *Journal of Communication* 29: 177–196.

GILBERG, S., EYAL, C., McCOMBS, M., & NICHOLAS, D. (1980) "The State of the Union Address and the Press Agenda." *Journalism Quarterly* 57: 584–588.

GILMORE, W. H. (1980) "Arraignment by Television: A New Way to Bring Defendants to the Courtroom." *Judicature* 63, no. 8 (March): 396–401.

GOFFMAN, E. (1959) *The Presentation of Self in Everyday Life.* Garden City, N. Y.: Doubleday.

GOFFMAN, E. (1961) *Asylums.* Garden City, N. Y.: Anchor Books.

GOFFMAN, E. (1967) *Interaction Ritual.* Garden City, N. Y.: Doubleday.

GOLDSTEIN, M., KANT, H., JUDD, L., RICE, C., & GREEN, R. (1972) "Exposure to Pornography and Sexual Behavior in Deviant and Normal Groups." In *Erotica and Antisocial Behavior,* vol. VII, pp. 1–90. Washington, D. C.: U. S. Government Printing Office. U. S. Commission on Obscenity and Pornography.

GORDON, M., & HEATH, L. (1981) "The News Business, Crime and Fear." In *Reaction to Crime,* edited by D. Lewis, pp. 227–250. Newbury Park, Calif.: Sage.

GORDON, M., & RIGER, S. (1989) *The Female Fear.* New York: Free Press.

GORELICK, S. (1989) "Join Our War: The Construction of Ideology in a Newspaper Crime-fighting Campaign." *Crime and Delinquency* 35: 421–436.

GOTTFREDSON, M., & GOTTFREDSON, D. (1980) *Decision Making in Criminal Justice.* Cambridge, Mass.: Ballinger Press.

GOTTFREDSON, M., & HIRSCHI, T. (1990) *A General Theory of Crime.* Palo Alto, Calif.: Stanford University Press.

GOULD, M., & SHAFFER, D. (1986) "The Impact of Suicide in Television Movies." *New England Journal of Medicine* 315: 690–694.

GRABER, D. (1979) "Evaluating Crime-Fighting Policies." In *Evaluating Alternative Law Enforcement Policies,* edited by R. Baker and F. Meyer, pp. 179–200. Lexington, Mass.: Lexington Books.

GRABER, D. (1980) *Crime News and the Public.* New York: Praeger.

GRABER, D. (1989) *Mass Media and American Politics.* Washington, D. C.: CQ Press.

GRANT, A. (1987) *The Audio-Visual Taping of Police Interviews with Suspects and Accused Persons by Halton Regional Police Force, Ontario, Canada: An Evaluation.* Ottawa, Ontario: Law Reform Commission of Canada.

GRANT, A. (1990) "The Videotaping of Police Interrogations in Canada." In *The Media and*

Criminal Justice Policy, edited by R. Surette, pp. 265–276. Springfield, Ill.: Charles C Thomas.

GRAY, S. (1982) "Exposure to Pornography and Aggression toward Women: The Case of the Angry Male." *Social Problems* 29: 387–398.

GREENBERG, B. (1969) "The Content and Context of Violence in the Media." In *Violence and the Media,* edited by R. Baker and S. Ball, pp. 423–449. Washington, D. C.: U. S. Government Printing Office.

GREENBERG, S. (1987) "Why People Take Precautions against Crime: A Review of the Literature on Individual and Collective Responses to Crime." In *Taking Care: Understanding and Encouraging Self-Protective Behavior,* edited by N. Weinstein, pp. 231–253. New York: Cambridge University Press.

GREENE, E. (1990) "Media Effects on Jurors." *Law and Human Behavior* 14, no. 5: 439–450.

GREENE, E., & LOFTUS, E. (1984) "What's New in the News? The Impact of Well-Publicized News Events on Psychological Research and Courtroom Trials." *Basic and Applied Social Psychology* 5: 211–221.

GREENE, E., & WADE, R. (1988) "Of Private Talk and Public Print: General Pre-Trial Publicity and Juror Decision-Making." *Applied Cognitive Psychology* 2: 123–135.

GREENE, J., & BYNUM, T. (1982) "TV Crooks: Implications of Latent Role Models for Theories of Delinquency." *Journal of Criminal Justice* 10: 177–190.

GREENWOOD, M. J., SKUPSKY, D., TOLLAR, J., JESKE, C., & VEREMKO, P. (1978) "Audio/Video Technology and the Courts." *State Court Journal* 2, no. 1 (Winter): 26–28.

GRENANDER, M. (1976) "The Heritage of Cain: Crime in American Fiction." *Annals of the American Academy of Political and Social Science* 423: 48–55.

HAAS, M. (1988) "TV in the Courts: Evaluation of Experiments." Memorandum, National Center for State Courts, Williamsburg, Va., February 3.

HALL, S., CHRITCHER, C., JEFFERSON, T., CLARKE, J., & ROBERTS, B. (1981) "The Social Production of News: Mugging in the Media." In *The Manufacture of News,* edited by S. Cohen and J. Young, pp. 335–367. Newbury Park, Calif.: Sage.

HALLIN, D. (1984) "The Media, the War in Vietnam, and Political Support." *Journal of Politics* 46: 2–24.

HANNEMAN, G., & McEWEN, W. (1973) "Televised Drug Abuse Appeals: A Content Analysis." *Journalism Quarterly* 50: 329–333.

HANRATTY, M., O'NEAL, E., & SULZER, J. (1972) "The Effects of Frustration upon the Imitation of Aggression." *Journal of Personality and Social Psychology* 21: 30–34.

HANS, V. (1990) "Law and the Media: An Overview and Introduction." *Law and Human Behavior* 14, no. 5: 399–407.

HANS, V., & SLATER, D. (1983) "John Hinckley, Jr., and the Insanity Defense: The Public's Verdict." *Public Opinion Quarterly* 47: 202–212.

HANS, V., & VIDMAR, N. (1982) "Jury selection." In *The Psychology of the Courtroom,* edited by Bray and Kerr, pp. 39–82. New York: Academic Press.

HANS, V., & VIDMAR, N. (1986) *Judging the Jury.* New York: Plenum.

HARPER, T. (1982) "When Your Case Hits the Front Page." *American Bar Association Journal* 70: 78–82.

HARTMAN, M. J. (1978) "Second Thoughts on Videotaped Trials." *Judicature* 61, no. 6 (December–January): 256–257.

HARTSFIELD, L. (1985) *The American Response to Professional Crime, 1870–1917.* Westport, Conn.: Greenwood Press.

HASKINS, J. (1969) "The Effects of Violence in the Printed Media." In *Mass Media and Violence,* edited by R. Baker and S. Ball, pp. 493–502. Washington, D.C.: U.S. Government Printing Office.

HASKINS, S. (1969) "Too Much Crime and Violence in the Press." *Editor and Publisher* 102: 12.

HAUGE, R. (1965) "Crime and the Press." *Scandinavian Studies in Criminology* 1: 147–164.

HAWKINS, G., & ZIMRING, F. (1988) *Pornography in a Free Society.* New York: Cambridge University Press.

HAWKINS, R., & PINGREE, S. (1981) "Uniform Messages and Habitual Viewing: Unnecessary Assumptions in Social Reality Effects." *Human Communications Research* 7: 291–301.

HAYS, W. (1932) President's Report to the Motion Picture Producers and Distributors' Association, Washington, D. C.

HEATH, L. (1984) "Impact of Newspaper Crime Reports on Fear of Crime: Multimethodological Investigation." *Journal of Personality and Social Psychology* 47: 263–276.

HELLER, M., & POLSKY, S. (1976) *Studies in Violence and Television.* New York: American Broadcasting Company.

HENDRICK, G. (1977) "When TV Is a School for Criminals." *TV Guide,* January 29, pp. 10–14.

HENNIGAN, K., HEATH, L., WHARTON, J., DEL ROSARIO, M., COOK, T., & CALDER, B. (1982) "Impact of the Introduction of Television on Crime in the United States." *Journal of Personality and Social Psychology* 42: 461–477.

HICKEY, J. (1976) "Terrorism and Television." *TV Guide,* July, pp. 8–13.

HIGBEE, K. (1969) "Fifteen Years of Fear Arousal: Research on Threat Appeals, 1953–1968." *Psychological Bulletin* 72: 426–444.

HIMMELWITT, H. T. (1980) "Social Influence and Television." In *Television and Social Behavior: Beyond Violence and Children,* edited by S. Withey and R. Abeles, pp. 135–160. Hillside, N. J.: Erlbaum.

HIRSCH, P. (1980) "The 'Scary World' of the Nonviewer and Other Anomalies." *Communications Research* 7: 403–456.

HIRSCH, P. (1981) "On Not Learning from One's Own Mistakes: A Reanalysis of Gerbner et al.'s Findings on Cultivation Analysis, Part II." *Communications Research* 8: 3–37.

HOCKING, J., MILLER, G., & FONTES, N. (1978) "Videotape in the Courtroom: Witness Deception." *Trial* 14, no. 4 (April): 52–53.

HOIBERG, B., & STIRES, L. (1973) "The Effect of Several Types of Pretrial Publicity on the Guilty Attributions of Simulated Jurors." *Journal of Applied Social Psychology* 3: 267–275.

HOLADAY, P., & STODDARD, G. (1933) *Getting Ideas from the Movies.* New York: Macmillan.

HOROWITZ, I., & WILLGING, T. (1984) *The Psychology of Law: Integrations and Applications.* Boston: Little, Brown.

HOVLAND, C., LUMSDAINE, A., & SHEFFIELD, F. (1949) *Experiments on Mass Communication.* Princeton, N. J.: Princeton University Press.

HOWITT, D., & CUMBERBATCH, G. (1975) *Mass Media Violence and Society.* New York: Wiley.

"HOW JURORS FEEL ABOUT VIDEOTAPED TRIALS" (1980) *Criminal Justice Newsletter* 11: 7–8.

HUESMANN, L. (1982) "Television Violence and Aggressive Behavior." In *Television and Behavior, vol. 2, Technical Reviews,* edited by D. Pearl, L. Bouthilet, and J. Lazar, pp. 126–137. Washington, D. C.: National Institute of Mental Health.

HUGHES, H. (1940) *News and the Human Interest Story.* Chicago: University of Chicago Press.

HUGHES, M. (1980) "The Fruits of Cultivation Analysis: A Reexamination of Some Effects of Television Watching." *Public Opinion Quarterly* 44: 287–302.

HUGHES, S. (1987) "The Reporting of Crime in the Press: A Study of Newspaper Reports in 1985." *Cambrian Law Review* 18: 35–51.

HUMPHRIES, D. (1981) "Serious Crime, News Coverage and Ideology: A Content Analysis of Crime Coverage in a Metropolitan Paper." *Crime and Delinquency* 27: 191–205.

HYMAN, H., & SHEATSLEY, P. (1947) "Some Reasons Why Information Campaigns Fail." *Public Opinion Quarterly* 11: 412–423.

IMRICH, D., MULLIN, C., & LINZ, D. (1990) "Sexually Violent Media and Criminal Justice Policy." In *The Media and Criminal Justice Policy,* edited by R. Surette, pp. 103–123. Springfield, Ill.: Charles C Thomas.

"IN RE JUDICIAL CONFERENCE GUIDELINES." (1990) *Media Law Reporter* 18: 1270–1272.

ISAACS, N. (1961) "The Crime of Crime Reporting." *Crime and Delinquency* 7: 312–320.

IYENGAR, S., & KINDER, D. (1987) *News That Matters: Agenda-Setting and Priming in a Television Age.* Chicago: University of Chicago Press.

IYENGAR, S., PETERS, M., & KINDER, D. (1982) "Experimental Demonstrations of the 'Not-So-Minimal' Consequences of Television News Programs." *American Political Science Review* 76: 848–858.

JACOBS, H., & LINBERRY, R. (1982) *Governmental Response to Crime: Crime and Governmental Responses in American Cities.* Washington, D. C.: National Institute of Justice.

JACOBS, J. (1961) *The Death and Life of Great American Cities.* New York: Random House.

JACOBS, T. (1980) "The Chilling Effect in Press Cases: Judicial Thumb on the Scales." *Harvard Civil Rights–Civil Liberties Law Review* 15: 685–712.

JAEHNIG, W., WEAVER, D., & FICO, F. (1981) "Reporting and Fearing Crime in Three Communities." *Journal of Communication* 31: 88–96.

JAFFE, L. (1965) "Trial by Newspaper." *New York University Law Review* 40: 504–524.

JANIS, I., & FESHBACH, S. (1953) "Effects of Fear-Arousing Communications." *Journal of Abnormal and Social Psychology* 48: 78–92.

JEFFERY, C. R. (1990) "Media Technology in Crime Control: History and Implications." In *Media and Criminal Justice Policy,* edited by R. Surette, pp. 289–298. Springfield, Ill.: Charles C Thomas.

JENKINS, B. (1975) *International Terrorism: A New Mode of Conflict.* Los Angeles: Crescent Publishers.

JOHNSON, C. (1978) "Perspectives on Terrorism." In *The Terrorist Reader: A Historical Anthology,* edited by L. Laqueur, pp. 267–285. Philadelphia: Temple University Press.

JONES, E. T. (1976) "The Press as Metropolitan Monitor." *Public Opinion Quarterly* 40: 239–244.

JONES, S. E. (1987) "Judge versus Attorney Conducted Voir Dire: An Empirical Investigation of Juror Candor." *Law and Human Behavior* 11: 131–146.

JOSEPH, G. (1982) "Videotapes as Evidence: Reviewing the Cases." *National Law Journal* 6: 1–3.

JOSEPH, G. (1986) "Demonstrative Videotape Evidence." *Trial* 22, no. 6: 60–66.

JOWETT, G., & LINTON, J. (1980) *Movies as Mass Communication.* Newbury Park, Calif.: Sage.

"JUDGES DENY COURT CAMERA USE" (1990) *News Media and the Law* 14, no. 2: 40–42.

JUNKE, R., VOUGHT, C., PYSZCZYNSKI, T., DANE, F., LOSURE, B., & WRIGHTSMAN, L. (1979) "Effects of Presentation Mode upon Mock Jurors' Reactions to a Trial." *Personality and Social Psychology Bulletin* 5: 36–39.

KAMINSKI, E., FONTES, N., & MILLER, G. (1978) "Videotape in the Courtroom." *Trial* 14, no. 5: 38–42, 64.

KANIA, R., & TANHAN, R. (1987) "Rise and Fall of Television Crime." Paper presented at the annual meeting of the American Society of Criminology, November, Montreal, Canada.

KAPLAN, J., & SKOLNICK, J. (1982) *Criminal Justice.* Mineola, N. Y.: Foundation Press.

KATSH, M. (1989) *The Electronic Media and the Transformation of Law.* New York: Oxford University Press.

KATZ, E., & LAZARSFELD, P. (1955) *Personal Influence.* Glencoe, Ill.: The Free Press.

KENNEDY, D. (1985) "Reporters and the Shield Law: A Differing Viewpoint." *Editor and Publisher* 118: 44–45.

KERR, N., KRAMER, G., CARROLL, J., & ALFINI, J. (1990) "On the Effectiveness of Voir Dire in Criminal Cases with Prejudicial Pretrial Publicity: An Empirical Study." Unpublished manuscript, Northwestern University.

KESSLER, R., DOWNEY, G., MILAVSKY, J., & STIPP, H. (1988) "Clustering of Teenage Suicides after Television News Stories about Suicide: A Reconsideration." *American Journal of Psychiatry* 145: 1379–1383.

KESSLER, R., & STIPP, H. (1984) "The Impact of Fictional Television Suicide Stories on American Fatalities." *American Journal of Sociology* 90: 151–167.

KIRTLEY, J. (1990) "Shield Laws and Reporter's Privilege—A National Assessment." In *The Media and Criminal Justice Policy,* edited by R. Surette. Springfield, Ill.: Charles C Thomas.

KLAIN, J. (1989) *International Television and Video Almanac.* New York: Quigley.

KLAPPER, J. (1960) *The Effects of Mass Communication.* Glencoe, Ill.: The Free Press.

KLEIN, F., & JESS, P. (1966) "Prejudicial Publicity: Its Effects on Law School Mock Juries." *Journalism Quarterly* 43: 113–116.

KOHN, P., GOODSTADT, M., COOK, G., SHEPPARD, M., & CHAN, G. (1982) "The Ineffectiveness of Threat Appeals about Drinking and Driving." *Accident Analysis and Prevention* 14: 458–466.

KOSKY, I. (1975) "Videotape in Ohio: Take 2." *Judicature* 59, no. 5 (December): 220–238.

KRAFKA, C. (1985) "Sexually Explicit, Sexually Violent, and Violent Media: Effects of Multiple Naturalistic Exposures and Debriefing on Female Viewers." Ph.D. diss., University of Wisconsin–Madison.

KRAMER, G., KERR, N., & CARROLL, J. (1990) "Pretrial Publicity, Judicial Remedies, and Jury Bias." *Law and Human Behavior* 14, no. 5: 409–438.

KRAUS, S., & DAVIS, D. (1976) *The Effects of Mass Communication on Political Behavior.* University Park: Pennsylvania State University Press.

KRAUSS, G., & BONORA, B. (1983) *Jurywork: Systematic Techniques* (2nd ed.). New York: Clark Broadman.

KUBEY, R., & CSIKSZENTMIHALYI, M. (1990) *Television and the Quality of Life: How Viewing Shapes Everyday Experience.* Hillsdale, N. J.: Erlbaum.

KUTCHINSKY, B. (1972) "Towards an Explanation of the Decrease in Registered Sex Crimes in Copenhagen." *Erotica and Antisocial Behavior,* vol. VII, pp. 263–310. Washington, D. C.: U. S. Government Printing Office. U. S. Commission on Obscenity and Pornography.

KUTCHINSKY, B. (1985) "Pornography and Its Effects in Denmark and the United States: A Rejoinder and Beyond." *Comparative Social Research* 8: 301–330.

LANCASTER, D. (1984) *Cameras in the Courtroom: A Study of Two Trials.* Bloomington: Indiana University, Center for New Communications, Research Report no. 14.

LANG, D., & LANG, K. (1983) *The Battle for Public Opinion.* New York: Columbia University Press.

LANGER, S. (1980) *Fear in the Deterrence of Delinquency: A Critical Analysis of the Rahway State Prison Lifers' Program.* Ann Arbor, Mich.: University Microfilms International Dissertation, City University of New York.

LAS VEGAS, NEVADA (1978) "Video Arraignment Demonstration Project." Grant proposal to the Law Enforcement Assistance Administration.

LAVRAKAS, P., ROSENBAUM, D., & LURIGIO, A. (1990) "Media Cooperation with Police: The Case of Crime Stoppers." In *Media and Criminal Justice Policy,* edited by R. Surette, pp. 225–242. Springfield, Ill.: Charles C Thomas.

"LAWYERS AREN'T CONVINCED THAT TV BELONGS IN COURTROOMS" (1979) *American Bar Association Journal* 65 (September): 1306–1308.

LAZARSFELD, P., BERELSON, B., & GAUDET, H. (1948) *The People's Choice.* New York: Columbia University Press.

LEE, A. (1937) *The Daily Newspaper in American.* New York: Macmillan.

LEFCOURT, H., BARNES, K., PARKE, R., & SCHWATZ, F. (1966) "Anticipated Social Censure and Aggression-Conflict as Mediators of Response to Aggression Induction." *Journal of Social Psychology* 70: 251–263.

LEFF, D., PROTESS, D., & BROOKS, S. (1986) "Crusading Journalism: Changing Public Attitudes and Policy-Making Agendas." *Public Opinion Quarterly* 50: 300–315.

LEIFER, A., & ROBERTS, D. (1972) "Children's Responses to Television Violence." In *Television and Social Behavior, vol. 2, Television and Social Learning,* edited by J. Murray, E. Rubinstein, and G. Comstock, pp. 43–180. Washington, D. C.: U. S. Government Printing Office. National Institute of Mental Health.

LESSER, G. (1974) *Children and Television: Lessons from "Sesame Street."* New York: Vintage.

LESYNA, K., & PHILLIPS, D. (1989) "Suicide and the Media: Research and Policy Implication." In *Preventive Strategies on Suicide.* New York: World Health Organization Publication.

LETKEMANN, P. (1973) *Crime as Work.* Englewood Cliffs, N. J.: Prentice-Hall.

LEVINE, P. (1987) "Invasion of Privacy and the News Media." In *The Reporter's Handbook.* Tallahassee: Florida Bar Association.

LEVINE, P., & BUSSIAN, J. (1987) "Through the Long Lens—Legitimate News or Invasion of Privacy." In *The Reporter's Handbook.* Tallahassee: Florida Bar Association.

LEWIS, R. (1984) "The Media, Violence and Criminal Behavior." In *Justice and the Media,* edited by R. Surette, pp. 51–69. Springfield, Ill.: Charles C Thomas.

LICHTER, L., & LICHTER, S. (1983) *Prime Time Crime.* Washington, D. C.: Media Institute.

LICHTER, S. (1988) "Media Power: The Influence of Media on Politics and Business." *Florida Policy Review* 4: 35–41.

LIEBERMAN, J. K. (1976) "Will Courts Meet the Challenge of Technology?" *Judicature* 60, no. 2 (August–September): 84–91.

LIEBERT, R. M., NEALE, J., & DAVIDSON, E.

(1973) *The Early Window: Effects of Television on Children and Youth.* New York: Pergamon Press.

LINDESMITH, A. (1965) *The Addict and the Law.* Bloomington: Indiana University Press.

LINZ, D. (1989) "Exposure to Sexually Explicit Materials and Attitudes toward Rape: A Comparison of Study Results." *Journal of Sex Research* 26, no. 1: 50–84.

LINZ, D., DONNERSTEIN, E., & PENROD, S. (1984) "The Effects of Long-Term Exposure to Filmed Violence against Women." *Journal of Communication* 34: 130–147.

LINZ, D., DONNERSTEIN, E., & PENROD, S. (1988) "The Effects of Long-Term Exposure to Violent and Sexually Degrading Depictions of Women." *Journal of Personality and Social Psychology* 55: 100–110.

LIPETZ, M. (1980) "Routine and Deviations: The Strength of the Courtroom Work Group in the Misdemeanor Court." *International Journal of Sociology of the Law* 8: 47–60.

LISKE, A., & BACCAGLINI, W. (1990) "Feeling Safe by Comparison: Crime in the Newspapers." *Social Problems* 37, no. 3: 360–374.

LIVINGSTONE, N. (1982) *The War against Terrorism.* Lexington, Mass.: D. C. Heath.

LOFTEN, J. (1966) *Justice and the Press.* Boston: Beacon Press.

LOTZ, R. (1979) "Public Anxiety about Crime." *Pacific Sociology Review* 22: 241–254.

LOWERY, S., & DeFLEUR, M. (1983) *Milestones in Mass Communication Research.* New York: Longman.

LOWRY, D. (1971) "Gresham's Law and Network TV News Selection." *Journal of Broadcasting* 15: 397–408.

MACKUEN, M. (1981) "Social Communication and the Mass Policy Agenda." In *More Than News: Media Power in Public Affairs,* edited by M. MacKuen and S. Coombs, pp. 19–146. Newbury Park, Calif.: Sage.

MACKUEN, M. (1984) "Exposure to Information, Belief Integration, and Individual Responsiveness to Agenda Change." *American Political Science Review* 78: 372–391.

MADDEN, W. (1969) "Illinois Pioneers Videotaping of Trials." *American Bar Association Journal* 55: 457–459.

MAGUIRE, W. (1980) " 'Scared Straight!' Discussion." In *Forensic Psychology and Psychiatry,* edited by F. Wright, C. Bahn, and R. Rieber. New York: Academy of Sciences.

"MAJOR SETBACK FOR THE NEWS MEDIA" (1983) *Crime Control Digest* 17, no. 13, p. 9.

MALAMUTH, N. (1981) "Rape Proclivity among Males." *Journal of Social Issues* 37: 138–157.

MALAMUTH, N. (1983) "Factors Associated with Rape as Predictors of Laboratory Aggression against Women." *Journal of Personality and Social Psychology* 45: 432–442.

MALAMUTH, N. (1986) "Predictors of Naturalistic Sexual Aggression." *Journal of Personality and Social Psychology* 50: 953–962.

MALAMUTH, N., & BRIERE, J. (1986) "Sexual Violence in the Media: Indirect Effects on Aggression against Women." *Journal of Social Issues* 42: 75–92.

MALAMUTH, N., & CENITI, J. (1986) "Repeated Exposure to Violent and Nonviolent Pornography: Likelihood of Raping Ratings and Laboratory Aggression against Women." *Aggressive Behavior* 12: 129–137.

MALAMUTH, N., & CHECK, J. (1980) "Penile Tumescence and Perceptual Responses to Rape as a Function of Victim's Perceived Reactions." *Journal of Applied Social Psychology* 10: 528–547.

MALAMUTH, N., & CHECK, J. (1983) "Sexual Arousal to Rape Depictions: Individual Differences." *Journal of Abnormal Psychology* 92: 55–67.

MALAMUTH, N., & CHECK, J. (1985) "The Effects of Aggressive Pornography on Beliefs of Rape Myths: Individual Differences." *Journal of Research in Personality* 19: 299–320.

MALAMUTH, N., CHECK, J., & BRIERE, J. (1986) "Sexual Arousal in Response to Aggression: Ideological, Aggressive and Sexual Correlates." *Journal of Personality and Social Psychology* 14: 399–408.

MALAMUTH, N., & DONNERSTEIN, E. (1982) "The Effects of Aggressive Pornographic Mass Media Stimuli." In *Advances in Experimental Social Psychology,* vol. 15, edited by L. Berkowitz, pp. 104–132. New York: Academic Press.

MALAMUTH, N., & DONNERSTEIN, E. (eds.) (1984) *Pornography and Sexual Aggression.* New York: Academic Press.

MALAMUTH, N., HABER, S., & FESHBACH, S. (1980) "Testing Hypotheses Regarding Rape: Exposure to Sexual Violence, Sex Differences, and the 'Normality' of Rapists." *Journal of Research in Personality* 14: 121–137.

MALAMUTH, N., HEIM, M., & FESHBACH, S. (1980) "The Sexual Responsiveness of College Students to Rape Depictions: Inhibitory and Disinhibitory Effects." *Journal of Personality and Social Psychology* 38: 399–408.

MALAMUTH, N., & SPINNER, B. (1980) "A Longitudinal Content Analysis of Sexual Violence in the Best-Selling Erotic Magazines." *Journal of Sex Research* 16: 226–237.

MANNHEIM, K. (1952) *Essays on the Sociology of Knowledge*. Ed. P. Kecskemeti. London: Routledge & Kegan Paul.

MANNHEIM, K. (1953) *Essays on the Sociology of Culture*. Ed. and trans. E. Mannheim and P. Kecskemeti. London: Routledge & Kegan Paul.

MARCUS, P. (1982) "The Media in the Courtroom: Attending, Reporting, Televising Criminal Cases." *Indiana Law Journal* (Spring): 235–287.

MARCUSE, H. (1972) *One-Dimensional Man*. London: Abacus.

MARIGHELLA, C. (n.d.) *Minimanual of the Urban Guerilla*. Havana: Tricontinental.

MARKS, A. (1987) *Television Exposure, Fear of Crime, and Concern about Serious Illness*. Ph.D. diss., Northwestern University.

MARSHALL, L. (1983) *Juror, Judge and Counsel Voir Dire Perceptions and Behavior in Two Illinois State Courts*. Ph.D. diss., Boston University.

MARSHALL, W. (1988) "The Use of Sexually Explicit Stimuli by Rapists, Child Molesters, and Nonoffenders." *Journal of Sex Research* 25: 267–280.

MARTENS, F., & CUNNINGHAM-NIEDERER, M. (1985) "Media Magic, Mafia Mania." *Federal Probation* 49, no. 2 (June): 60–68.

MARX, G. (1985) "The Surveillance Society." *The Futurist,* June, pp. 21–26.

MAYHEW, P., CLARKE, R., BURROWS, J., HOUGH, J., & WINCHESTER, S. (1979) *Crime in Public View*. Home Office Research Study no. 49. London: Her Majesty's Stationery Office.

MAZUR, A. (1982) "Bomb Threats and the Mass Media: Evidence for a Theory of Suggestion." *American Sociological Review* 47: 407–411.

McARTHUR, C. (1972) *Underworld U. S. A.* New York: Viking Press.

McCLOSKY, H., & ZALLER, J. (1984) *The American Ethos: Public Attitudes toward Capitalism and Democracy*. Cambridge, Mass.: Harvard University Press.

McCOMBS, M., & SHAW, D. (1972) "The Agenda-Setting Function of Mass Media." *Public Opinion Quarterly* 36: 176–187.

McCOMBS, M., & WEAVER, D. (1973) "Voters' Need for Orientation and Use of Mass Communication." Paper presented at the annual meeting of the International Communication Association, Montreal.

McCONNELL, G. (1967) *Private Power and American Democracy*. New York: Knopf.

McCRYSTAL, J. L. (1976) "The Case for PRVTTs." *Trial* 12, no. 7 (July): 56–57.

McCRYSTAL, J. L. (1978) "Videotaped Trials: A Primer." *Judicature* 61, no. 6 (December–January): 250–256.

McGRUFF CAMPAIGN TEAM (n.d.) "National Citizens' Crime Prevention Three-Year Public Education Program, FY 1990–FY 1992." Photocopy, planning document provided by the National Crime Prevention Council, Washington, D. C.

McGUIRE, W. (1986) "The Myth of Massive Media Impact: Savagings and Salvagings." In *Public Communication and Behavior,* edited by G. Comstock, pp. 175–257. New York: Academic Press.

McLEOD, J., BECKER, L., & BYRNES, J. (1974) "Another Look at the Agenda-Setting Function of the Press." *Communication Research* 1: 137–144.

McLUHAN, M. (1962) *The Gutenberg Galaxy: The Making of Typographical Man*. Toronto: University of Toronto Press.

McLUHAN, M. (1964) *Understanding Media: The Extensions of Man*. New York: McGraw-Hill.

McLUHAN, M., & FIORE, Q. (1967) *The Medium Is the Message: An Inventory of Effects*. New York: Random House.

MENDELSOHN, H. (1973) "Some Reasons Why Information Campaigns Can Succeed." *Public Opinion Quarterly* 37: 50–61.

MERTON, R. (1946) *Mass Persuasion: The Social Pathology of a War Bond Drive*. Westport, Conn.: Greenwood Press.

MEYER, T. (1972) "Effects of Viewing Justified and Unjustified Real Film Violence on Aggressive Behavior." *Journal of Personality and Social Psychology* 23: 21–29.

MEYROWITZ, J. (1985a) *No Sense of Place.* New York: Oxford University Press.

MEYROWITZ, J. (1985b) Interview by Connie Lauerman, Chicago Tribune Service, *The Miami Herald,* May 21, p. F1.

"MIAMI BEACH GIVES UP ON STREET ANTI-CRIME CAMERAS" (1984) *Crime Control Digest,* 18, no. 24: 2–3.

MIAMI BEACH POLICE DEPARTMENT (1983) *Micro-Video Project Yearly Report.*

MIAMI BEACH PUBLIC INFORMATION OFFICE (1982) News release. February.

MILAVSKY, J., KESSLER, R., STIPP, H., & RUBINS, W. (1982) "Television and Aggression: Results of a Panel Study." In *Television and Behavior, vol. 2, Technical Reviews,* edited by D. Pearl, L. Bouthilet, and J. Lazar, pp. 138–157. Washington, D.C.: U.S. Department of Health and Human Services. National Institute of Public Health.

MILGRAM, S., & SHOTLAND, R. (1973) *Television and Antisocial Behavior: Field Experiments.* New York: Academic Press.

MILLER, G. (1976) "The Effects of Videotaped Trial Materials on Juror Response." In *Psychology and the Law,* edited by C. Nemeth and N. Vidmar, pp. 185–208. Lexington, Mass.: D. C. Heath.

MILLER, G., & FONTES, N. (1979a) "Trial by Videotape." *Psychology Today,* May, pp. 92, 95–96, 99–100, 112.

MILLER, G., & FONTES, N. (1979b) *Videotape on Trial.* Newbury Park, Calif.: Sage.

MILLER, G., & SIEBERT, F. (1974) *Effects of Videotaped Testimony on Information Processing and Decision-Making in Jury Trials.* Progress Report no. 1, February. NSF-RANN Grant #GI 38398, Dept. of Communications. East Lansing: Michigan State University.

MILLER, G., & SIEBERT, F. (1975) *Effects of Videotaped Testimony on Information Processing and Decision-Making in Jury Trials.* Progress Report no. 2, February. NSF-RANN Grant #GI 38398, Dept. of Communications. East Lansing: Michigan State University.

MISCHEL, W. (1981) *Introduction to Personality.* New York: Holt, Rinehart & Winston.

MOHR, D., & ZANNA, M. (in press) "Treating Women as Sexual Objects: Look to the (Gender Schematic) Male Who Has Viewed Pornography." *Personality and Social Psychology Bulletin.*

MOLOTCH, H., & LESTER, M. (1981) "News as Purposive Behavior: On the Strategic Use of Routine Events, Accidents and Scandals." In *The Manufacture of News,* edited by S. Cohen and J. Young, pp. 118–137. Newbury Park, Calif.: Sage.

MOLOTCH, H., PROTESS, D., & GORDON, M. (1987) "The Media–Policy Connections: Ecologies of News." In *Political Communication Research,* edited by D. L. Paletz, pp. 26–48. Norwood, N.J.: Ablex.

MONTELEONE, C. D. (1982) "Videotape Depositions: Basic Pointers for a Skilled Presentation." *American Bar Association Journal* 68 (July): 863–865.

MOONEY, L., & FEWELL, C. (1989) "Crime in One Long-Lived Comic Strip: An Evaluation of Chestor Gould's 'Dick Tracy.'" *American Journal of Economics and Sociology* 48 (1): 89–100.

MORAN, G., & CUTLER, B. (in press) "The Prejudicial Impact of Pretrial Publicity." *Journal of Applied Social Psychology.*

MOS, L. (1980) "A Theoretical Perspective on Juvenile Intervention Programs: Discussion." In *Forensic Psychology and Psychiatry,* edited by F. Wright, C. Bahn, and R. Rieber. New York: Academy of Sciences.

MOULD, D. (1988) "The Pornography–Sexual Crime Debate." *Journal of Sex Research* 25: 267–288.

MURDOCK, G., & GOLDING, P. (1977) "Capitalism, Communication and Class Relations." In *Mass Communication and Society,* edited by J. Curran, M. Gurevitch, and J. Woollacott. London: Edward Arnold.

MURRAY, J. (1980) *Television and Youth: 25 Years of Research.* Stanford, Wash.: Boys Town Center for the Study of Youth Development.

MURRAY, J. (1984) "Cross-Cultural TV: Implications for Policy." In *Justice and the Media,* edited by R. Surette, pp. 233–244. Springfield, Ill.: Charles C Thomas.

MURRAY, J., & CLARKE, P. (1980) "Television and Story Telling: Media Influences on Children's Fantasies." *College and School Innovator* 11: 4–7.

MURRAY, J., HAYES, A., & SMITH, J. (1978) "Sequential Analysis: Another Approach to Describing the Stream of Behavior in Children's Interactions." *Australian Journal of Psychology* 30: 207–215.

MURRAY, T. (1978) "Videotaped Depositions: The Ohio Experience." *Judicature* 61, no. 6 (December–January): 258–261.

NATIONAL COMMISSION ON THE CAUSES AND PREVENTION OF VIOLENCE (NCCPV) (1969) *Mass Media and Violence,* vol. 9. Washington, D. C.: U. S. Government Printing Office.

NATIONAL INSTITUTE OF MENTAL HEALTH (NIMH) (1982) *Television and Behavior: Ten Years of Scientific Progress and Implications for the Eighties, vol. 1, Summary Report.* Rockville, Md.: Author.

NEALE, S. (1980) *Genre.* England: British File Institute (distributed by University of Illinois Press, Champagne–Urbana.

NELSON, S. (1989) "Crime-Time Television." *Law Enforcement Bulletin* 58, no. 8, pp. 1–9.

NESSON, C., & KOBLENZ, A. (1981) "The Image of Justice: *Chandler* v. *Florida.*" *Harvard Civil Rights–Civil Liberties Law Review* 16: 405–413.

NETTLER, G. (1982) *Killing One Another.* Cincinnati, Ohio: Anderson.

NEWMAN, G. (1990) "Popular Culture and Criminal Justice: A Preliminary Analysis." *Journal of Criminal Justice* 18: 261–274.

NEWMAN, O. (1972) *Defensible Space: Crime Prevention through Urban Design.* New York: Macmillan.

NEWMAN, O. (1975) "Community of Interest-Design for Community Control." In *Architecture, Planning and Urban Crime.* Report to NACRO Conference, 12/6/74, London.

NEWMAN, O. (1976) *Design Guidelines for Creating Defensible Space.* NIJ/LEAA. Washington, D. C.: U. S. Government Printing Office.

NEW YORK CITY (1983) "Television Arraignment: Feasibility for New York City Criminal Courts." Photocopy, February.

NIENSTEDT, B. (1990) "The Policy Effects of a DUI Law and a Publicity Campaign." In *The Media and Criminal Justice Policy,* edited by R. Surette. Springfield, Ill.: Charles C Thomas.

NOBLE, G. (1983) "Social Learning from Everyday Television (Children in Front of the Small Screen)." In *Learning from Television Psychological and Educational Research,* ed-

ited by M. Howe, pp. 101–124. New York: Academic Press.

NOELLE-NEUMANN, E. (1974) "The Spiral of Silence." *Journal of Communication* 24: 3–51.

NOELLE-NEUMANN, E. (1980) "Mass Media and Social Change in Developed Societies." In *Mass Communication Review Yearbook, vol. 1,* edited by H. Wilhoit and L. de Bock, pp. 657–678. Newbury Park, Calif.: Sage.

NOELLE-NEUMANN, E. (1983) "The Effect of Media on Media Effects Research." *Journal of Communication* 33: 157–165.

O'KEEFE, G. (1984) "Public Views on Crime: Television Exposure and Media Credibility." In *Communication Yearbook* 8, edited by R. N. Bostrum, pp. 514–537. Newbury Park, Calif.: Sage.

O'KEEFE, G. (1985a) "Taking a Bite Out of Crime: The Impact of a Public Information Campaign." *Communication Research* 12: 147–178.

O'KEEFE, G. (1985b) "Taking a Bite Out of Crime." *Society* 22: 56–64.

O'KEEFE, G., & MENDELSOHN, H. (1984) *"Taking a Bite Out of Crime": The Impact of a Mass Media Crime Prevention Campaign.* Washington, D. C.: U. S. Department of Justice, National Institute of Justice.

O'KEEFE, G., & REID-NASH, K. (1987a) "Crime News and Real-World Blues: The Effects of the Media on Social Reality." *Communication Research* 14: 147–173.

O'KEEFE, G., & REID-NASH, K. (1987b) *Promoting Crime Prevention Competence among the Elderly.* Washington, D. C.: U. S. Department of Justice, National Institute of Justice.

O'KEEFE, G., & REID, K. (1990) "Media Public Information Campaigns and Criminal Justice Policy: Beyond 'McGruff.'" In *Media and Criminal Justice Policy,* edited by R. Surette. Springfield, Ill.: Charles C Thomas.

O'KEEFE, T. (1971) "The Anti-Smoking Commercials: A Study of Television's Impact on Behavior." *Public Opinion Quarterly* 35: 242–248.

O'NEILL, J. (1990) "Computer to Handle Police Mugs." *The Miami Herald,* March 3, p. 4B.

OSTROFF, M., & BOYD, J. (1987) "Television and Suicide." *New England Journal of Medicine* 3, no. 6: 876–877.

OSTROFF, R., BEHRENDS, R., LEE, K., & OLIPH-

ANT, J. (1985) "Adolescent Suicides Modeled after Television Movie." *American Journal of Psychiatry* 142: 989–999.

OTTO, H. A. (1962) "Sex and Violence on the American Newsstand." *Journalism Quarterly* 40: 19–26.

OWENS, D. (1983) "Crime Stoppers Generates Valuable Tips." *The Miami Herald,* February 17, p. 15C.

PACKER, H. (1968) *The Limits of the Criminal Sanction.* Palo Alto, Calif.: Stanford University Press.

PADAWER-SINGER, A., & BARTON, H. (1975) "Free Press, Fair Trial." In *The Jury System: A Critical Analysis,* edited by R. Simon. Newbury Park, Calif.: Sage.

PADAWER-SINGER, A., & BARTON, H. (1975) "The Impact of Pretrial Publicity on Jurors' Verdicts." In *The Jury System in America: A Critical Overview,* edited by R. Simon, pp. 123–139. Newbury Park, Calif.: Sage.

PADAWER-SINGER, A., SINGER, A., & SINGER, R. (1974) "Voir Dire by Two Lawyers: An Essential Safeguard." *Judicature* 57: 386–391.

PADDON, A. (1985) "Television Coverage of Criminal Trials with Cameras and Microphones: A Laboratory Experiment of Audience Effects." Ph.D. diss., University of Tennessee.

PADGETT, V., & BRISLIN-SLUTZ, J. (1987) *Pornography, Erotica and Negative Attitudes towards Women: The Effects of Repeated Exposure.* Unpublished manuscript, Marshall University.

PAGE, B., SHAPIRO, R., & DEMPSEY, G. (1987) "What Moves Public Opinion?" *American Political Science Review* 81: 23–43.

PAISLEY, W. (1981) "Public Communication Campaigns: The American Experience." In *Public Communication Campaigns,* edited by R. Rice and W. Paisley, pp. 15–38. Newbury Park, Calif.: Sage.

PALMER, E. (1973) "Formative Research in the Production of Television for Children." In *Communications Technology and Social Policy,* edited by G. Gerbner, L. Gross, and R. Melody, pp. 229–245. New York: Wiley.

PANDIANI, J. (1978) "Crime Time TV: If All We Knew Is What We Saw. . ." *Contemporary Crises* 2: 437–458.

PAPKE, D. (1987) *Framing the Criminal.* Hamden, Conn.: Archon Books.

PARENTI, M. (1978) *Power and the Powerless.* New York: St. Martin Press.

PARISH, J., & PITTS, M. (1976) *The Great Gangster Pictures.* Metuchen, N. J.: Scarecrow Press.

PARK, R. (1940) "News as a Form of Knowledge." *American Journal of Sociology* 45: 669–686.

PARKE, R. D., BERKOWITZ, L., LEYENS, J., WEST, S., & SEBASTIAN, R. (1977) "Some Effects of Violent and Non-Violent Movies on the Behavior of Juvenile Delinquents." In *Advances in Experimental Social Psychology,* vol. 10, edited by L. Berkowitz, pp. 135–172. New York: Academic Press.

PATE, J. (1978) *The Great Villains.* New York: Oxford University Press.

PAULIN, D. (1988) "TV Tips Reap Innocent Suspects." *The Miami News,* November 29, p. 9A.

PAYNE, D. (1974) "Newspapers and Crime: What Happens During Strike Periods." *Journalism Quarterly* 51: 607–612.

PAYNE, D., & PAYNE, K. (1970) "Newspapers and Crime in Detroit." *Journalism Quarterly* 47: 233–238.

PEARL, D. (1984) "Violence and Aggression." *Society* 21: 17–20.

PEARL, D., BOUTHILET, L., & LAZAR, J. (eds.) (1982) *Television and Behavior: Ten Years of Scientific Progress and Implications for the Eighties,* vols. 1–3. Washington, D. C.: U. S. Government Printing Office, National Institute of Mental Health.

PEASE, S., & LOVE, C. (1984a) "The Prisoner's Perspective of Copycat Crime." Paper presented at the annual meeting of the American Society of Criminology, November, Cincinnati, Ohio.

PEASE, S., & LOVE, C. (1984b) "The Copy-Cat Crime Phenomenon." In *Justice and the Media,* edited by R. Surette, pp. 199–211. Springfield, Ill.: Charles C Thomas.

PEMBER, D. (1984) *Mass Media Law.* 3rd ed. Dubuque, Iowa: William C. Brown.

PEMBER, D. (1987) *Mass Media Law,* 4th ed. Dubuque, Iowa: William C. Brown.

PETERSON, P., & ZILL, T. (1980) "Television Viewing and Children's Intellectual, Social and Emotional Development." Paper presented at the annual meeting of the American Association for Public Opinion Research, May, Washington, D. C.

PETERSON, R., & THURSTONE, L. (1933) *Motion Pictures and the Social Attitudes of Children.* New York: Macmillan.

"PHILADELPHIA'S POPULAR POLICE STATION" (1979) *Target* 8, no. 2 (March/April), p. 1. Washington, D. C.: International City Management Association.

PHILLIPS, D. (1974) "The Influence of Suggestion on Suicide: Substantive and Theoretical Implications of the Werther Effect." *American Sociological Review* 39: 340–354.

PHILLIPS, D. (1977) "Motor Vehicle Fatalities Increase Just after Publicized Suicide Stories." *Science* 196: 1464–1465.

PHILLIPS, D. (1978) "Airplane Accident Fatalities Increase Just after Newspaper Stories about Murder and Suicide." *Science* 201: 148–150.

PHILLIPS, D. (1979) "Suicide, Motor Vehicle Fatalities, and the Mass Media: Evidence toward a Theory of Suggestion." *American Journal of Sociology* 84: 1150–1174.

PHILLIPS, D. (1980) "Airplane Accidents, Murder, and the Mass Media: Toward a Theory of Imitation." *Social Forces* 58: 1001–1024.

PHILLIPS, D. (1982a) "The Behavioral Impact of Violence in the Mass Media: A Review of the Evidence from Laboratory and Non-Laboratory Investigations." *Sociology and Social Research* 66: 387–398.

PHILLIPS, D. (1982b) "The Impact of Fictional Television Stories on U. S. Adult Fatalities: New Evidence of the Effect of Mass Media on Violence." *American Journal of Sociology* 87: 1340–1359.

PHILLIPS, D. (1983) "The Impact of Mass Media Violence on Homicide." *American Sociological Research* 48: 560–568.

PHILLIPS, D., & BOLLEN, K. (1985) "Same Time Last Year: Selective Data Dredging for Negative Findings." *American Sociological Review* 50: 364–371.

PHILLIPS, D., & CARSTENSEN, L. (1986) "Clustering of Teenage Suicides after Television News Stories about Suicide." *New England Journal of Medicine* 315: 685–689.

PHILLIPS, D., & CARSTENSEN, L. (1988) "The Effect of Suicide Stories on Various Demographic Groups, 1968–1985." *Suicide and Life-Threatening Behavior* 18: 100–114.

PHILLIPS, D., & HENSLEY, J. (1984) "When Violence Is Rewarded or Punished: The Impact of Mass Media Stories on Homicide." *Journal of Communication* 34, no. 3 (Summer): 101–116.

PHILLIPS, D., & PAIGHT, D. (1987) "The Impact of Televised Movies about Suicide." *New England Journal of Medicine* 315: 809–811.

PIERCE, G., & BOWERS, W. (1979) *The Impact of the Bartley-Fox Gun Law on Crime in Massachusetts.* Boston: Northeastern University, Center for Applied Social Research.

PLATT, D. (1987) "The Aftermath of Angie's Overdose: Is Soap (Opera) Damaging to Your Health?" *British Medical Journal* 294: 954–957.

POLAND, J. (1988) *Understanding Terrorism.* Englewood Cliffs, N. J.: Prentice-Hall.

"POLICE ADOPT MEDIA GUIDELINES" (1985) *News Media and the Law* 9, no. 3: 31–32.

"POLICE TAKE SHOTS AT STREET CRIME" (1983) *Security World* 20, no. 9: 13, 15.

POWERS, R. (1990) Review of *The Police Mystique,* by A. Bouza. *New York Times Review of Books,* May 6, p. G8.

"PRETRIAL PUBLICITY—HABEAS CORPUS" (1984) *Criminal Law Reporter* 35, no. 20: 2366.

PRITCHARD, D. (1985) "Race, Homicide and Newspapers." *Journalism Quarterly* 62: 500–507.

PRITCHARD, D. (1986) "Homicide and Bargained Justice: The Agenda-Setting Effect of Crime News on Prosecutors." *Public Opinion Quarterly* 50: 143–159.

PRITCHARD, D., DILTS, J., & BERKOWITZ, D. (1987) "Prosecutors' Use of External Agendas in Prosecuting Pornography Cases." *Journalism Quarterly* 64: 392–398.

"PRIVACY EXEMPTION SURMOUNTABLE" (1985) *News Media and the Law* 9, no. 1: 33–35.

"PROBLEMS FREQUENT WHEN SEEKING ACCESS TO INMATES" (1989) *News Media and the Law* 13, no. 4: 6–7.

PROTESS, D., COOK, S., CURTIN, T., GORDON, M., LEFF, D., McCOMBS, M., & MILLER, P. (1987) "The Impact of Investigative Reporting on Public Opinion and Policymaking: Targeting Toxic Waste." *Public Opinion Quarterly* 51: 166–185.

PROTESS, D., LEFF, D., BROOKS, S., & GORDON, M. (1985) "Uncovering Rape: The Watchdog Press and the Limits of Agenda Setting." *Public Opinion Quarterly* 49: 19–37.

"PUBLICITY DIDN'T REQUIRE VENUE CHANGES FOR FEDERAL DEFENDANTS" (1984) *Criminal Law Reporter* 36, no. 8: 2140–2141.

QUINNEY, R. (1970) *The Social Reality of Crime.* Boston: Little, Brown.

QUINNEY, R. (1974) *Critique of Legal Order.* Boston: Little, Brown.

QUINSEY, V. (in press) "Sexual Aggression: Studies of Offenders against Women." *International Yearbook on Law and Mental Health.*

RADIN, E. (1964) *The Innocents.* Fairfield, N.J.: Morrow.

"RADIO, TV, NEWSPAPERS REJECTED IN BID TO USE CAMERAS IN COURT" (1984) *Criminal Justice Newsletter* 15, no. 20: 3–4.

RANDALL, D., LEE-SIMMONS, L., & HAGNER, P. (1988) "Common versus Elite Crime Coverage in Network News." *Social Science Quarterly* 69: 910–929.

RAY, M., & WILKIE, W. (1970) "Fear: The Potential of an Appeal Neglected in Marketing." *Journal of Marketing* 34: 54–62.

REAL, M. (1989) *Super Media: A Cultural Studies Approach.* Newbury Park, Calif.: Sage.

REINER, R. (1985) *The Politics of the Police,* New York: St. Martin's.

REPPETTO, R. (1974) *Residential Crime.* Cambridge, Mass.: Ballinger.

RILEY, D., & MAYHEW, P. (1980) *Crime Prevention Publicity: An Assessment.* London: Her Majesty's Stationery Office, Study no. 63.

RILEY, S. (1973) "Pretrial Publicity: A Field Study." *Journalism Quarterly* 50: 17–23.

ROBERTS, D., & BACHEN, C. (1981) "Mass Communication Effects." *Annual Review of Psychology* 32: 307–356.

ROBERTS, D., HEROLD, C., HORNBY, M., KING, S., STERNE, D., WHITELEY, S., & SILVERMAN, T. (1974) *Earth's a Big Blue Marble: A Report on the Impact of a Children's Television Series on Children's Opinions.* Palo Alto, Calif.: Stanford University Press.

ROBERTS, J., & DOOB, A. (1990) "News Media Influences on Public Views on Sentencing." *Law and Human Behavior* 14, no. 5: 451–468.

ROBERTS, J., & EDWARDS, D. (1989) "Contextual Effects in Judgements of Crimes, Crimi-

nals and the Purpose of Sentencing." *Journal of Applied Social Psych* 19, no. 11: 902–917.

ROBERTS, J., & GROSSMAN, M. (1990) "Crime Prevention and Public Opinion." *Canadian Journal of Criminology* 32: 75–90.

ROBINSON, J. (1972) "Mass Communication and Information Diffusion." In *Current Perspectives in Mass Communication Research,* edited by F. G. Kline and P. J. Tichenor, pp. 71–93. Newbury Park, Calif.: Sage.

ROBINSON, J. (1976) "Interpersonal Influence in Election Campaigns: Two Step-Flow Hypotheses." *Public Opinion Quarterly* 40: 304–319.

ROBINSON, M. (1974) "The Impact of the Televised Watergate Hearings." *Journal of Communication* 24: 17–30.

ROBINSON, M. (1976) "Public Affairs Television and the Growth of Political Malaise." *American Political Science Review* 70: 425–445.

ROCKWELL, J. H. (1983) "Videophones and Closed-Circuit Television in Pretrial Proceedings." Memorandum, National Center for State Courts, Research and Information Service, Williamsburg, Va., May 6, Ref. no. RIS 83.056.

ROGERS, E. (1973) *Communication Strategies for Family Planning.* New York: Free Press.

ROGERS, E., & DEARING, J. (1988) "Agenda-Setting Research: Where Has It Been, Where Is It Going?" In *Communication Yearbook 11,* edited by J. Anderson, pp. 555–594. Newbury Park, Calif.: Sage.

ROGERS, E., & STOREY, J. (1987) "Effects of Mass Communications." In *The Handbook of Social Psychology,* 3rd ed., vol. 2, edited by G. Lindzey and E. Aronson, pp. 539–598. New York: Random House.

ROLLINGS, H., & BLASCOVICH, J. (1977) "The Case of Patricia Hearst: Pretrial Publicity and Opinion." *Journal of Communication* (Spring): 58–65.

ROSEKRANS, M. (1967) "Imitation in Children as a Function of Perceived Similarities to a Social Model of Vicarious Reinforcement." *Journal of Personality and Social Psychology* 7: 307–315.

ROSEKRANS, M., & HARTUP, W. (1967) "Imitative Influences of Consistent and Inconsistent Response Consequences to a Model of Aggressive Behavior in Children." *Journal of Personality and Social Psychology* 7: 429–434.

ROSEN, R. (1989) "Ethical Soap: 'L. A. Law' and the Privileging of Character." *University of Miami Law Review* 43: 1229–1261.

ROSENBAUM, D., & LURIGIO, A. (1985) "Crime Stoppers: Paying the Price." *Psychology Today,* June, pp. 56–61.

ROSENBAUM, D., LURIGIO, A., & LAVRAKAS, P. (1986) *Crime Stoppers: A National Evaluation of Program Operations and Effects.* Evanston, Ill.: Northwestern University, Center for Urban Affairs and Policy Research.

ROSENBAUM, D., LURIGIO, A., & LAVRAKAS, P. (1989) "Enhancing Citizen Participation and Solving Serious Crime: A National Evaluation of Crime Stoppers Programs." *Crime and Delinquency* 35: 401–420.

ROSENBERG, H. (1990) "Talk Shows Retry McMartin Case." Los Angeles Times Service, *The Miami Herald,* February 3, pp. 1E–2E.

ROSENSTOCK, I. (1960) "What Research in Motivation Suggests for Public Health." *American Journal of Public Health* 50: 22–33.

ROSENTHAL, R. (1986) "Media Violence, Antisocial Behavior, and the Social Consequences of Small Effects." *Journal of Social Issues* 42: 141–154.

ROSENTHAL, T., & ZIMMERMAN, B. (1978) *Social Learning and Cognition.* New York: Academic Press.

ROSHIER, B. (1981) "The Selection of Crime News in the Press." In *The Manufacture of News,* edited by S. Cohen and J. Young, pp. 40–51. Newbury Park, Calif.: Sage.

ROSOW, E. (1978) *Born to Lose.* New York: Oxford University Press.

ROSS, H., CAMPBELL, D., & GLASS, G. (1970) "The British 'Breathalyser' Crackdown of 1967." *American Behavioral Scientist* 13: 493–509.

ROTHMAN, D. (1971) *The Discovery of the Asylum.* Boston: Little, Brown.

ROTTENBERG, D. (1976) "Do News Reports Bias Juries?" *Columbia Journalism Review* (May/June), pp. 128–131.

RUBINSTEIN, E., LIEBERT, R., NEALE, J., & POULOS, R. (1974) *Assessing Television's Influence on Children's Prosocial Behavior.* Stony

Brook, N. Y.: Brookdale International Institute.

RUBINSTEIN, J. (1973) *City Police.* New York: Farrar, Straus & Giroux.

RUSHTON, J. P. (1976a) "Socialization and the Altruistic Behavior of Children." *Psychological Bulletin* 83: 893–913.

RUSHTON, J. P. (1976b) "Television and Prosocial Behavior." In *Report of the Royal Commission on Violence in the Communications Industry,* vol. 4. Ontario: Queen's Printer.

RUSHTON, J. P. (1980) *Altruism, Socialization, and Society.* Englewood Cliffs, N. J.: Prentice-Hall.

RUSHTON, J. P. (1982a) "Imagination, Creativity, and Prosocial Behavior." In *Television and Behavior: Ten Years of Scientific Research and Implications for the Eighties, vol 1, Summary Report,* edited by D. Pearl, L. Bouthilet, and J. Lazar, pp. 45–53. Washington, D. C.: National Institute of Mental Health.

RUSHTON, J. P. (1982b) "Television and Prosocial Behavior." In *Television and Behavior, vol. 2, Technical Review,* edited by D. Pearl, L. Bouthilet, & J. Lazar, pp. 248–257. Washington, D. C.: National Institute of Mental Health.

RYPINSKI, I. (1982) "Videotaping Depositions." *Hawaii Bar Journal* (Winter): 67–76.

SACCO, V. (1982) "The Effects of Mass Media on Perceptions of Crime." *Pacific Sociological Review* 25: 475–493.

SACCO, V., & SILVERMAN, R. (1981) "Selling Crime Prevention: The Evaluation of a Mass Media Campaign." *Canadian Journal of Criminology* 23: 191–201.

SACCO, V., & SILVERMAN, R. (1982) "Crime Prevention through Mass Media: Prospects and Problems." *Journal of Criminal Justice* 10: 257–269.

SALAS, L. (1984) "The Press and the Criminal Justice System: Controversies over Acquisition and Distribution of Information." In *Justice and the Media,* edited by R. Surette, pp. 91–105. Springfield, Ill.: Charles C Thomas.

SALCEDO, R., READ, H., EVANS, J., & KONG, A. (1974) "A Successful Information Campaign on Pesticides." *Journalism Quarterly* 51: 91–95, 110.

SALVAN, S. A. (1975) "Videotape for the Legal

Community." *Judicature* 59, no. 5 (December): 222–229.

SALWIN, M. (1986) "Time in Agenda-Setting: The Accumulation of Media Coverage on Audience Issue Salience." Paper presented at the annual meeting of the International Communication Association, November, Chicago.

SCHATTSCHNEIDER, D. (1960) *The Semi-Sovereign People.* Hinsdale, Ill.: Dryden Press.

SCHELER, M. [1926] (1980) *Problems of a Sociology of Knowledge.* Reprint, translated by M. Frings. London: Routledge & Kegan Paul.

SCHMELING, D., & WOTRING, C. (1976) "Agenda-Setting Effects of Drug Abuse Public Service Ads." *Journalism Quarterly* 53: 743–746.

SCHMELING, D., & WOTRING, C. (1980) "Making Anti-Drug-Abuse Advertising Work." *Journal of Advertising Research* 20: 33–37.

SCHMID, A., & de GRAAF, J. (1982) *Violence as Communication.* Newbury Park, Calif.: Sage.

SCHMIDTKE, A., & HAFNER, H. (1988) "The Werther Effect after Television Films: New Evidence for an Old Hypothesis." *Psychiatric Medicine* 18: 665–676.

SCHWARTZ, J. (1989) "Promoting a Good Public Image." *Corrections Today* 51: 38–42.

SCOTT, J. (1985) "Sexual Violence in *Playboy* Magazine: Longitudinal Analysis." Paper presented at the meeting of the American Society of Criminology, November, Atlanta.

SCOTT, J., & SCHWALM, L. (1988) "Pornography and Rape: An Examination of Adult Theater Rapes and Rape Rates by State." In *Controversial Issues in Crime and Justice,* edited by J. Scott and T. Hirschi, pp. 40–53. Newbury Park, Calif.: Sage.

SCOTT, J., & SCHWALM, L. (forthcoming) "Rape Rates and the Circulation Rates of Adult Magazines." *Journal of Sex Research.*

SCOTT, W., & HART, D. (1979) *Organizational America.* Boston: Houghton Mifflin.

SECHREST, D., LIQUORI, W., & PERRY, J. (1990) "Using Video Technology in Police Patrol." In *The Media and Criminal Justice Policy,* edited by R. Surette, pp. 255–264. Springfield, Ill.: Charles C Thomas.

"SECRET COURT WATCH" (1979) *News Media and the Law* 3, no. 4: 17–23.

SENNET, R., & COBB, J. (1973) *The Hidden Inquiries of Class.* New York: Vintage Books.

SHAABER, M. (1929) *Some Forerunners of the Newspaper in England.* Philadelphia: University of Pennsylvania Press.

SHADOIAN, J. (1977) *Dreams and Dead Ends.* Cambridge, Mass.: MIT Press.

SHARP, A. (1983) "Postverdict Interviews with Jurors." *Case and Comment* 88: 3–15.

SHAW, D. (1990a) "McMartin Verdict: Not Guilty. Where Was Skepticism in the Media?" *Los Angeles Times,* January 19, pp. A1, A20–A21.

SHAW, D. (1990b) "Reporter's Early Exclusives Triggered a Media Frenzy." *Los Angeles Times,* January 20, pp. A1, A30–A31.

SHAW, D. (1990c) "Media Skepticism Grew as McMartin Case Lingered." *Los Angeles Times,* January 21, pp. A1, A32–A34.

SHAW, D., & McCOMBS, M. (1977) *The Emergence of American Political Issues: The Agenda-Setting Function of the Press.* St. Paul, Minn.: West Publishing.

SHELEY, J., & ASHKINS, C. (1981) "Crime, Crime News, and Crime Views." *Public Opinion Quarterly* 45: 492–506.

SHERIZEN, S. (1978) "Social Creation of Crime News." In *Deviance and Mass Media,* edited by C. Winick, pp. 203–224. Newbury Park, Calif.: Sage.

SHUTKIN, J. (1973) "Videotape Trials: Legal and Practical Implications." *Columbia Journal of Law and Social Problems* 9: 363–393.

SHUTTLEWORTH, F., & MAY, M. (1933) *The Social Conduct and Attitudes of Movie Fans.* New York: Macmillan.

SIEBERT, F., WILCOX, P., HOUGH, W., & BUSH, T. (1970) *Free Press and Fair Trial.* Athens.: University of Georgia Press.

SIEGEL, A. (1974) "The Effects of Media Violence on Social Learning." In *Where Do You Draw the Line? An Exploration into Media Violence, Pornography, and Censorship,* edited by V. B. Cline, pp. 129–146. Provo, Utah: Brigham Young University Press.

SIGAL, L. (1973) *Reporters and Officials.* Lexington, Mass.: D. C. Heath.

SIMON, R. (1966) "Murder, Juries, and the Press." *Transaction* (May–June): 40–42.

SIMON, R. (1977) "Does the Court's Decision in Nebraska Press Association Fit the Research Evidence on the Impact on Jurors of News Coverage?" *Sanford Law Review* 29: 515–528.

SIMON, R., & EIMERMANN, T. (1971) "The Jury

Finds Not Guilty: Another Look at Media Influence on the Jury." *Journalism Quarterly* 48: 343.

SIMONETT, T. (1966) "The Trial as One of the Arts." *American Bar Association Journal* 552: 1145–1160.

SKOGAN, W., & MAXFIELD, M. (1981) *Coping with Crime.* Newbury Park, Calif.: Sage.

SLATER, D., & ELLIOTT, W. (1982) "Television's Influence on Social Reality." *Quarterly Journal of Speech* 68: 69–79.

SLIFE, B., & RYCHIAK, J. (1976) "Role of Affective Assessment in Modeling Aggressive Behavior." *Journal of Personality and Social Psychology* 43: 861–868.

SMITH, D. (1976) "The Social Content of Pornography." *Journal of Communication* 26: 16–24.

SMITH, S. (1984) "Crime in the News." *British Journal of Criminology* 24: 289–295.

SNEED, D. (1985) "How to Improve Crime Reporting." *Editor and Publisher,* November 9, pp. 39, 56.

SNOW, R. (1984) "Crime and Justice in Prime-Time News: The John Hinckley, Jr., Case." In *Justice and the Media,* edited by R. Surette, pp. 212–232. Springfield, Ill.: Charles C Thomas.

SOHN, A. (1976) "Determining Guilt or Innocence of Accused from Pretrial News Stories." *Journalism Quarterly* 53: 100–105.

SPANIOLO, J., & TERILLI, S. (1987) "The Freedom of Information Act: A Reporters' Map to a Federal Maze." In *The Reporter's Handbook.* Tallahassee: Florida Bar Association.

SPARKS, G., & OGLES, R. (1990) "The Difference between Fear of Victimization and the Probability of Being Victimized: Implications for Cultivation." *Journal of Broadcasting and Electronic Media* 34, no. 3: 351–358.

SPRAFKIN, J., LIEBERT, R., & POULOS, R. (1975) "Effects of a Pro-Social Televised Example on Children's Helping." *Journal of Experimental Child Psychology* 20: 119–126.

SPRAFKIN, J., & RUBINSTEIN, E. (1982) "Using Television to Improve the Social Behavior of Institutionalized Children." *Prevention in Human Services* 2: 107–114.

STACK, S. (1987) "Celebrities and Suicide: A Taxonomy and Analysis, 1948–1983." *American Sociological Review* 52: 401–412.

STAR, S., & HUGHES, H. (1950) "Report on an Educational Campaign: The Cincinnati Plan for the United States." *American Journal of Sociology* 55: 389–400.

STARK, S. (1987) "Perry Mason Meets Sonny Crockett: The History of Lawyers and the Police as Television Heroes." *University of Miami Law Review* 42: 229–283.

"STATE SHIELD LAWS: DO THEY WORK" (1982) *News Media and the Law* 6, no. 3: 31–33.

STEIGLEMAN, W. (1971) *The Newspaperman and the Law.* Westport, Conn.: Greenwood Press.

STEIN, A., & FRIEDRICH, L. (1972) "Television Content and Young Children's Behavior." In *Television and Social Behavior, vol. 2, Television and Social Learning,* edited by J. Murray, E. Rubinstein, and G. Comstock, pp. 202–317. Washington, D.C.: U.S. Government Printing Office. National Institute of Mental Health.

STEIN, A., FRIEDRICH, L., & TAHSLER, S. (1973) *The Effects of Prosocial Television and Environmental Cues on Children's Task Persistence and Conceptual Tempo.* University Park: Pennsylvania State University Press.

STEMPL, G. (1962) "Content Patterns of Small Metropolitan Dailies." *Journalism Quarterly* 39: 88–90.

STEVENS, J., & GARCIA, H. (1980) *Communication History.* Newbury Park, Calif.: Sage.

STINCHCOMBE, A., ADAMS, R., HEIMER, C., SCHEPPLE, K., SMITH, T., & TAYLOR, G. (1980) *Crime and Punishment: Changing Attitudes in America.* San Francisco: Jossey Bass.

STROMAN, C., & SELTZER, R. (1985) "Media Use and Perceptions of Crime." *Journalism Quarterly* 62: 340–345.

SUE, S., SMITH R., & GILBERT, R. (1974) "Biasing Effects of Pretrial Publicity on Judicial Decisions." *Journal of Criminal Justice* 2: 163–171.

SULLIVAN, H. (1961) *Trial by Newspaper.* Hyannis, Mass.: Patriot Press.

SURETTE, R. (1984a) Ed. *Justice and the Media.* Springfield, Ill.: Charles C Thomas.

SURETTE, R. (1984b) "Two Media-Based Crime-Control Programs: Crime Stoppers and Video Street Patrol." In *Justice and the*

Media, edited by R. Surette, pp. 275–290. Springfield, Ill.: Charles C Thomas.

SURETTE, R. (1985a) "Video Street Patrol: Media Technology and Street Crime." *Journal of Police Science and Administration* 13: 78–85.

SURETTE, R. (1985b) "Television Viewing and Support of Punitive Criminal Justice Policy." *Journalism Quarterly* 62: 373–377, 450.

SURETTE, R. (1986) "The Mass Media and Criminal Investigations: Crime Stoppers in Dade County, Florida." *Journal of Justice Issues* 1: 21–38.

SURETTE, R. (1988) "Video Technology in Criminal Justice: Live Judicial Proceedings and Patrol and Surveillance." In *New Technologies and Criminal Justice,* edited by M. LeBlanc, P. Tremblay, and A. Blumstein, pp. 407–440. Montreal: University of Montreal.

SURETTE, R. (1989) "Media Trials." *Journal of Criminal Justice* 17: 293–308.

SURETTE, R. (1990a) "Law Enforcement Surveillance Projects Employing Media Technology." In *Media and Criminal Justice Policy,* edited by R. Surette, pp. 277–288. Springfield, Ill.: Charles C Thomas.

SURETTE, R. (1990b) "Media Trials and Echo Effects." In *Media and Criminal Justice Policy,* edited by R. Surette, pp. 177–192. Springfield, Ill.: Charles C Thomas.

SURETTE, R., & TERRY, C. (1984) "Videotaped Misdemeanor First Appearances: Fairness from the Defendant's Perspective." In *Justice and the Media,* edited by R. Surette, pp. 305–320. Springfield, Ill.: Charles C Thomas.

SWANSON, C. (1953) "What They Read in 130 Daily Newspapers." *Journalism Quarterly* 32: 411–421.

SWANSON, D. (1988) "Feeling the Elephant: Some Observations on Agenda-Setting Research." *Communication Yearbook* 11: 603–619.

TAJGMAN, D. (1981) "From *Estes* to *Chandler:* The Distinction between Television and Newspaper Trial Coverage." *Communication/Entertainment Law Journal* 3: 503–541.

TANICK, M., & SHIELDS, T. (1985) "Courts Wrestle with Venue Problems. . ." *Bench and Bar of Minnesota* 42: 15–20.

TANNENBAUM, P., & ZILLMANN, D. (1975) "Emotional Arousal in the Facilitation of Aggression through Communication." In *Advances in Experimental Social Psychology,* edited by L. Berkowitz, vol. 8, pp. 149–192. New York: Academic Press.

TANS, M., & CHAFFEE, S. (1966) "Pretrial Publicity and Juror Prejudice." *Journalism Quarterly* 43: 647–654.

TARDE, G. (1912) *Penal Philosophy.* Boston: Little, Brown.

TERRY, W. (1984) "Crime and the News: Gatekeeping and Beyond." In *Justice and the Media,* edited by R. Surette, pp. 31–50. Springfield, Ill.: Charles C Thomas.

TERRY, W., & SURETTE, R. (1985) "Video in the Misdemeanor Court." *Judicature* 69, no. 1: 13–19.

TEUCHMAN, G., & ORME, M. (1981) "Effects of Aggression and Prosocial Film Material on Altruistic Behavior of Children." *Psychological Reports,* June, pp. 699–702.

THOMAS, W. I. (1908) "The Psychology of Yellow Journalism." *American Magazine,* March, p. 491.

THOMPSON, W., FONG, G., & ROSENHAN, D. (1981) "Inadmissable Evidence and Juror Verdicts." *Journal of Personality and Social Psychology* 40: 453–483.

THRASHER, F. (1949) "The Comics and Delinquency: Cause or Scapegoat?" *Journal of Educational Sociology* 23: 195–205.

TOPLIN, R. (1975) *Unchallenged Violence: An American Ordeal.* Westport, Conn.: Greenwood Press.

TREEVAN, J., & HARTNAGEL, P. (1976) "The Effect of Television Violence on the Perceptions of Crime by Adolescents." *Journal of Sociology and Sociological Research* 60: 337–348.

TREUHAFT, D. (1957) "Trial by Headline." *The Nation,* October, pp. 279–282.

"TRIAL BY MEDIA" (1984) *U. S. Press* 10, no. 30, p. 4.

"TRIAL COURT MAY ORDER TRIAL PROCEEDINGS CLOSED TO PUBLIC IF IT FOLLOWS CERTAIN PROCEDURAL SAFEGUARDS" (1985) *Criminal Law Bulletin* 21 no. 2: 180.

TUCHMAN, G. (1973) "Making News by Doing Work." *American Journal of Sociology* 79: 110–131.

TUCHMAN, G. (1978) *Making News: A Study in*

the Construction of Reality. New York: Free Press.

TUSKA, J. (1987) *The Detective in Hollywood.* Garden City, N. Y.: Doubleday.

TYLER, T. (1980) "Impact of Directly and Indirectly Experienced Events: The Origin of Crime-Related Judgments and Behavior." *Journal of Personality and Social Psychology* 39: 13–28.

TYLER, T. (1984) "Assessing the Risk of Crime Victimization: The Integration of Personal Victimization Experience and Socially Transmitted Information." *Journal of Social Issues* 40: 27–38.

TYLER, T., & COOK, F. (1984) "The Mass Media and Judgments of Risk: Distinguishing Impact on Personal and Societal Level Judgments." *Journal of Personality and Social Psychology* 47: 693–708.

TYLER, T., & LAVRAKAS, P. (1985) "Cognitions Leading to Personal and Political Behaviors: The Case of Crime." In *Mass Media and Political Thought: An Information Processing Approach,* edited by S. Hraus and R. M. Perloff, pp. 141–156. Newbury Park, Calif.: Sage.

U. S. COMMISSION ON OBSCENITY AND PORNOGRAPHY (1972) *Erotica and Anti-Social Behavior,* vol. 7. Washington, D. C.: U. S. Government Printing Office.

U. S. DEPARTMENT OF JUSTICE (1986) *Final Report of the Attorney General's Commission on Pornography,* vols. 1–2. Washington, D. C.: U. S. Government Printing Office.

U. S. SENATE JUDICIARY COMMITTEE ON JUVENILE DELINQUENCY (1969) *Interim Report on Judiciary Investigation of Juvenile Delinquency in the U. S.* Reprint. Westport, Conn.: Greenwood Press.

VAN ALSTYNE, S. (1977) "The Hazards to the Press of Claiming a Preferred Position." *Hastings Law Journal* 28: 761–781.

VAN DIJK, J. (1978) "The Extent of Public Information and the Nature of Public Attitudes Toward Crime." In *Public Opinion on Crime and Criminal Justice,* edited by A. Coenen and J. van Dijk, pp. 7–42. *Vol. XVII, Collected Studies in Criminological Research.* Strasbourg Cedex (France): Council of Europe.

VAN DYKE, J. (1977) *Jury Selection Procedures.* Cambridge, Mass: Ballinger.

"VIDEO TRANSMISSION TO COUNTER HIJACKING" (1986) *Security World* 23, no. 7, p. 18.

"VIOLENT MOVIE DIDN'T CAUSE YOUTH'S DEATH." (1989) *News Media and the Law* 13, no. 4: 33–34.

WALKER, S. (1985) *Sense and Nonsense about Crime.* Pacific Grove, Calif.: Brooks/Cole.

WARR, M. (1980) "The Accuracy of Public Beliefs about Crime." *Social Forces* 59: 456–470.

WARREN, S., & BRANDEIS, L. (1890) "The Right to Privacy." *Harvard Law Review* 4: 193–199.

WATT, J., & KRULL, R. (1978) "Examination of Three Models of Television Viewing and Aggression." *Human Communication Research* 3: 99–112.

WEAVER, D. (1980) "Audience Need for Orientation and Media Effects." *Communications Research* 7: 361–376.

WEAVER, J. (1987) *Effects of Portrayals of Female Sexuality and Violence against Women on Perceptions of Women.* Ph.D. diss., University of Indiana.

WEINSTEIN, N. (1987) "Cross-Hazard Consistencies: Conclusions about Self-Protective Behavior." In *Taking Care: Understanding and Encouraging Self-Protective Behavior,* edited by N. Weinstein, pp. 325–336. New York: Cambridge University Press.

WEIS, J. (1977) "Electronics Expand Courtrooms' Walls." *American Bar Association Journal* 63: 1713–1716.

WEIS, K., & BORGES, S. (1973) "Victimology and Rape: The Case of the Legitimate Victim." *Issues in Criminology* 8: 71–115.

WEISS, M. J. (1982) "Trial by Tape." *American Film,* June, pp. 61–64.

WERTHAM, R. (1954) *Seduction of the Innocent.* New York: Rinehart.

WEST, S., HEPWORTH, J., McCALL, M., & REICH, J. (1989) "An Evaluation of Arizona's July 1982 Drunk Driving Law: Effects on the City of Phoenix." *Journal of Applied Social Psychology* 19, no. 14: 1212–1237.

WESTIN, A. (1982) *Newswatch: How TV Decides the News.* New York: Simon & Schuster.

WHEATLEY, J. (1971) "Marketing and the Use of Fear or Anxiety-Arousing Appeals." *Journal of Marketing* 35: 62–64.

WHITE, D. M. (1950) "The Gatekeepers: A Case Study in the Selection of News." *Journalism Quarterly* 27: 383–390.

WHITE, T., REGAN, K., WALLER, J., & WHOLEY, J. (1975) *Police Burglary Prevention Programs.* Washington, D. C.: U. S. Department of Justice, Law Enforcement Assistance Administration.

WILCOX, W. (1970) "The Press, the Jury, and the Behavioral Sciences." In *Free Press and Fair Trial: Some Dimensions of the Problem,* edited by C. R. Bush, pp. 49–105. Athens: University of Georgia Press.

WILLARD, D., & ROWLANEL, J. (1983) *The Politics of TV Violence.* Newbury Park, Calif.: Sage.

WILLIAMS, J., LAWTON, C., ELLIS, S., WALSH, S., & REED, J. (1987) "Copycat Suicide Attempts." *Lancet* vol. i: 102–103.

WILLS, G. (1977) "Measuring the Impact of Erotica." *Psychology Today,* November, pp. 30–34.

WILMER, L. [1859] (1970) *Our Press Gang.* New York: Lloyd Pub. Reprint. Arno.

WILSON, G., & O'LEARY, K. (1980) *Principles of Behavior Theory.* Englewood Cliffs, N. J.: Prentice-Hall.

WILSON, J. Q. (1975) *Thinking about Crime.* New York: Basic Books.

WILSON, J. Q., & HERRNSTEIN, R. (1985) *Crime and Human Behavior.* New York: Simon & Schuster.

WISE, D. (1986) "Bar Report Recommends Curbs on Pretrial Comments to Media." *New York Law Journal* 196: 1, 3.

WOOLDRIDGE, F. (1981) *Micro Video Patrol.* Grant application, Community Development Block Grant Program (HUD), August, Miami Beach.

WORCHEL, S., HARDY, T., & HURLEY, R. (1976) "The Effects of Commercial Interruption of Violent and Nonviolent Films on Viewers' Subsequent Aggression." *Journal of Experimental Psychology* 12: 220–232.

WURTZEL, A., & LOMETTI, G. (1984a) "Researching Television Violence." *Society* 21: 22–30.

WURTZEL, A., & LOMETTI, G. (1984b) "Smoking Out the Critics." *Society* 21: 36–40.

YANKELOVICH, D., SKELLY, S., & WHITE, A., INC. (1978) "The Public Image of Courts: Highlights of a National Survey of the General Public, Judges, Lawyers, and Community Leaders." In *State Courts: A Blueprint for the Future,* proceedings of the Second National Conference on the Judiciary, edited by T. J. Fetter, pp. 5–69. Williamsburg, Va.: National Center for State Courts.

ZANER, L. (1989) "The Screen Test: Has Hollywood Hurt Corrections' Image?" *Corrections Today* 51: 64–66, 94, 95, 98.

ZEISEL, H., & DIAMOND, S. (1978) "The Effect of Peremptory Challenges on Jury and Verdict: An Experiment in a Federal District Court." *Stanford Law Review* 30: 491–531.

ZILLMAN, D. (1971) "Excitation Transfer in Communication-Mediated Aggressive Behavior." *Journal of Experimental Social Psychology* 7: 419–434.

ZILLMAN, D., & BRYANT, J. (1982) "Pornography, Sexual Callousness, and the Trivialization of Rape." *Journal of Communication* 32: 10–21.

ZILLMAN, D., JOHNSON, R., & HANRAHAM, J. (1973) "Pacifying Effect of Happy Ending of Communication Involving Aggression." *Psychological Reports* 32: 967–970.

ZUCKER, H. (1978) "The Variable Nature of News Media Influence." In *Communication Yearbook* vol. 2, edited by B. Ruben, pp. 225–240. New Brunswick, N.J.: Transaction Books.

Index

TO THE OWNER OF THIS BOOK:

We hope that you have found Ray Surette's *Media, Crime, and Criminal Justice* useful. So that this book can be improved in a future edition, would you take the time to complete this sheet and return it? Thank you.

Instructor's name: _____

Department: _____

School and address: _____

_____

1. The name of the course in which I used this book is: _____

_____

2. My general reaction to this book is: _____

_____

_____

3. What I like most about this book is: _____

_____

_____

4. What I like least about this book is: _____

_____

_____

5. Were all of the chapters of the book assigned for you to read?   Yes   No

   If not, which ones weren't? _____

6. Do you plan to keep this book after you finish the course?   Yes   No

   Why or why not? _____

_____

7. On a separate sheet of paper, please write specific suggestions for improving this book and anything else you'd care to share about your experience in using the book.

Optional:

Your name: _____ Date: _____

May Brooks/Cole quote you, either in promotion for *Media, Crime, and Criminal Justice* or in future publishing ventures?

Yes: _____ No: _____

Sincerely,
Ray Surette